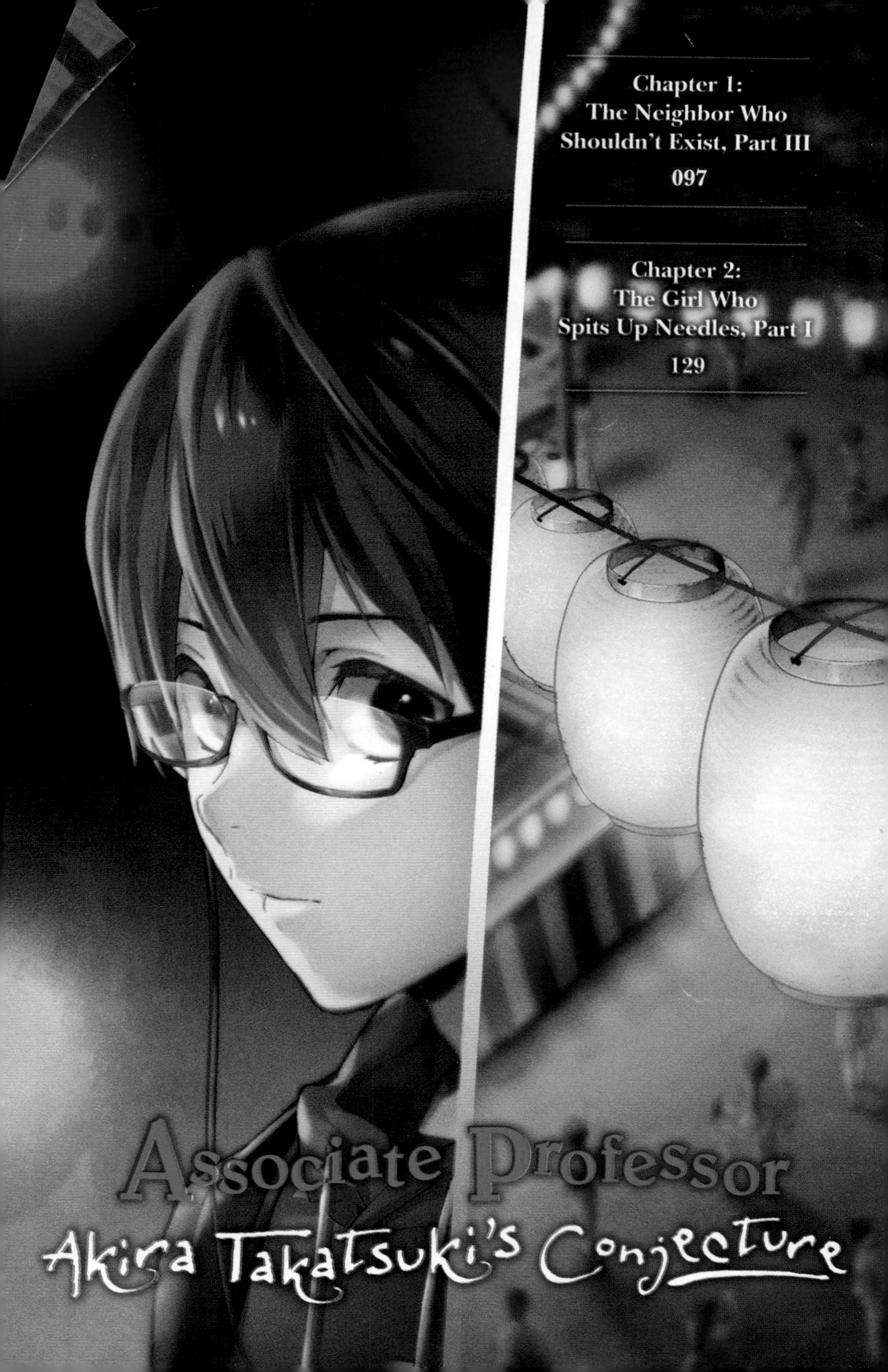
Associate Professor
Akira Takatsuki's Conjecture

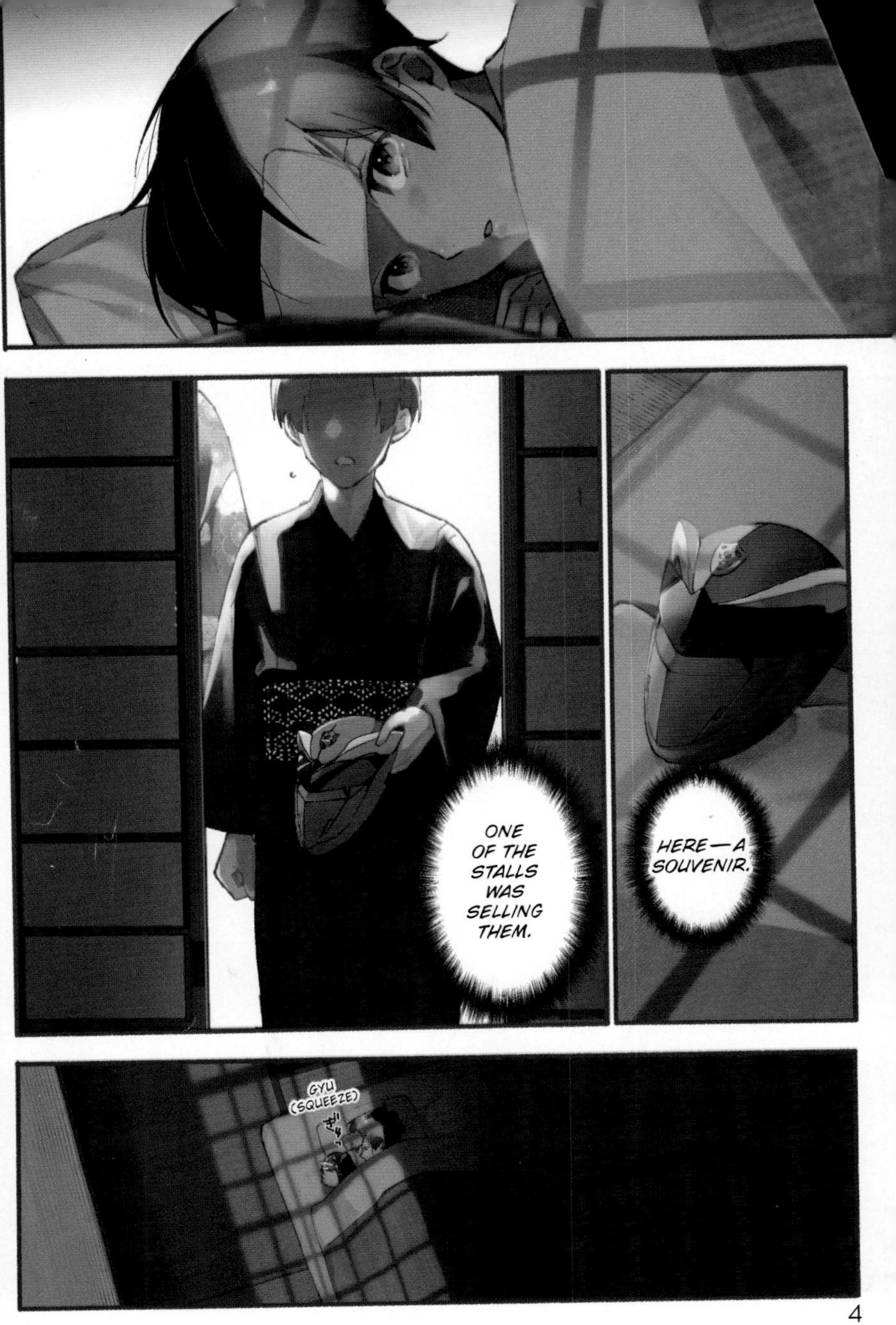
HERE—A SOUVENIR.
ONE OF THE STALLS WAS SELLING THEM.
GYU (SQUEEZE)

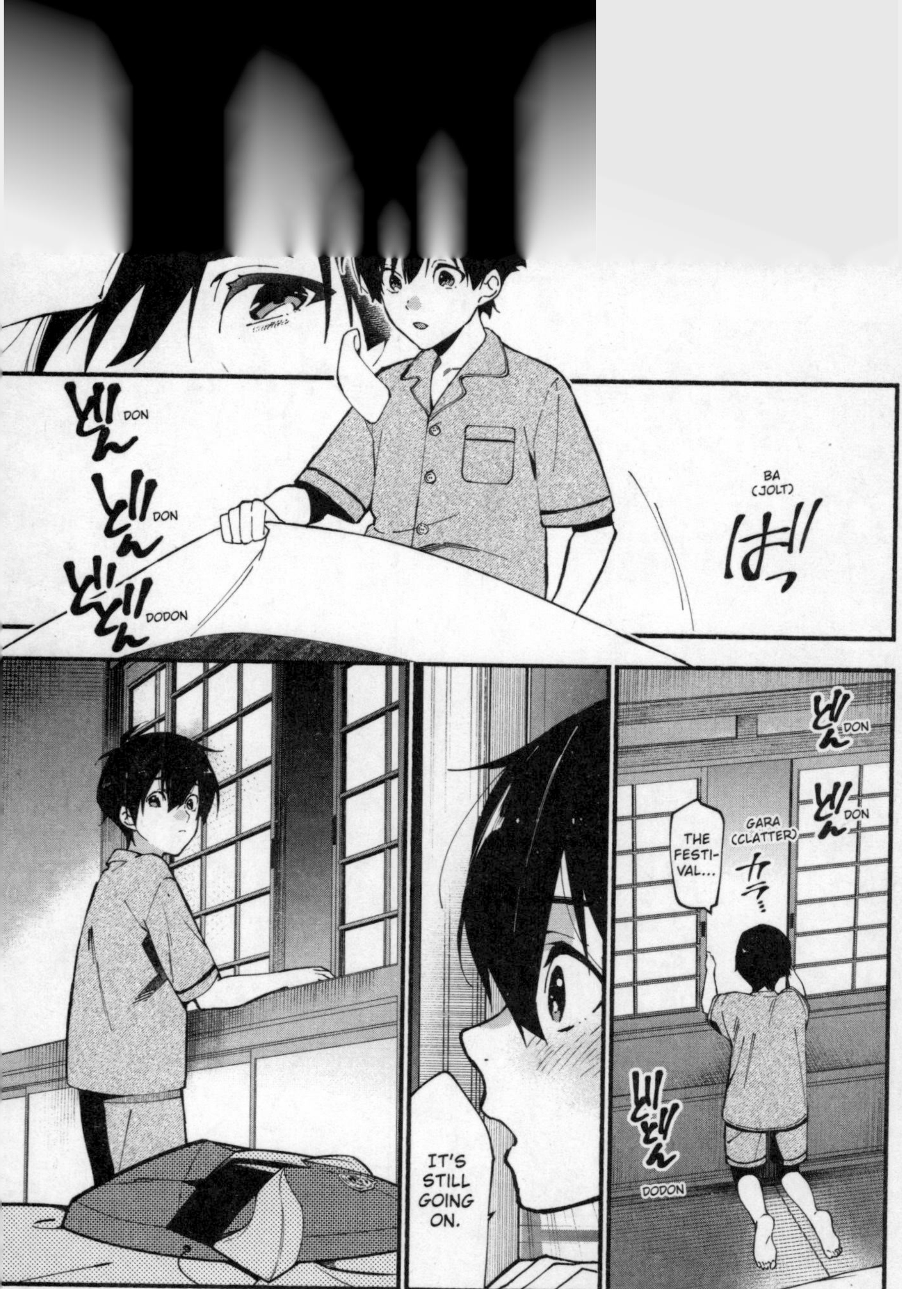

BA (JOLT)
DON
DON
DODON
DON
DON
GARA (CLATTER)
THE FESTIVAL...
DODON
IT'S STILL GOING ON.

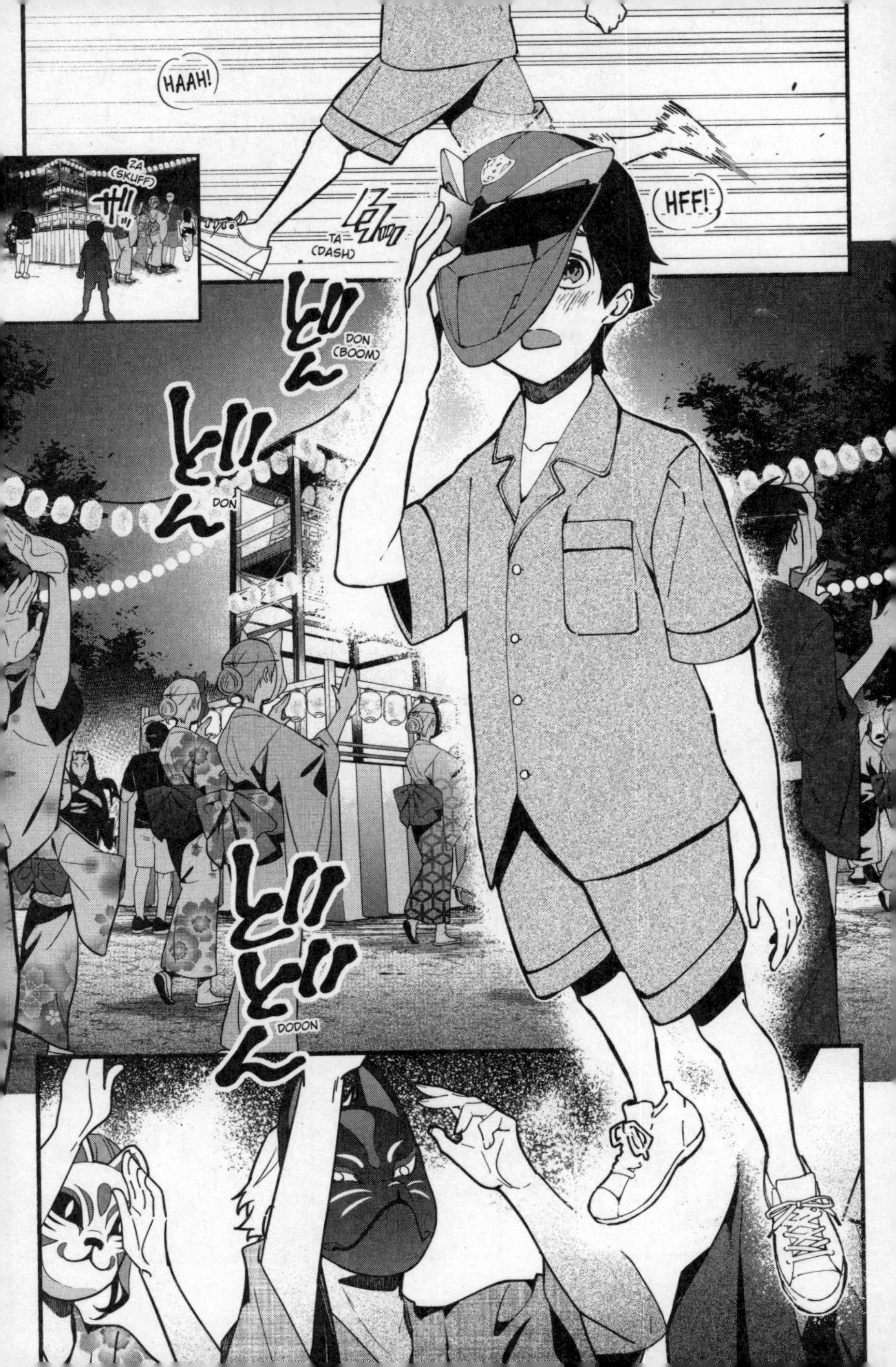
HAAH!
HFF!
TA (DASH)
ZA (SKUFF)
どん
DON (BOOM)
どん
DON
どどん
DODON

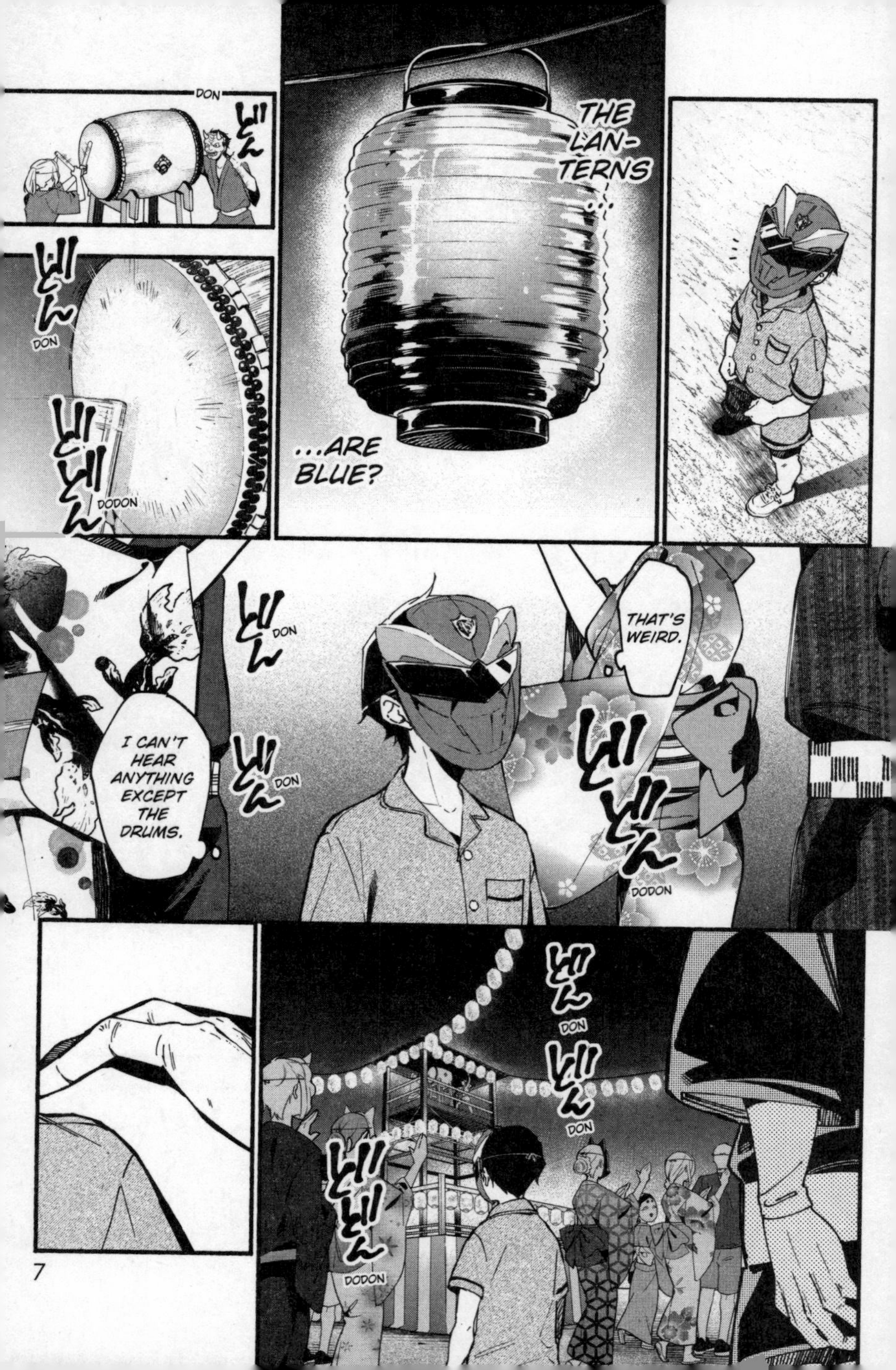
THE LAN-TERNS...
...ARE BLUE?
どん
DON
どん
DON
どどん
DODON
THAT'S WEIRD.
どどん
DODON
どん
DON
どん
DON
I CAN'T HEAR ANYTHING EXCEPT THE DRUMS.
どん
DON
どん
DON
どどん
DODON

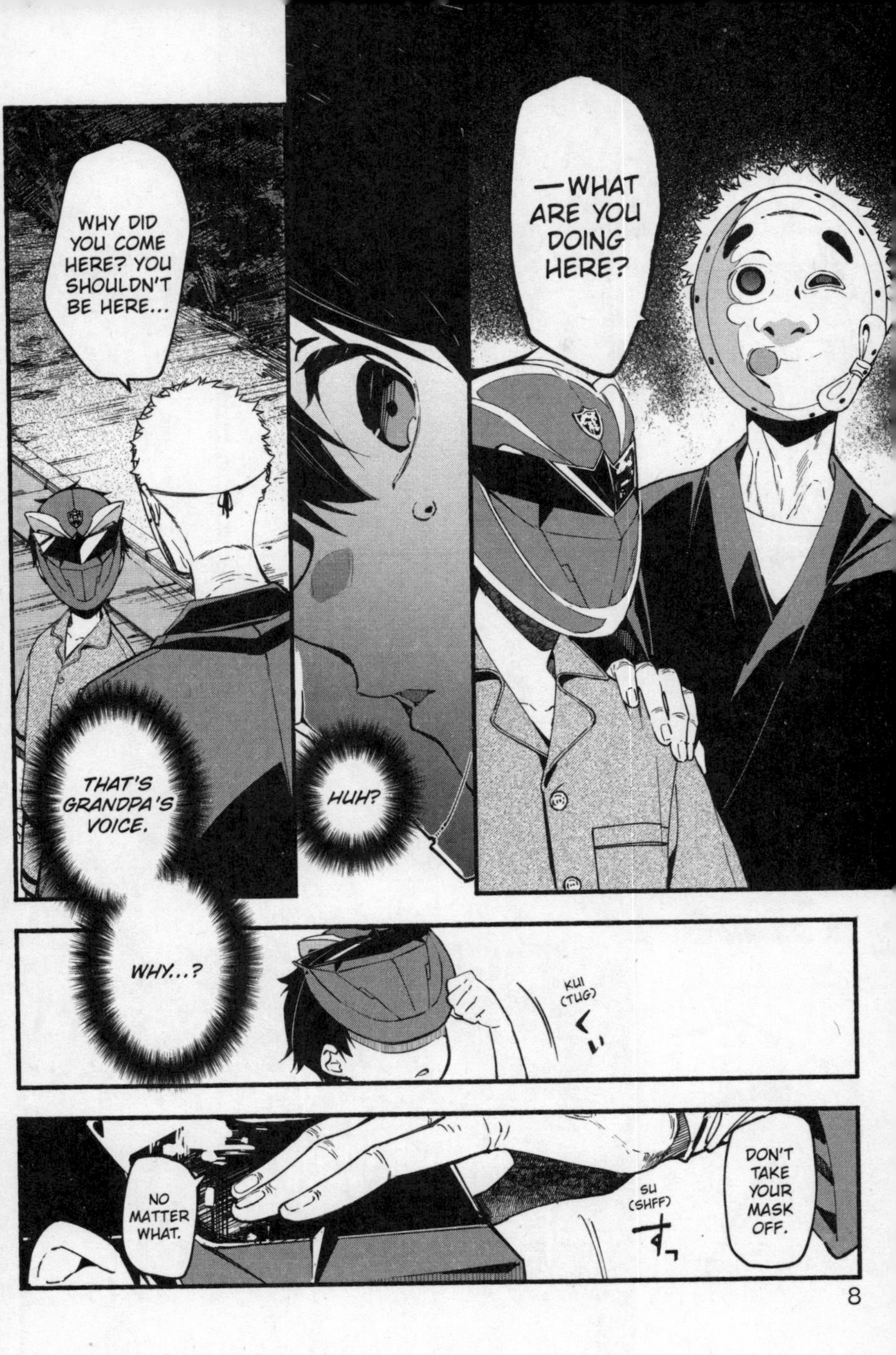
—WHAT ARE YOU DOING HERE?
HUH?
WHY DID YOU COME HERE? YOU SHOULDN'T BE HERE...
THAT'S GRANDPA'S VOICE.
WHY...?
KUI (TUG)
DON'T TAKE YOUR MASK OFF.
SU (SHFF)
NO MATTER WHAT.

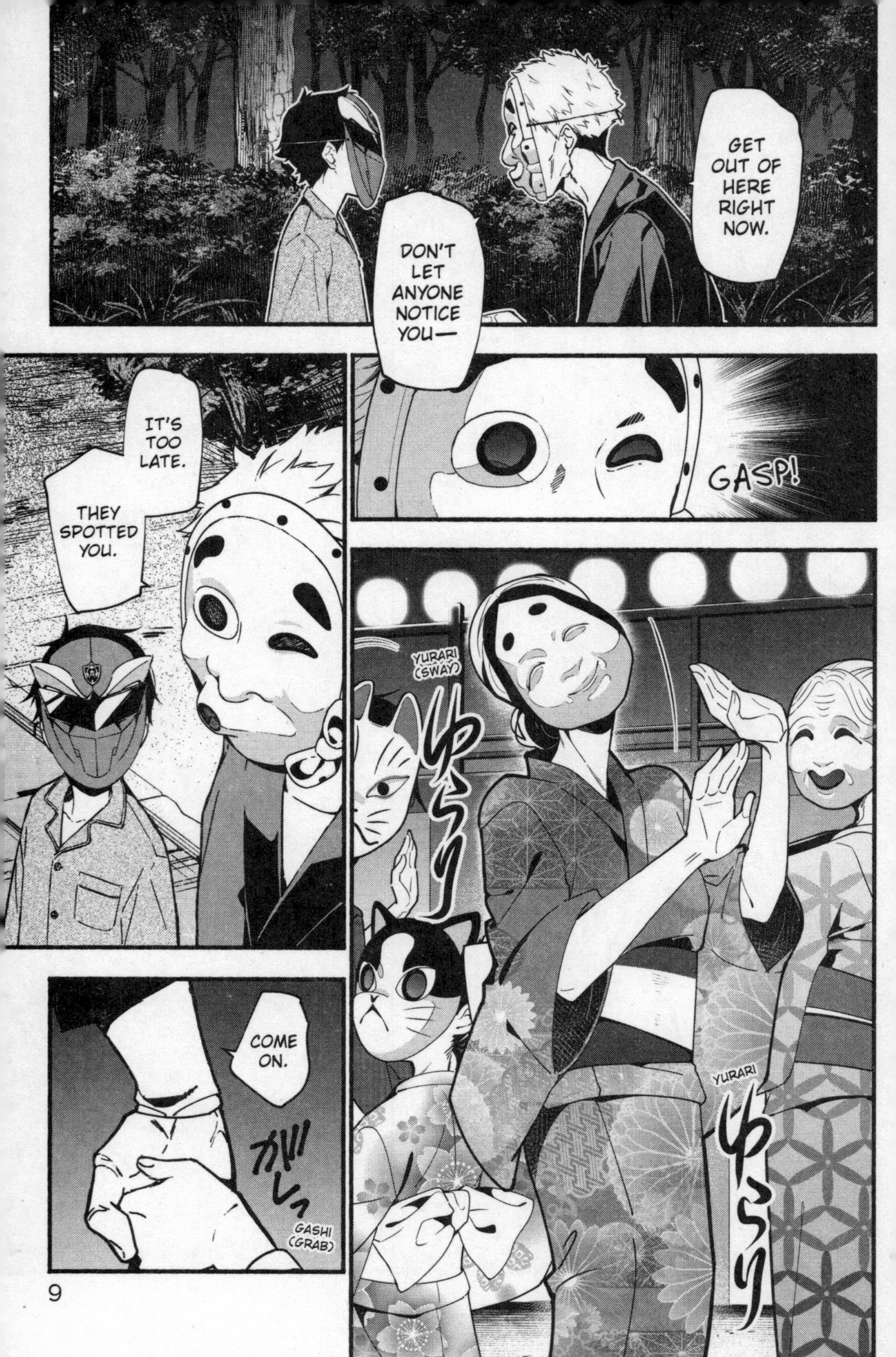
GET OUT OF HERE RIGHT NOW.
DON'T LET ANYONE NOTICE YOU—
GASP!
IT'S TOO LATE.
THEY SPOTTED YOU.
ゆらり
YURARI (SWAY)
ゆらり
YURARI
COME ON.
ガシッ
GASHI (GRAB)

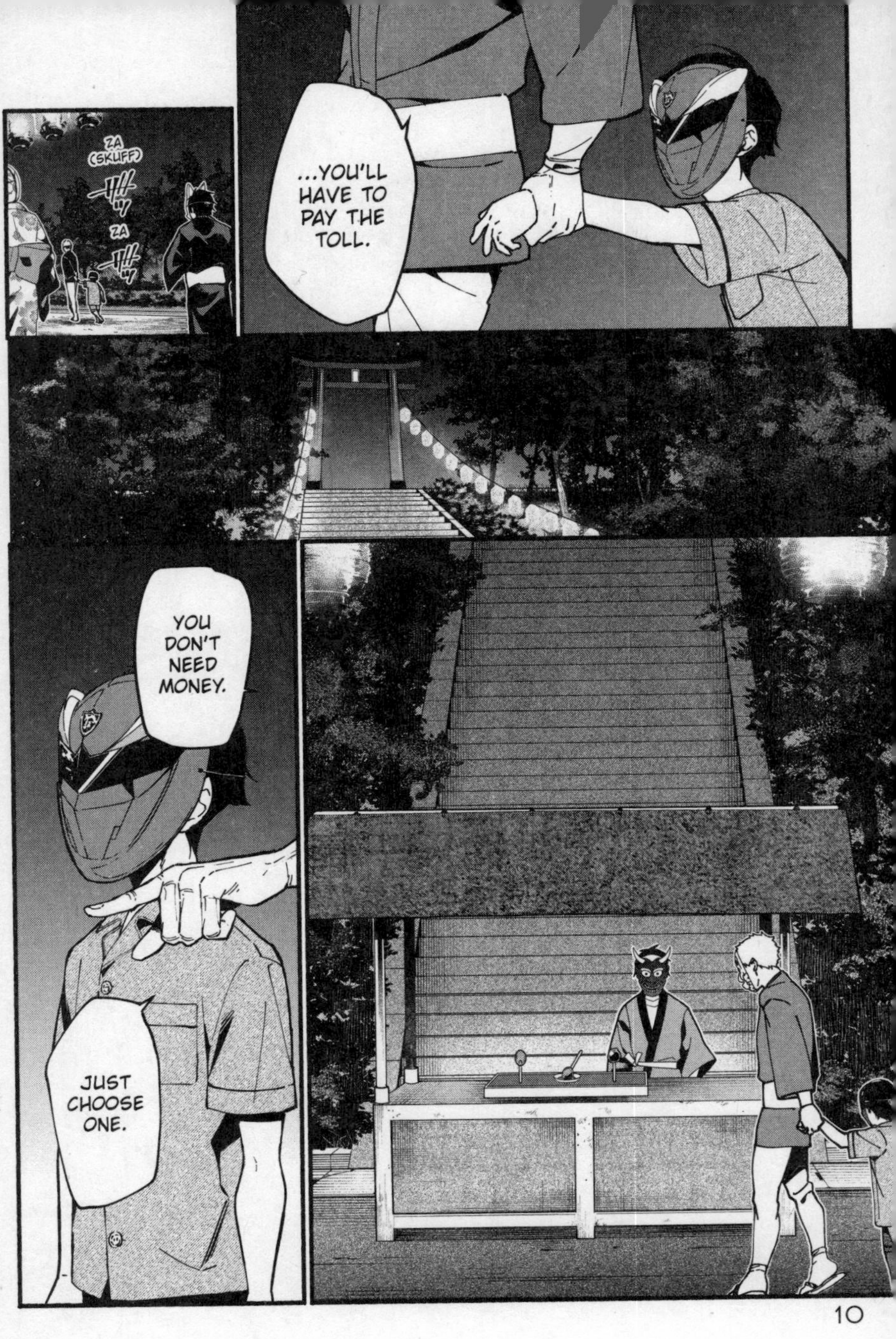
...YOU'LL HAVE TO PAY THE TOLL.
ZA (SKUFF)
ZA
YOU DON'T NEED MONEY.
JUST CHOOSE ONE.

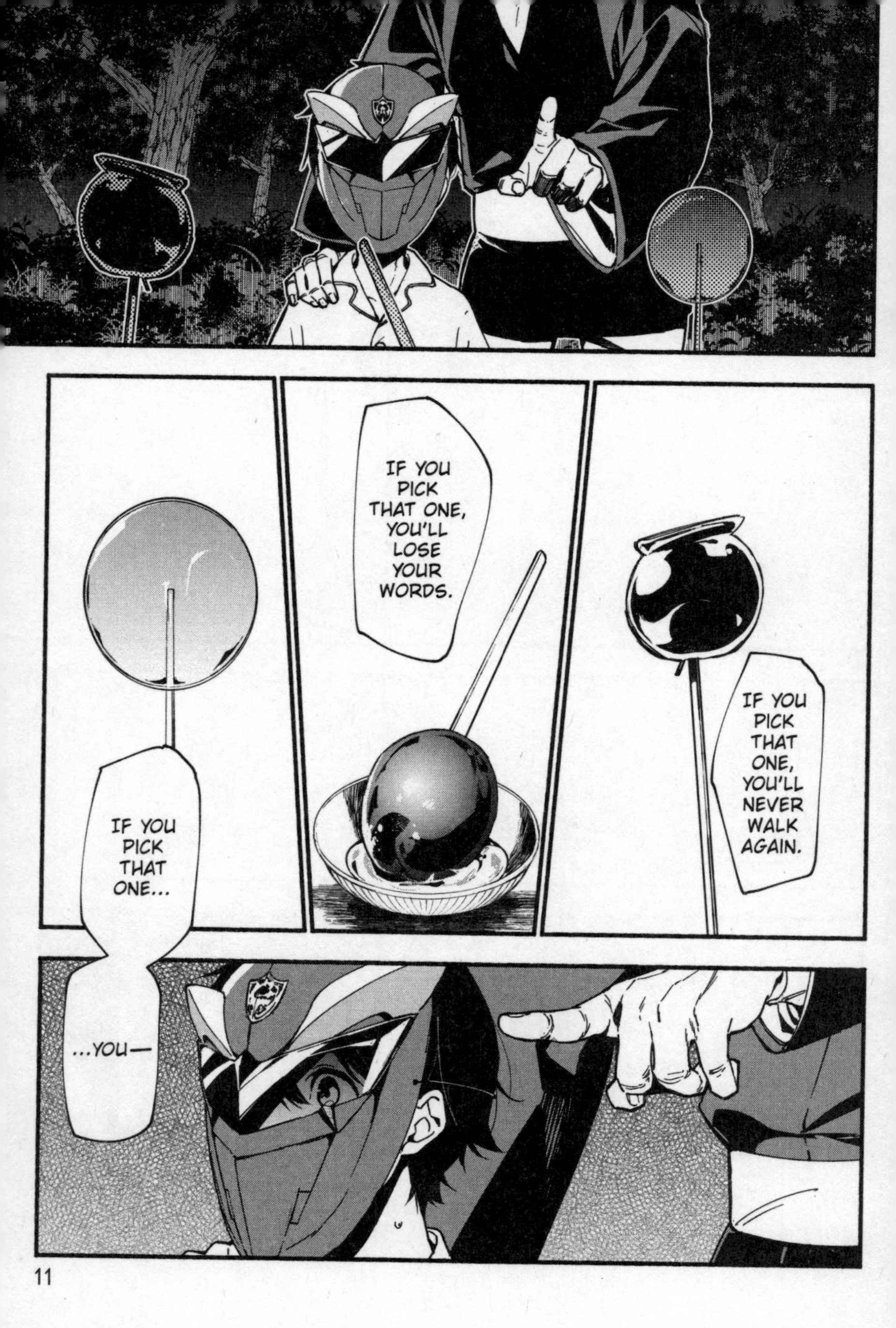
IF YOU PICK THAT ONE, YOU'LL NEVER WALK AGAIN.
IF YOU PICK THAT ONE, YOU'LL LOSE YOUR WORDS.
IF YOU PICK THAT ONE...
...YOU—

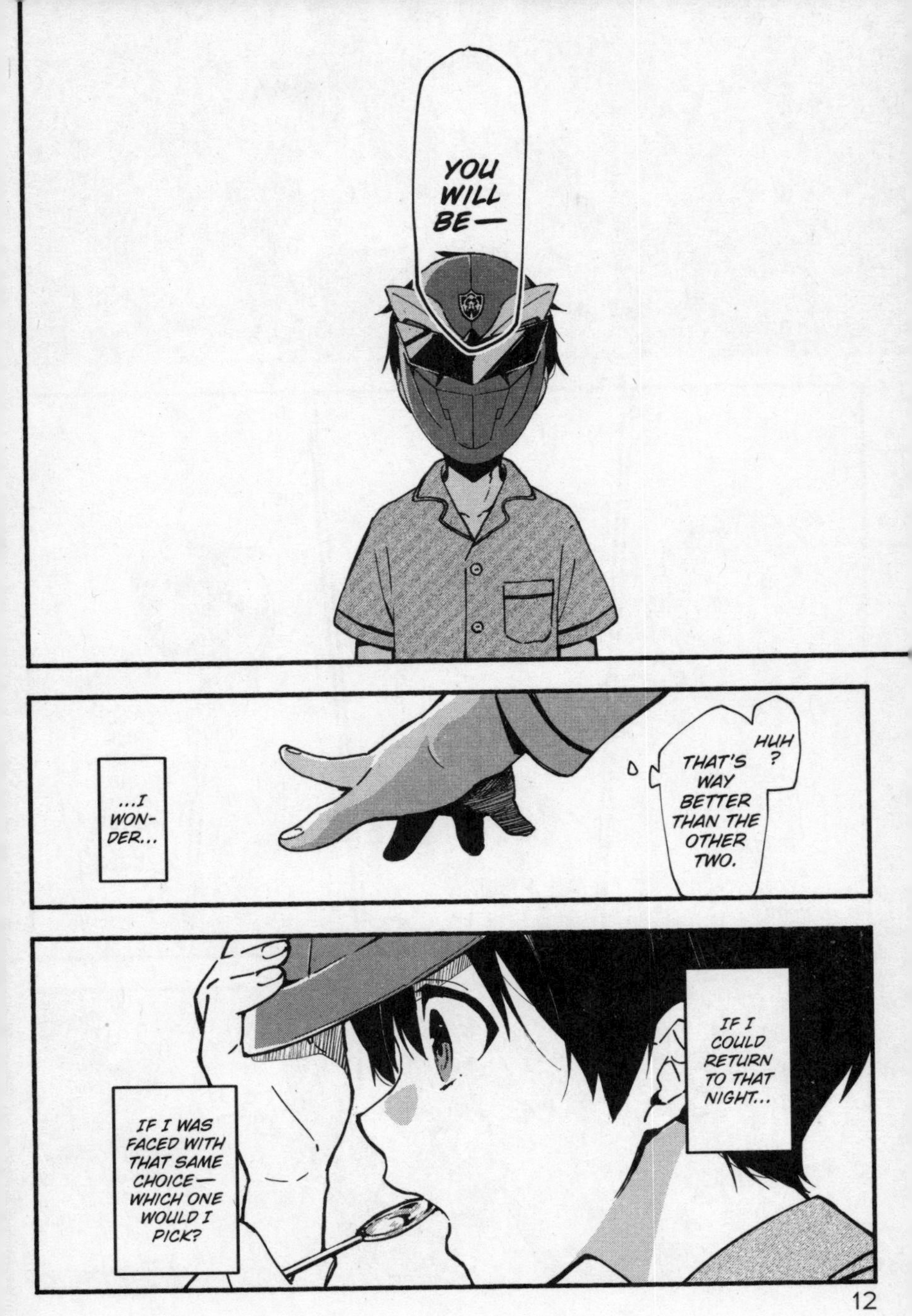
YOU WILL BE—
HUH? THAT'S WAY BETTER THAN THE OTHER TWO.
...I WONDER...
IF I COULD RETURN TO THAT NIGHT...
IF I WAS FACED WITH THAT SAME CHOICE—WHICH ONE WOULD I PICK?

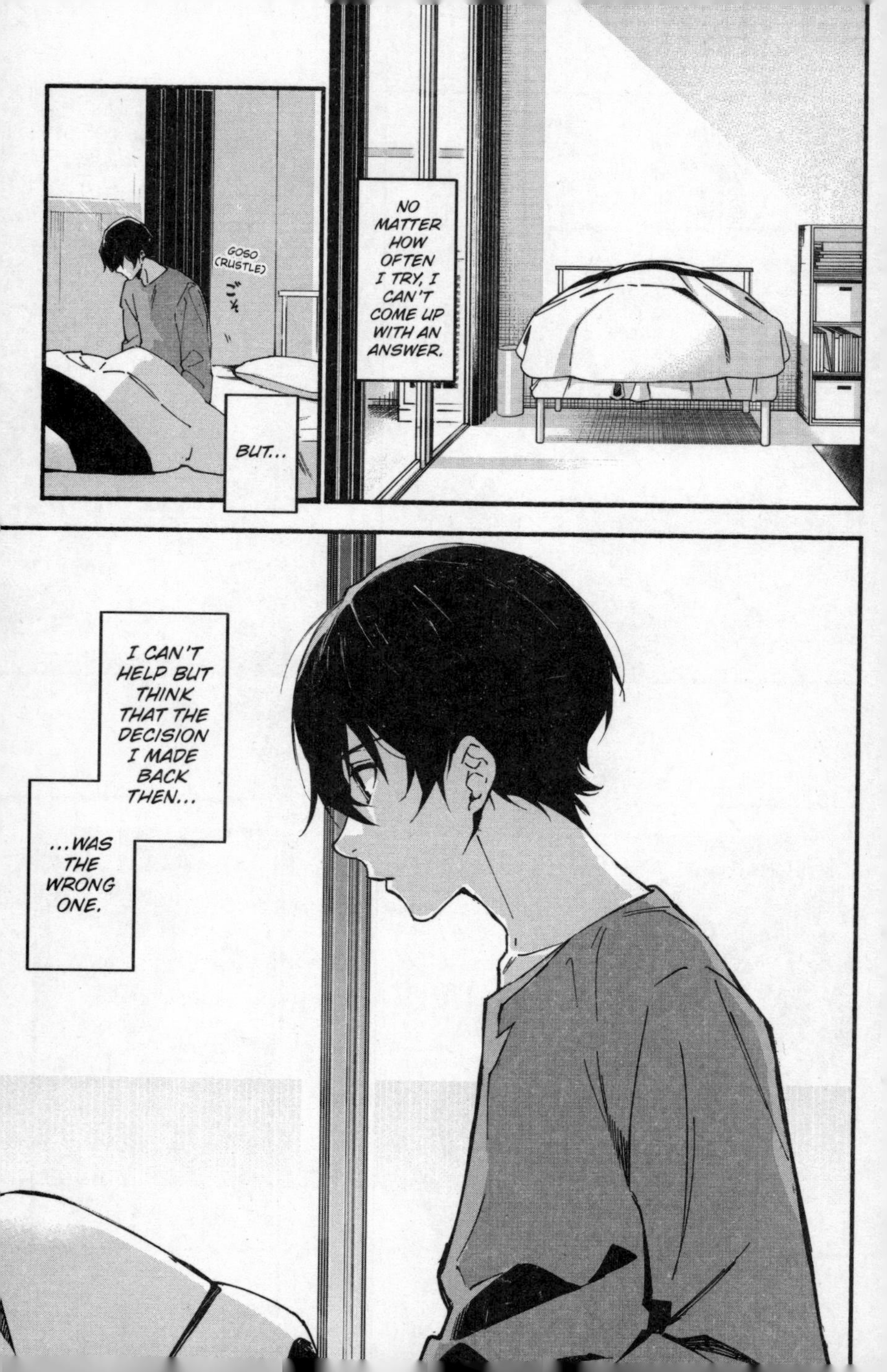
NO MATTER HOW OFTEN I TRY, I CAN'T COME UP WITH AN ANSWER.
GOSO (RUSTLE)
BUT...
I CAN'T HELP BUT THINK THAT THE DECISION I MADE BACK THEN...
...WAS THE WRONG ONE.

SIGN: SEIWA UNIVERSITY

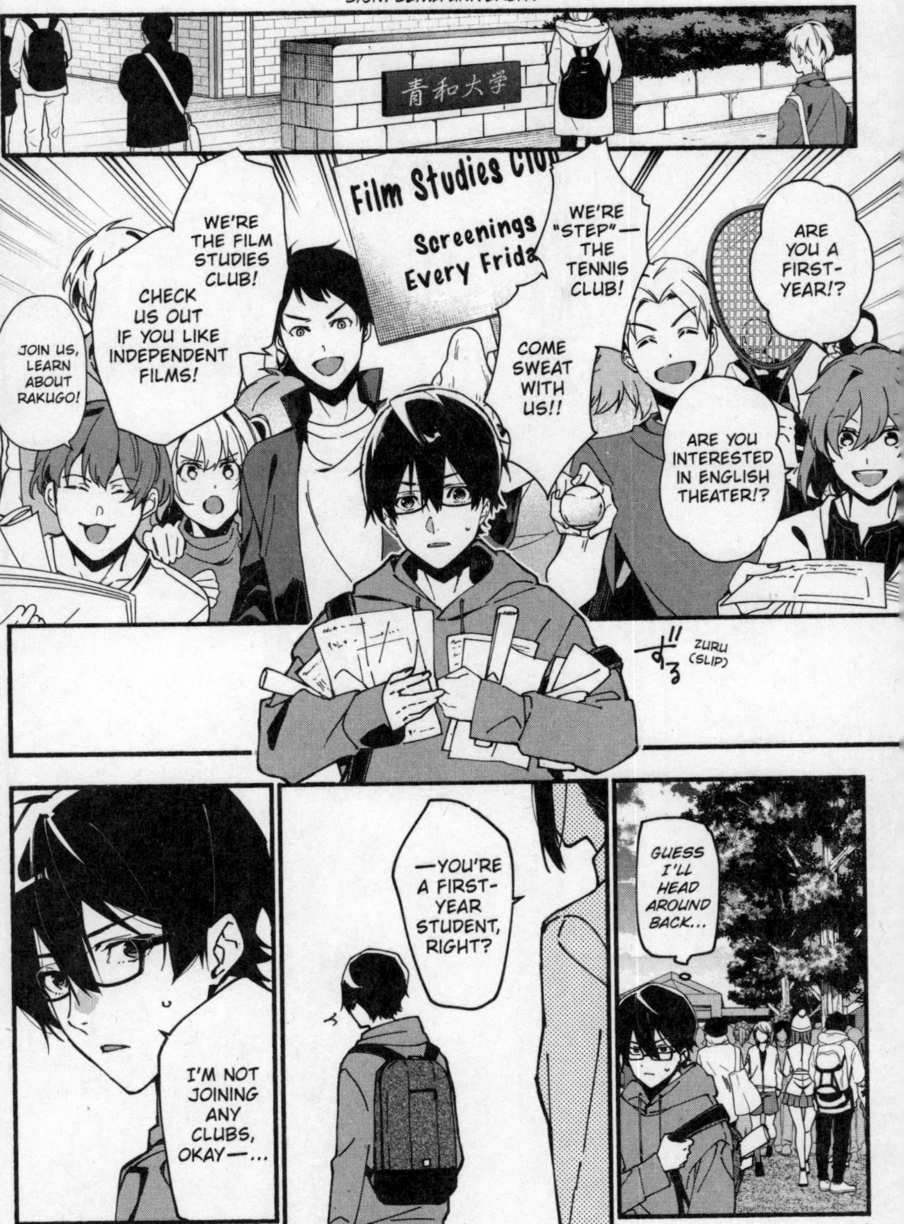
青和大学
ARE YOU A FIRST-YEAR!?
WE'RE "STEP"— THE TENNIS CLUB!
COME SWEAT WITH US!!
ARE YOU INTERESTED IN ENGLISH THEATER!?
Film Studies Clu
Screenings Every Frida
WE'RE THE FILM STUDIES CLUB!
CHECK US OUT IF YOU LIKE INDEPENDENT FILMS!
JOIN US, LEARN ABOUT RAKUGO!
ずる
ZURU (SLIP)
GUESS I'LL HEAD AROUND BACK...
—YOU'RE A FIRST-YEAR STUDENT, RIGHT?
I'M NOT JOINING ANY CLUBS, OKAY—...

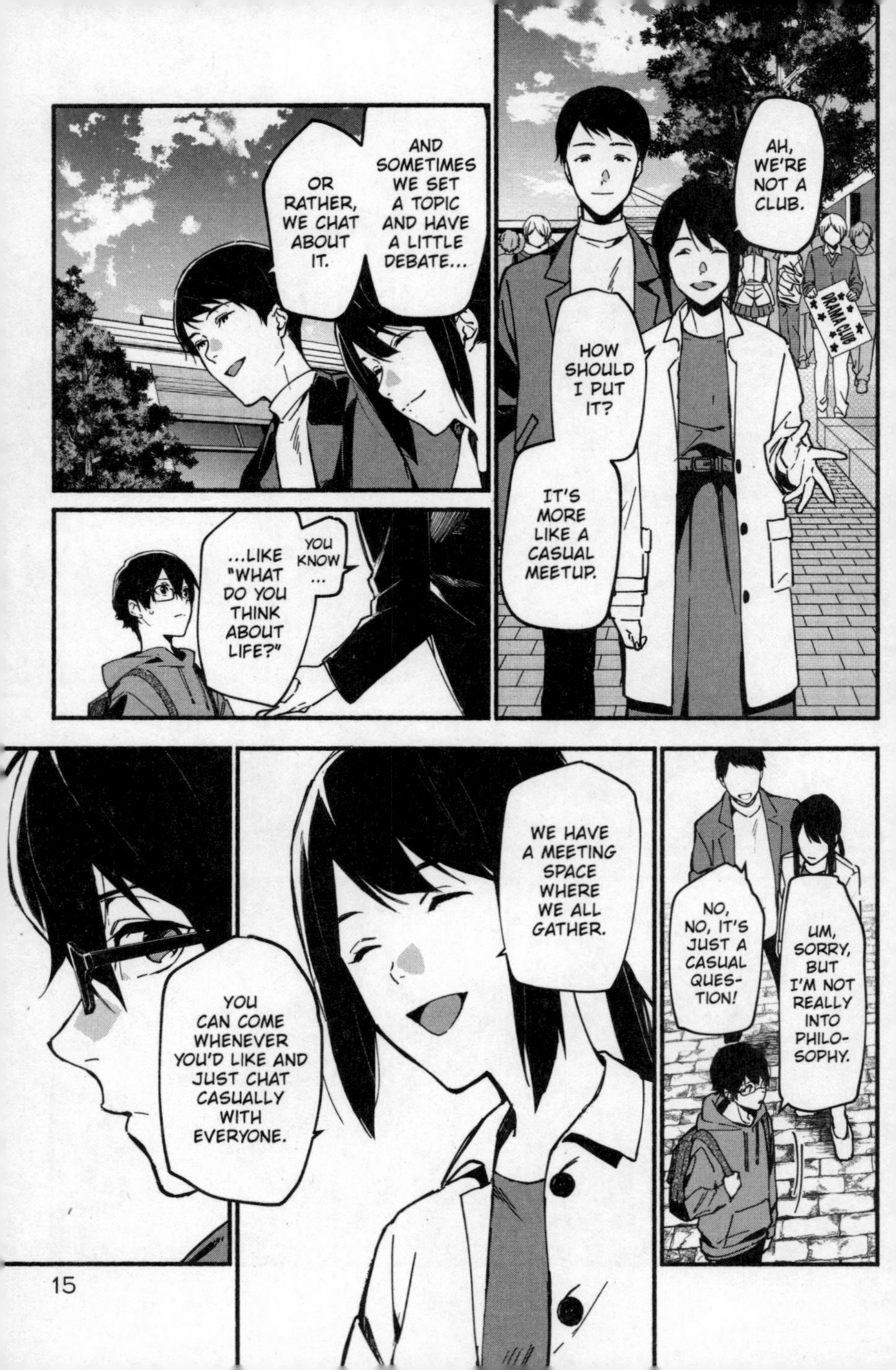
AH, WE'RE NOT A CLUB.
HOW SHOULD I PUT IT?
IT'S MORE LIKE A CASUAL MEETUP.
DRAMA CLUB
AND SOMETIMES WE SET A TOPIC AND HAVE A LITTLE DEBATE...
OR RATHER, WE CHAT ABOUT IT.
YOU KNOW ...
...LIKE "WHAT DO YOU THINK ABOUT LIFE?"
UM, SORRY, BUT I'M NOT REALLY INTO PHILO-SOPHY.
NO, NO, IT'S JUST A CASUAL QUES-TION!
WE HAVE A MEETING SPACE WHERE WE ALL GATHER.
YOU CAN COME WHENEVER YOU'D LIKE AND JUST CHAT CASUALLY WITH EVERYONE.

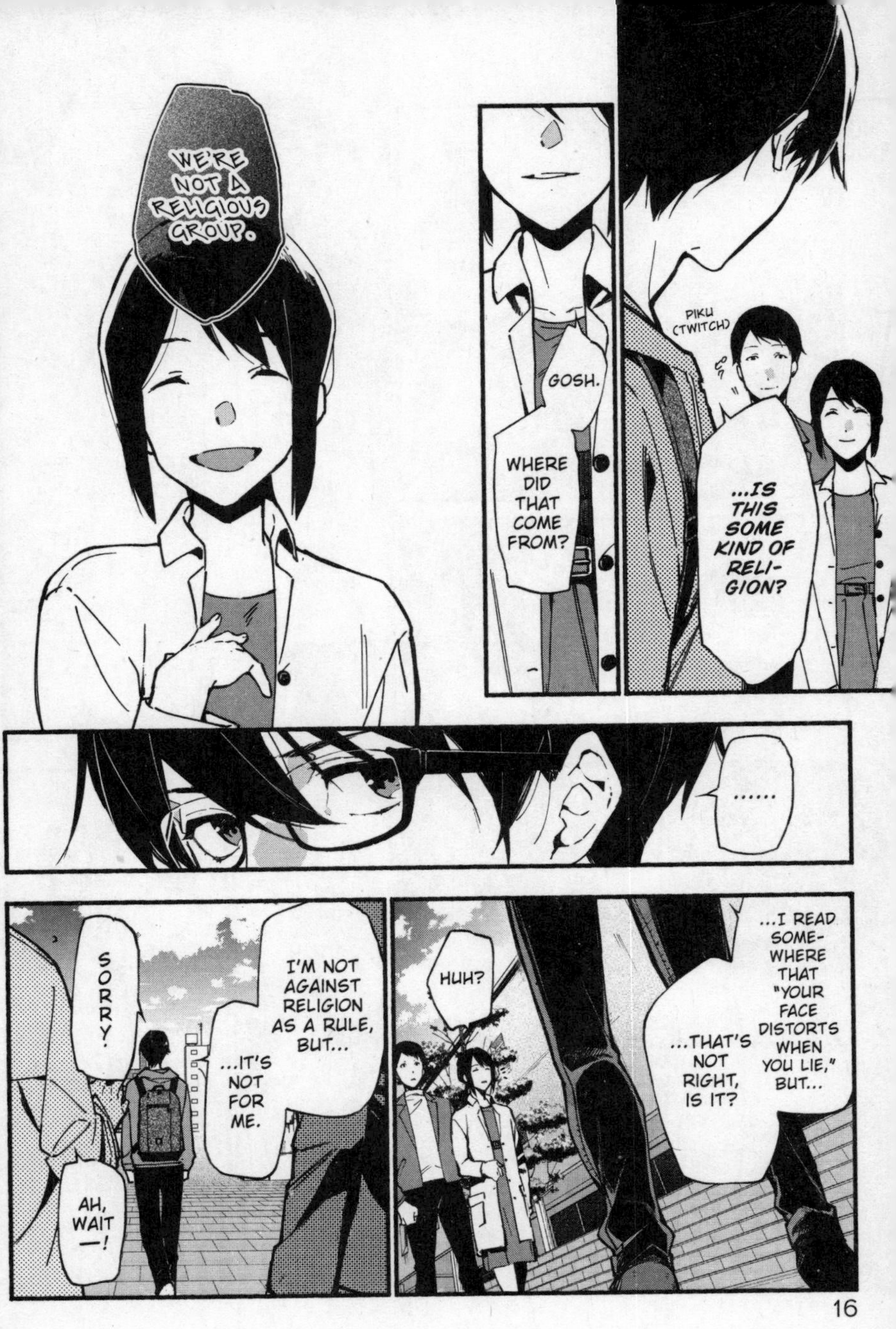
PIKU (TWITCH)
...IS THIS SOME KIND OF RELIGION?
GOSH.
WHERE DID THAT COME FROM?
WE'RE NOT A RELIGIOUS GROUP.
......
...I READ SOMEWHERE THAT "YOUR FACE DISTORTS WHEN YOU LIE," BUT...
...THAT'S NOT RIGHT, IS IT?
HUH?
I'M NOT AGAINST RELIGION AS A RULE, BUT...
...IT'S NOT FOR ME.
SORRY.
AH, WAIT—!

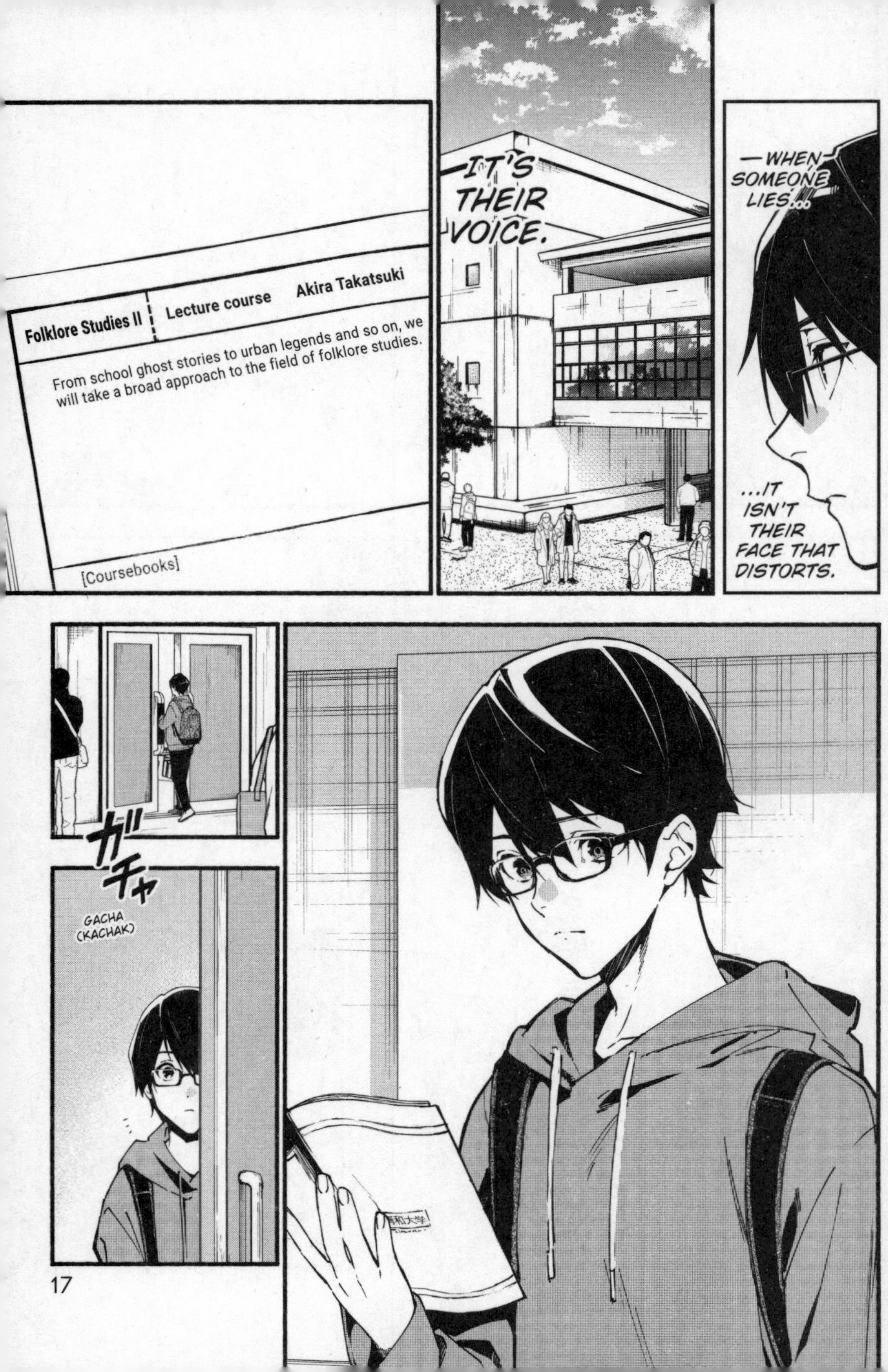
—WHEN SOMEONE LIES...
...IT ISN'T THEIR FACE THAT DISTORTS.
IT'S THEIR VOICE.
Folklore Studies II
Lecture course
Akira Takatsuki
From school ghost stories to urban legends and so on, we will take a broad approach to the field of folklore studies.
[Coursebooks]
ガチャ
GACHA (KACHAK)

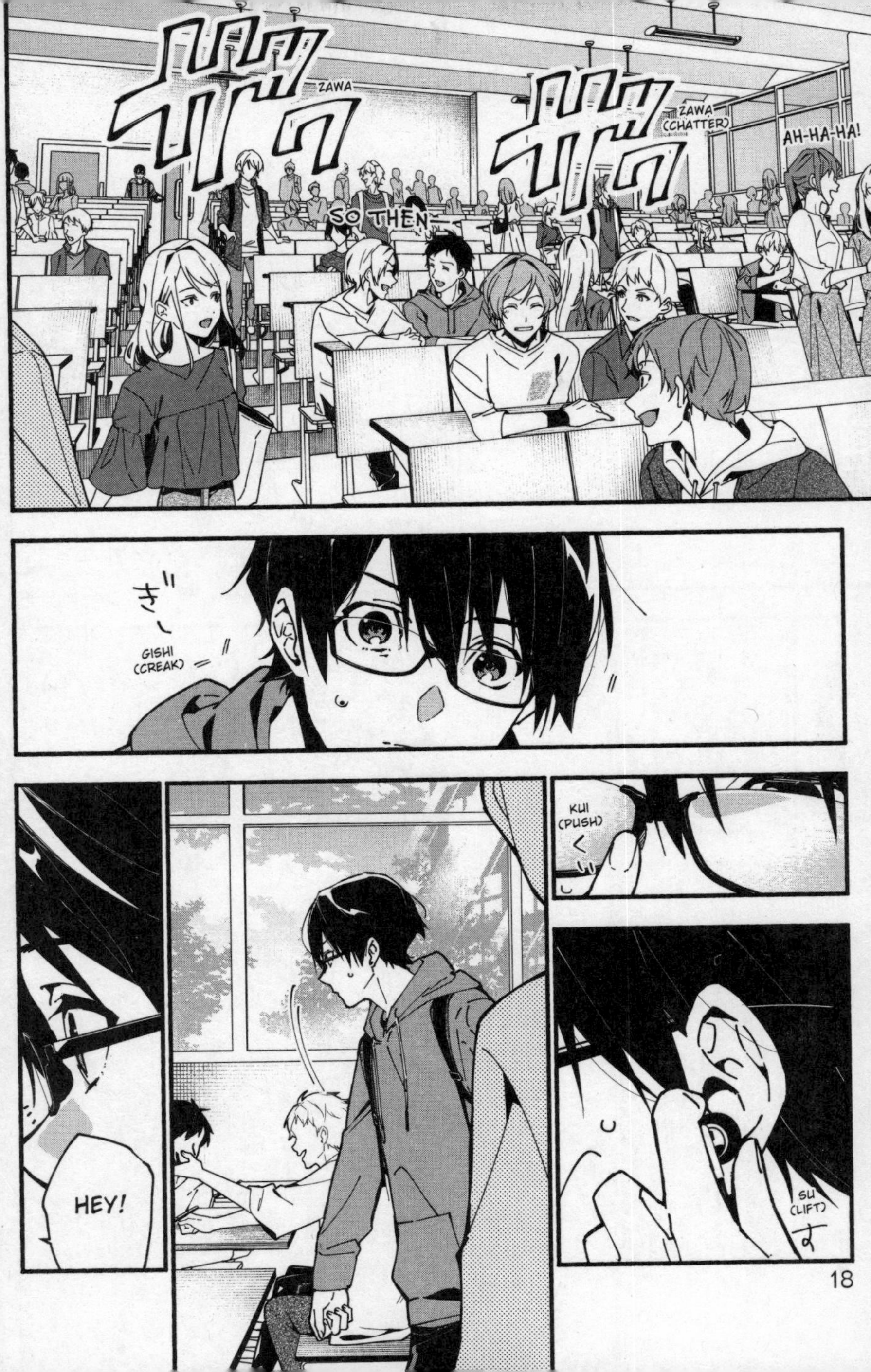
AH-HA-HA!
ZAWA (CHATTER)
SO THEN—
ZAWA
ぎし
GISHI (CREAK)
KUI (PUSH)
く
SU (LIFT)
す
HEY!

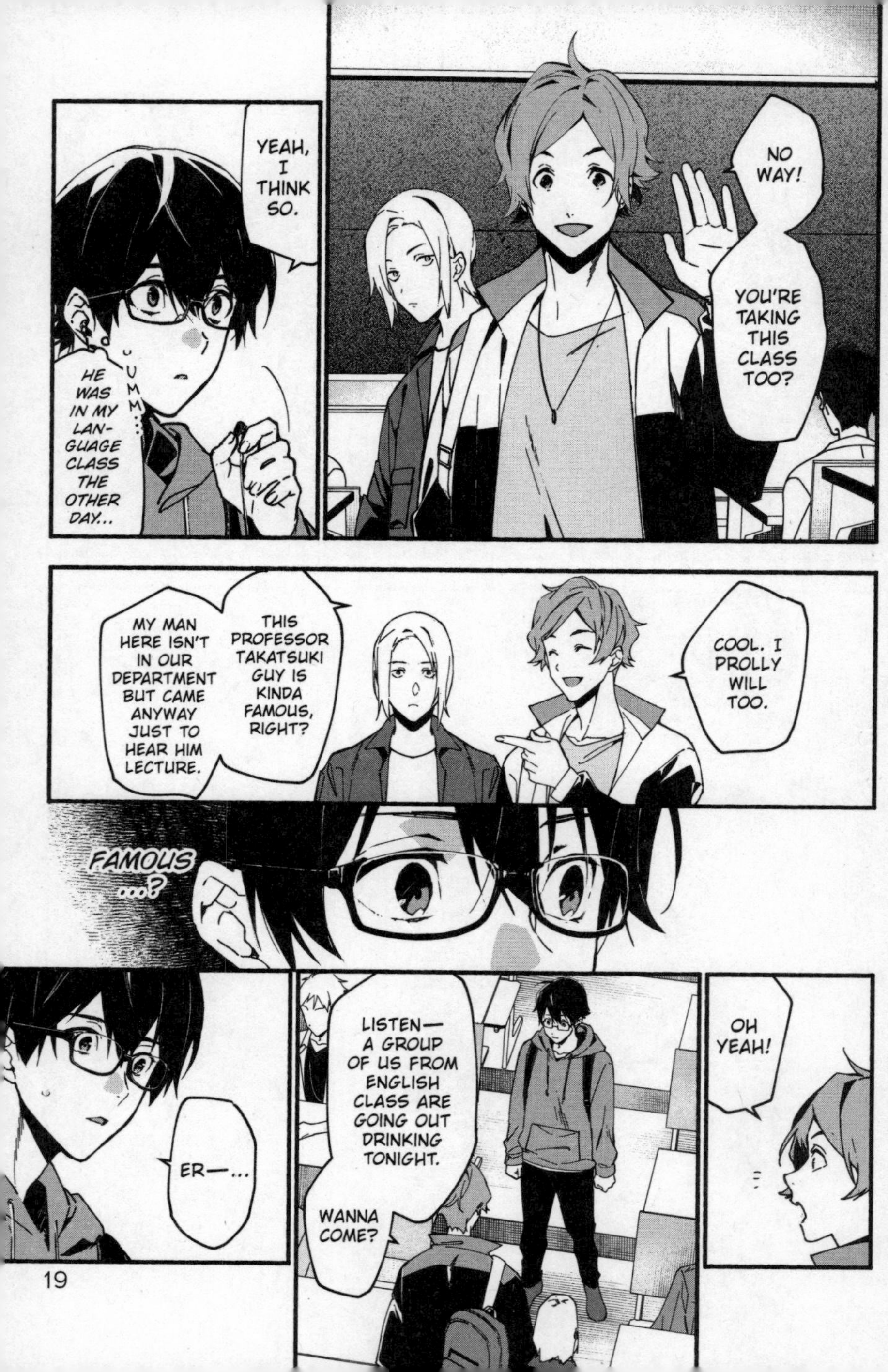
NO WAY!
YOU'RE TAKING THIS CLASS TOO?
YEAH, I THINK SO.
HE WAS IN MY LAN-GUAGE CLASS THE OTHER DAY...
UMM...
COOL. I PROLLY WILL TOO.
THIS PROFESSOR TAKATSUKI GUY IS KINDA FAMOUS, RIGHT?
MY MAN HERE ISN'T IN OUR DEPARTMENT BUT CAME ANYWAY JUST TO HEAR HIM LECTURE.
FAMOUS ...?
OH YEAH!
LISTEN— A GROUP OF US FROM ENGLISH CLASS ARE GOING OUT DRINKING TONIGHT.
WANNA COME?
ER—...

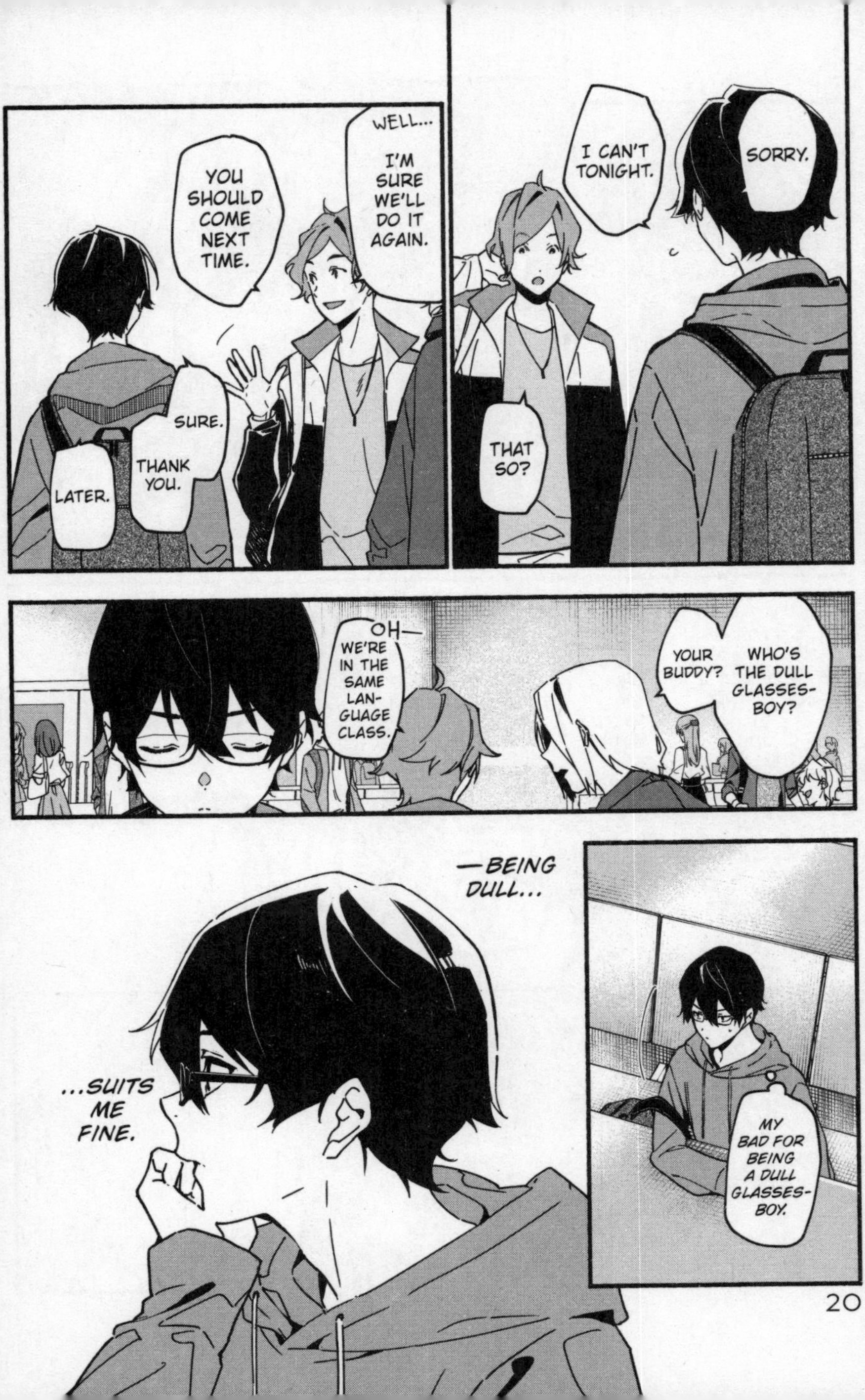
SORRY.
I CAN'T TONIGHT.
THAT SO?
WELL... I'M SURE WE'LL DO IT AGAIN.
YOU SHOULD COME NEXT TIME.
SURE. THANK YOU.
LATER.
WHO'S THE DULL GLASSES-BOY?
YOUR BUDDY?
OH— WE'RE IN THE SAME LAN-GUAGE CLASS.
MY BAD FOR BEING A DULL GLASSES-BOY.
—BEING DULL...
...SUITS ME FINE.

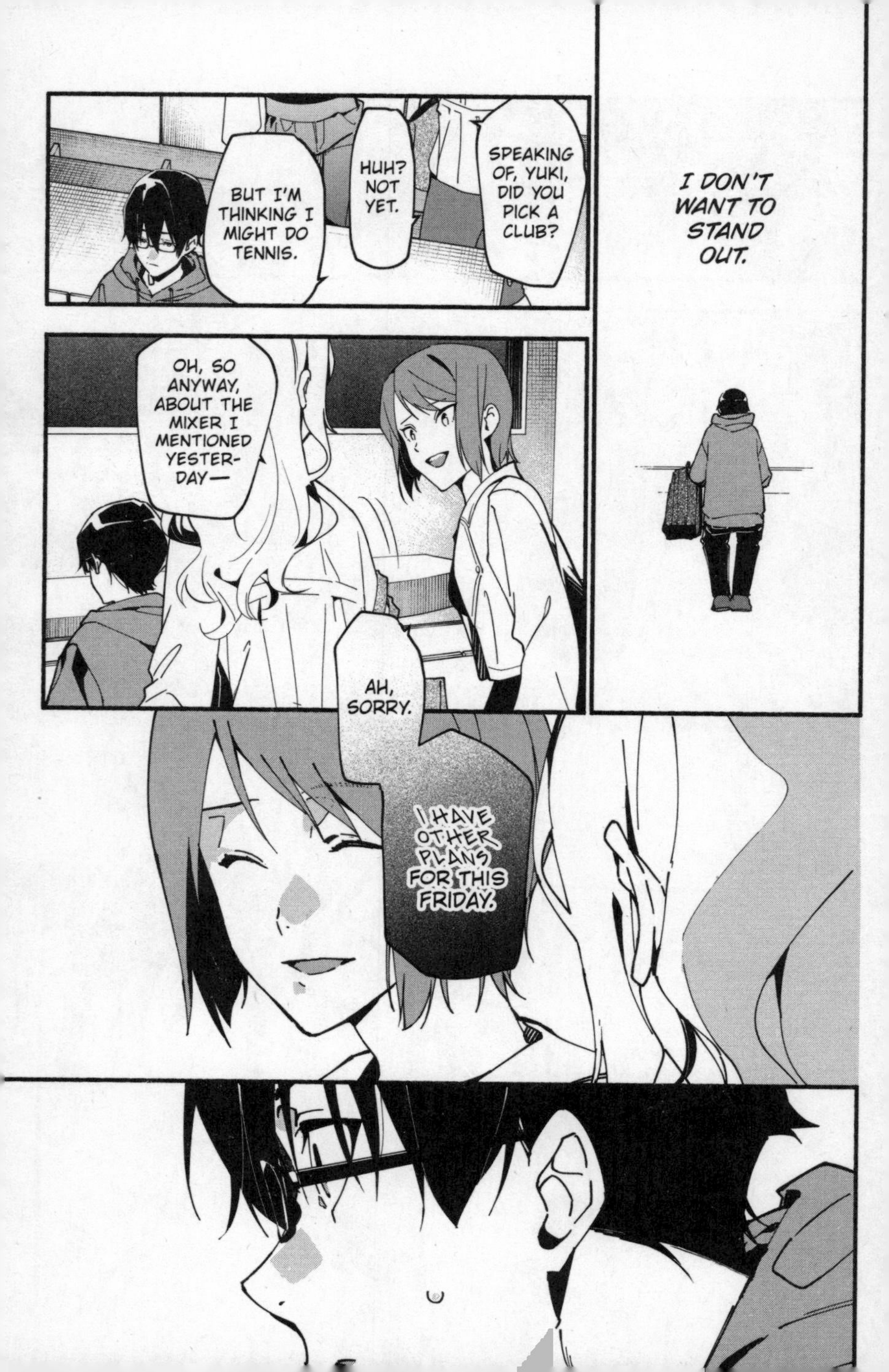
I DON'T WANT TO STAND OUT.
SPEAKING OF, YUKI, DID YOU PICK A CLUB?
HUH? NOT YET.
BUT I'M THINKING I MIGHT DO TENNIS.
OH, SO ANYWAY, ABOUT THE MIXER I MENTIONED YESTER-DAY—
AH, SORRY.
I HAVE OTHER PLANS FOR THIS FRIDAY.

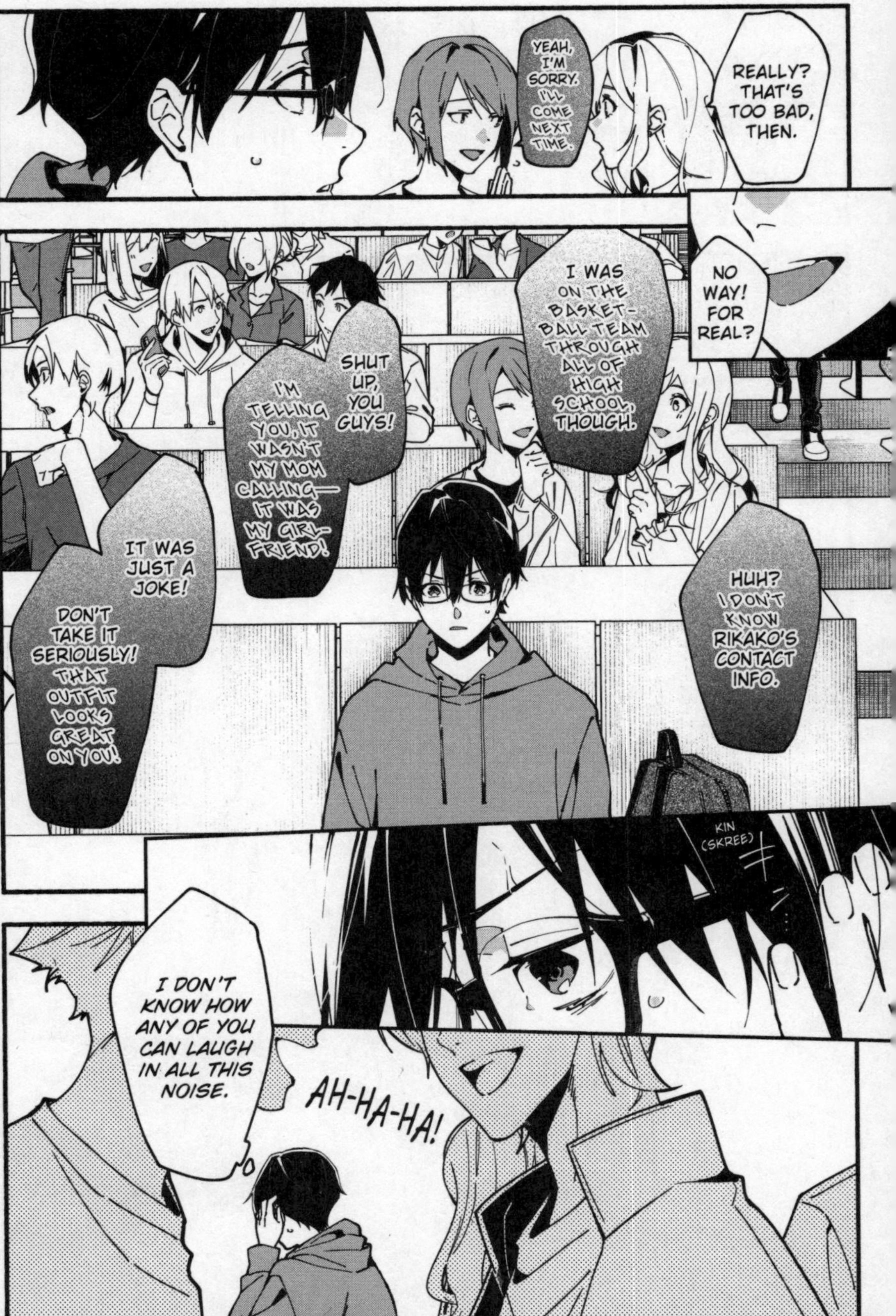

REALLY? THAT'S TOO BAD, THEN.
YEAH, I'M SORRY. I'LL COME NEXT TIME.
NO WAY! FOR REAL?
I WAS ON THE BASKETBALL TEAM THROUGH ALL OF HIGH SCHOOL, THOUGH.
HUH? I DON'T KNOW RIKAKO'S CONTACT INFO.
SHUT UP, YOU GUYS!
I'M TELLING YOU, IT WASN'T MY MOM CALLING—IT WAS MY GIRLFRIEND!
IT WAS JUST A JOKE!
DON'T TAKE IT SERIOUSLY! THAT OUTFIT LOOKS GREAT ON YOU!
KIN (SKREE)
AH-HA-HA!
I DON'T KNOW HOW ANY OF YOU CAN LAUGH IN ALL THIS NOISE.

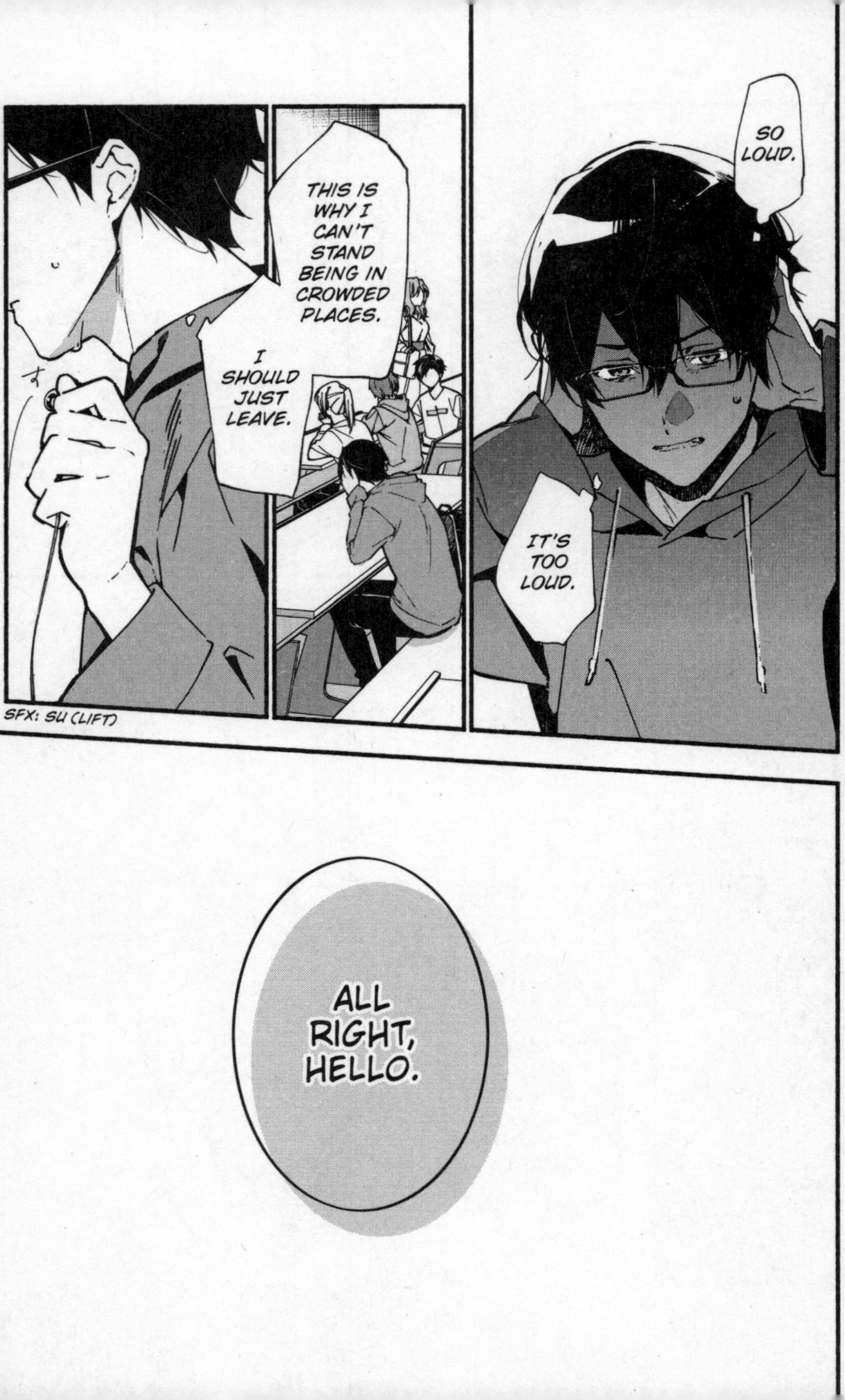
SO LOUD.
IT'S TOO LOUD.
THIS IS WHY I CAN'T STAND BEING IN CROWDED PLACES.
I SHOULD JUST LEAVE.
SFX: SU (LIFT)
ALL RIGHT, HELLO.

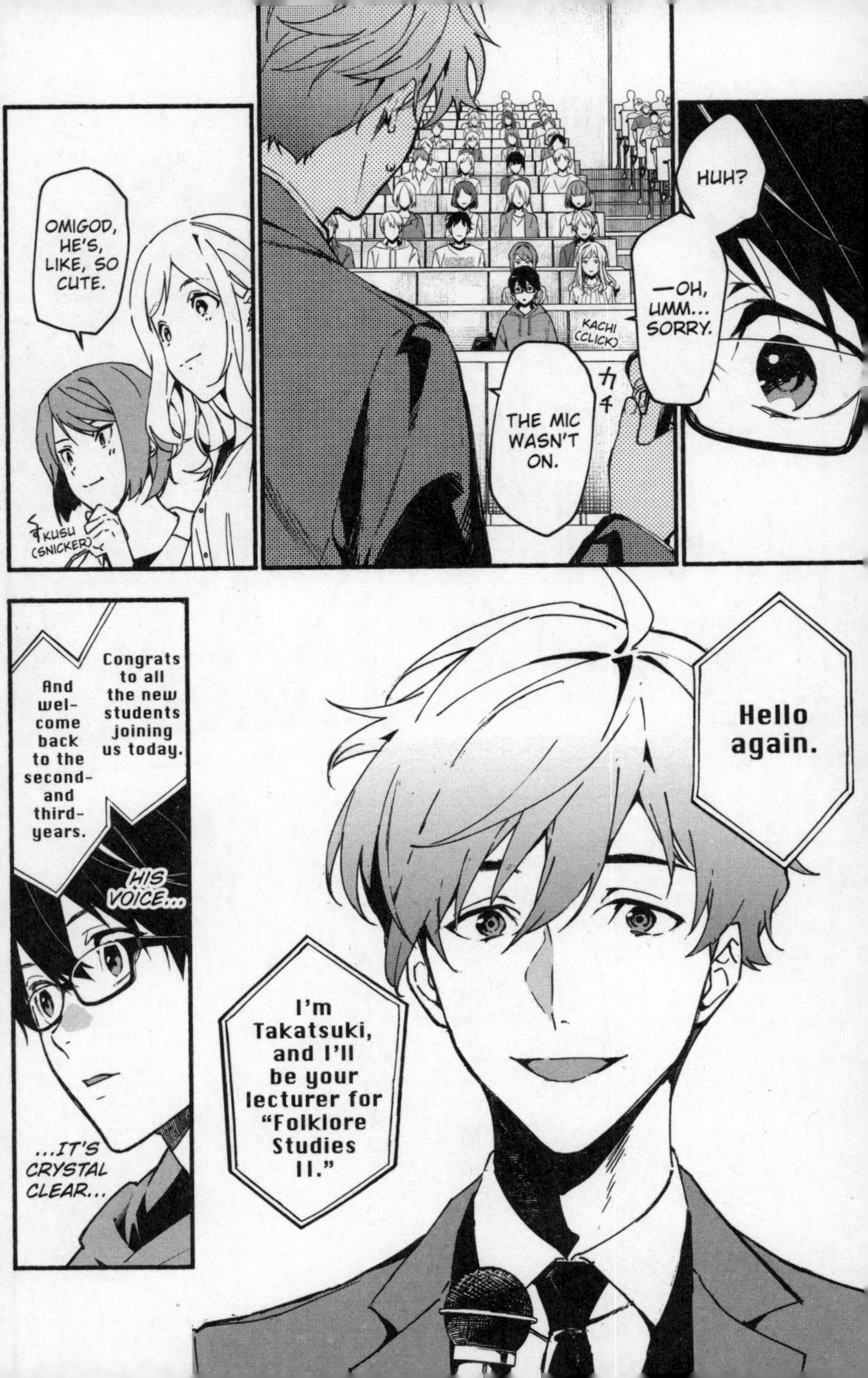
HUH?
—OH, UMM... SORRY.
KACHI (CLICK)
カチ
THE MIC WASN'T ON.
OMIGOD, HE'S, LIKE, SO CUTE.
す KUSU (SNICKER)
Hello again.
I'm Takatsuki, and I'll be your lecturer for "Folklore Studies II."
Congrats to all the new students joining us today.
And wel-come back to the second- and third-years.
HIS VOICE...
...IT'S CRYSTAL CLEAR...

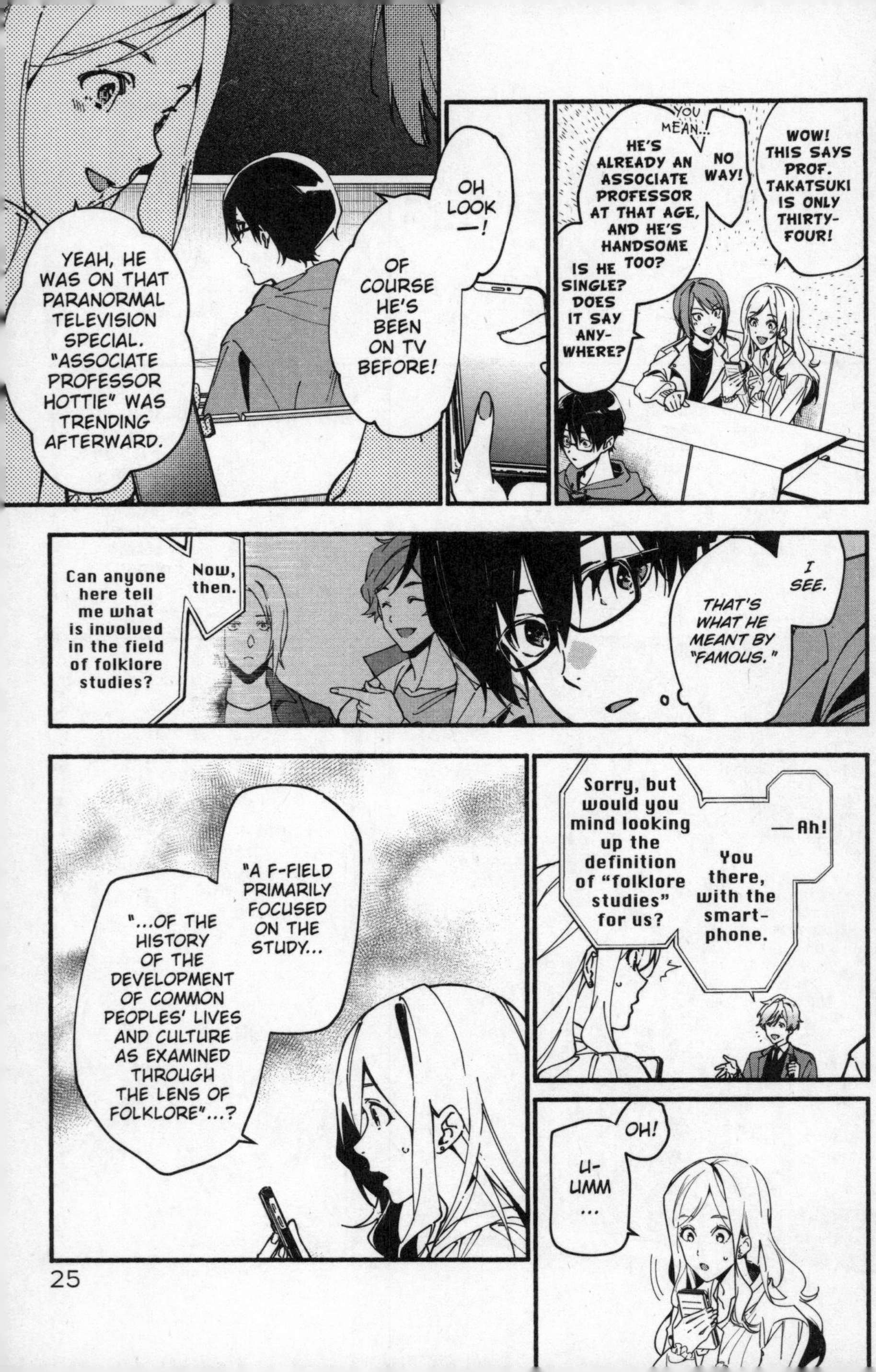

WOW! THIS SAYS PROF. TAKATSUKI IS ONLY THIRTY-FOUR!
YOU MEAN...
NO WAY!
HE'S ALREADY AN ASSOCIATE PROFESSOR AT THAT AGE, AND HE'S HANDSOME TOO?
IS HE SINGLE? DOES IT SAY ANYWHERE?
OH LOOK—!
OF COURSE HE'S BEEN ON TV BEFORE!
YEAH, HE WAS ON THAT PARANORMAL TELEVISION SPECIAL. "ASSOCIATE PROFESSOR HOTTIE" WAS TRENDING AFTERWARD.
I SEE.
THAT'S WHAT HE MEANT BY "FAMOUS."
Now, then.
Can anyone here tell me what is involved in the field of folklore studies?
—Ah!
You there, with the smartphone.
Sorry, but would you mind looking up the definition of "folklore studies" for us?
OH!
U-UMM...
"A F-FIELD PRIMARILY FOCUSED ON THE STUDY...
"...OF THE HISTORY OF THE DEVELOPMENT OF COMMON PEOPLES' LIVES AND CULTURE AS EXAMINED THROUGH THE LENS OF FOLKLORE"...?

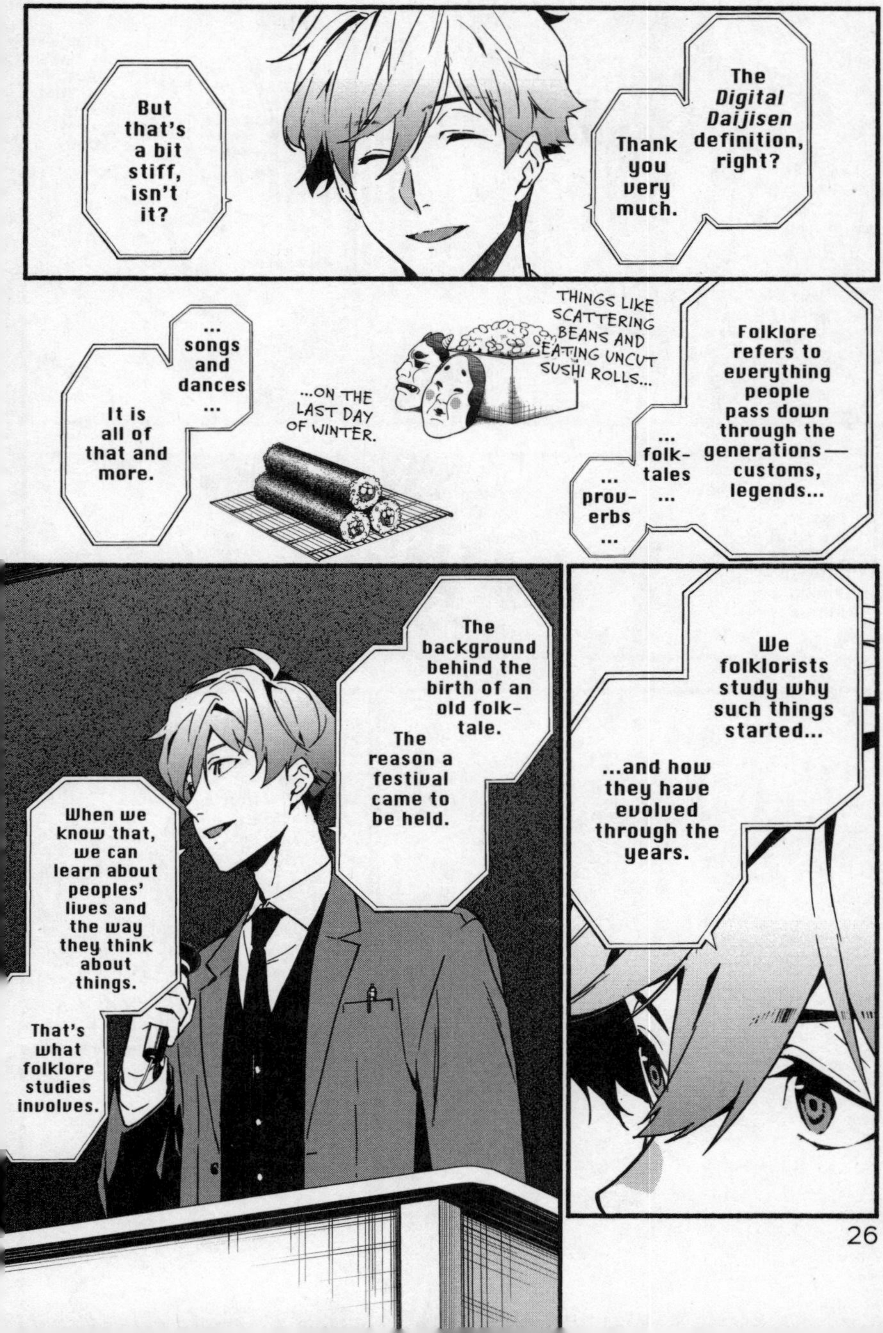
The Digital Daijisen definition, right?
Thank you very much.
But that's a bit stiff, isn't it?
Folklore refers to everything people pass down through the generations—customs, legends...
...folk-tales...
...prov-erbs...
THINGS LIKE SCATTERING BEANS AND EATING UNCUT SUSHI ROLLS...
...ON THE LAST DAY OF WINTER.
...songs and dances...
It is all of that and more.
We folklorists study why such things started...
...and how they have evolved through the years.
The background behind the birth of an old folk-tale.
The reason a festival came to be held.
When we know that, we can learn about peoples' lives and the way they think about things.
That's what folklore studies involves.

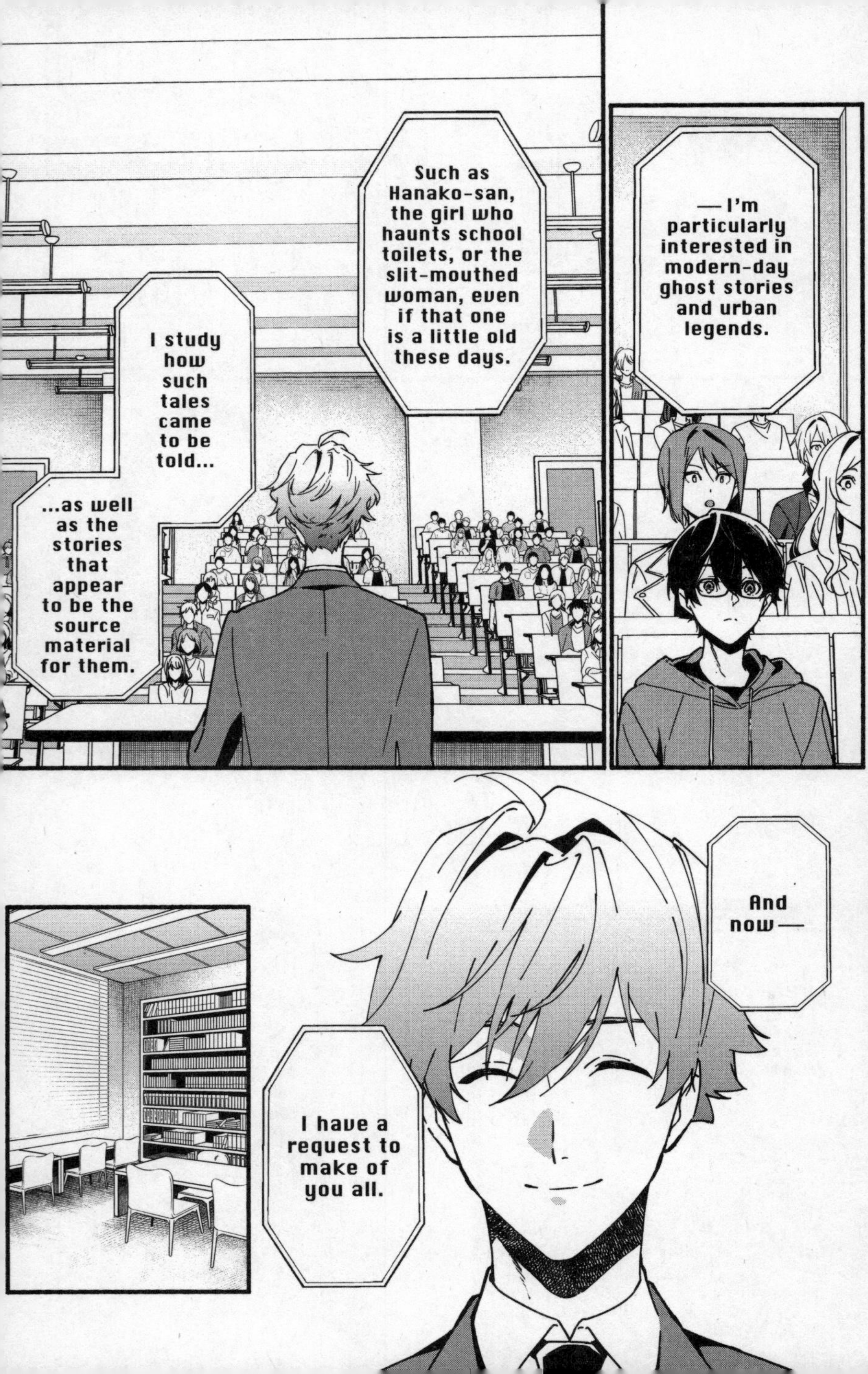
—I'm particularly interested in modern-day ghost stories and urban legends.
Such as Hanako-san, the girl who haunts school toilets, or the slit-mouthed woman, even if that one is a little old these days.
I study how such tales came to be told...
...as well as the stories that appear to be the source material for them.
And now—
I have a request to make of you all.

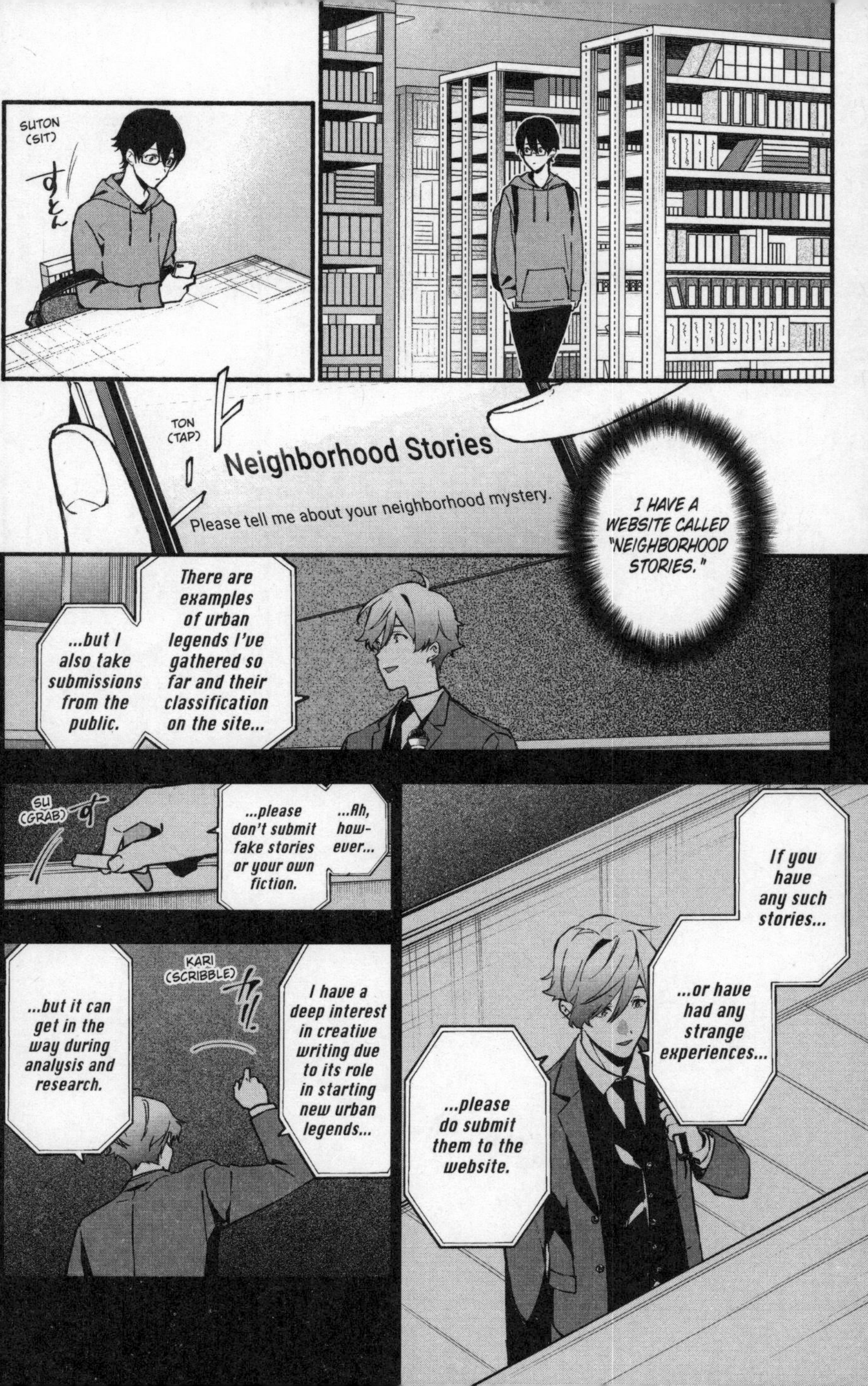
SUTON (SIT)
すとん
TON (TAP)
Neighborhood Stories
Please tell me about your neighborhood mystery.
I HAVE A WEBSITE CALLED "NEIGHBORHOOD STORIES."
There are examples of urban legends I've gathered so far and their classification on the site...
...but I also take submissions from the public.
If you have any such stories...
...or have had any strange experiences...
...please do submit them to the website.
...Ah, how-ever...
...please don't submit fake stories or your own fiction.
SU (GRAB)
す
I have a deep interest in creative writing due to its role in starting new urban legends...
KARI (SCRIBBLE)
...but it can get in the way during analysis and research.

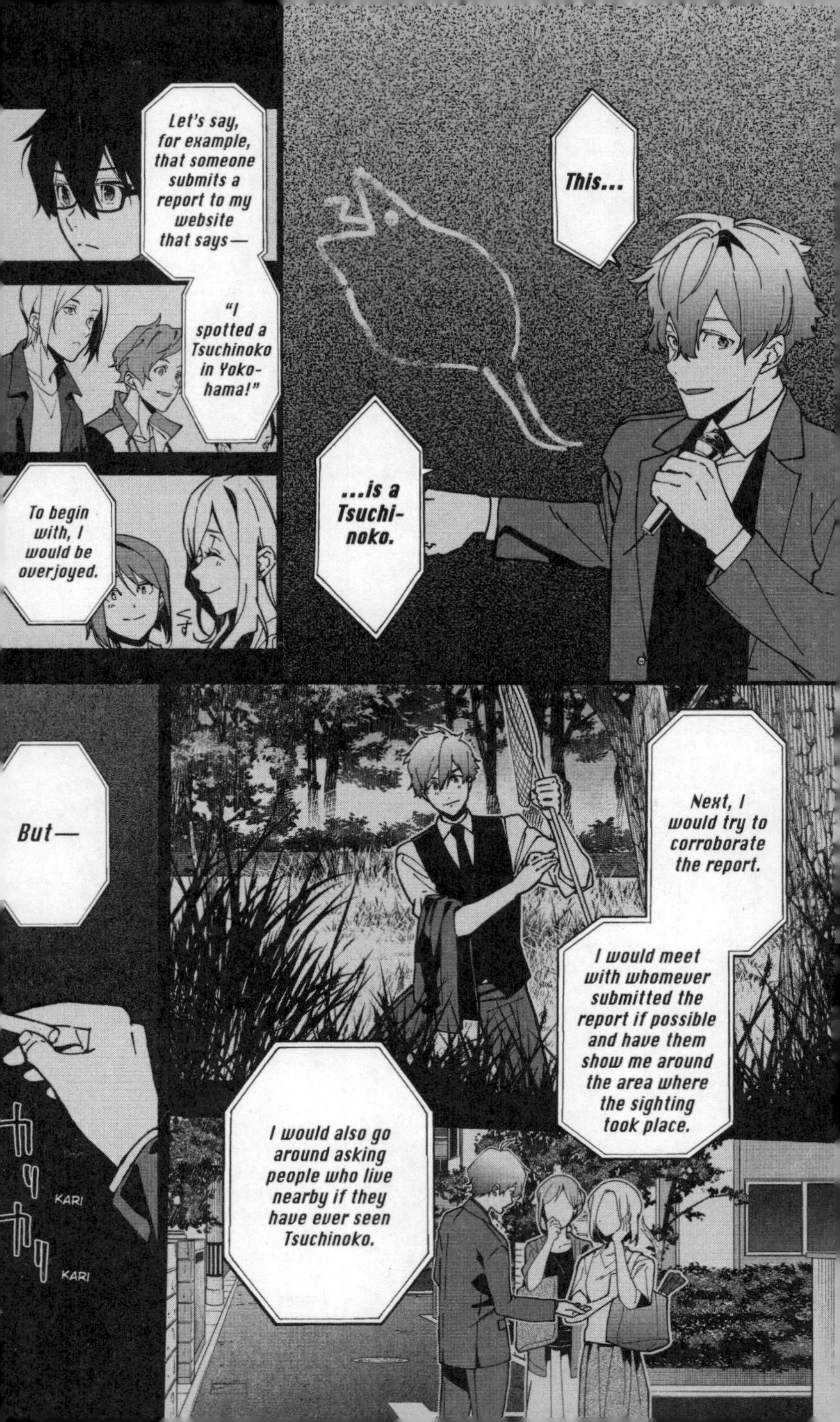
This...
...is a Tsuchinoko.
Let's say, for example, that someone submits a report to my website that says—
"I spotted a Tsuchinoko in Yokohama!"
To begin with, I would be overjoyed.
Next, I would try to corroborate the report.
I would meet with whomever submitted the report if possible and have them show me around the area where the sighting took place.
I would also go around asking people who live nearby if they have ever seen Tsuchinoko.
But—
カリ KARI
カリ KARI

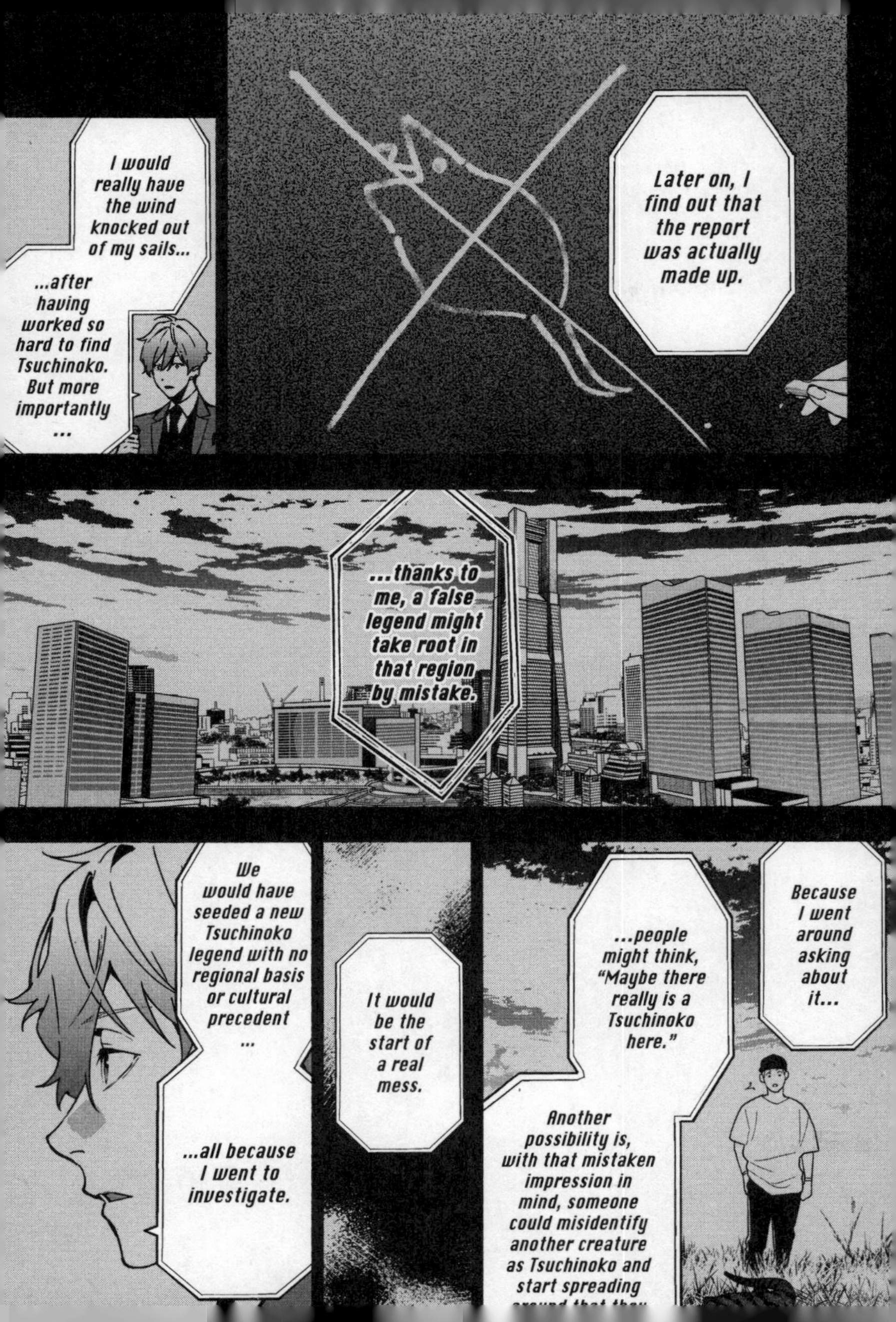
Later on, I find out that the report was actually made up.
I would really have the wind knocked out of my sails...
...after having worked so hard to find Tsuchinoko. But more importantly ...
...thanks to me, a false legend might take root in that region by mistake.
Because I went around asking about it...
...people might think, "Maybe there really is a Tsuchinoko here."
Another possibility is, with that mistaken impression in mind, someone could misidentify another creature as Tsuchinoko and start spreading
It would be the start of a real mess.
We would have seeded a new Tsuchinoko legend with no regional basis or cultural precedent ...
...all because I went to investigate.

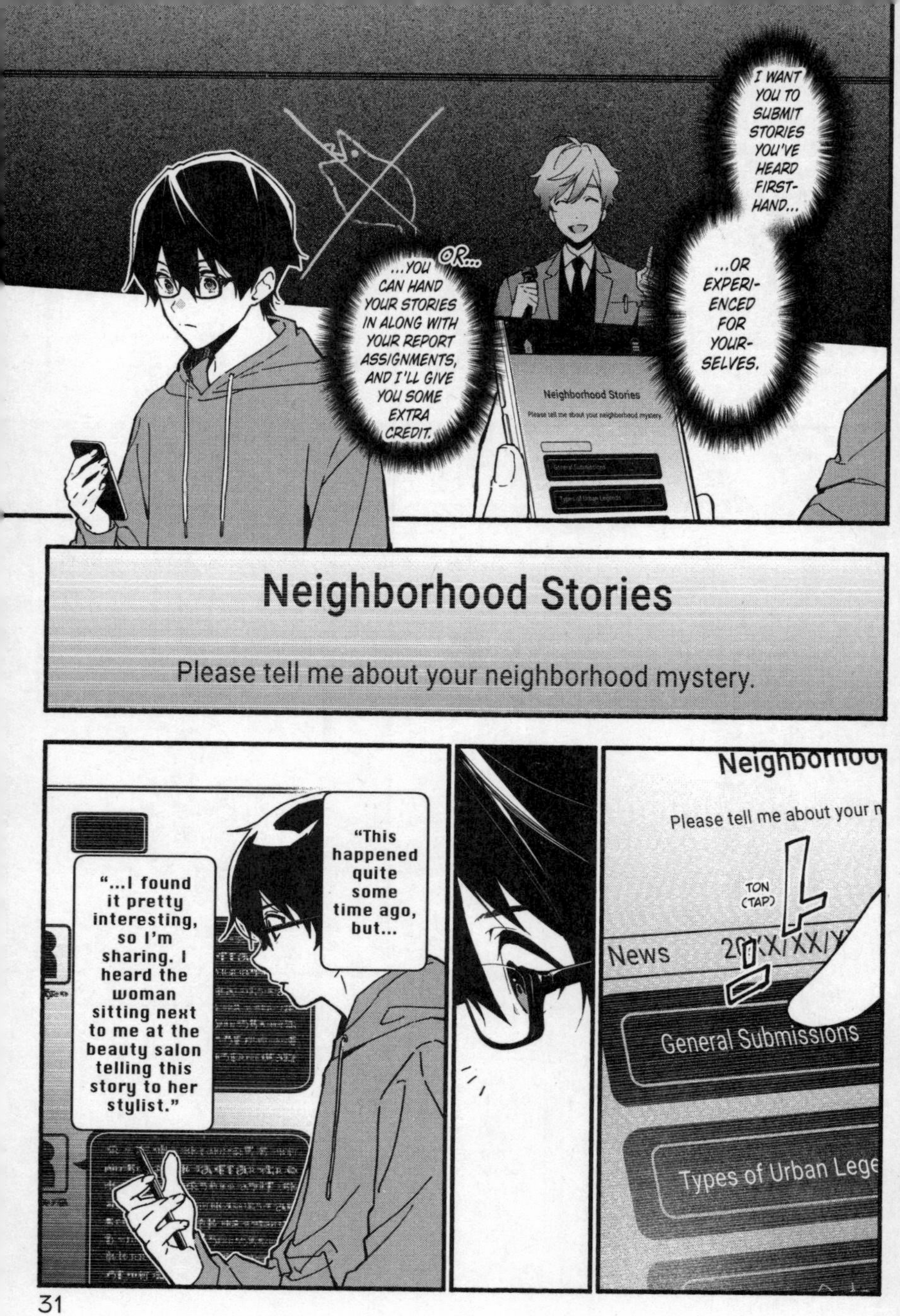
I WANT YOU TO SUBMIT STORIES YOU'VE HEARD FIRST-HAND...
...OR EXPERIENCED FOR YOURSELVES.
OR...
...YOU CAN HAND YOUR STORIES IN ALONG WITH YOUR REPORT ASSIGNMENTS, AND I'LL GIVE YOU SOME EXTRA CREDIT.
Neighborhood Stories
Please tell me about your neighborhood mystery.
TON (TAP)
News
General Submissions
"This happened quite some time ago, but...
"...I found it pretty interesting, so I'm sharing. I heard the woman sitting next to me at the beauty salon telling this story to her stylist."

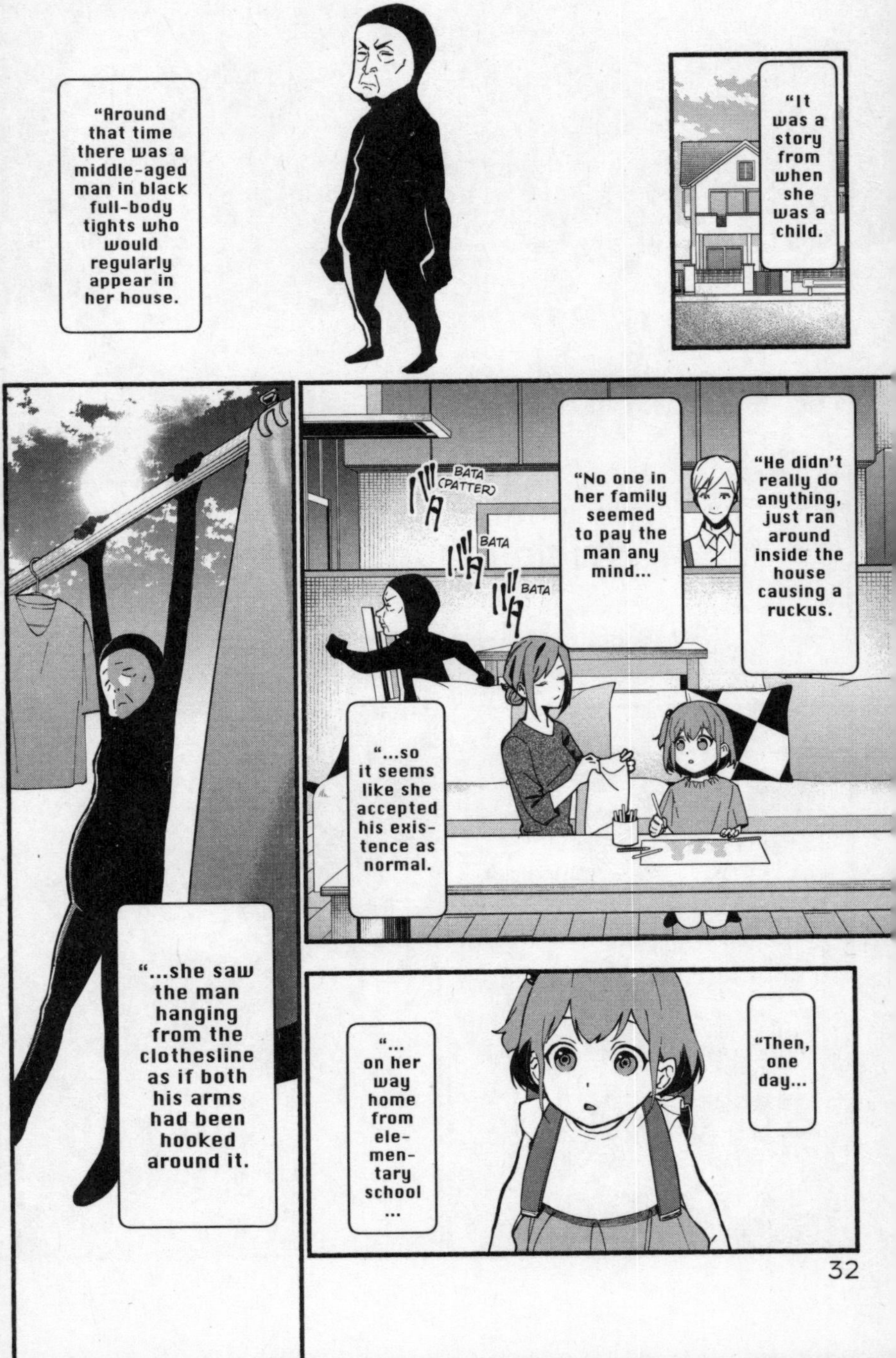
"It was a story from when she was a child.
"Around that time there was a middle-aged man in black full-body tights who would regularly appear in her house.
"He didn't really do anything, just ran around inside the house causing a ruckus.
"No one in her family seemed to pay the man any mind...
BATA (PATTER)
BATA
BATA
"...so it seems like she accepted his existence as normal.
"Then, one day...
"...on her way home from elementary school...
"...she saw the man hanging from the clothesline as if both his arms had been hooked around it.

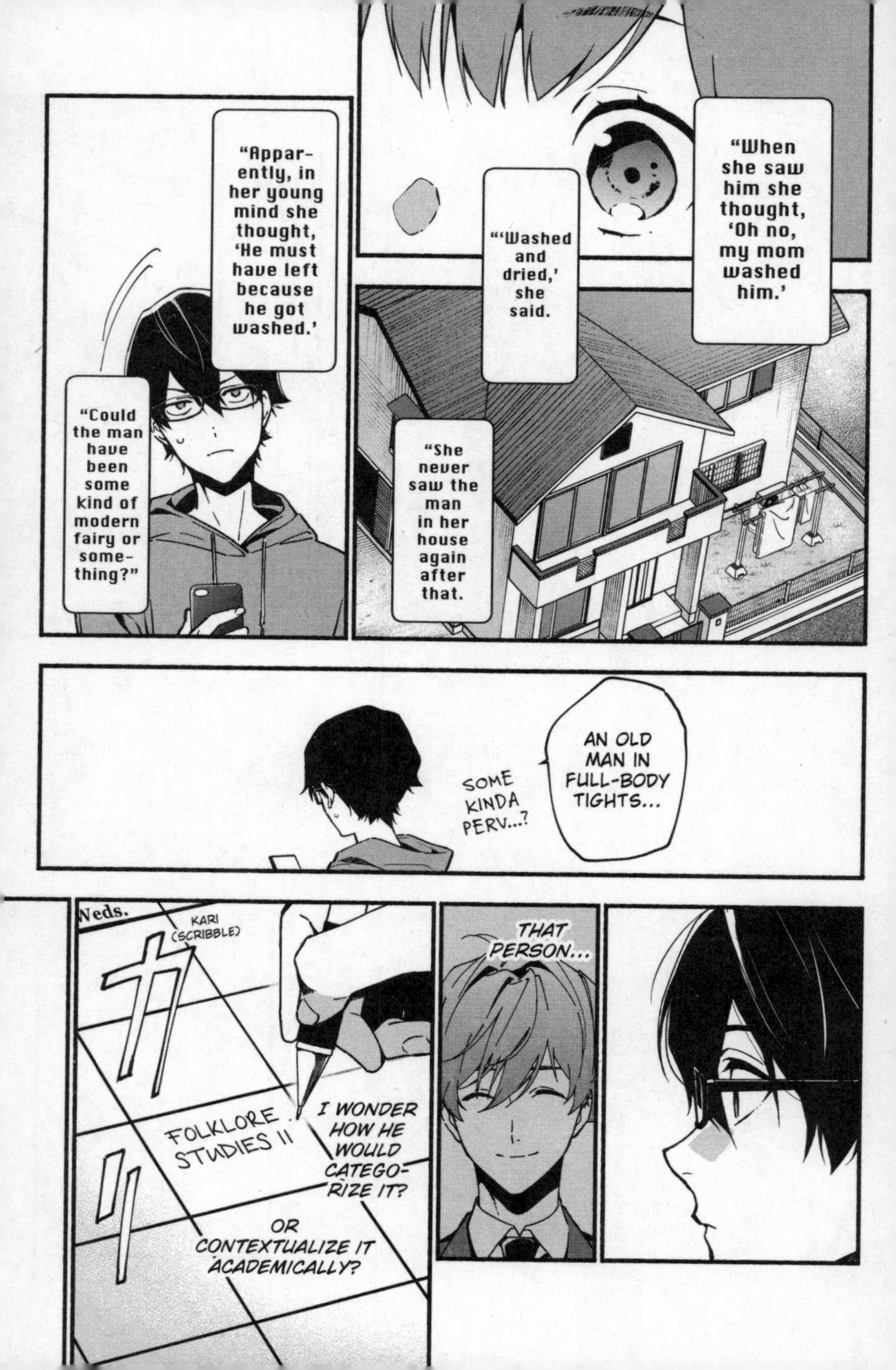
"When she saw him she thought, 'Oh no, my mom washed him.'
"'Washed and dried,' she said.
"She never saw the man in her house again after that.
"Apparently, in her young mind she thought, 'He must have left because he got washed.'
"Could the man have been some kind of modern fairy or something?"
AN OLD MAN IN FULL-BODY TIGHTS...
SOME KINDA PERV...?
THAT PERSON...
I WONDER HOW HE WOULD CATEGORIZE IT?
OR CONTEXTUALIZE IT ACADEMICALLY?
Weds.
KARI (SCRIBBLE)
カ
リ
FOLKLORE STUDIES II

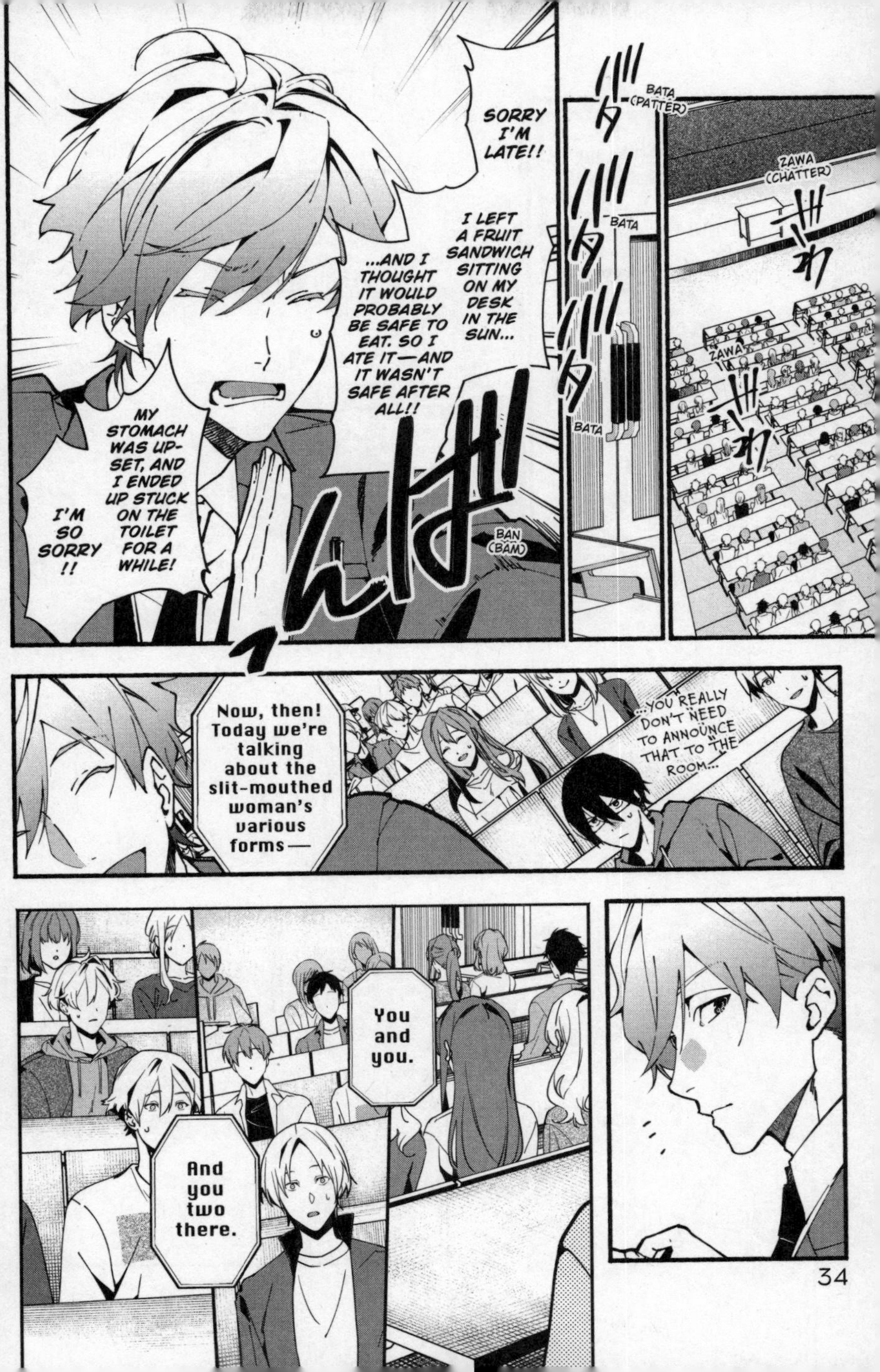
ZAWA (CHATTER)
ZAWA
BATA (PATTER)
BATA
BATA
SORRY I'M LATE!!
I LEFT A FRUIT SANDWICH SITTING ON MY DESK IN THE SUN...
...AND I THOUGHT IT WOULD PROBABLY BE SAFE TO EAT. SO I ATE IT—AND IT WASN'T SAFE AFTER ALL!!
BAN (BAM)
MY STOMACH WAS UPSET, AND I ENDED UP STUCK ON THE TOILET FOR A WHILE!
I'M SO SORRY!!
...YOU REALLY DON'T NEED TO ANNOUNCE THAT TO THE ROOM...
Now, then! Today we're talking about the slit-mouthed woman's various forms—
...
You and you.
And you two there.

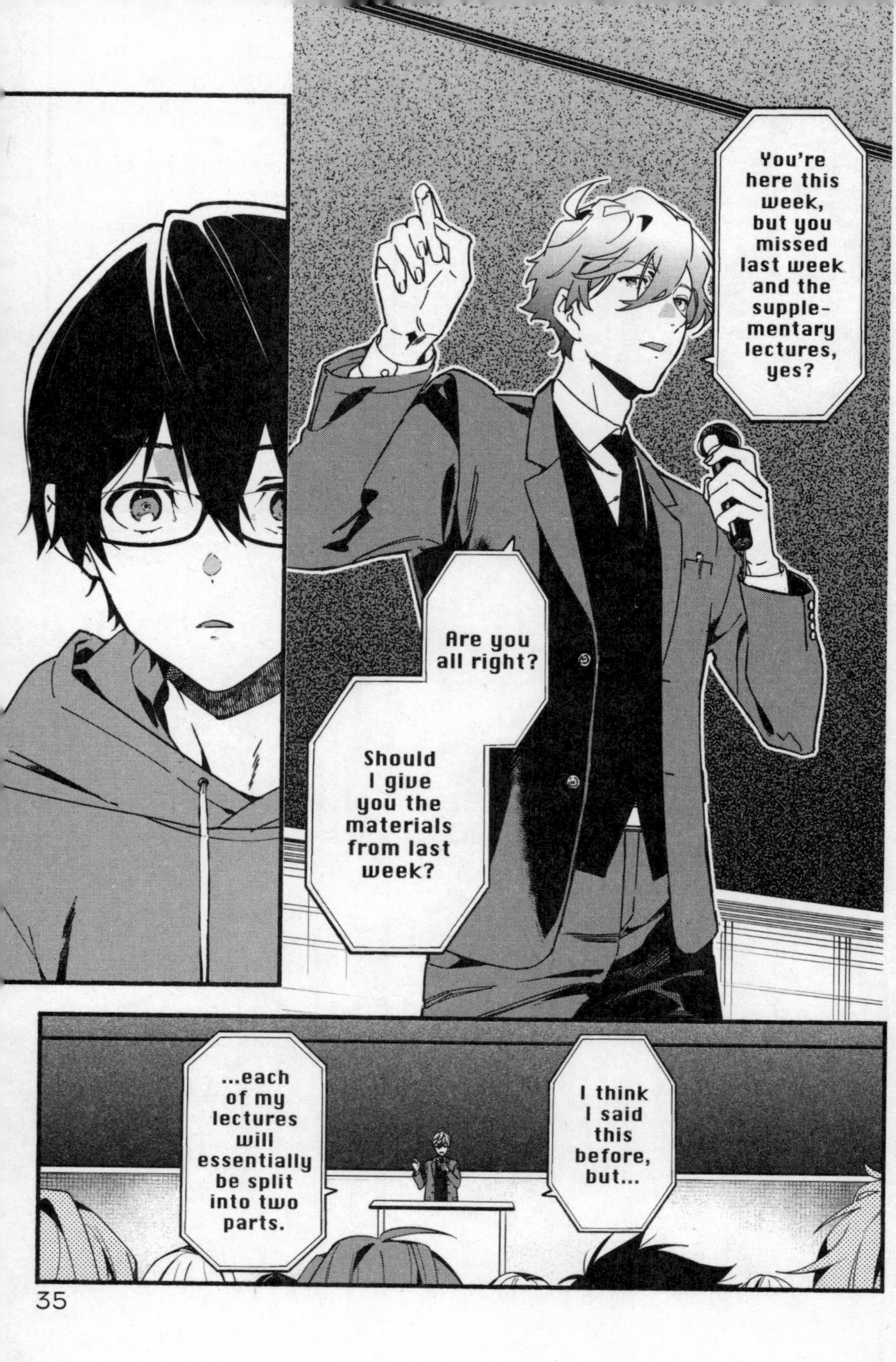
You're here this week, but you missed last week and the supple-mentary lectures, yes?
Are you all right?
Should I give you the materials from last week?
I think I said this before, but...
...each of my lectures will essentially be split into two parts.

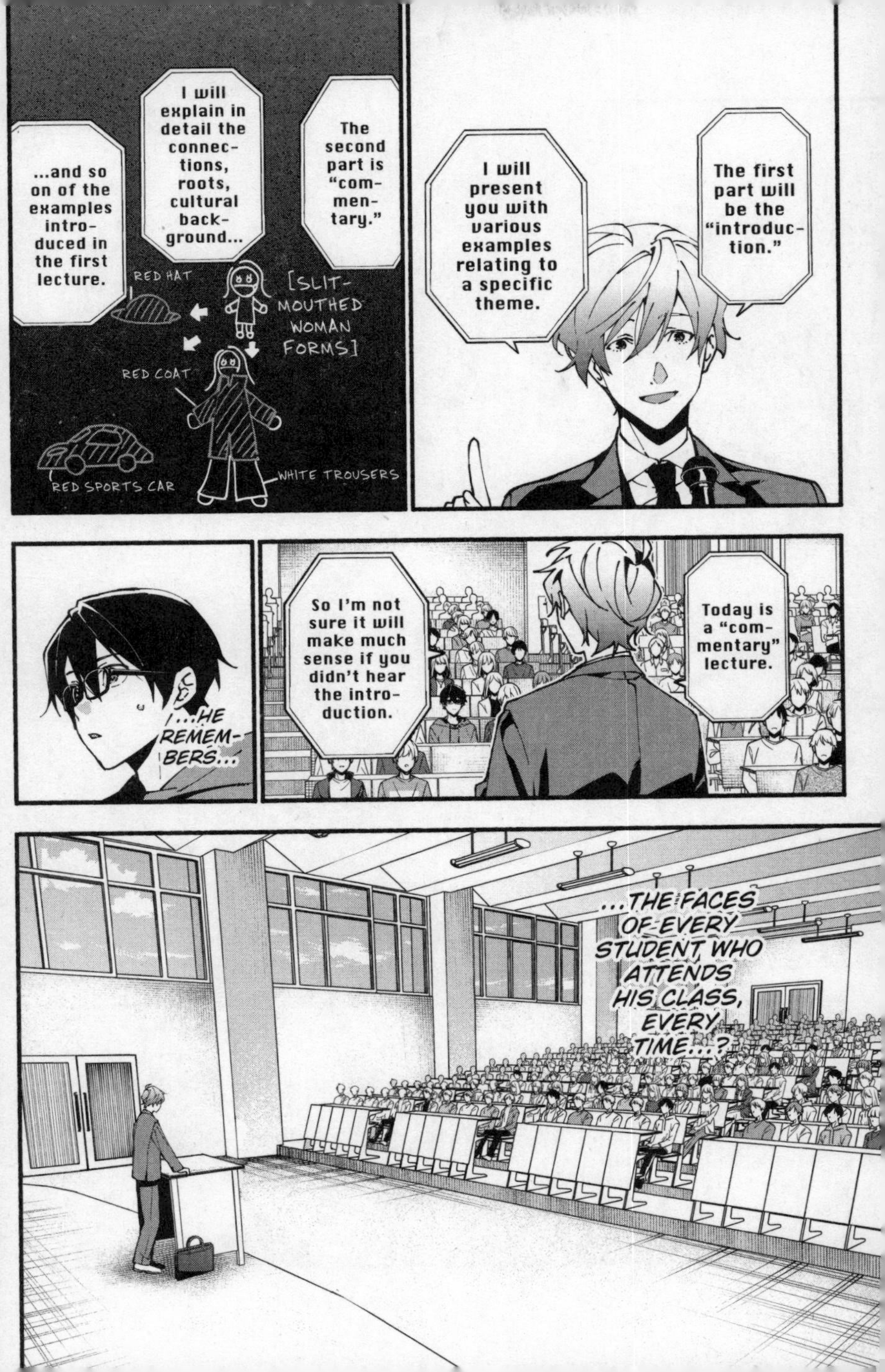
The first part will be the "introduction."
I will present you with various examples relating to a specific theme.
The second part is "commentary."
I will explain in detail the connections, roots, cultural background...
...and so on of the examples introduced in the first lecture.
[SLIT-MOUTHED WOMAN FORMS]
RED HAT
RED COAT
RED SPORTS CAR
WHITE TROUSERS
Today is a "commentary" lecture.
So I'm not sure it will make much sense if you didn't hear the introduction.
...HE REMEMBERS...
...THE FACES OF EVERY STUDENT WHO ATTENDS HIS CLASS, EVERY TIME...?

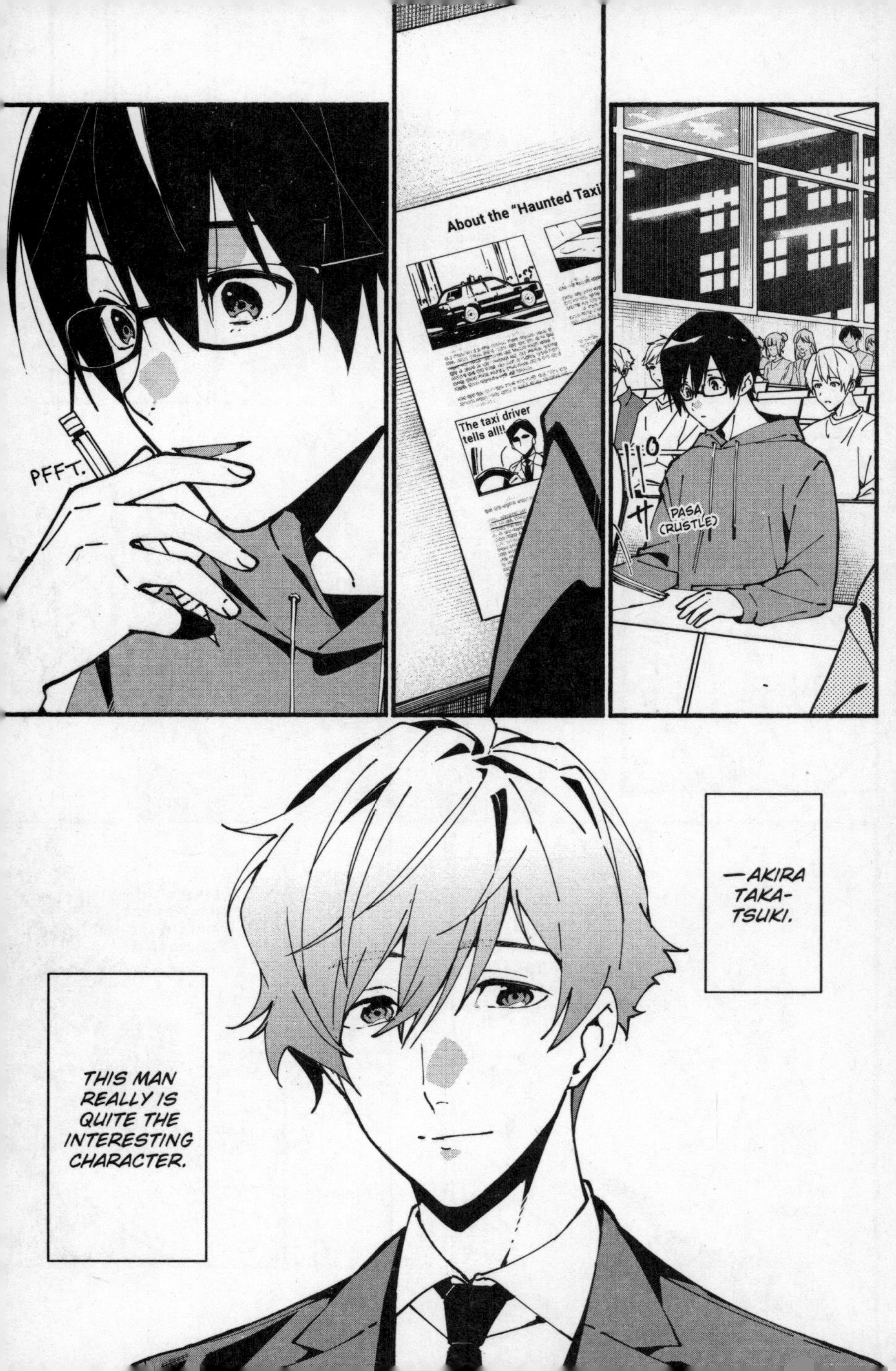
PASA (RUSTLE)
About the “Haunted Taxi
The taxi driver tells all!!
PFFT.
—AKIRA TAKA-TSUKI.
THIS MAN REALLY IS QUITE THE INTERESTING CHARACTER.

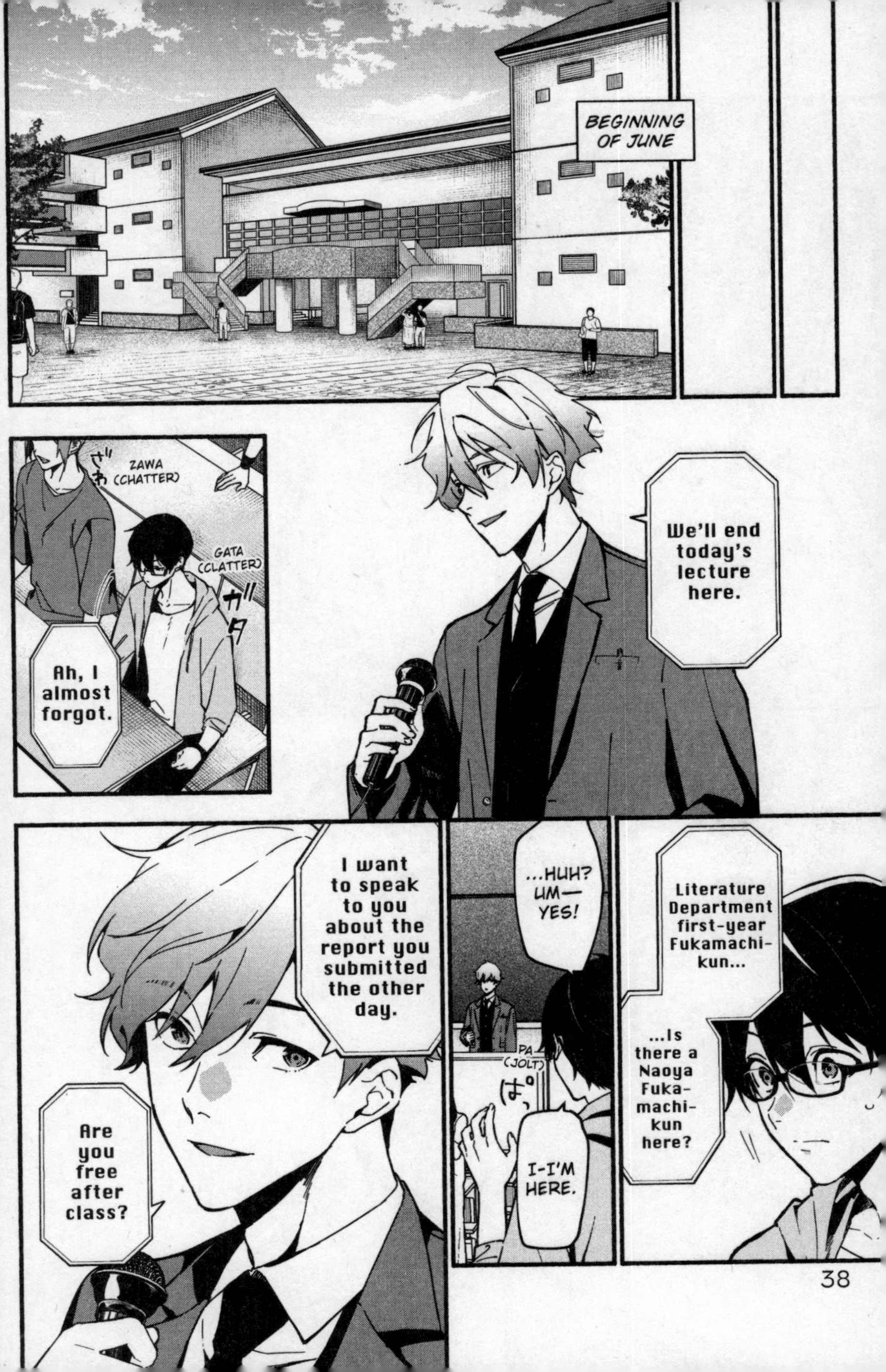
BEGINNING OF JUNE
We'll end today's lecture here.
ざわ
ZAWA (CHATTER)
GATA (CLATTER)
ガタ
Ah, I almost forgot.
Literature Department first-year Fukamachi-kun...
...Is there a Naoya Fukamachi-kun here?
...HUH? UM— YES!
PA (JOLT)
ぱ
I-I'M HERE.
I want to speak to you about the report you submitted the other day.
Are you free after class?

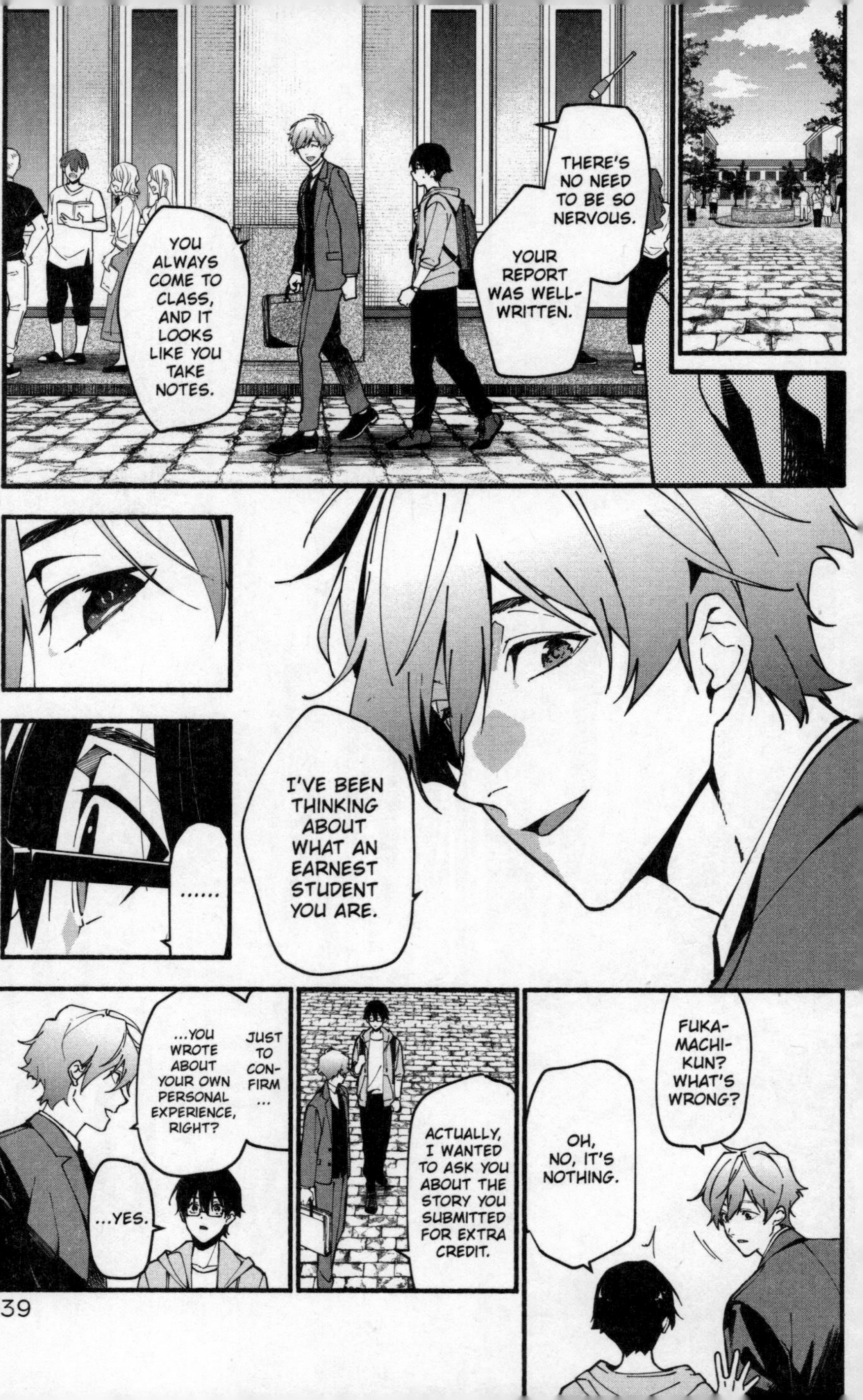
THERE'S NO NEED TO BE SO NERVOUS.
YOUR REPORT WAS WELL-WRITTEN.
YOU ALWAYS COME TO CLASS, AND IT LOOKS LIKE YOU TAKE NOTES.
I'VE BEEN THINKING ABOUT WHAT AN EARNEST STUDENT YOU ARE.
......
FUKAMACHI-KUN? WHAT'S WRONG?
OH, NO, IT'S NOTHING.
ACTUALLY, I WANTED TO ASK YOU ABOUT THE STORY YOU SUBMITTED FOR EXTRA CREDIT.
JUST TO CONFIRM...
...YOU WROTE ABOUT YOUR OWN PERSONAL EXPERIENCE, RIGHT?
...YES.

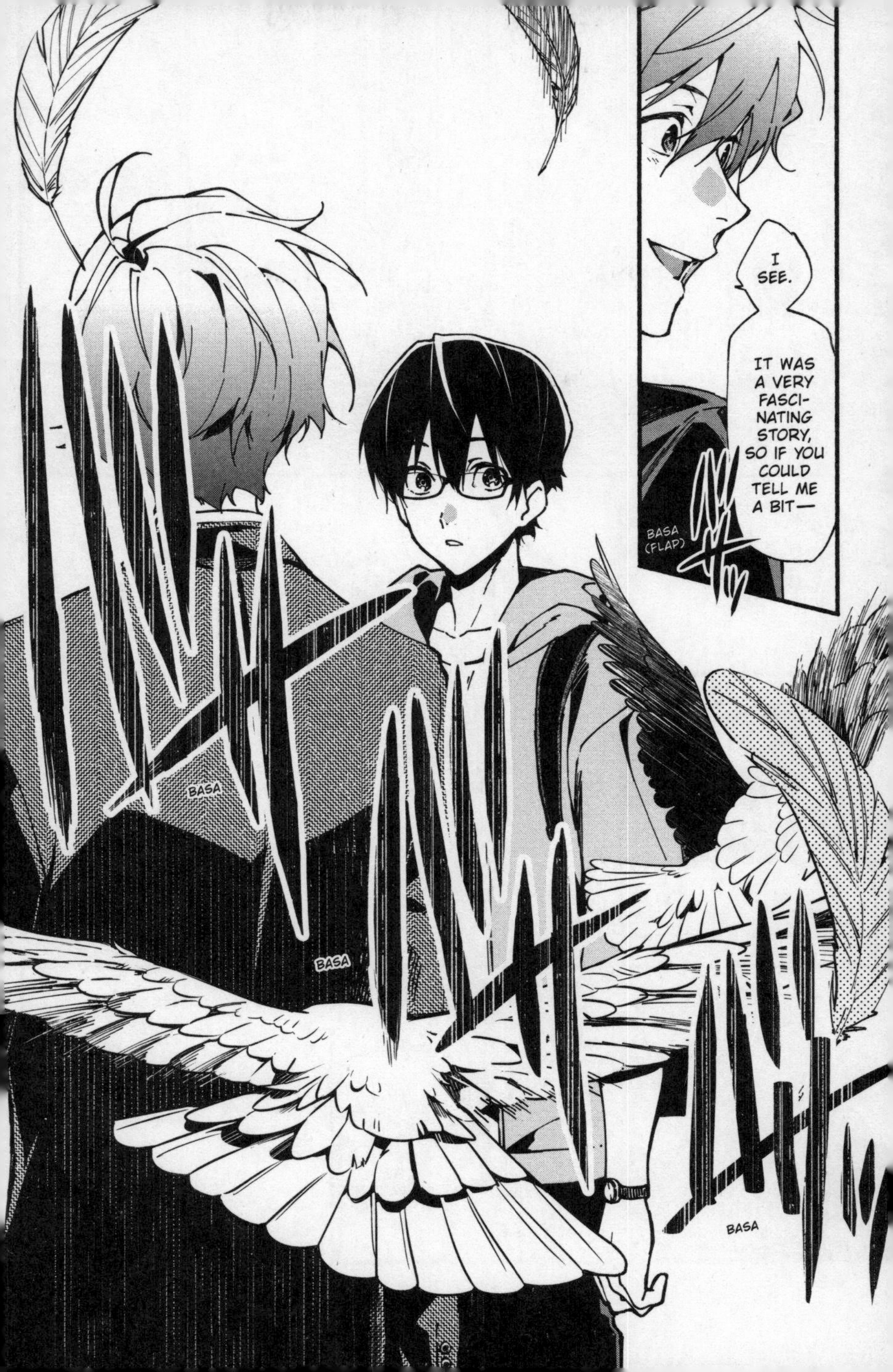
I SEE.
IT WAS A VERY FASCI-NATING STORY, SO IF YOU COULD TELL ME A BIT—
BASA (FLAP)
BASA
BASA
BASA

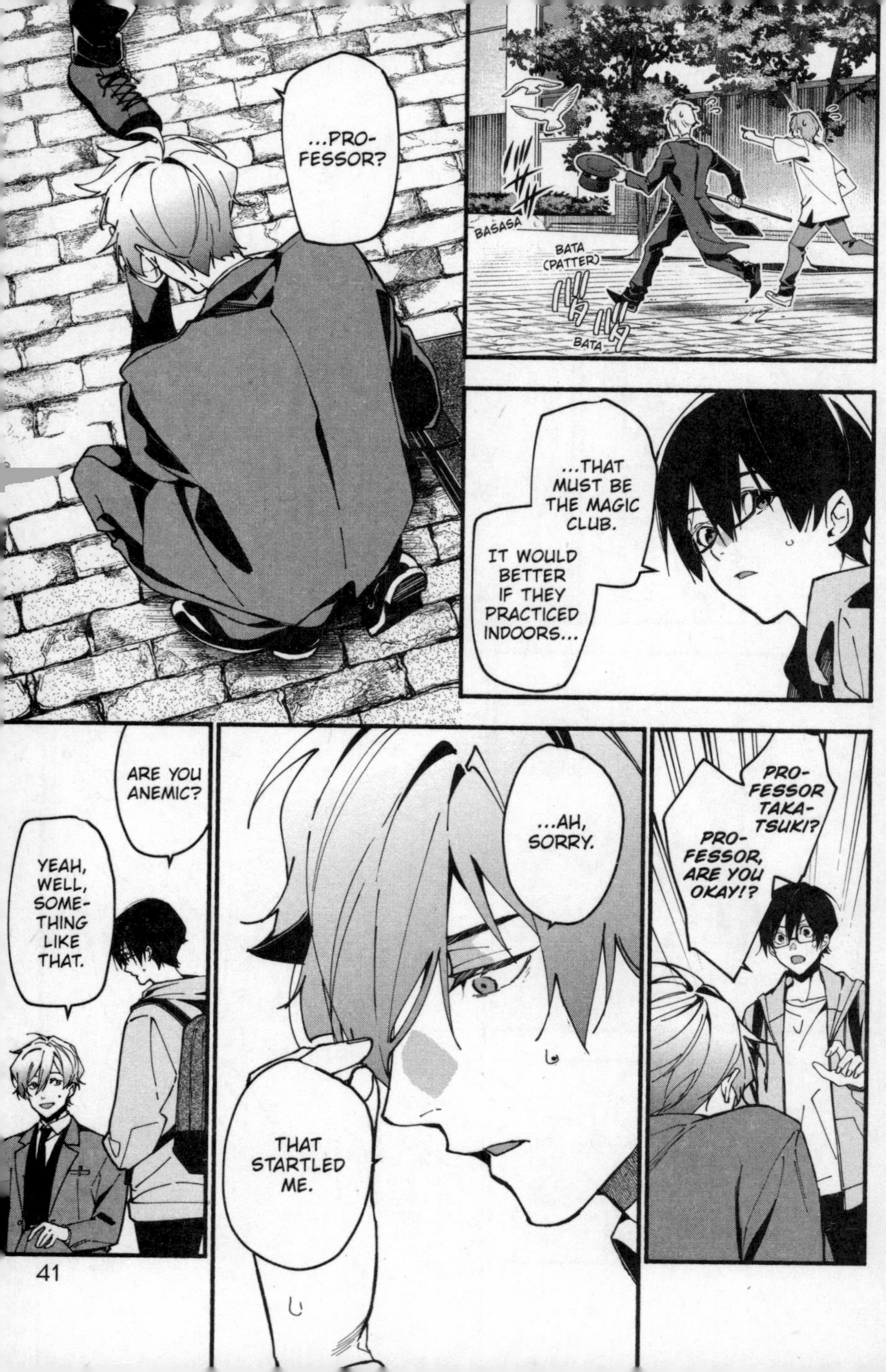
BASASA
BATA (PATTER)
BATA
...THAT MUST BE THE MAGIC CLUB.
IT WOULD BETTER IF THEY PRACTICED INDOORS...
...PRO-FESSOR?
PRO-FESSOR TAKA-TSUKI?
PRO-FESSOR, ARE YOU OKAY!?
...AH, SORRY.
THAT STARTLED ME.
ARE YOU ANEMIC?
YEAH, WELL, SOMETHING LIKE THAT.

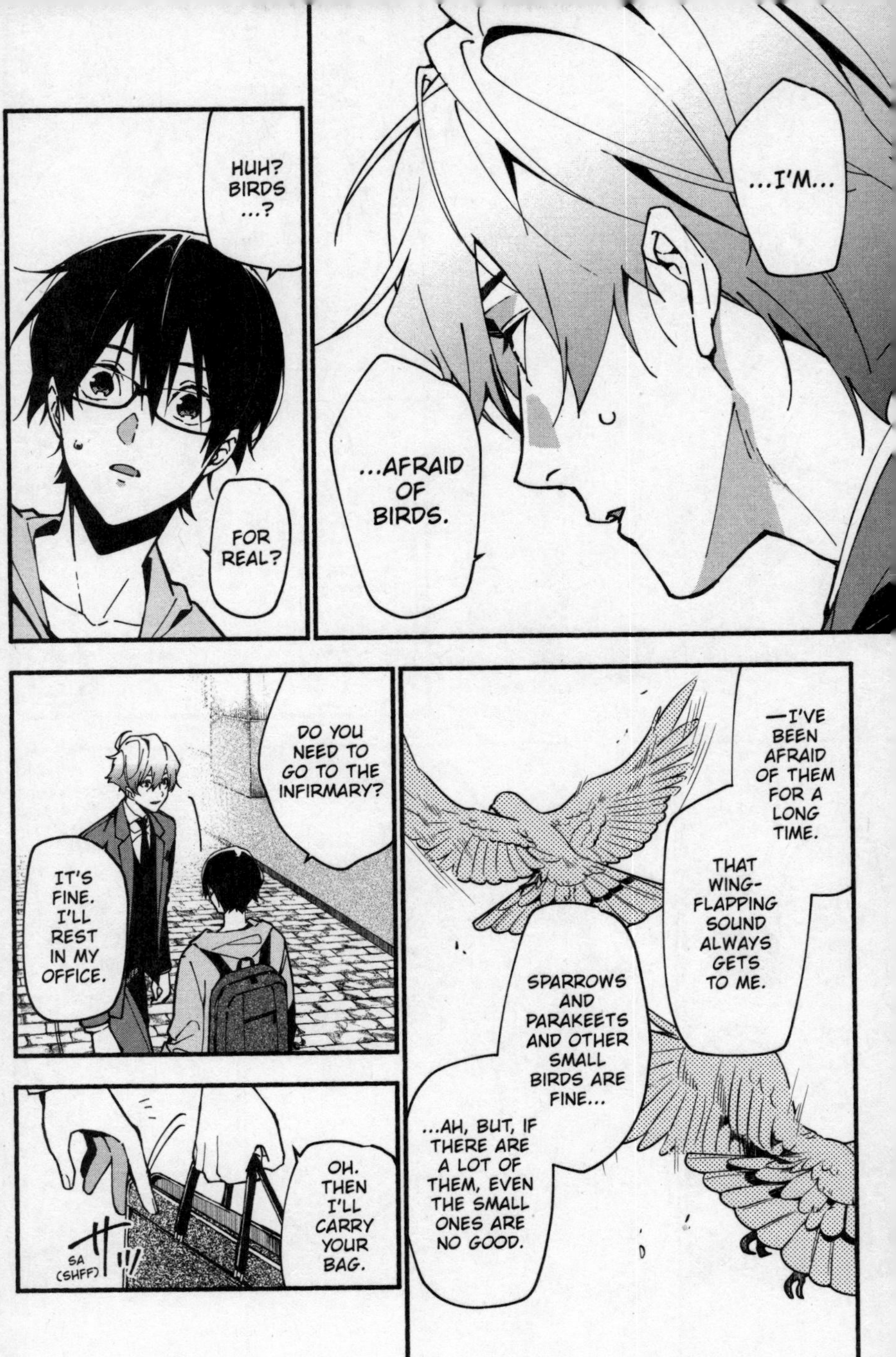
...I'M...
...AFRAID OF BIRDS.
HUH? BIRDS ...?
FOR REAL?
—I'VE BEEN AFRAID OF THEM FOR A LONG TIME.
THAT WING-FLAPPING SOUND ALWAYS GETS TO ME.
SPARROWS AND PARAKEETS AND OTHER SMALL BIRDS ARE FINE...
...AH, BUT, IF THERE ARE A LOT OF THEM, EVEN THE SMALL ONES ARE NO GOOD.
DO YOU NEED TO GO TO THE INFIRMARY?
IT'S FINE. I'LL REST IN MY OFFICE.
OH. THEN I'LL CARRY YOUR BAG.
SA (SHFF)

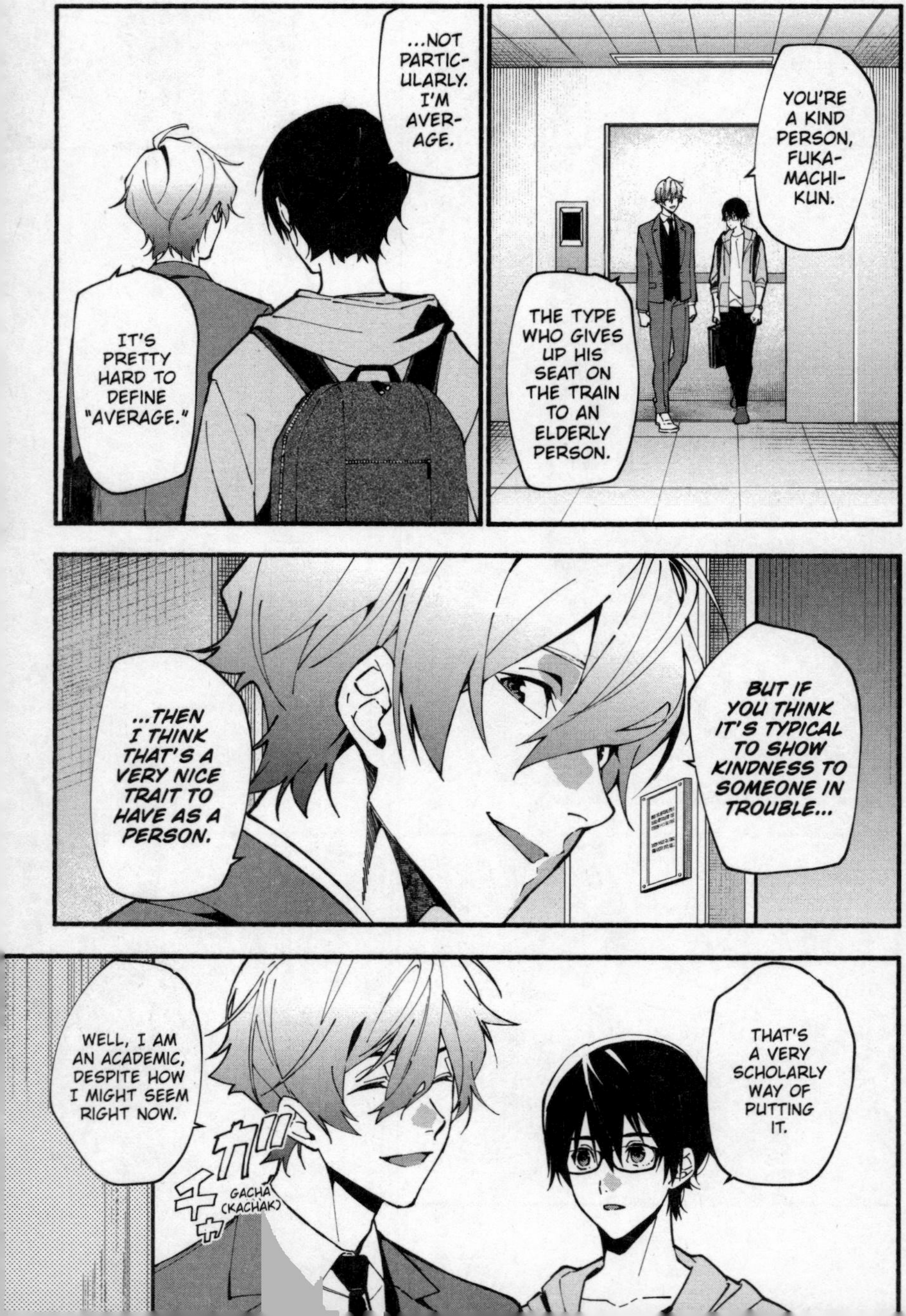
YOU'RE A KIND PERSON, FUKA-MACHI-KUN.
THE TYPE WHO GIVES UP HIS SEAT ON THE TRAIN TO AN ELDERLY PERSON.
...NOT PARTIC-ULARLY. I'M AVER-AGE.
IT'S PRETTY HARD TO DEFINE "AVERAGE."
BUT IF YOU THINK IT'S TYPICAL TO SHOW KINDNESS TO SOMEONE IN TROUBLE...
...THEN I THINK THAT'S A VERY NICE TRAIT TO HAVE AS A PERSON.
THAT'S A VERY SCHOLARLY WAY OF PUTTING IT.
WELL, I AM AN ACADEMIC, DESPITE HOW I MIGHT SEEM RIGHT NOW.
ガチャ
GACHA (KACHAK)

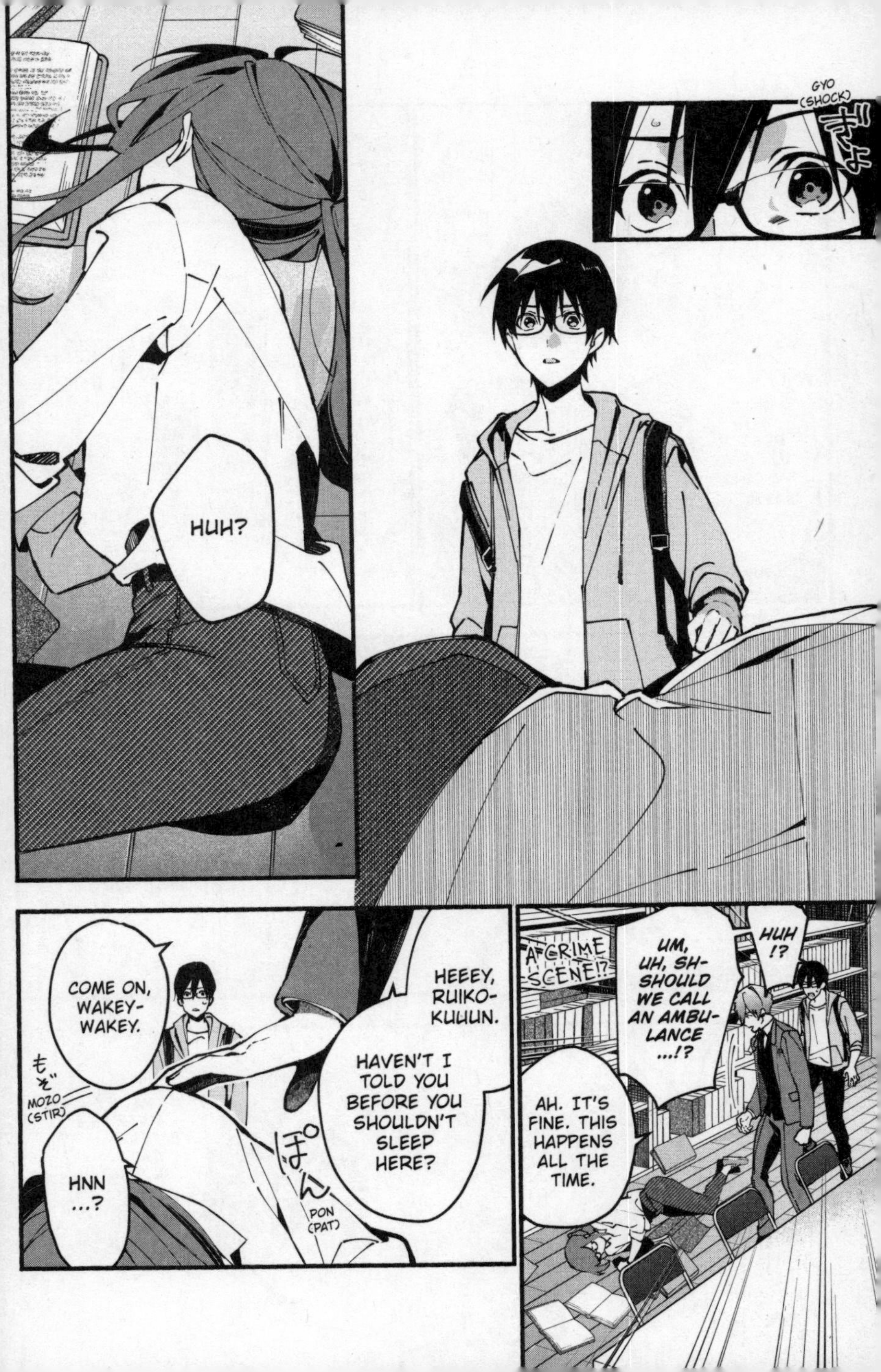
ぎょ
GYO (SHOCK)
HUH?
HUH!?
UM, UH, SH-SHOULD WE CALL AN AMBULANCE ...!?
A CRIME SCENE!?
AH. IT'S FINE. THIS HAPPENS ALL THE TIME.
HEEEY, RUIKO-KUUUN.
HAVEN'T I TOLD YOU BEFORE YOU SHOULDN'T SLEEP HERE?
ぽん
PON (PAT)
COME ON, WAKEY-WAKEY.
もぞ
MOZO (STIR)
HNN ...?

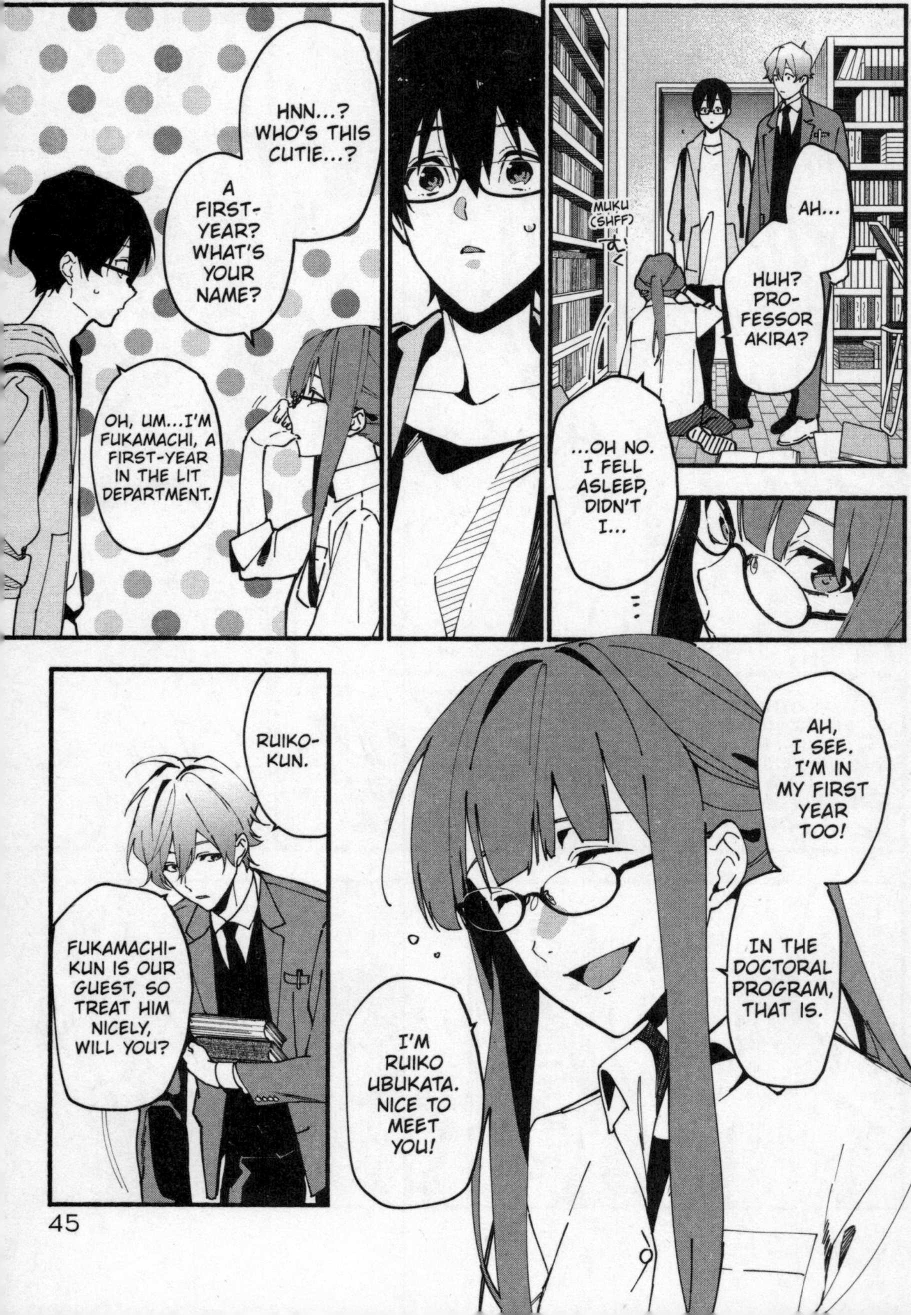
MUKU (SHFF)
AH...
HUH? PRO-FESSOR AKIRA?
...OH NO. I FELL ASLEEP, DIDN'T I...
HNN...? WHO'S THIS CUTIE...?
A FIRST-YEAR? WHAT'S YOUR NAME?
OH, UM...I'M FUKAMACHI, A FIRST-YEAR IN THE LIT DEPARTMENT.
AH, I SEE. I'M IN MY FIRST YEAR TOO!
IN THE DOCTORAL PROGRAM, THAT IS.
I'M RUIKO UBUKATA. NICE TO MEET YOU!
RUIKO-KUN.
FUKAMACHI-KUN IS OUR GUEST, SO TREAT HIM NICELY, WILL YOU?

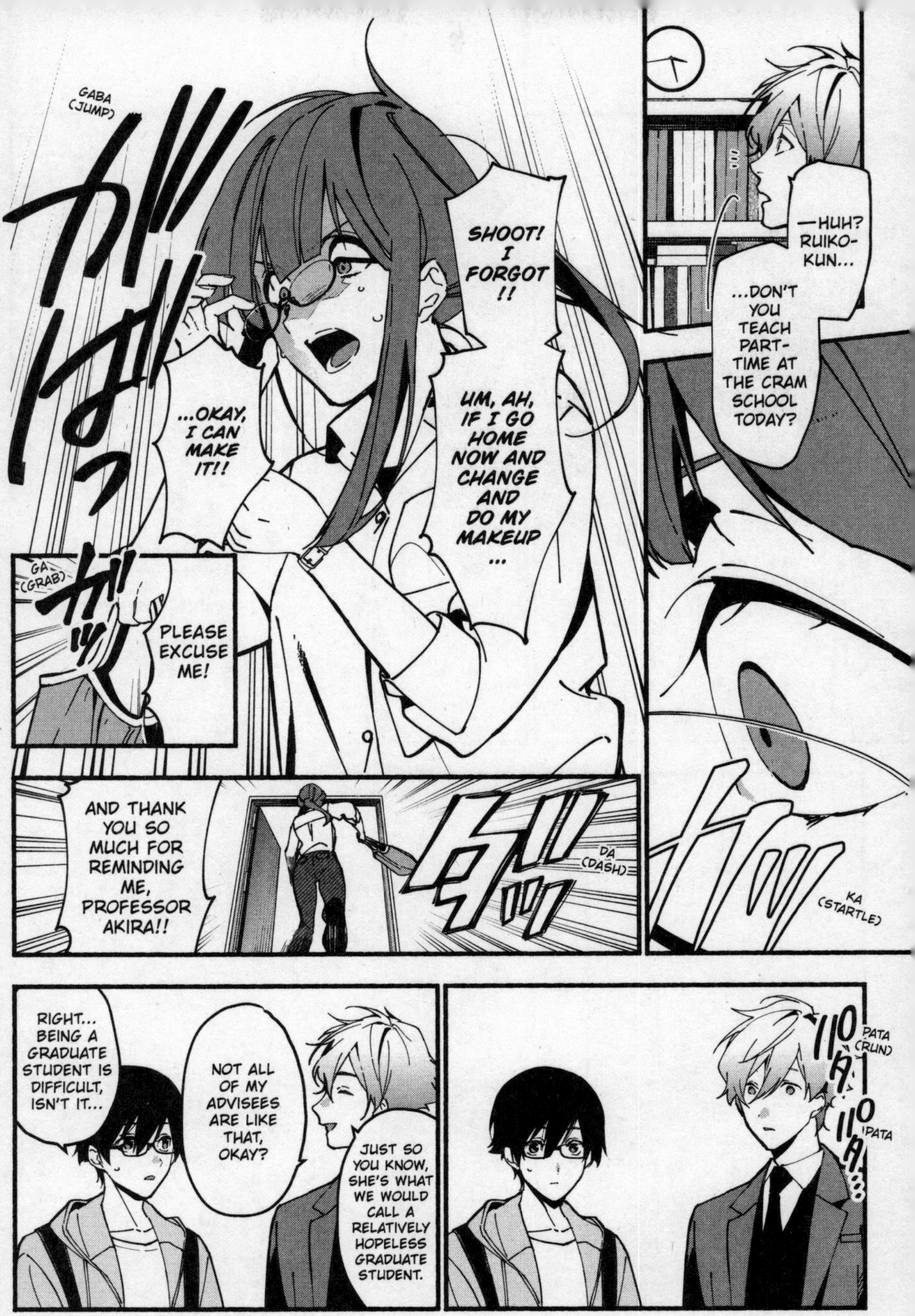

—HUH? RUIKO-KUN...
...DON'T YOU TEACH PART-TIME AT THE CRAM SCHOOL TODAY?
KA (STARTLE)
SHOOT! I FORGOT!!
GABA (JUMP)
UM, AH, IF I GO HOME NOW AND CHANGE AND DO MY MAKEUP...
...OKAY, I CAN MAKE IT!!
GA (GRAB)
PLEASE EXCUSE ME!
DA (DASH)
AND THANK YOU SO MUCH FOR REMINDING ME, PROFESSOR AKIRA!!
PATA (RUN)
PATA
RIGHT... BEING A GRADUATE STUDENT IS DIFFICULT, ISN'T IT...
NOT ALL OF MY ADVISEES ARE LIKE THAT, OKAY?
JUST SO YOU KNOW, SHE'S WHAT WE WOULD CALL A RELATIVELY HOPELESS GRADUATE STUDENT.

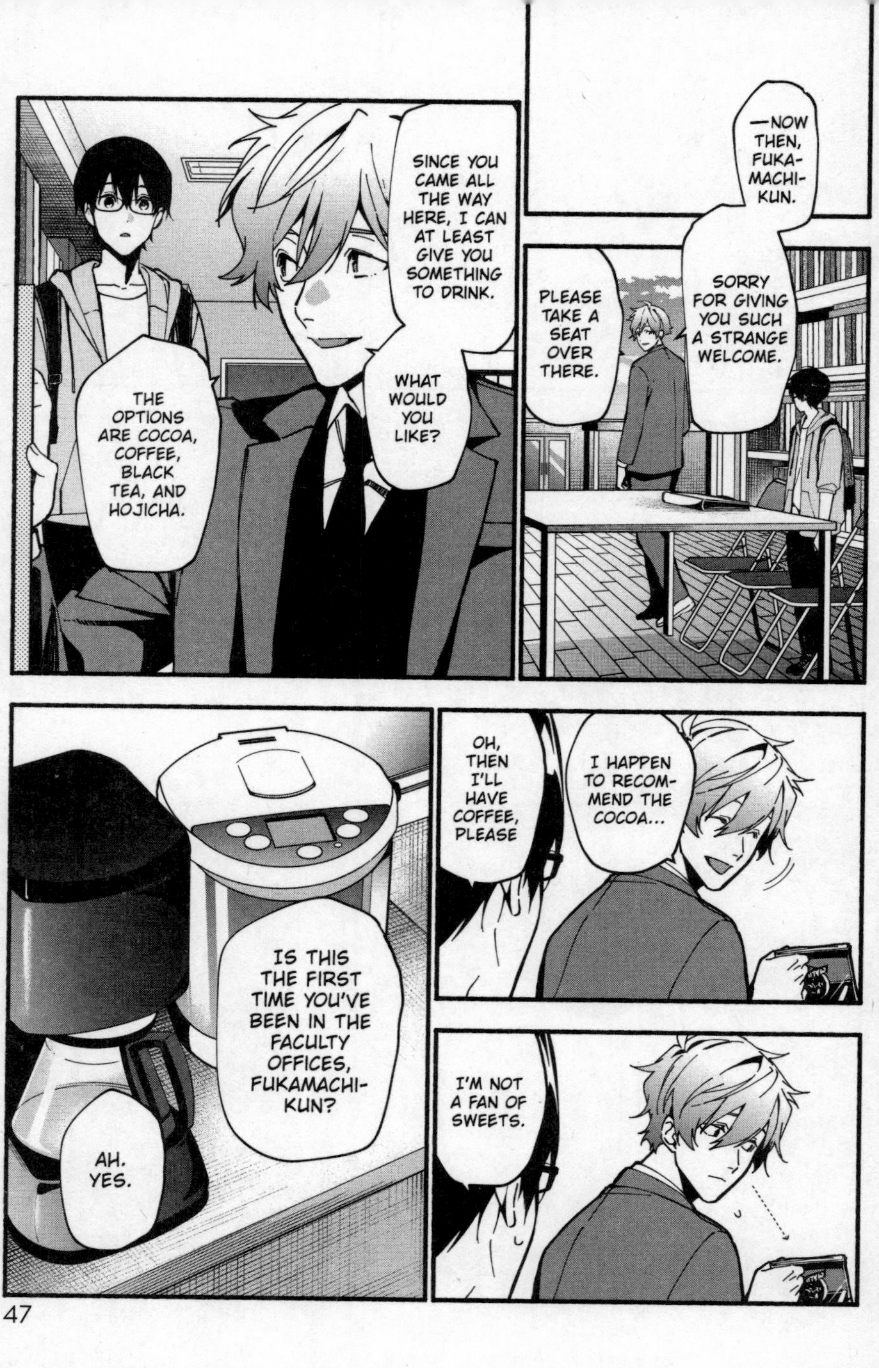
—NOW THEN, FUKAMACHI-KUN.
SORRY FOR GIVING YOU SUCH A STRANGE WELCOME.
PLEASE TAKE A SEAT OVER THERE.
SINCE YOU CAME ALL THE WAY HERE, I CAN AT LEAST GIVE YOU SOMETHING TO DRINK.
WHAT WOULD YOU LIKE?
THE OPTIONS ARE COCOA, COFFEE, BLACK TEA, AND HOJICHA.
I HAPPEN TO RECOMMEND THE COCOA...
OH, THEN I'LL HAVE COFFEE, PLEASE
I'M NOT A FAN OF SWEETS.
IS THIS THE FIRST TIME YOU'VE BEEN IN THE FACULTY OFFICES, FUKAMACHI-KUN?
AH. YES.

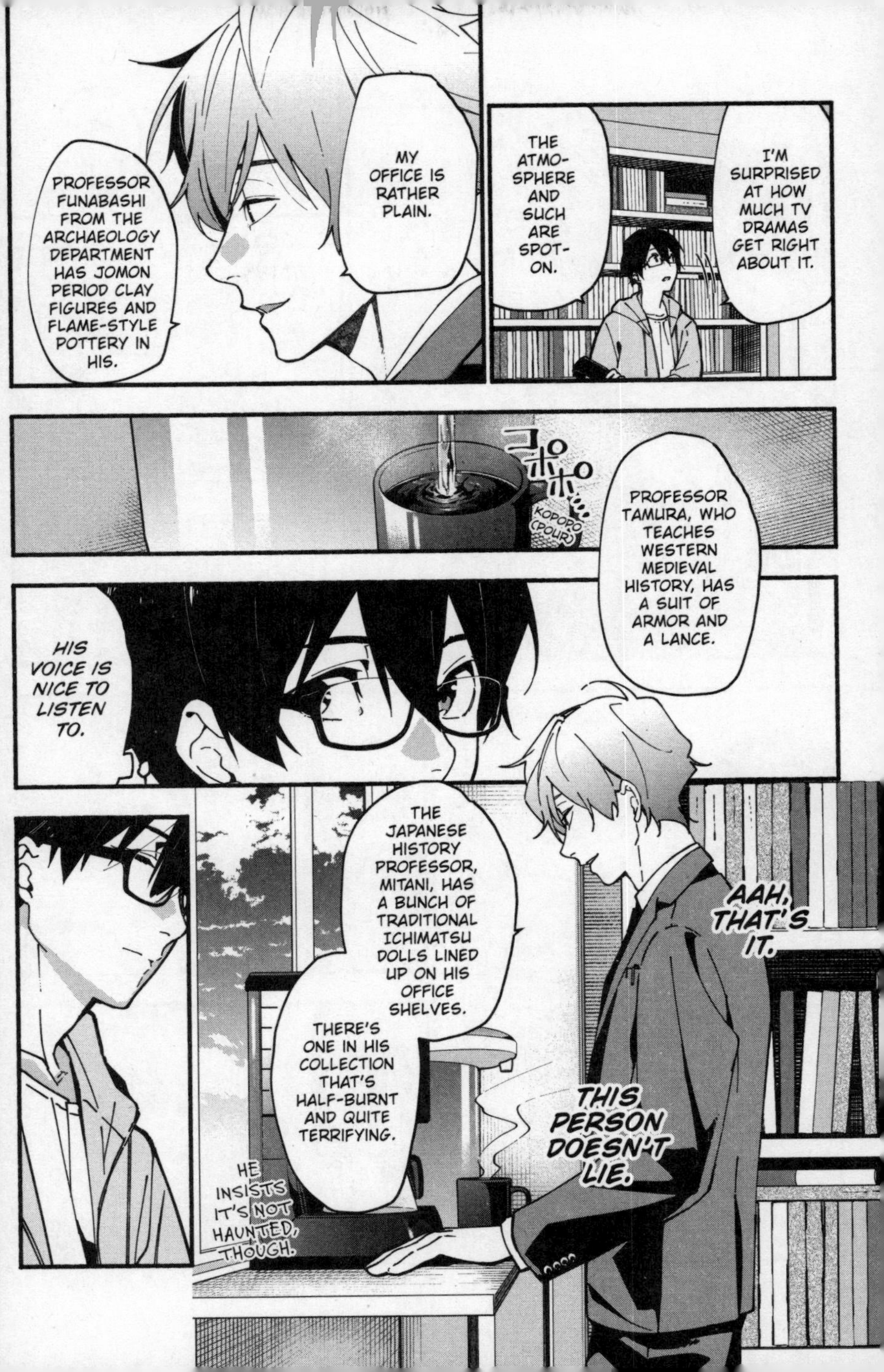
I'M SURPRISED AT HOW MUCH TV DRAMAS GET RIGHT ABOUT IT.
THE ATMOSPHERE AND SUCH ARE SPOT-ON.
MY OFFICE IS RATHER PLAIN.
PROFESSOR FUNABASHI FROM THE ARCHAEOLOGY DEPARTMENT HAS JOMON PERIOD CLAY FIGURES AND FLAME-STYLE POTTERY IN HIS.
PROFESSOR TAMURA, WHO TEACHES WESTERN MEDIEVAL HISTORY, HAS A SUIT OF ARMOR AND A LANCE.
コポポ…
KOPOPO (POUR)
HIS VOICE IS NICE TO LISTEN TO.
THE JAPANESE HISTORY PROFESSOR, MITANI, HAS A BUNCH OF TRADITIONAL ICHIMATSU DOLLS LINED UP ON HIS OFFICE SHELVES.
THERE'S ONE IN HIS COLLECTION THAT'S HALF-BURNT AND QUITE TERRIFYING.
HE INSISTS IT'S NOT HAUNTED, THOUGH.
AAH, THAT'S IT.
THIS PERSON DOESN'T LIE.

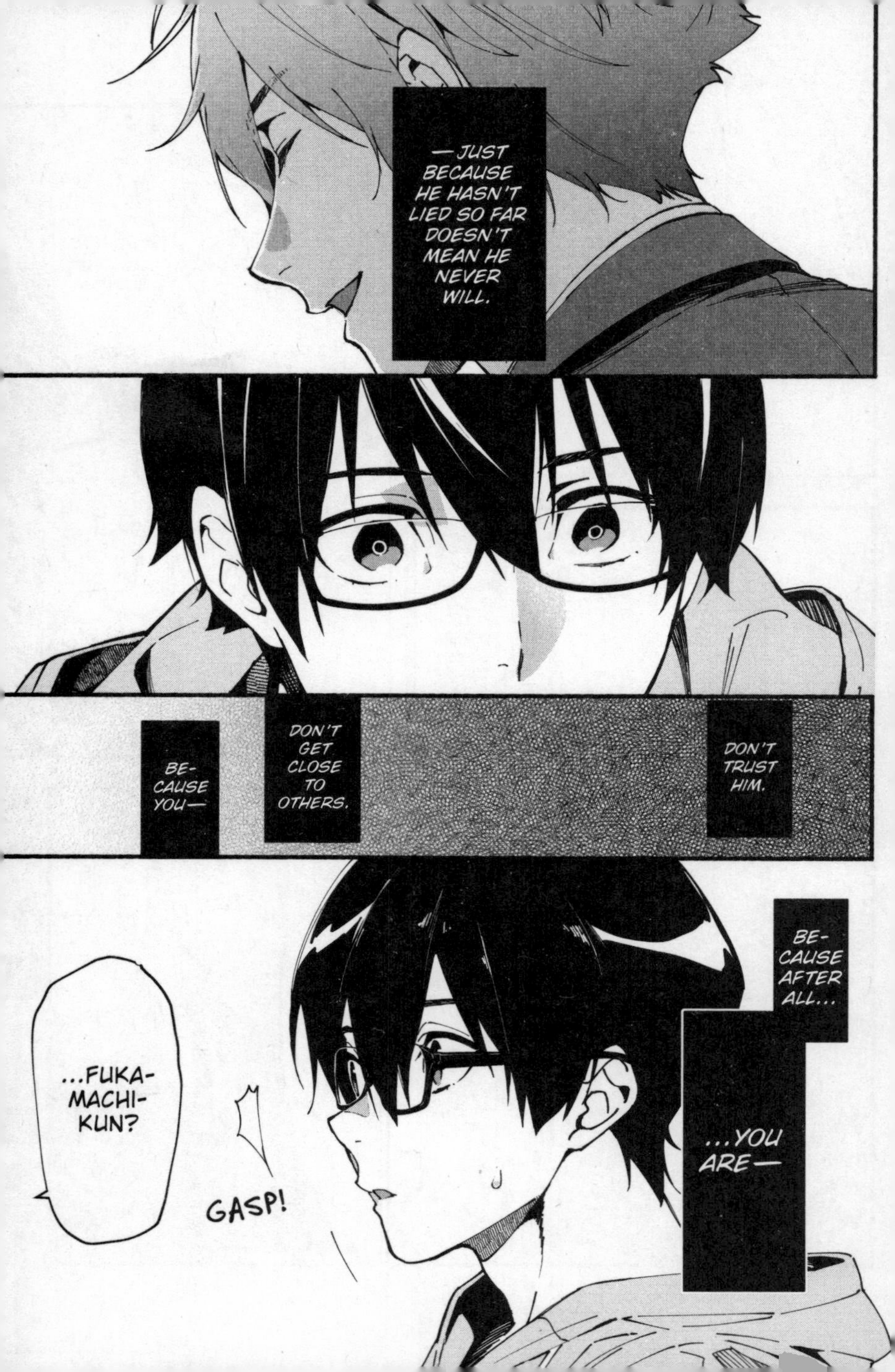
—JUST BECAUSE HE HASN'T LIED SO FAR DOESN'T MEAN HE NEVER WILL.
DON'T TRUST HIM.
DON'T GET CLOSE TO OTHERS.
BE-CAUSE YOU—
BE-CAUSE AFTER ALL...
...YOU ARE—
...FUKA-MACHI-KUN?
GASP!

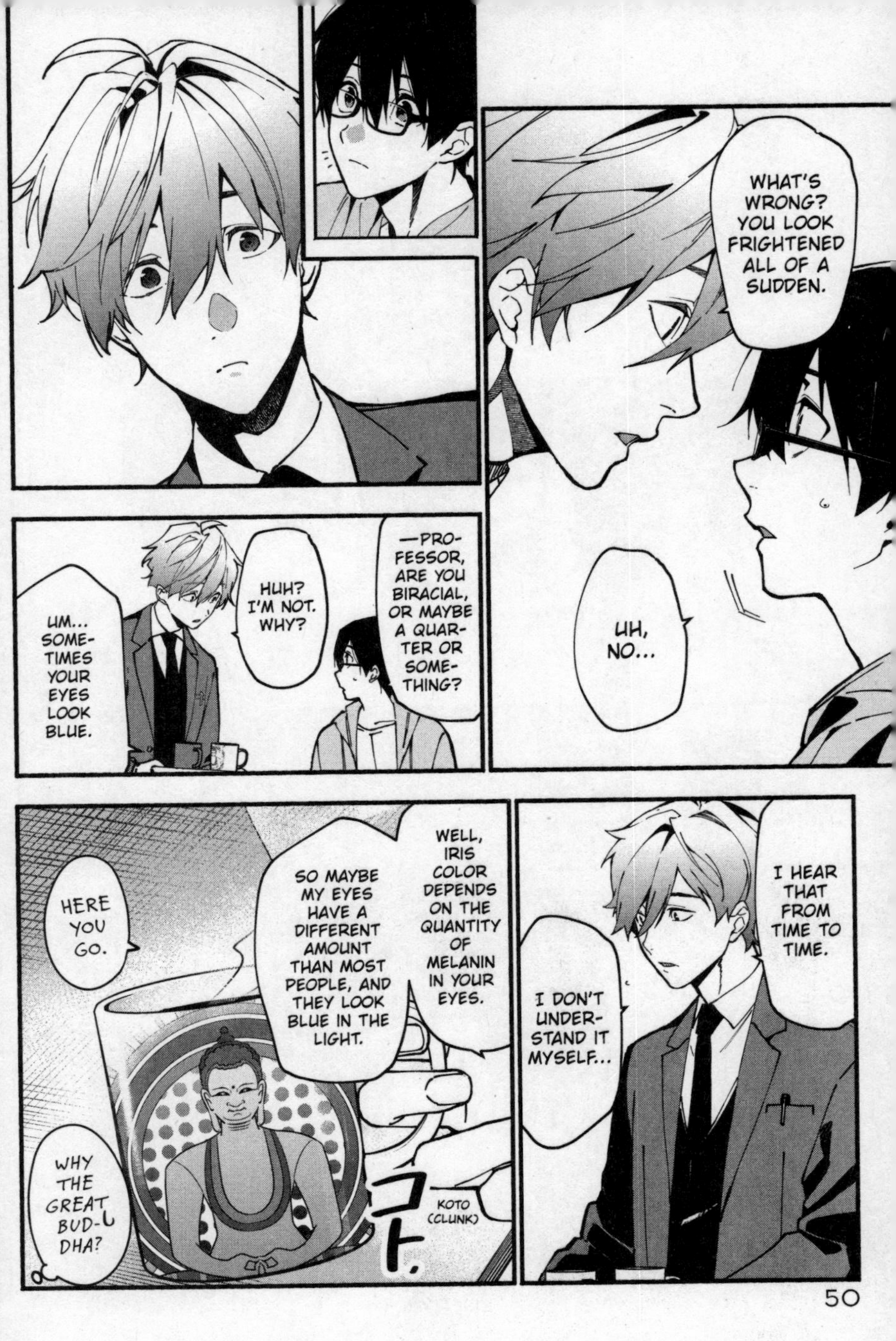
WHAT'S WRONG? YOU LOOK FRIGHTENED ALL OF A SUDDEN.
UH, NO...
—PRO-FESSOR, ARE YOU BIRACIAL, OR MAYBE A QUAR-TER OR SOME-THING?
HUH? I'M NOT. WHY?
UM... SOME-TIMES YOUR EYES LOOK BLUE.
I HEAR THAT FROM TIME TO TIME.
I DON'T UNDER-STAND IT MYSELF...
WELL, IRIS COLOR DEPENDS ON THE QUANTITY OF MELANIN IN YOUR EYES.
SO MAYBE MY EYES HAVE A DIFFERENT AMOUNT THAN MOST PEOPLE, AND THEY LOOK BLUE IN THE LIGHT.
HERE YOU GO.
KOTO (CLUNK)
WHY THE GREAT BUD-DHA?

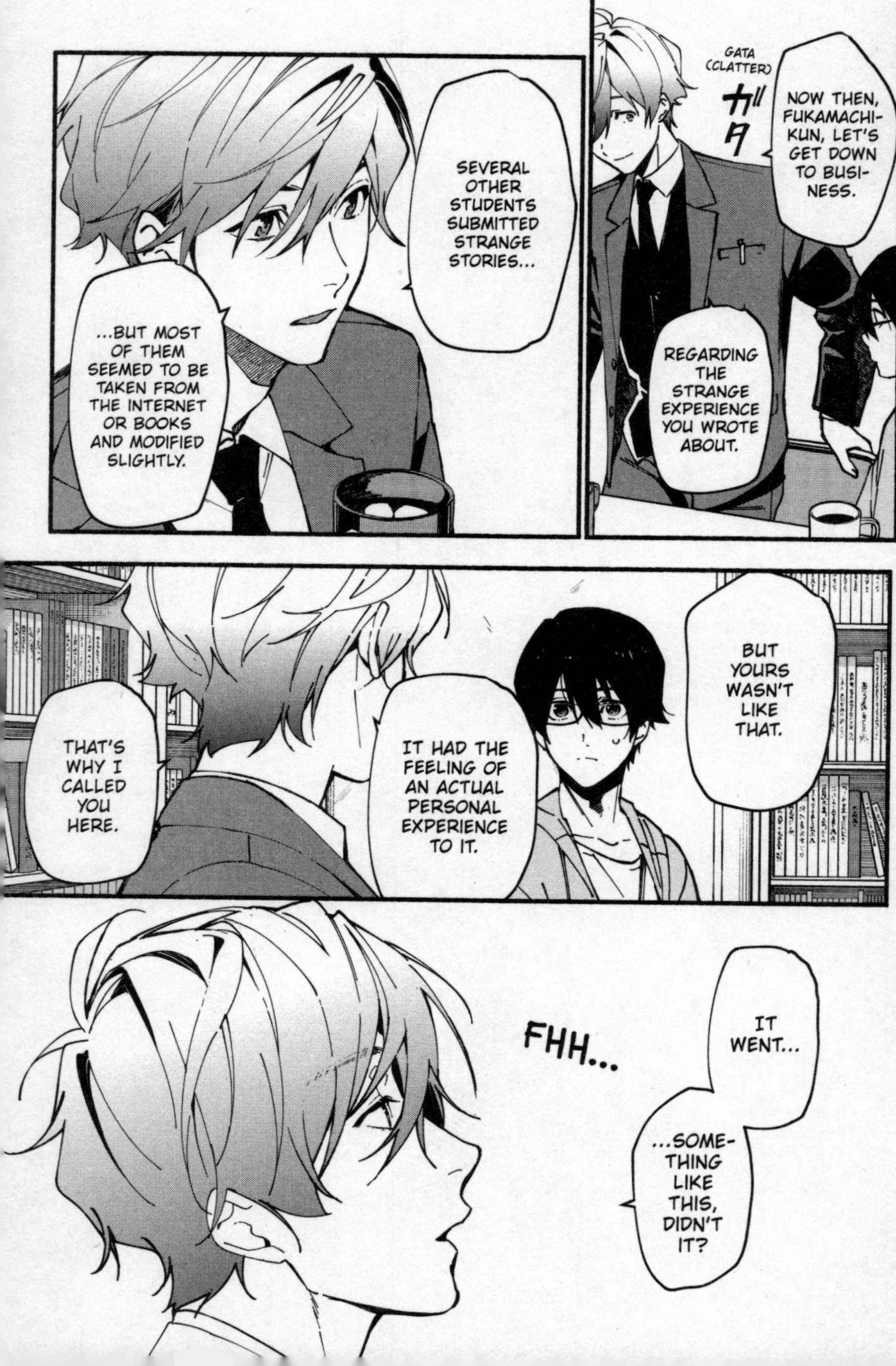
NOW THEN, FUKAMACHI-KUN, LET'S GET DOWN TO BUSI-NESS.
GATA (CLATTER)
ガタ
REGARDING THE STRANGE EXPERIENCE YOU WROTE ABOUT.
SEVERAL OTHER STUDENTS SUBMITTED STRANGE STORIES...
...BUT MOST OF THEM SEEMED TO BE TAKEN FROM THE INTERNET OR BOOKS AND MODIFIED SLIGHTLY.
BUT YOURS WASN'T LIKE THAT.
IT HAD THE FEELING OF AN ACTUAL PERSONAL EXPERIENCE TO IT.
THAT'S WHY I CALLED YOU HERE.
IT WENT...
FHH...
...SOME-THING LIKE THIS, DIDN'T IT?

"THIS HAPPENED WHEN I WAS IN ELEMENTARY SCHOOL.
"ONCE, WHILE I WAS VISITING MY GRANDMOTHER'S HOUSE IN THE COUNTRYSIDE, THERE WAS A FESTIVAL IN THE MIDDLE OF THE NIGHT.
"THE FESTIVAL ITSELF WAS HELD ANNUALLY, AND I HAD BEEN LOOKING FORWARD TO GOING. BUT I CAUGHT A FEVER THAT YEAR AND COULDN'T GO.
"HOWEVER, WHEN I AWOKE IN THE DEAD OF NIGHT, I COULD HEAR THE THUNDERING OF DRUMS, AND I THOUGHT THAT THE FESTIVAL MUST STILL BE IN FULL SWING...
"...SO I SNUCK OUT OF MY GRANDMOTHER'S HOUSE BY MYSELF.
"WHEN I GOT TO THE FESTIVAL GROUNDS, ALL THE STALLS WERE CLOSED, AND ONLY THE BON FESTIVAL DANCE WAS HAPPENING.
"EVERYONE WAS DANCING ALONG TO THE THUNDERING DRUMS BENEATH COUNTLESS BLUE PAPER LANTERNS, WHICH WERE UNLIKE ANY I HAD EVER SEEN BEFORE.
"STRANGEST OF ALL, THERE WAS NO MUSIC BESIDES THE DRUM BEAT, AND EVERYONE WAS WEARING SOME KIND OF MASK ON THEIR FACE.
"COME MORNING, I TRIED TO TELL MY PARENTS AND GRAND-MOTHER ABOUT WHAT I SAW ...
"...BUT THEY ALL TOLD ME, 'I DON'T KNOW WHAT YOU'RE TALKING ABOUT. THAT KIND OF THING WOULDN'T HAPPEN.'

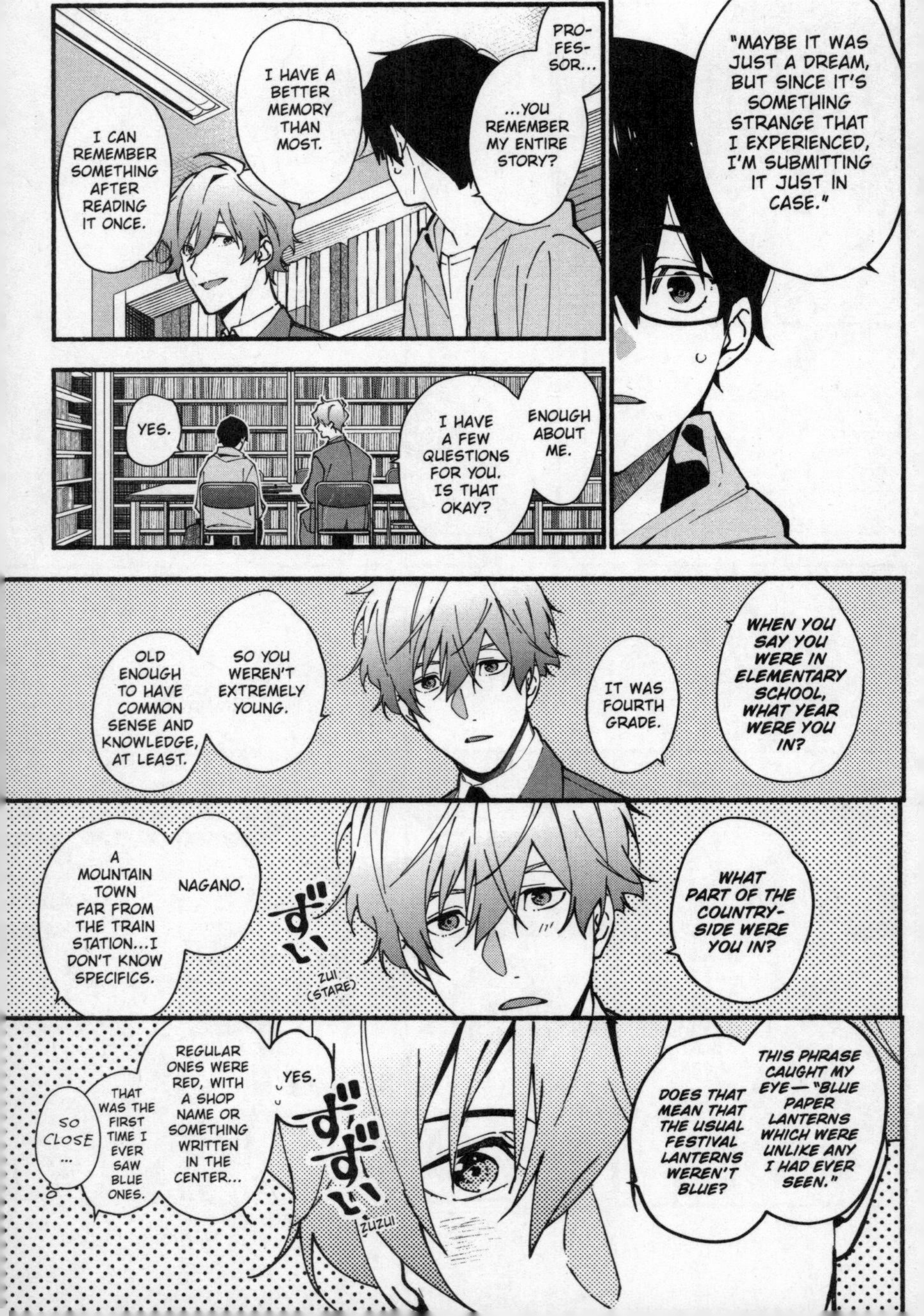
"MAYBE IT WAS JUST A DREAM, BUT SINCE IT'S SOMETHING STRANGE THAT I EXPERIENCED, I'M SUBMITTING IT JUST IN CASE."
PRO-FES-SOR...
...YOU REMEMBER MY ENTIRE STORY?
I HAVE A BETTER MEMORY THAN MOST.
I CAN REMEMBER SOMETHING AFTER READING IT ONCE.
ENOUGH ABOUT ME.
I HAVE A FEW QUESTIONS FOR YOU. IS THAT OKAY?
YES.
WHEN YOU SAY YOU WERE IN ELEMENTARY SCHOOL, WHAT YEAR WERE YOU IN?
IT WAS FOURTH GRADE.
SO YOU WEREN'T EXTREMELY YOUNG.
OLD ENOUGH TO HAVE COMMON SENSE AND KNOWLEDGE, AT LEAST.
WHAT PART OF THE COUNTRY-SIDE WERE YOU IN?
ずい
ZUI (STARE)
NAGANO.
A MOUNTAIN TOWN FAR FROM THE TRAIN STATION...I DON'T KNOW SPECIFICS.
THIS PHRASE CAUGHT MY EYE—"BLUE PAPER LANTERNS WHICH WERE UNLIKE ANY I HAD EVER SEEN."
DOES THAT MEAN THAT THE USUAL FESTIVAL LANTERNS WEREN'T BLUE?
ずずい
ZUZUI
YES.
REGULAR ONES WERE RED, WITH A SHOP NAME OR SOMETHING WRITTEN IN THE CENTER...
THAT WAS THE FIRST TIME I EVER SAW BLUE ONES.
SO CLOSE...

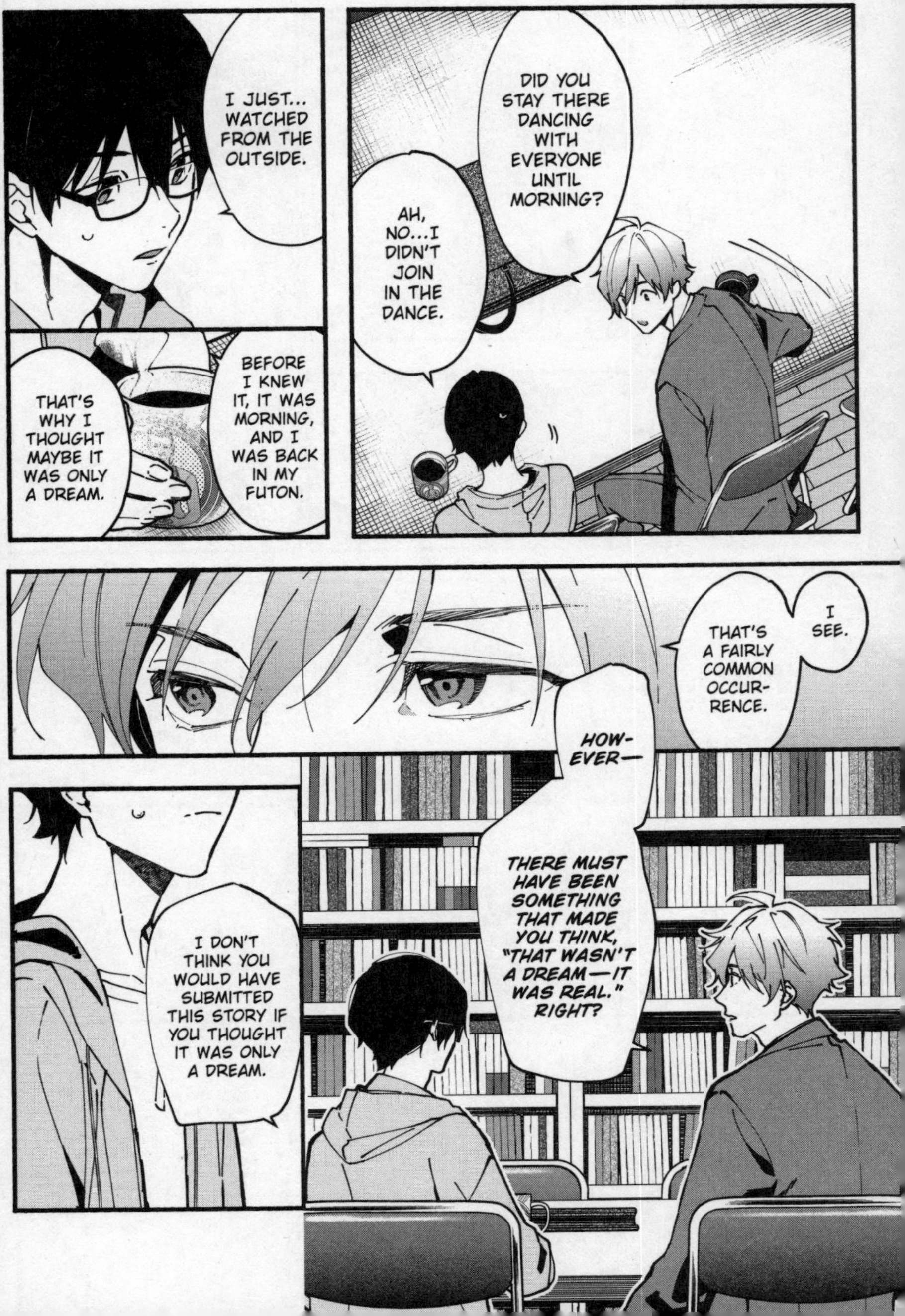
DID YOU STAY THERE DANCING WITH EVERYONE UNTIL MORNING?
AH, NO...I DIDN'T JOIN IN THE DANCE.
I JUST... WATCHED FROM THE OUTSIDE.
BEFORE I KNEW IT, IT WAS MORNING, AND I WAS BACK IN MY FUTON.
THAT'S WHY I THOUGHT MAYBE IT WAS ONLY A DREAM.
I SEE.
THAT'S A FAIRLY COMMON OCCUR-RENCE.
HOW-EVER—
THERE MUST HAVE BEEN SOMETHING THAT MADE YOU THINK, "THAT WASN'T A DREAM—IT WAS REAL." RIGHT?
I DON'T THINK YOU WOULD HAVE SUBMITTED THIS STORY IF YOU THOUGHT IT WAS ONLY A DREAM.

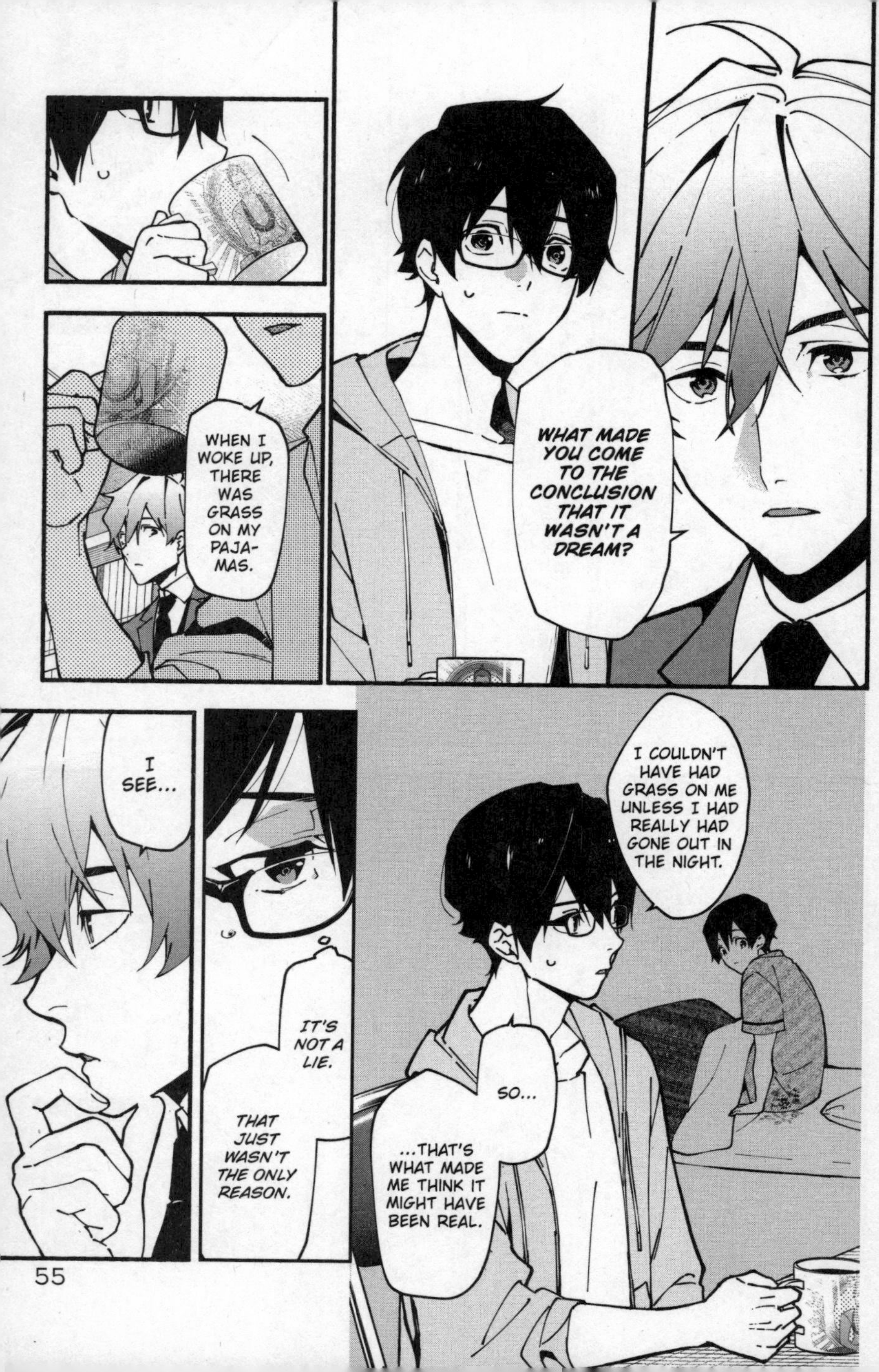
WHAT MADE YOU COME TO THE CONCLUSION THAT IT WASN'T A DREAM?
WHEN I WOKE UP, THERE WAS GRASS ON MY PAJA-MAS.
I COULDN'T HAVE HAD GRASS ON ME UNLESS I HAD REALLY HAD GONE OUT IN THE NIGHT.
SO...
...THAT'S WHAT MADE ME THINK IT MIGHT HAVE BEEN REAL.
IT'S NOT A LIE.
THAT JUST WASN'T THE ONLY REASON.
I SEE...

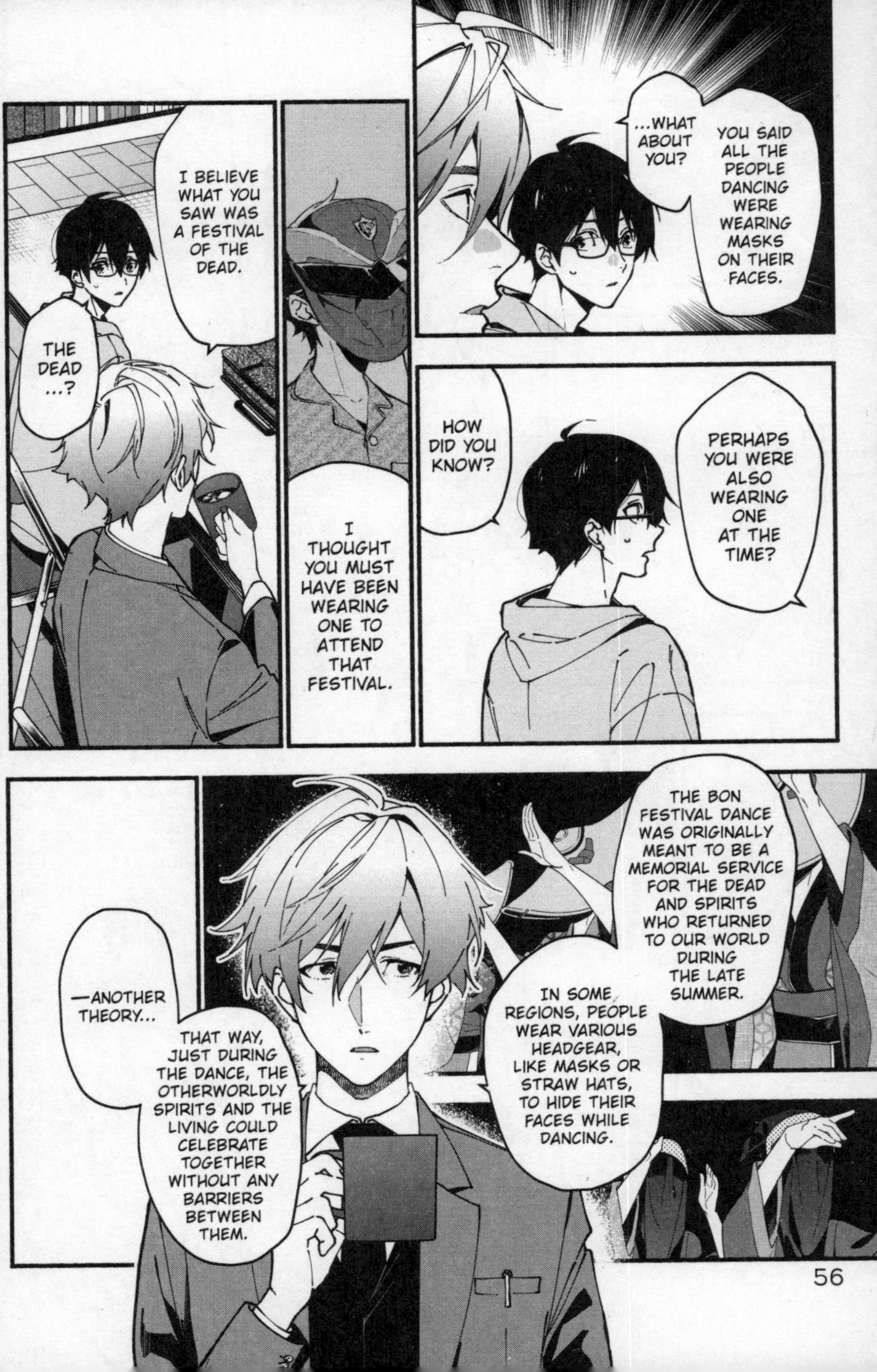
YOU SAID ALL THE PEOPLE DANCING WERE WEARING MASKS ON THEIR FACES.
...WHAT ABOUT YOU?
PERHAPS YOU WERE ALSO WEARING ONE AT THE TIME?
HOW DID YOU KNOW?
I THOUGHT YOU MUST HAVE BEEN WEARING ONE TO ATTEND THAT FESTIVAL.
I BELIEVE WHAT YOU SAW WAS A FESTIVAL OF THE DEAD.
THE DEAD ...?
THE BON FESTIVAL DANCE WAS ORIGINALLY MEANT TO BE A MEMORIAL SERVICE FOR THE DEAD AND SPIRITS WHO RETURNED TO OUR WORLD DURING THE LATE SUMMER.
IN SOME REGIONS, PEOPLE WEAR VARIOUS HEADGEAR, LIKE MASKS OR STRAW HATS, TO HIDE THEIR FACES WHILE DANCING.
THAT WAY, JUST DURING THE DANCE, THE OTHERWORLDLY SPIRITS AND THE LIVING COULD CELEBRATE TOGETHER WITHOUT ANY BARRIERS BETWEEN THEM.
—ANOTHER THEORY...

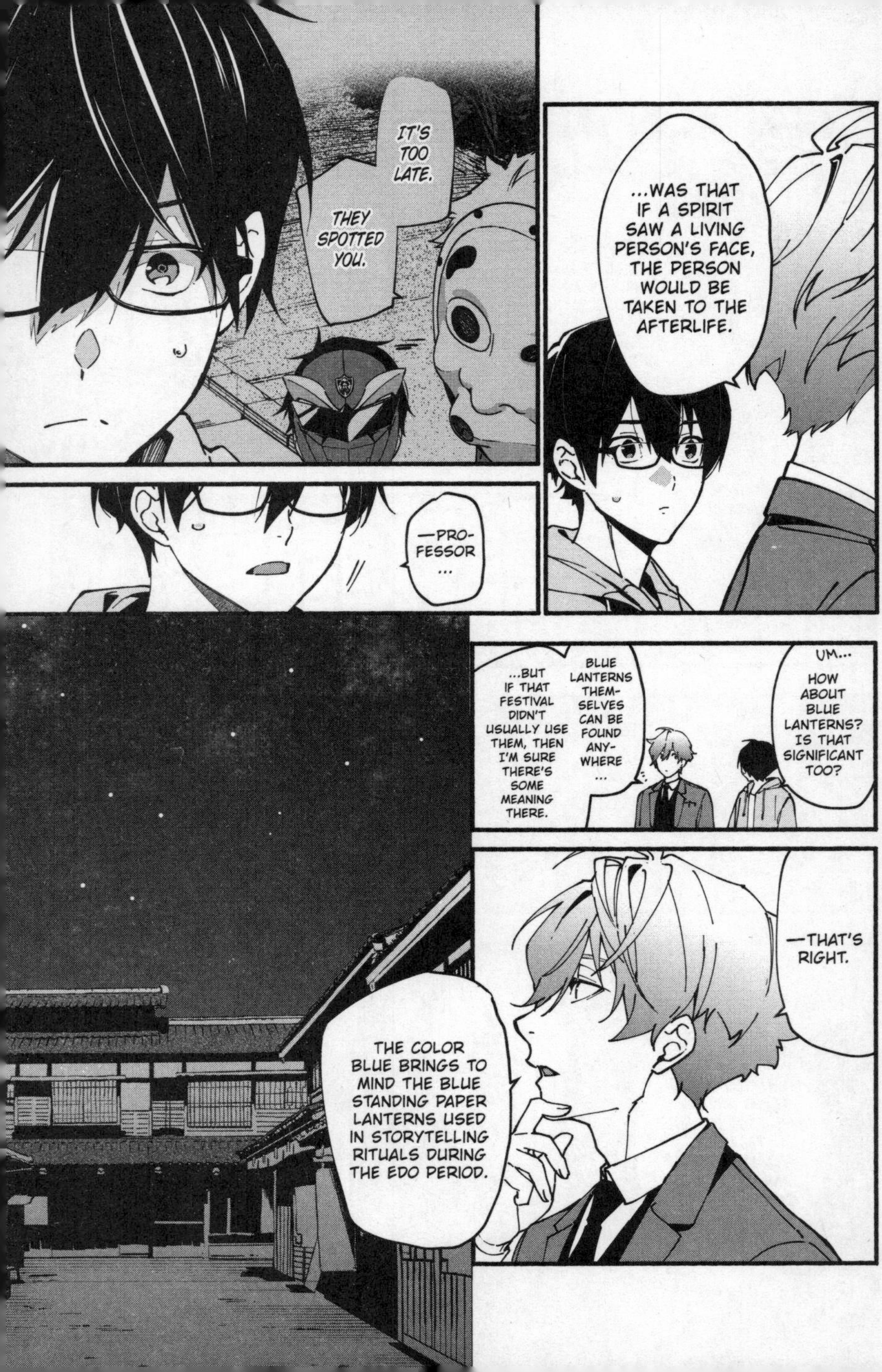
...WAS THAT IF A SPIRIT SAW A LIVING PERSON'S FACE, THE PERSON WOULD BE TAKEN TO THE AFTERLIFE.
IT'S TOO LATE.
THEY SPOTTED YOU.
—PRO-FESSOR...
UM...
HOW ABOUT BLUE LANTERNS? IS THAT SIGNIFICANT TOO?
BLUE LANTERNS THEM-SELVES CAN BE FOUND ANY-WHERE...
...BUT IF THAT FESTIVAL DIDN'T USUALLY USE THEM, THEN I'M SURE THERE'S SOME MEANING THERE.
—THAT'S RIGHT.
THE COLOR BLUE BRINGS TO MIND THE BLUE STANDING PAPER LANTERNS USED IN STORYTELLING RITUALS DURING THE EDO PERIOD.

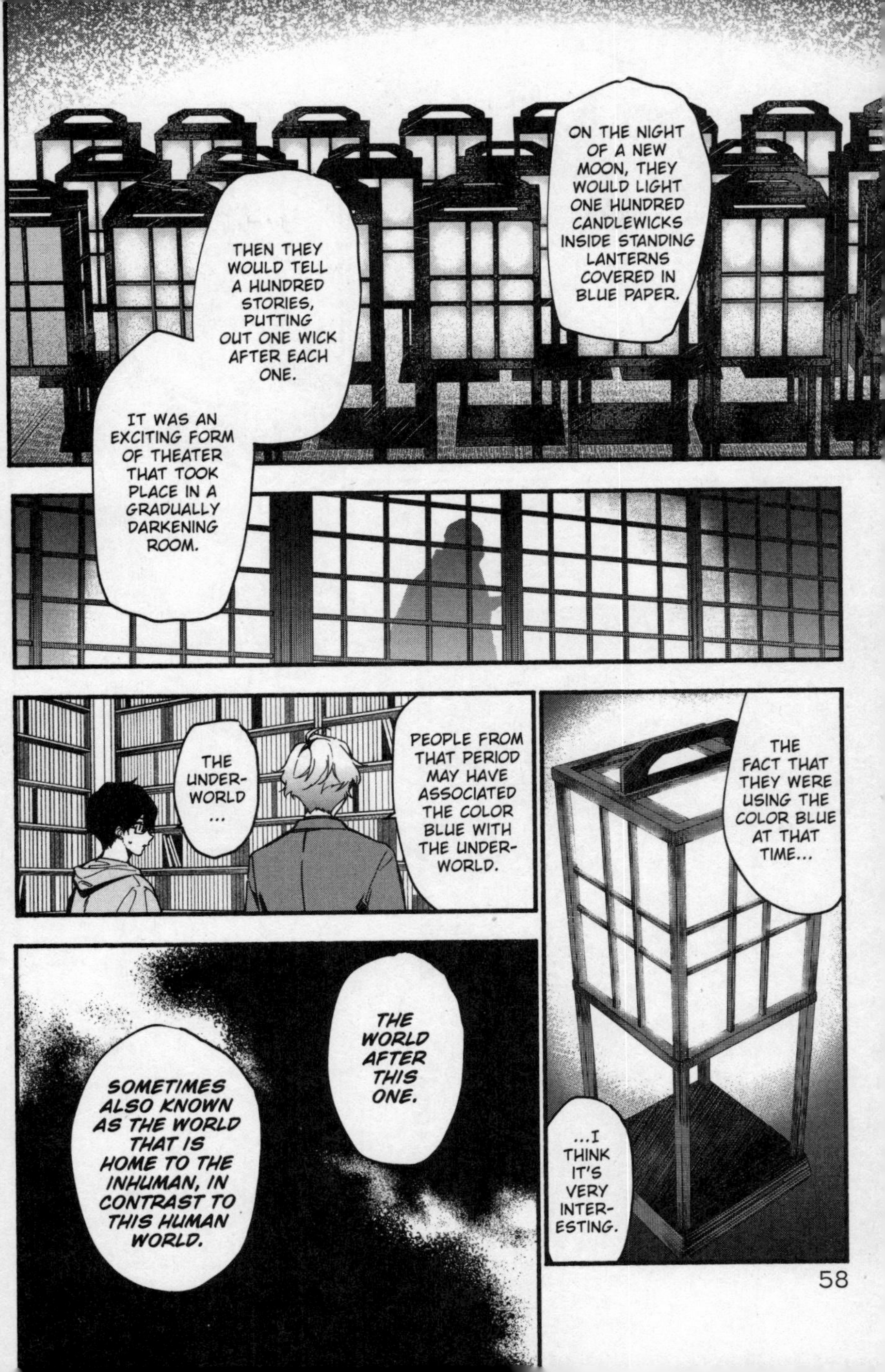
ON THE NIGHT OF A NEW MOON, THEY WOULD LIGHT ONE HUNDRED CANDLEWICKS INSIDE STANDING LANTERNS COVERED IN BLUE PAPER.
THEN THEY WOULD TELL A HUNDRED STORIES, PUTTING OUT ONE WICK AFTER EACH ONE.
IT WAS AN EXCITING FORM OF THEATER THAT TOOK PLACE IN A GRADUALLY DARKENING ROOM.
THE FACT THAT THEY WERE USING THE COLOR BLUE AT THAT TIME...
...I THINK IT'S VERY INTER-ESTING.
PEOPLE FROM THAT PERIOD MAY HAVE ASSOCIATED THE COLOR BLUE WITH THE UNDER-WORLD.
THE UNDER-WORLD...
THE WORLD AFTER THIS ONE.
SOMETIMES ALSO KNOWN AS THE WORLD THAT IS HOME TO THE INHUMAN, IN CONTRAST TO THIS HUMAN WORLD.

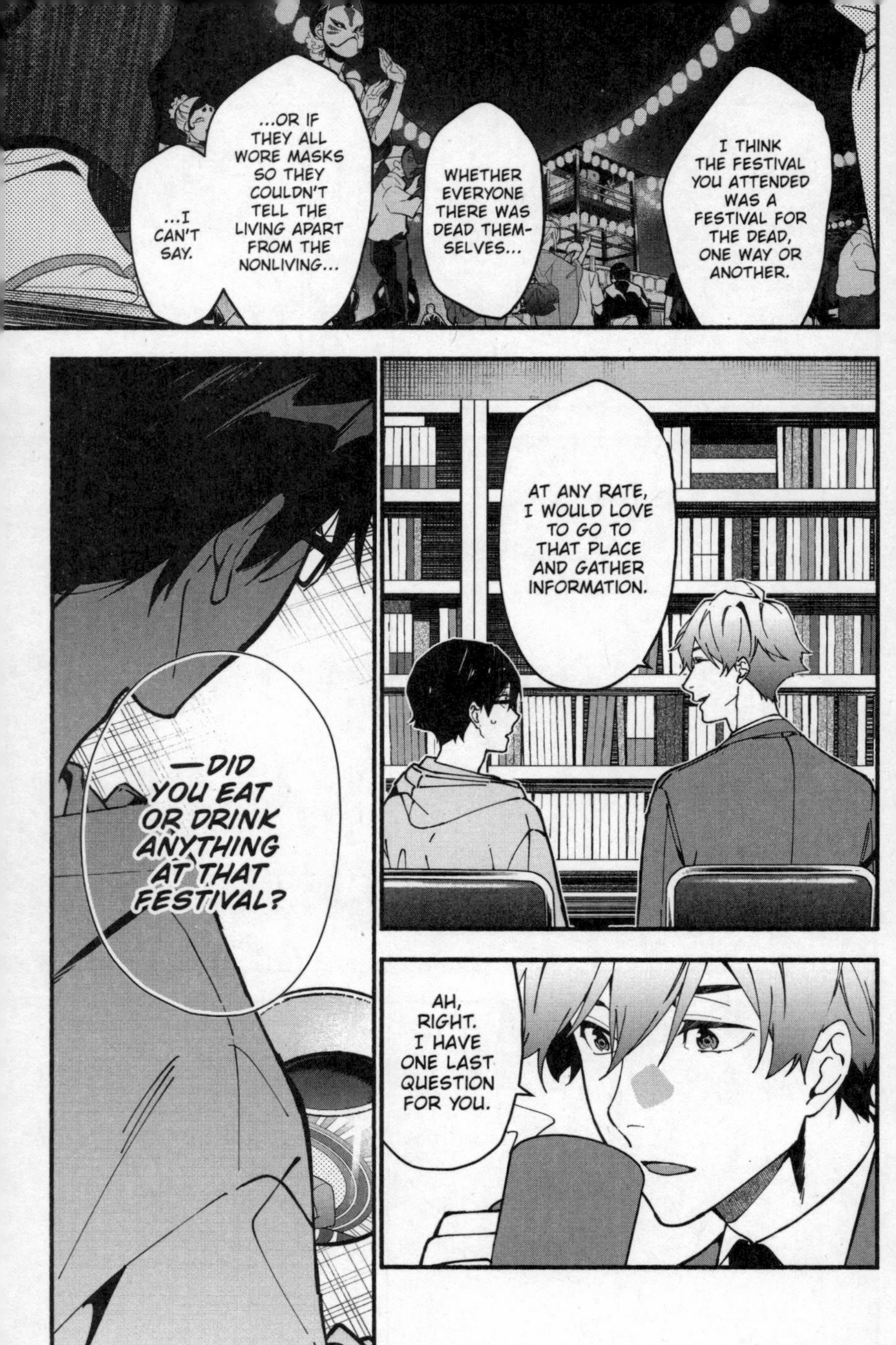
I THINK THE FESTIVAL YOU ATTENDED WAS A FESTIVAL FOR THE DEAD, ONE WAY OR ANOTHER.
WHETHER EVERYONE THERE WAS DEAD THEMSELVES...
...OR IF THEY ALL WORE MASKS SO THEY COULDN'T TELL THE LIVING APART FROM THE NONLIVING...
...I CAN'T SAY.
AT ANY RATE, I WOULD LOVE TO GO TO THAT PLACE AND GATHER INFORMATION.
AH, RIGHT. I HAVE ONE LAST QUESTION FOR YOU.
—DID YOU EAT OR DRINK ANYTHING AT THAT FESTIVAL?

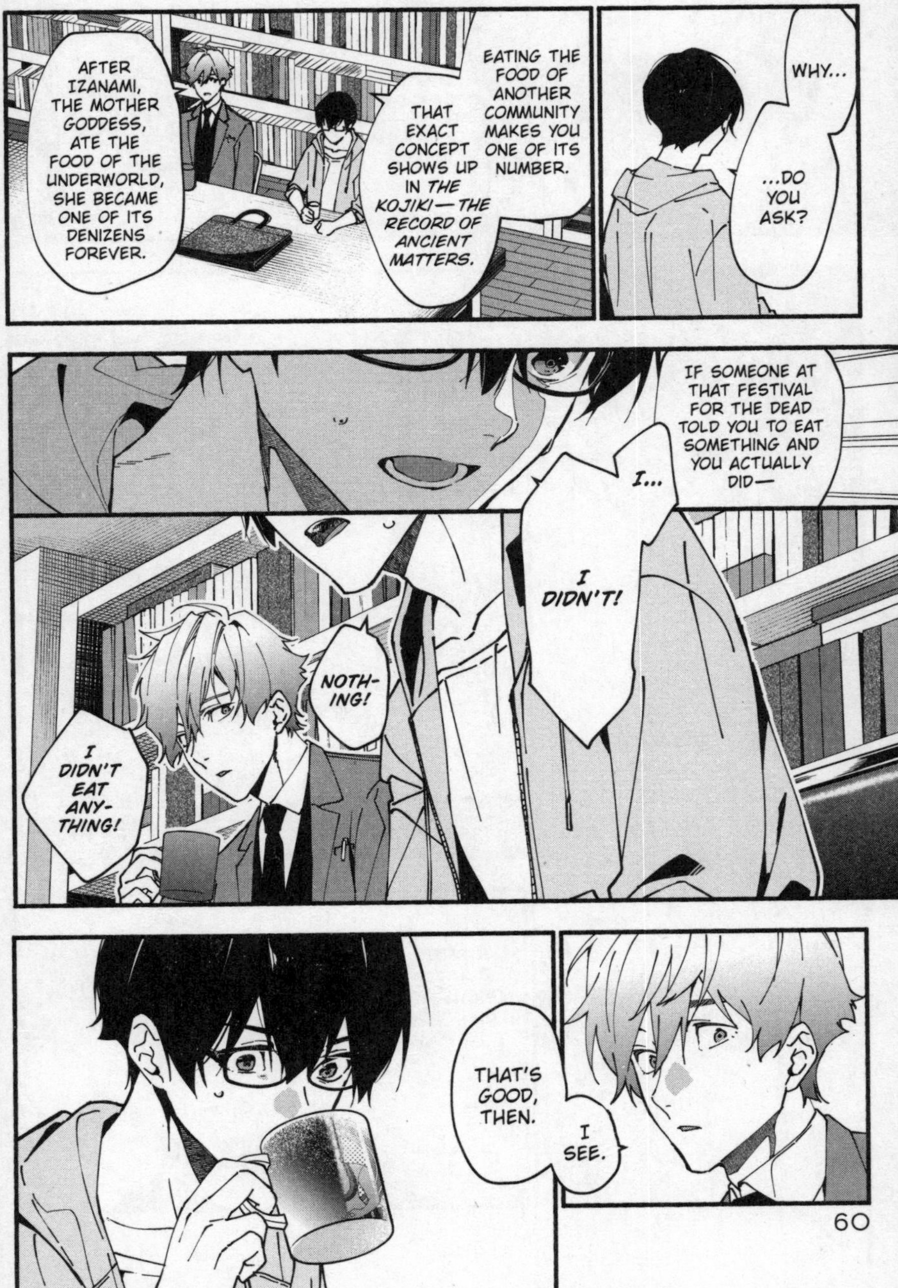
WHY...
...DO YOU ASK?
EATING THE FOOD OF ANOTHER COMMUNITY MAKES YOU ONE OF ITS NUMBER.
THAT EXACT CONCEPT SHOWS UP IN *THE KOJIKI—THE RECORD OF ANCIENT MATTERS.*
AFTER IZANAMI, THE MOTHER GODDESS, ATE THE FOOD OF THE UNDERWORLD, SHE BECAME ONE OF ITS DENIZENS FOREVER.
IF SOMEONE AT THAT FESTIVAL FOR THE DEAD TOLD YOU TO EAT SOMETHING AND YOU ACTUALLY DID—
I...
I DIDN'T!
NOTHING!
I DIDN'T EAT ANYTHING!
I SEE.
THAT'S GOOD, THEN.

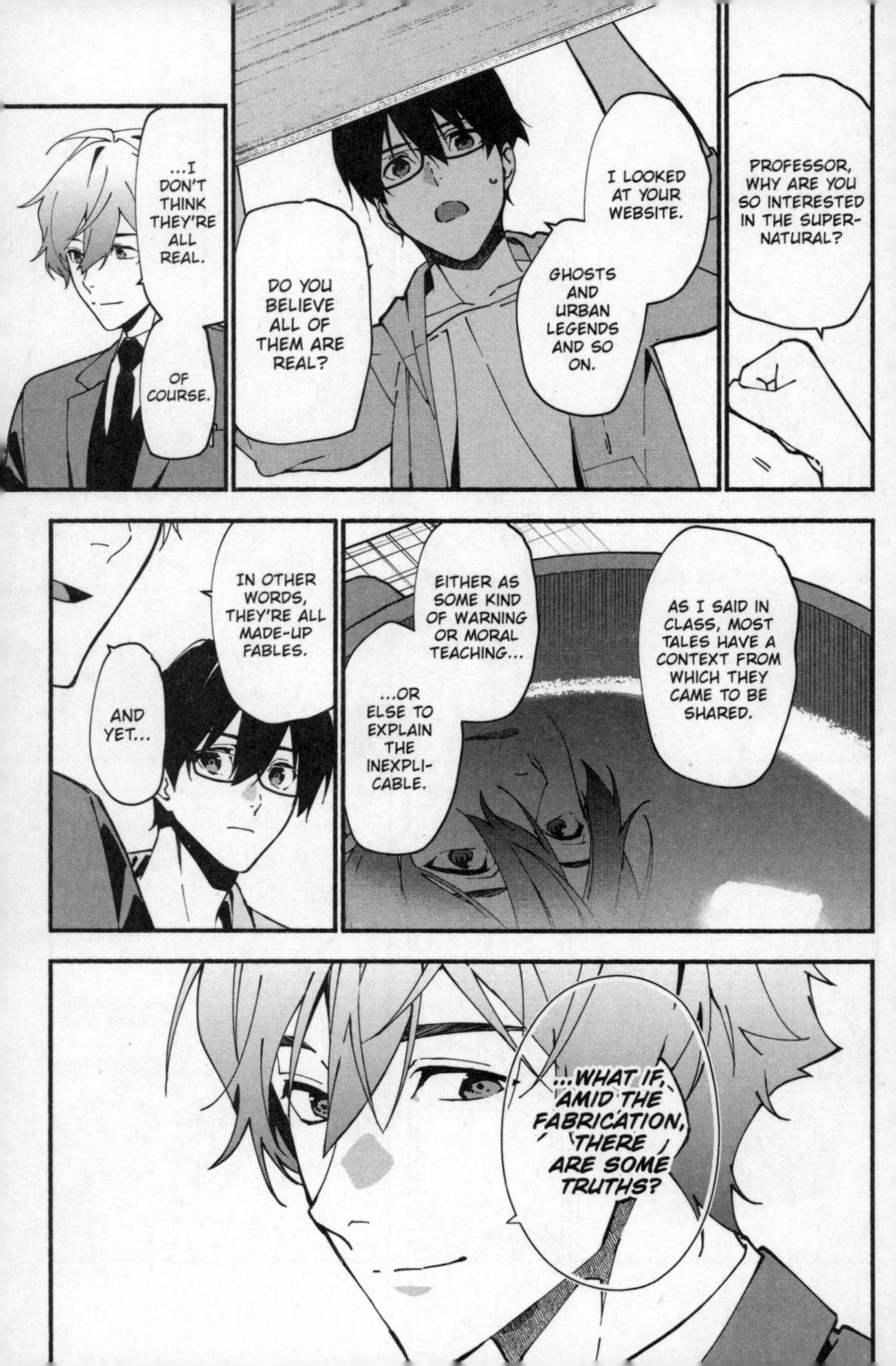
PROFESSOR, WHY ARE YOU SO INTERESTED IN THE SUPER-NATURAL?
I LOOKED AT YOUR WEBSITE.
GHOSTS AND URBAN LEGENDS AND SO ON.
DO YOU BELIEVE ALL OF THEM ARE REAL?
...I DON'T THINK THEY'RE ALL REAL.
OF COURSE.
AS I SAID IN CLASS, MOST TALES HAVE A CONTEXT FROM WHICH THEY CAME TO BE SHARED.
EITHER AS SOME KIND OF WARNING OR MORAL TEACHING...
...OR ELSE TO EXPLAIN THE INEXPLICABLE.
IN OTHER WORDS, THEY'RE ALL MADE-UP FABLES.
AND YET...
...WHAT IF, AMID THE FABRICATION, THERE ARE SOME TRUTHS?

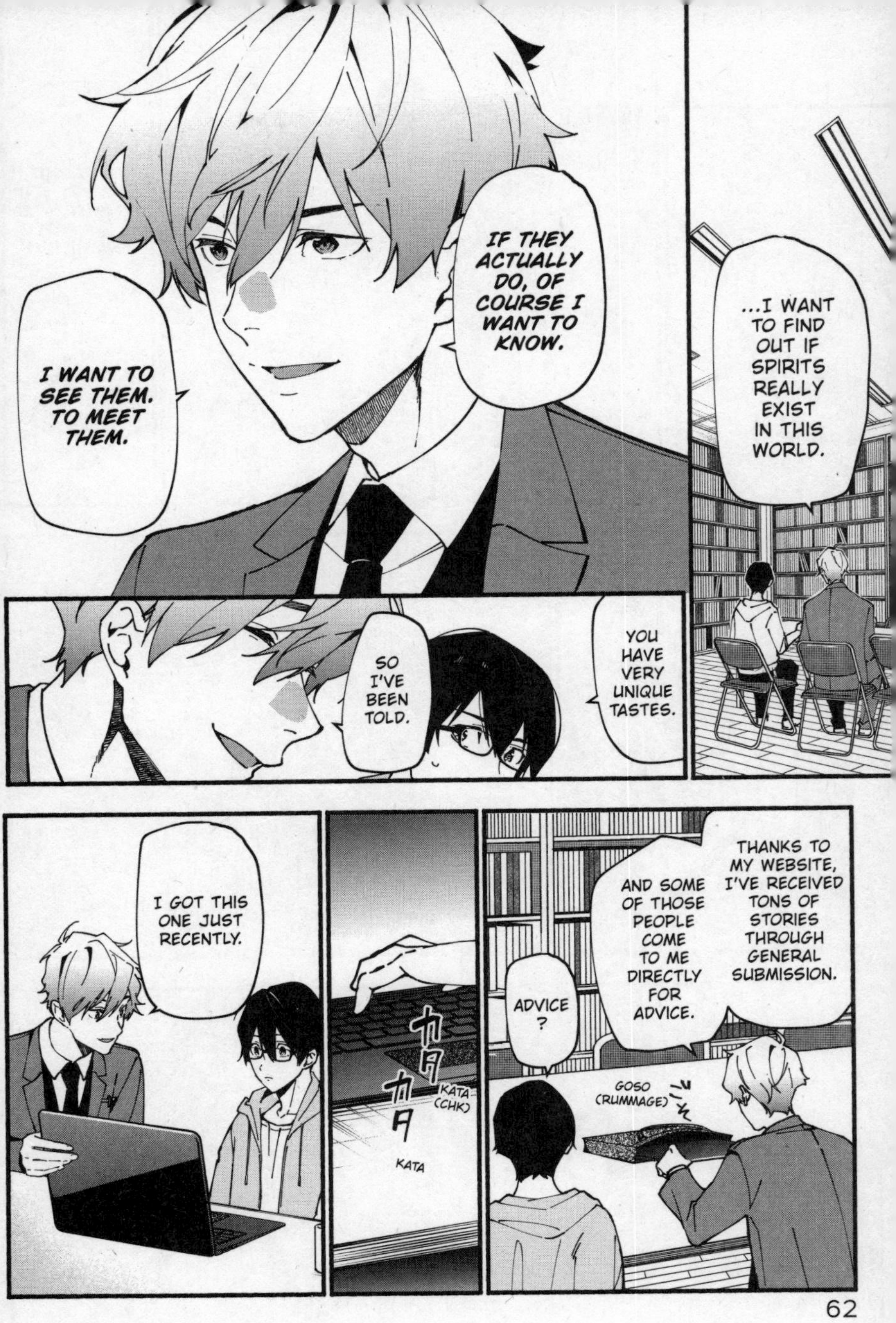

...I WANT TO FIND OUT IF SPIRITS REALLY EXIST IN THIS WORLD.
IF THEY ACTUALLY DO, OF COURSE I WANT TO KNOW.
I WANT TO SEE THEM. TO MEET THEM.
YOU HAVE VERY UNIQUE TASTES.
SO I'VE BEEN TOLD.
THANKS TO MY WEBSITE, I'VE RECEIVED TONS OF STORIES THROUGH GENERAL SUBMISSION.
AND SOME OF THOSE PEOPLE COME TO ME DIRECTLY FOR ADVICE.
ADVICE?
GOSO (RUMMAGE)
KATA (CHK)
KATA
I GOT THIS ONE JUST RECENTLY.

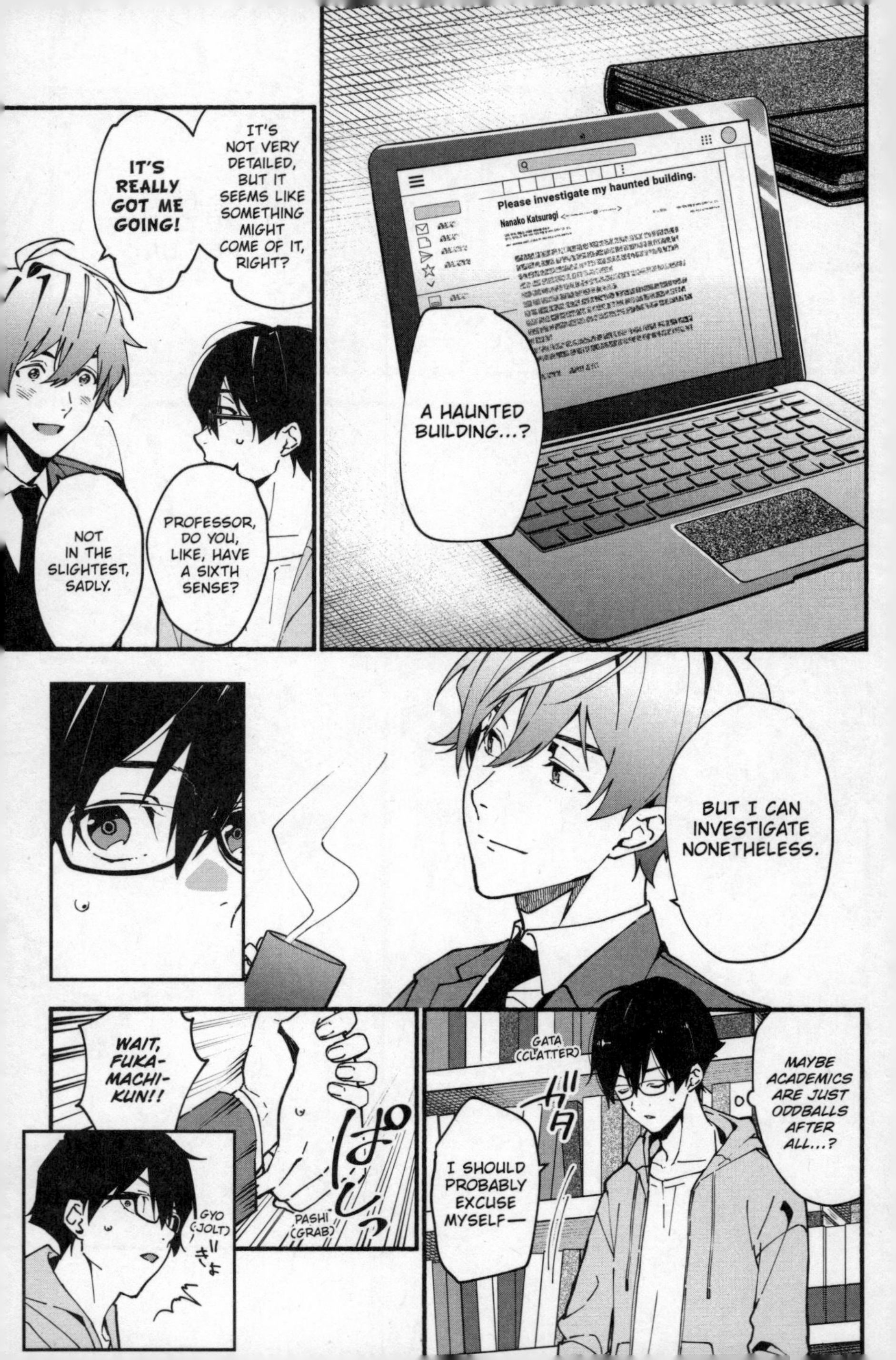
Please investigate my haunted building.
Nanako Katsuragi
A HAUNTED BUILDING...?
IT'S NOT VERY DETAILED, BUT IT SEEMS LIKE SOMETHING MIGHT COME OF IT, RIGHT?
IT'S REALLY GOT ME GOING!
PROFESSOR, DO YOU, LIKE, HAVE A SIXTH SENSE?
NOT IN THE SLIGHTEST, SADLY.
BUT I CAN INVESTIGATE NONETHELESS.
MAYBE ACADEMICS ARE JUST ODDBALLS AFTER ALL...?
GATA (CLATTER)
I SHOULD PROBABLY EXCUSE MYSELF—
WAIT, FUKA-MACHI-KUN!!
PASHI (GRAB)
GYO (JOLT)

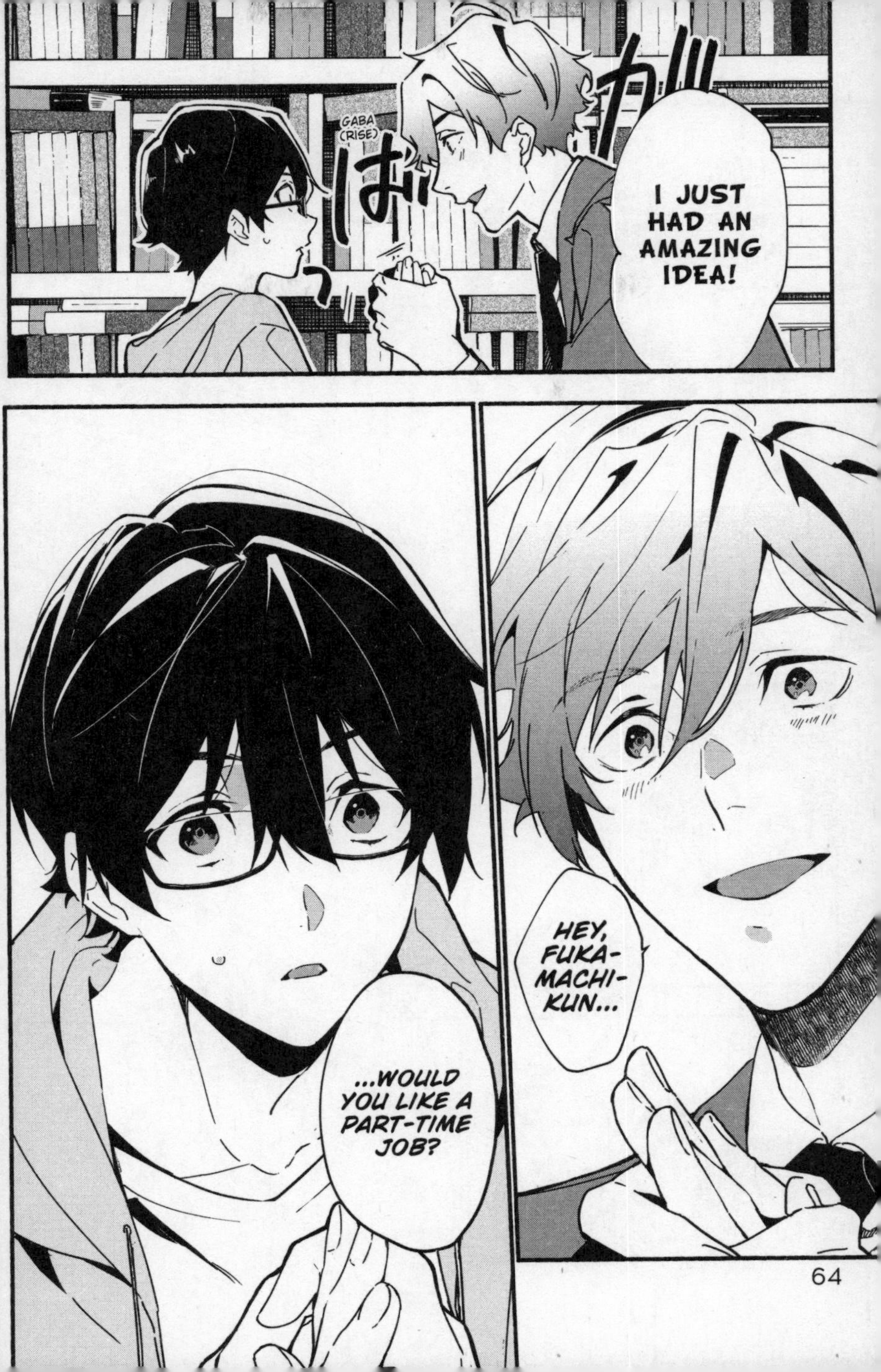
I JUST HAD AN AMAZING IDEA!
GABA (RISE)
HEY, FUKA-MACHI-KUN...
...WOULD YOU LIKE A PART-TIME JOB?

Associate Professor Akira Takatsuki's Conjecture

Associate Professor Akira Takatsuki's Conjecture

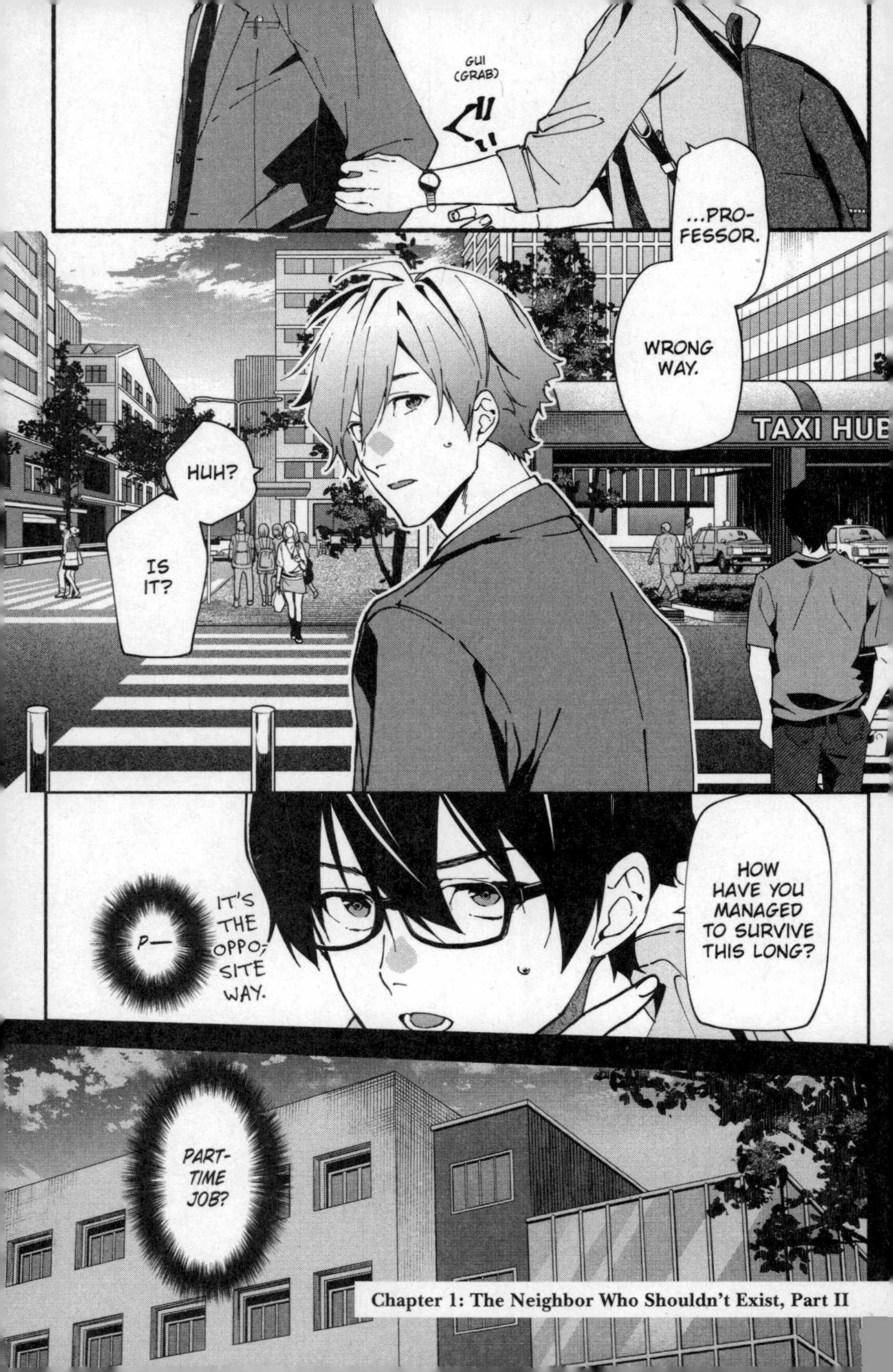
GUI (GRAB)
...PRO-FESSOR.
WRONG WAY.
TAXI HUB
HUH?
IS IT?
HOW HAVE YOU MANAGED TO SURVIVE THIS LONG?
IT'S THE OPPO-SITE WAY.
P—
PART-TIME JOB?

Chapter 1: The Neighbor Who Shouldn't Exist, Part II

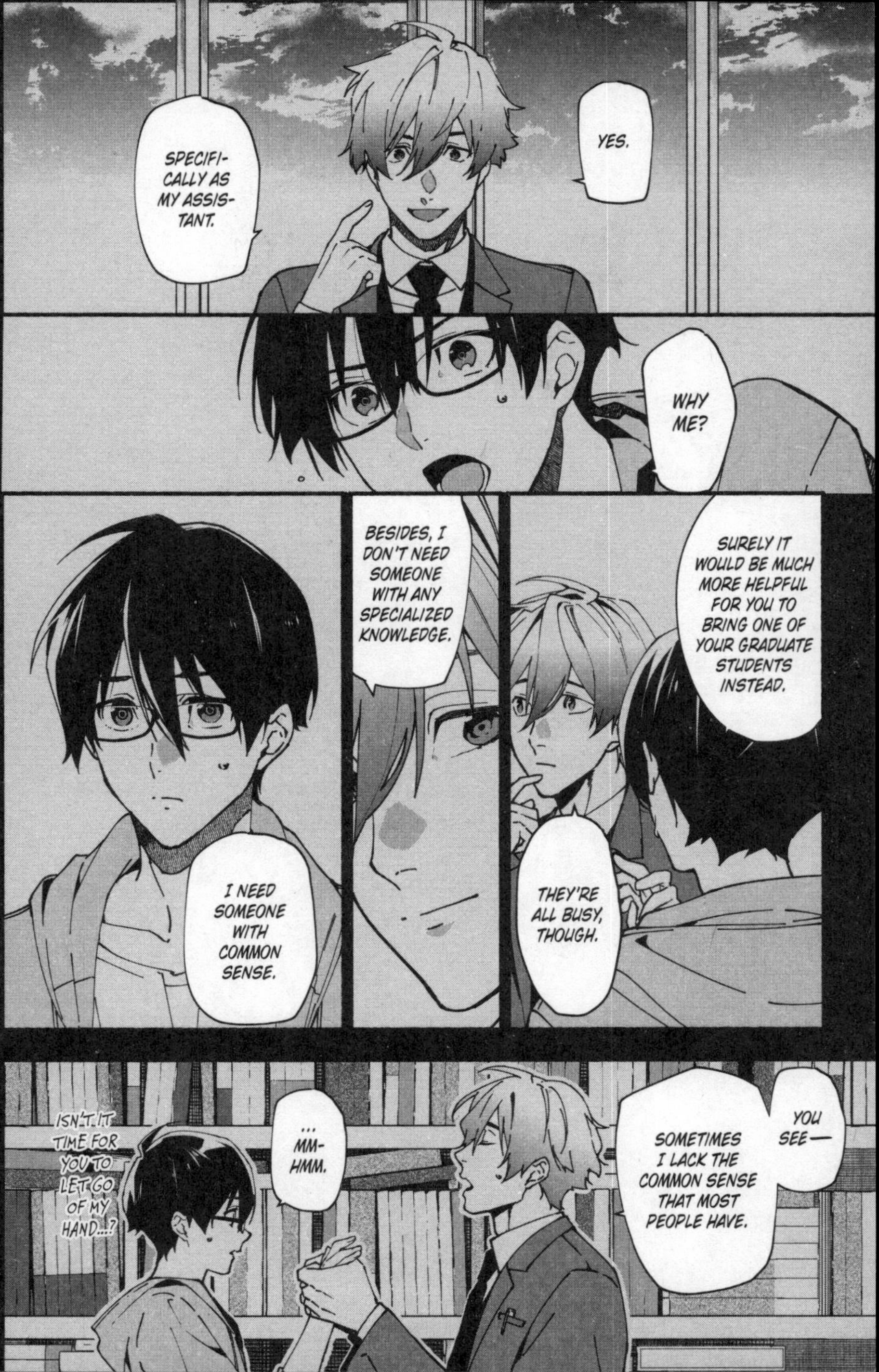
YES.
SPECIFI-CALLY AS MY ASSIS-TANT.
WHY ME?
SURELY IT WOULD BE MUCH MORE HELPFUL FOR YOU TO BRING ONE OF YOUR GRADUATE STUDENTS INSTEAD.
THEY'RE ALL BUSY, THOUGH.
BESIDES, I DON'T NEED SOMEONE WITH ANY SPECIALIZED KNOWLEDGE.
I NEED SOMEONE WITH COMMON SENSE.
YOU SEE—
SOMETIMES I LACK THE COMMON SENSE THAT MOST PEOPLE HAVE.
...MM-HMM.
ISN'T IT TIME FOR YOU TO LET GO OF MY HAND...?

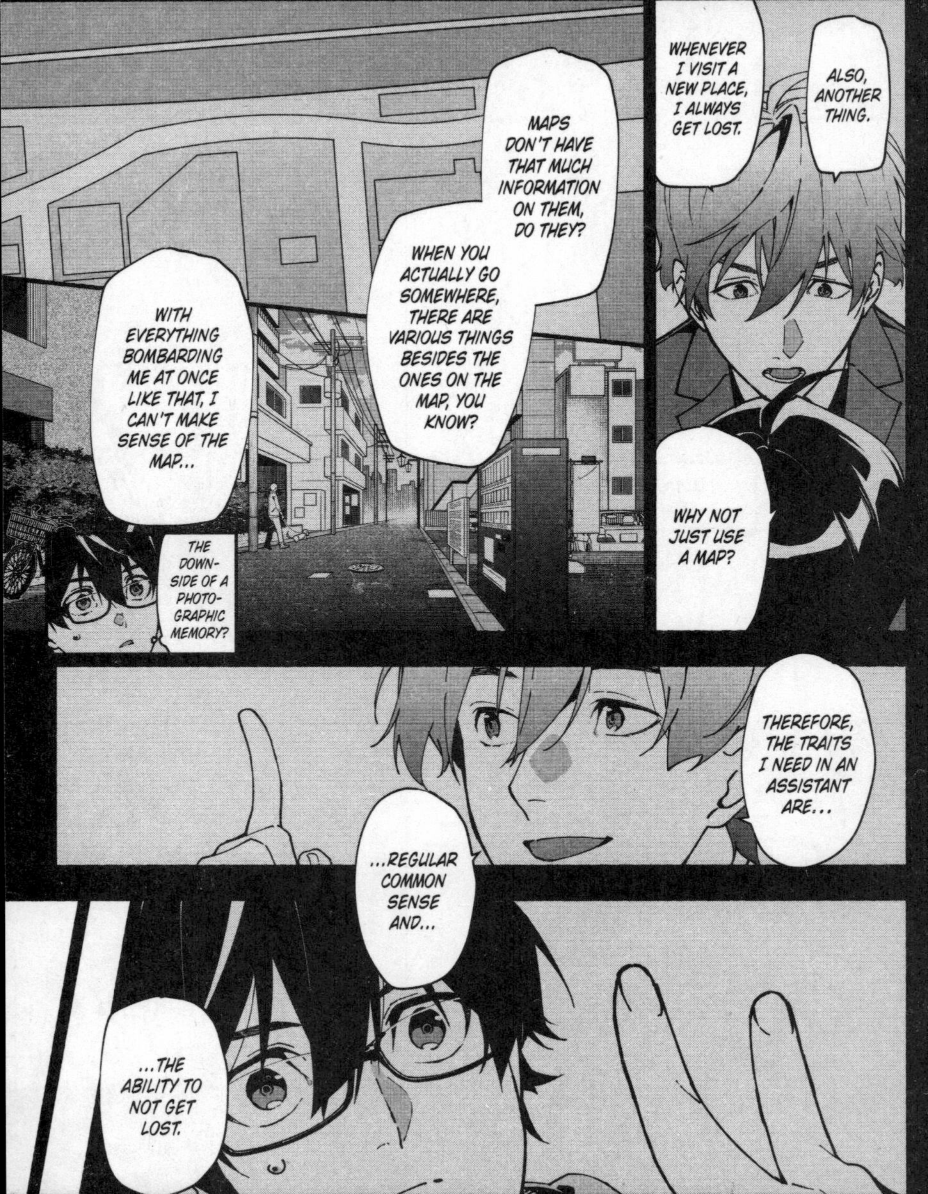
ALSO, ANOTHER THING.
WHENEVER I VISIT A NEW PLACE, I ALWAYS GET LOST.
WHY NOT JUST USE A MAP?
MAPS DON'T HAVE THAT MUCH INFORMATION ON THEM, DO THEY?
WHEN YOU ACTUALLY GO SOMEWHERE, THERE ARE VARIOUS THINGS BESIDES THE ONES ON THE MAP, YOU KNOW?
WITH EVERYTHING BOMBARDING ME AT ONCE LIKE THAT, I CAN'T MAKE SENSE OF THE MAP...
THE DOWN-SIDE OF A PHOTO-GRAPHIC MEMORY?
THEREFORE, THE TRAITS I NEED IN AN ASSISTANT ARE...
...REGULAR COMMON SENSE AND...
...THE ABILITY TO NOT GET LOST.

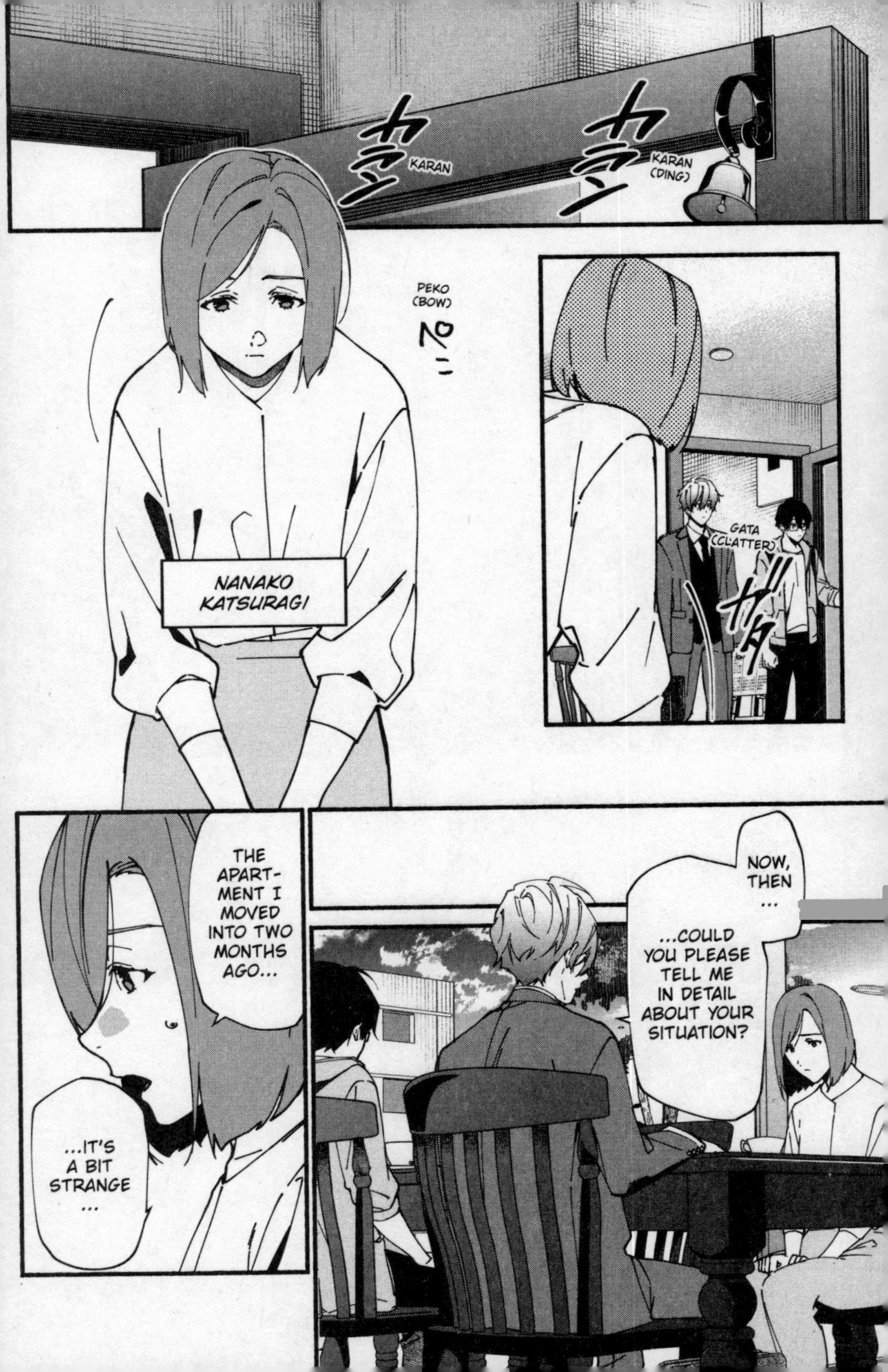
KARAN (DING)
KARAN
GATA (CLATTER)
PEKO (BOW)
NANAKO KATSURAGI
NOW, THEN ...
...COULD YOU PLEASE TELL ME IN DETAIL ABOUT YOUR SITUATION?
THE APARTMENT I MOVED INTO TWO MONTHS AGO...
...IT'S A BIT STRANGE ...

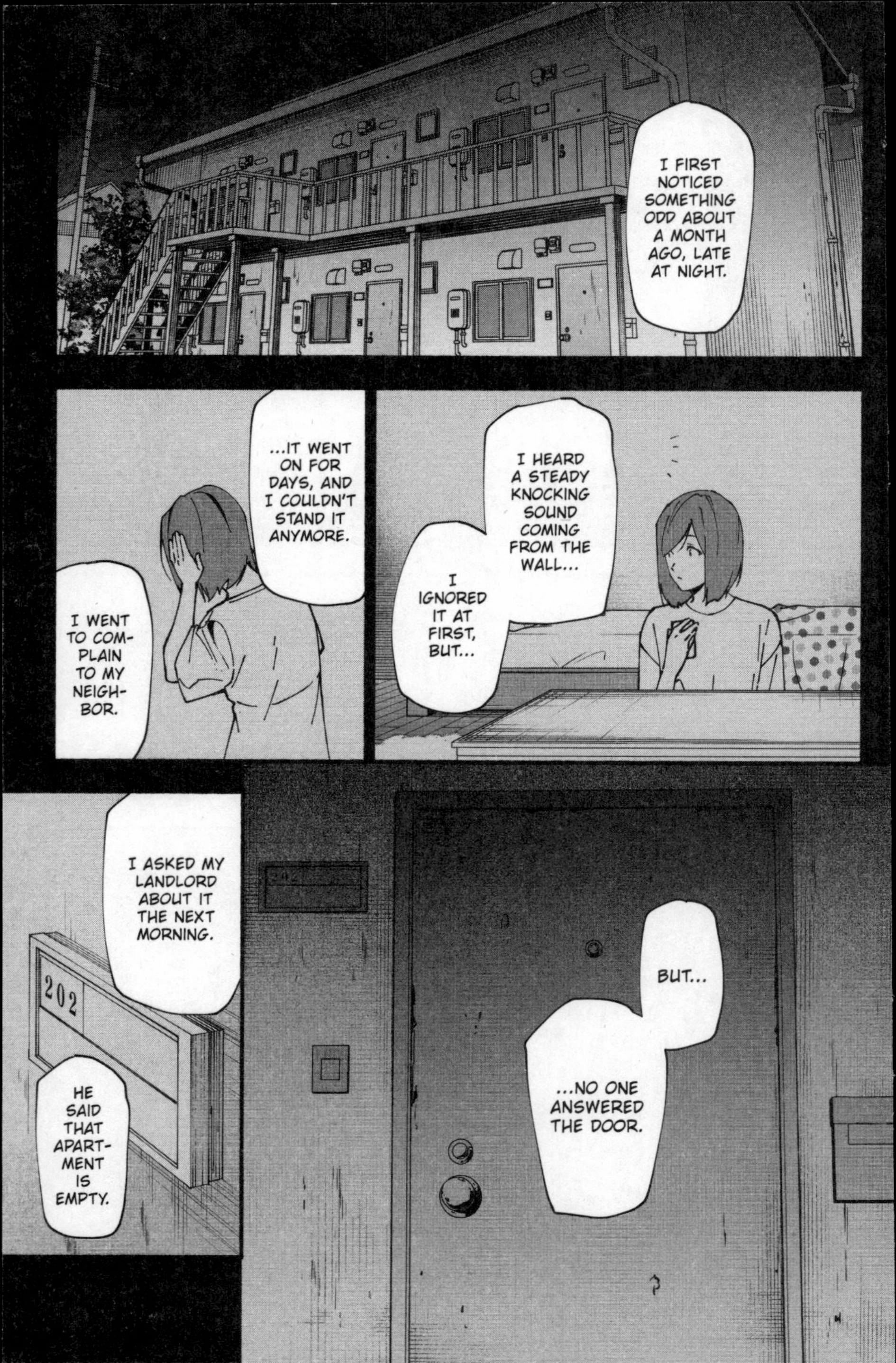
I FIRST NOTICED SOMETHING ODD ABOUT A MONTH AGO, LATE AT NIGHT.
I HEARD A STEADY KNOCKING SOUND COMING FROM THE WALL...
I IGNORED IT AT FIRST, BUT...
...IT WENT ON FOR DAYS, AND I COULDN'T STAND IT ANYMORE.
I WENT TO COM-PLAIN TO MY NEIGH-BOR.
BUT...
...NO ONE ANSWERED THE DOOR.
I ASKED MY LANDLORD ABOUT IT THE NEXT MORNING.
202
HE SAID THAT APART-MENT IS EMPTY.

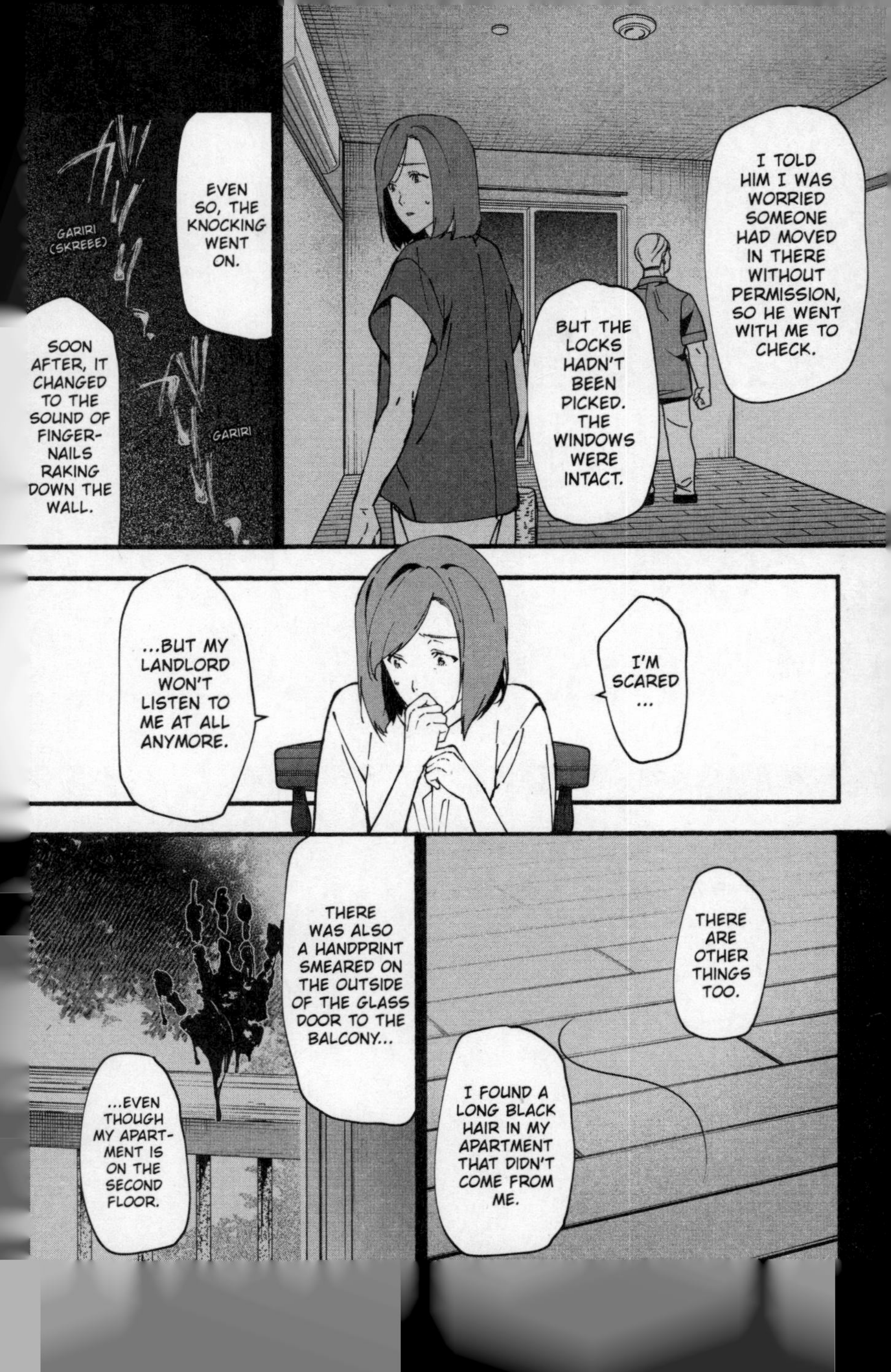
I TOLD HIM I WAS WORRIED SOMEONE HAD MOVED IN THERE WITHOUT PERMISSION, SO HE WENT WITH ME TO CHECK.
BUT THE LOCKS HADN'T BEEN PICKED. THE WINDOWS WERE INTACT.
EVEN SO, THE KNOCKING WENT ON.
GARIRI (SKREEE)
SOON AFTER, IT CHANGED TO THE SOUND OF FINGER-NAILS RAKING DOWN THE WALL.
GARIRI
I'M SCARED...
...BUT MY LANDLORD WON'T LISTEN TO ME AT ALL ANYMORE.
THERE ARE OTHER THINGS TOO.
I FOUND A LONG BLACK HAIR IN MY APARTMENT THAT DIDN'T COME FROM ME.
THERE WAS ALSO A HANDPRINT SMEARED ON THE OUTSIDE OF THE GLASS DOOR TO THE BALCONY...
...EVEN THOUGH MY APART-MENT IS ON THE SECOND FLOOR.

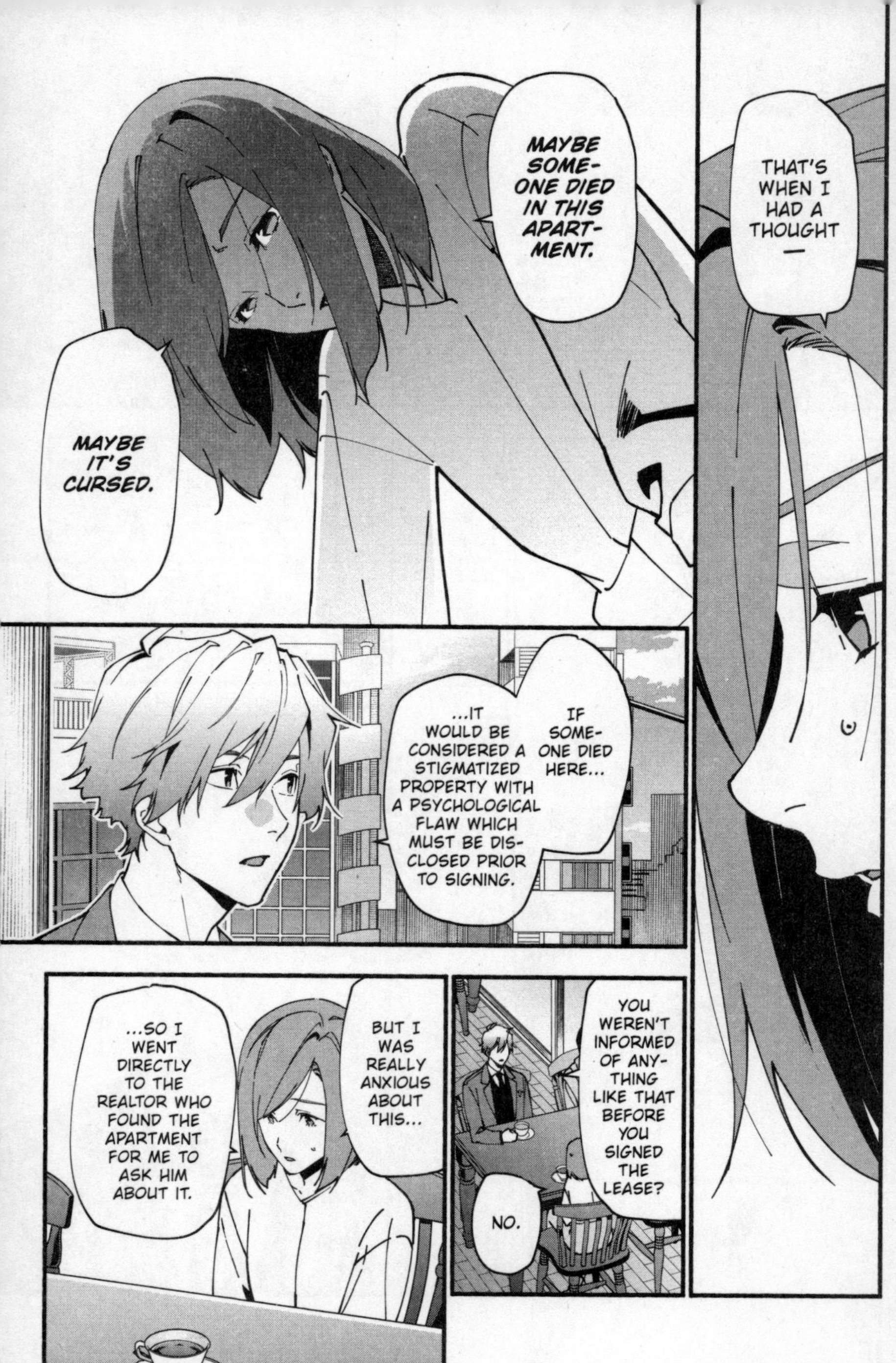
THAT'S WHEN I HAD A THOUGHT —
MAYBE SOME-ONE DIED IN THIS APART-MENT.
MAYBE IT'S CURSED.
IF SOME-ONE DIED HERE...
...IT WOULD BE CONSIDERED A STIGMATIZED PROPERTY WITH A PSYCHOLOGICAL FLAW WHICH MUST BE DIS-CLOSED PRIOR TO SIGNING.
YOU WEREN'T INFORMED OF ANY-THING LIKE THAT BEFORE YOU SIGNED THE LEASE?
NO.
BUT I WAS REALLY ANXIOUS ABOUT THIS...
...SO I WENT DIRECTLY TO THE REALTOR WHO FOUND THE APARTMENT FOR ME TO ASK HIM ABOUT IT.

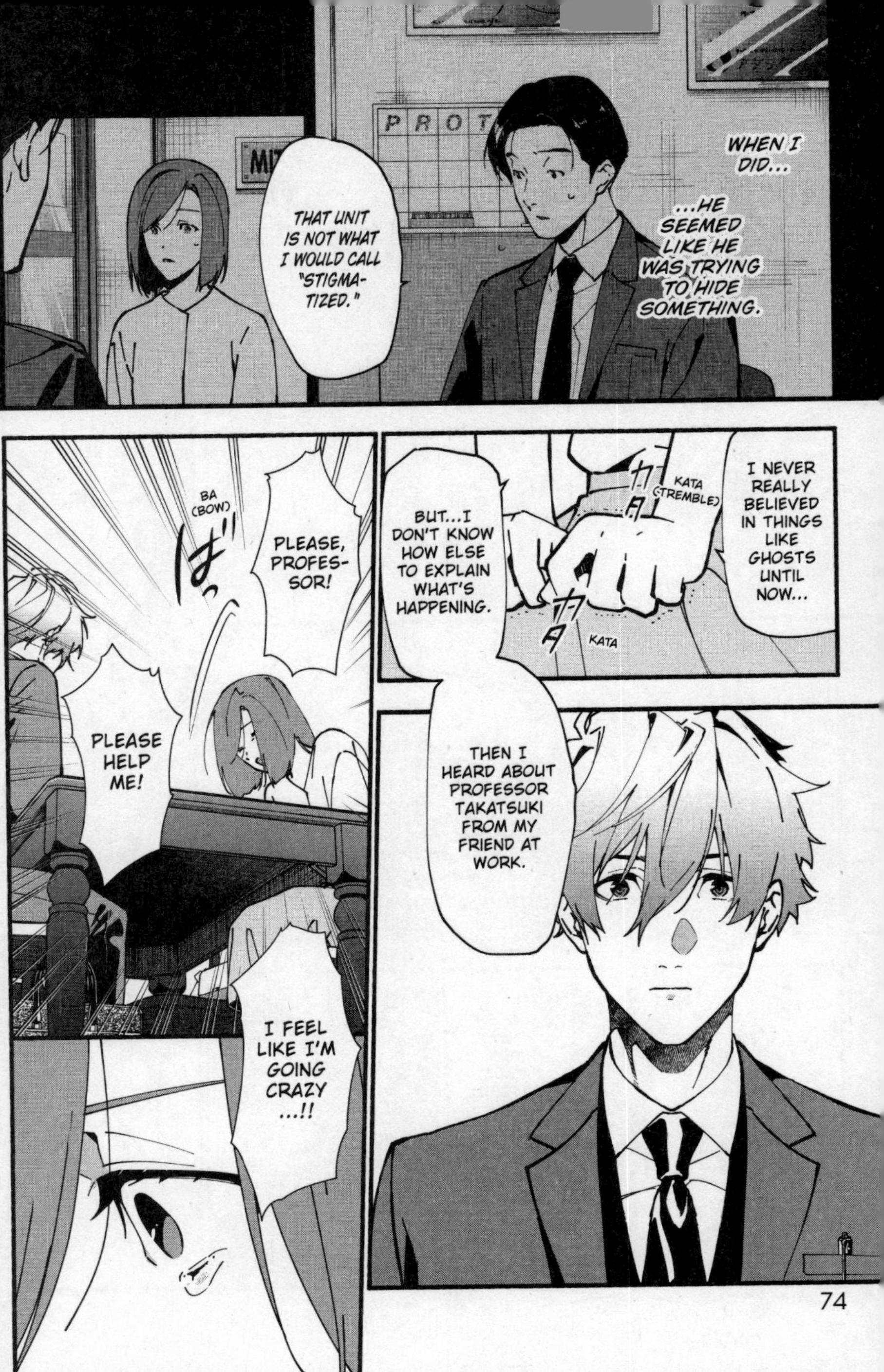
WHEN I DID...
...HE SEEMED LIKE HE WAS TRYING TO HIDE SOMETHING.
THAT UNIT IS NOT WHAT I WOULD CALL "STIGMATIZED."
I NEVER REALLY BELIEVED IN THINGS LIKE GHOSTS UNTIL NOW...
KATA (TREMBLE)
BUT...I DON'T KNOW HOW ELSE TO EXPLAIN WHAT'S HAPPENING.
KATA
THEN I HEARD ABOUT PROFESSOR TAKATSUKI FROM MY FRIEND AT WORK.
PLEASE, PROFESSOR!
BA (BOW)
PLEASE HELP ME!
I FEEL LIKE I'M GOING CRAZY ...!!

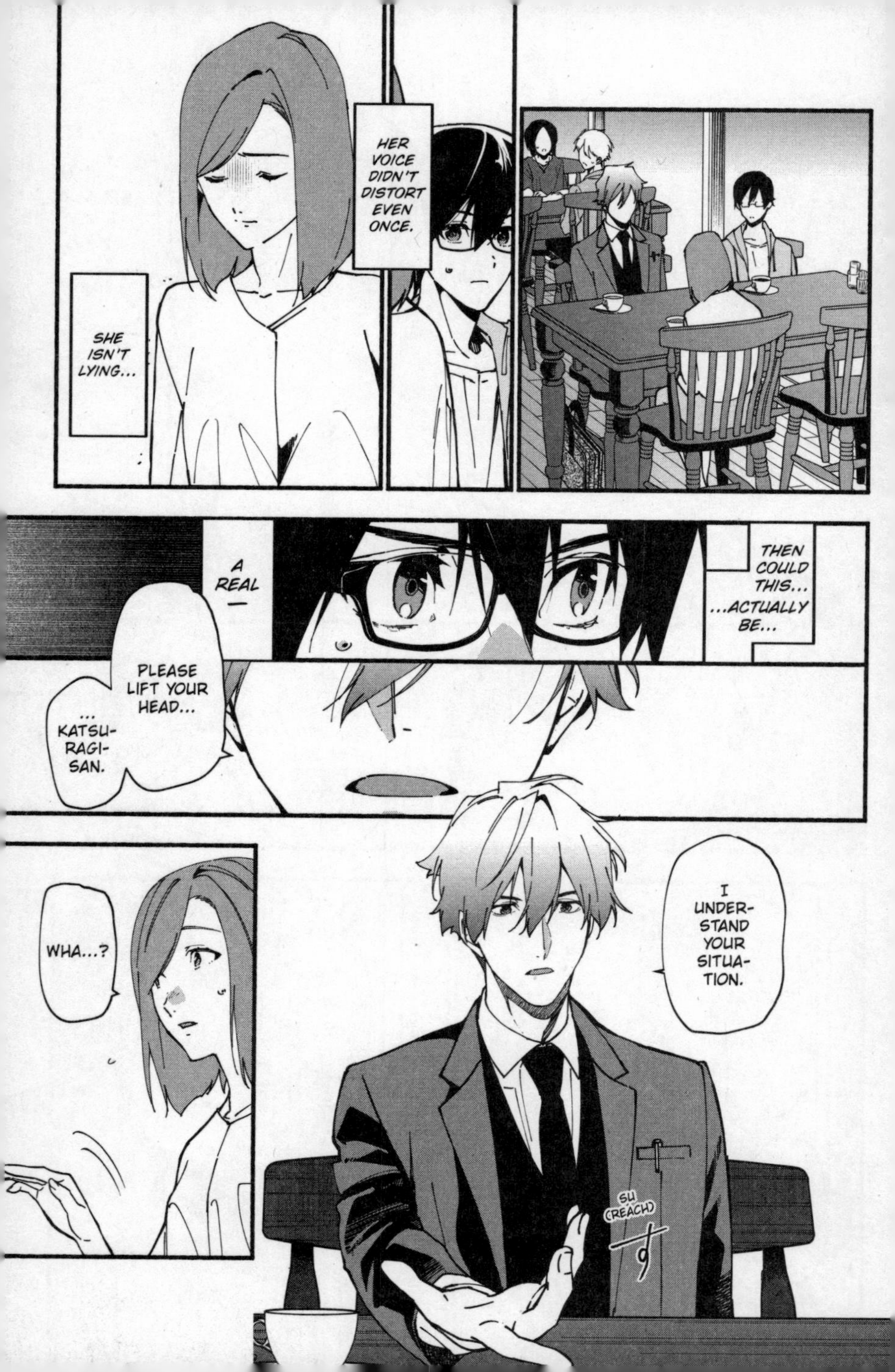
HER VOICE DIDN'T DISTORT EVEN ONCE.
SHE ISN'T LYING...
THEN COULD THIS... ...ACTUALLY BE...
A REAL —
PLEASE LIFT YOUR HEAD...
...KATSURAGI-SAN.
I UNDERSTAND YOUR SITUATION.
SU (REACH)
WHA...?

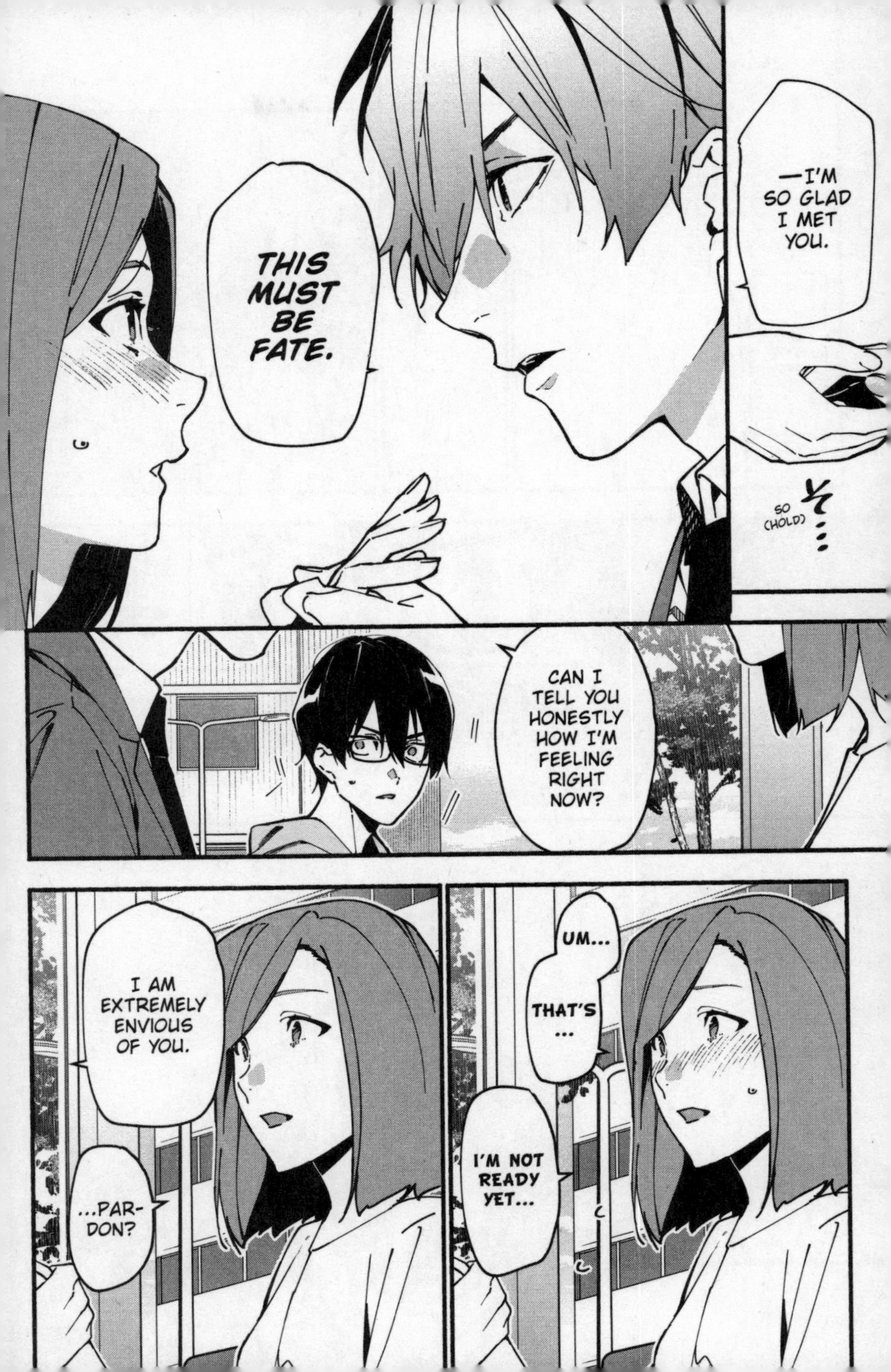
—I'M SO GLAD I MET YOU.
SO (HOLD)
THIS MUST BE FATE.
CAN I TELL YOU HONESTLY HOW I'M FEELING RIGHT NOW?
UM... THAT'S ...
I'M NOT READY YET...
I AM EXTREMELY ENVIOUS OF YOU.
...PAR-DON?

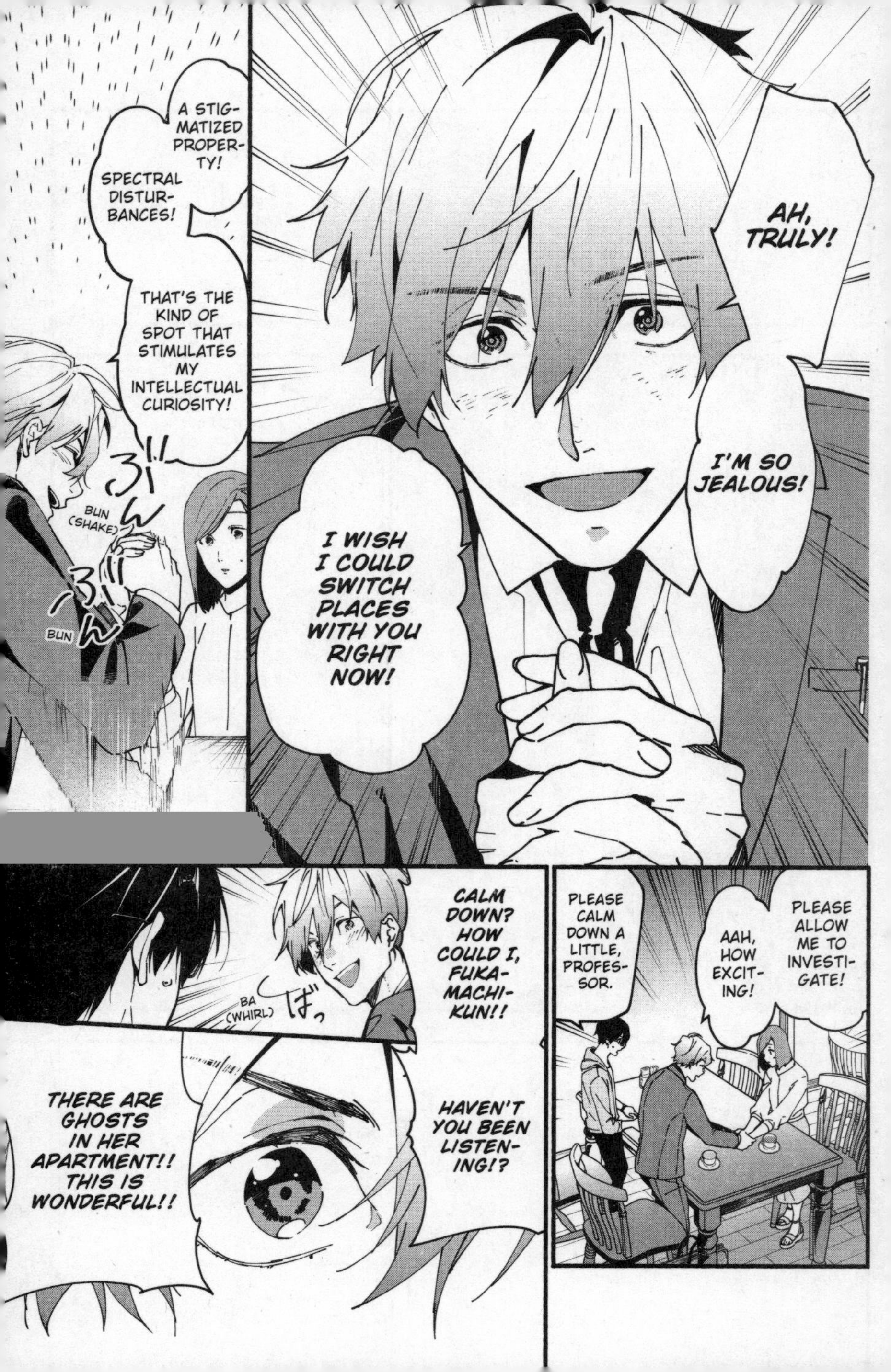

AH, TRULY!
I'M SO JEALOUS!
I WISH I COULD SWITCH PLACES WITH YOU RIGHT NOW!
A STIGMATIZED PROPERTY!
SPECTRAL DISTURBANCES!
THAT'S THE KIND OF SPOT THAT STIMULATES MY INTELLECTUAL CURIOSITY!
BUN (SHAKE)
BUN
PLEASE ALLOW ME TO INVESTIGATE!
AAH, HOW EXCITING!
PLEASE CALM DOWN A LITTLE, PROFESSOR.
CALM DOWN? HOW COULD I, FUKAMACHI-KUN!!
BA (WHIRL)
HAVEN'T YOU BEEN LISTENING!?
THERE ARE GHOSTS IN HER APARTMENT!! THIS IS WONDERFUL!!

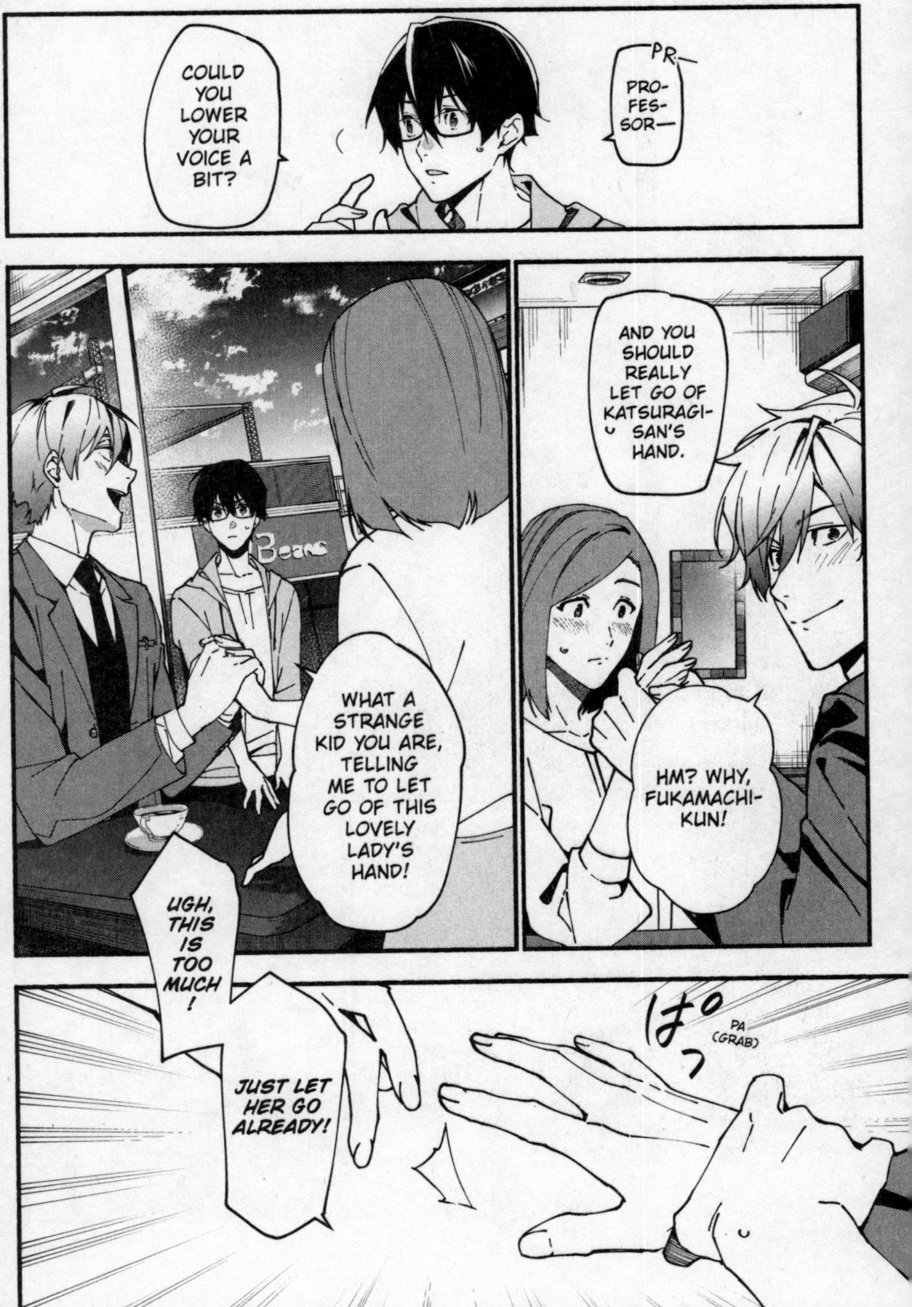
PR— PRO-FES-SOR—
COULD YOU LOWER YOUR VOICE A BIT?
AND YOU SHOULD REALLY LET GO OF KATSURAGI-SAN'S HAND.
HM? WHY, FUKAMACHI-KUN!
WHAT A STRANGE KID YOU ARE, TELLING ME TO LET GO OF THIS LOVELY LADY'S HAND!
UGH, THIS IS TOO MUCH!
ぱっ
PA (GRAB)
JUST LET HER GO ALREADY!

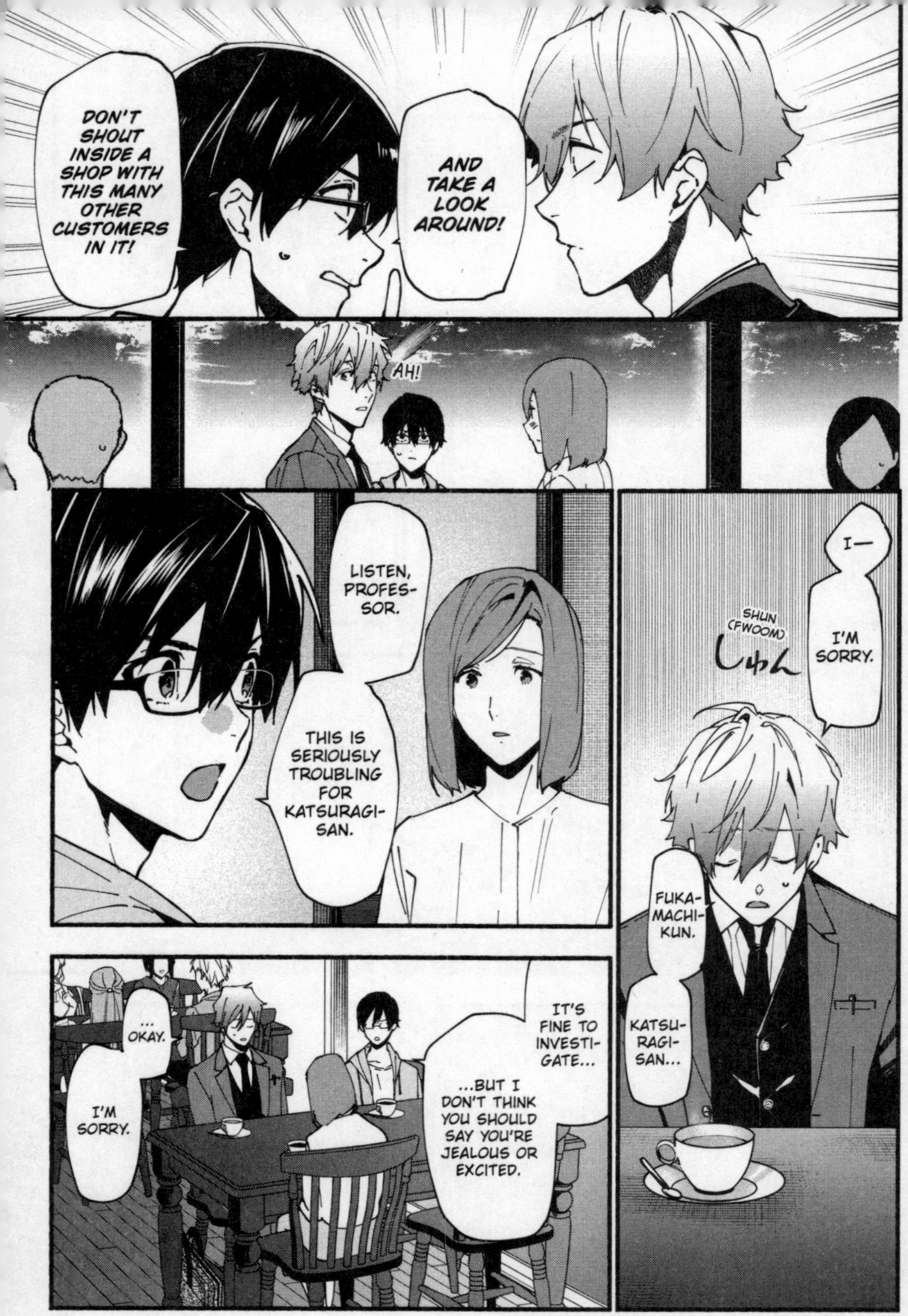
DON'T SHOUT INSIDE A SHOP WITH THIS MANY OTHER CUSTOMERS IN IT!
AND TAKE A LOOK AROUND!
AH!
I—
I'M SORRY.
SHUN (FWOOM)
しゅん
FUKA-MACHI-KUN.
KATSU-RAGI-SAN...
LISTEN, PROFES-SOR.
THIS IS SERIOUSLY TROUBLING FOR KATSURAGI-SAN.
IT'S FINE TO INVESTI-GATE...
...BUT I DON'T THINK YOU SHOULD SAY YOU'RE JEALOUS OR EXCITED.
...OKAY.
I'M SORRY.

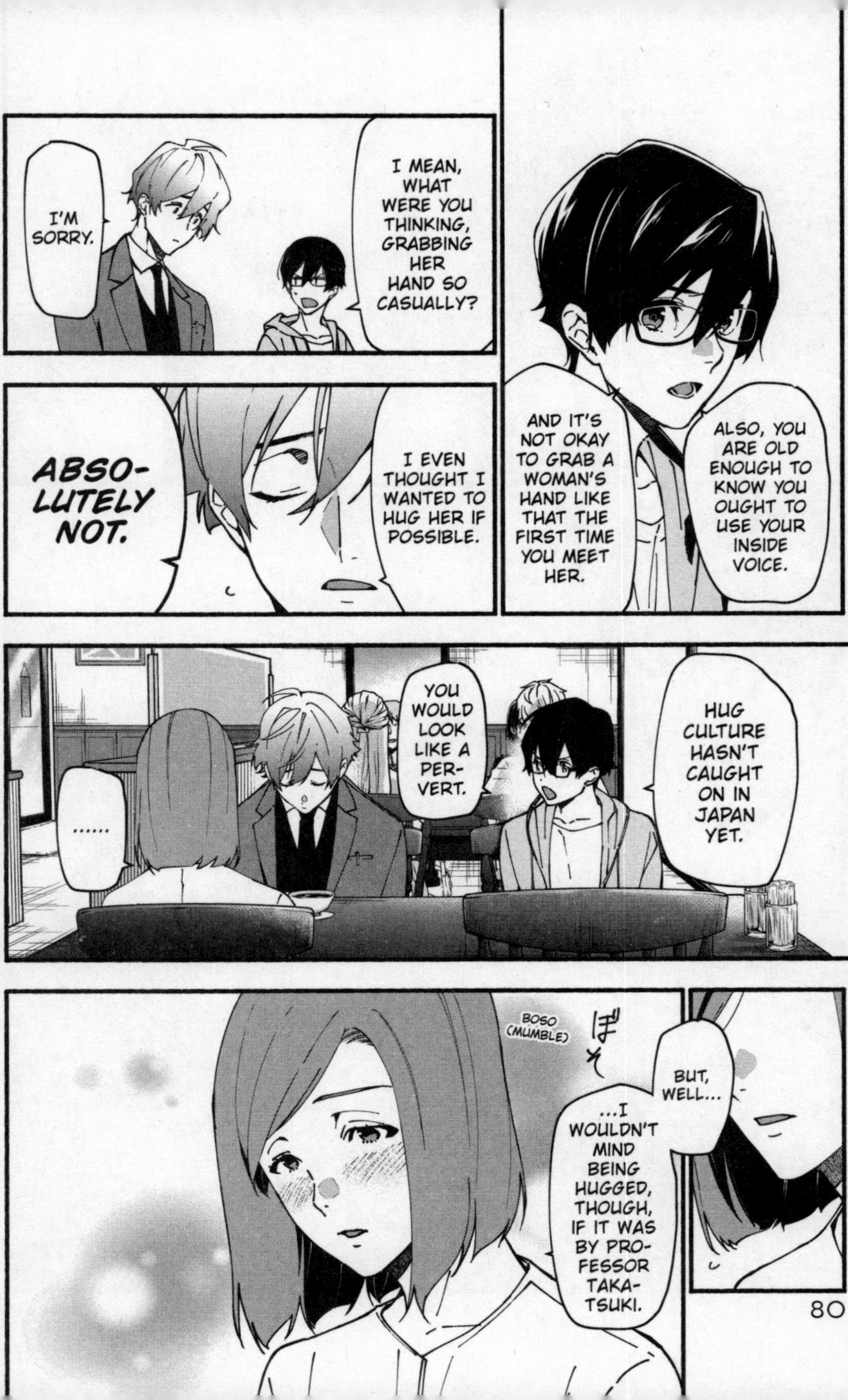
ALSO, YOU ARE OLD ENOUGH TO KNOW YOU OUGHT TO USE YOUR INSIDE VOICE.
AND IT'S NOT OKAY TO GRAB A WOMAN'S HAND LIKE THAT THE FIRST TIME YOU MEET HER.
I MEAN, WHAT WERE YOU THINKING, GRABBING HER HAND SO CASUALLY?
I'M SORRY.
I EVEN THOUGHT I WANTED TO HUG HER IF POSSIBLE.
ABSO-LUTELY NOT.
HUG CULTURE HASN'T CAUGHT ON IN JAPAN YET.
YOU WOULD LOOK LIKE A PER-VERT.
......
BUT, WELL...
BOSO (MUMBLE)
ぼそ
...I WOULDN'T MIND BEING HUGGED, THOUGH, IF IT WAS BY PRO-FESSOR TAKA-TSUKI.

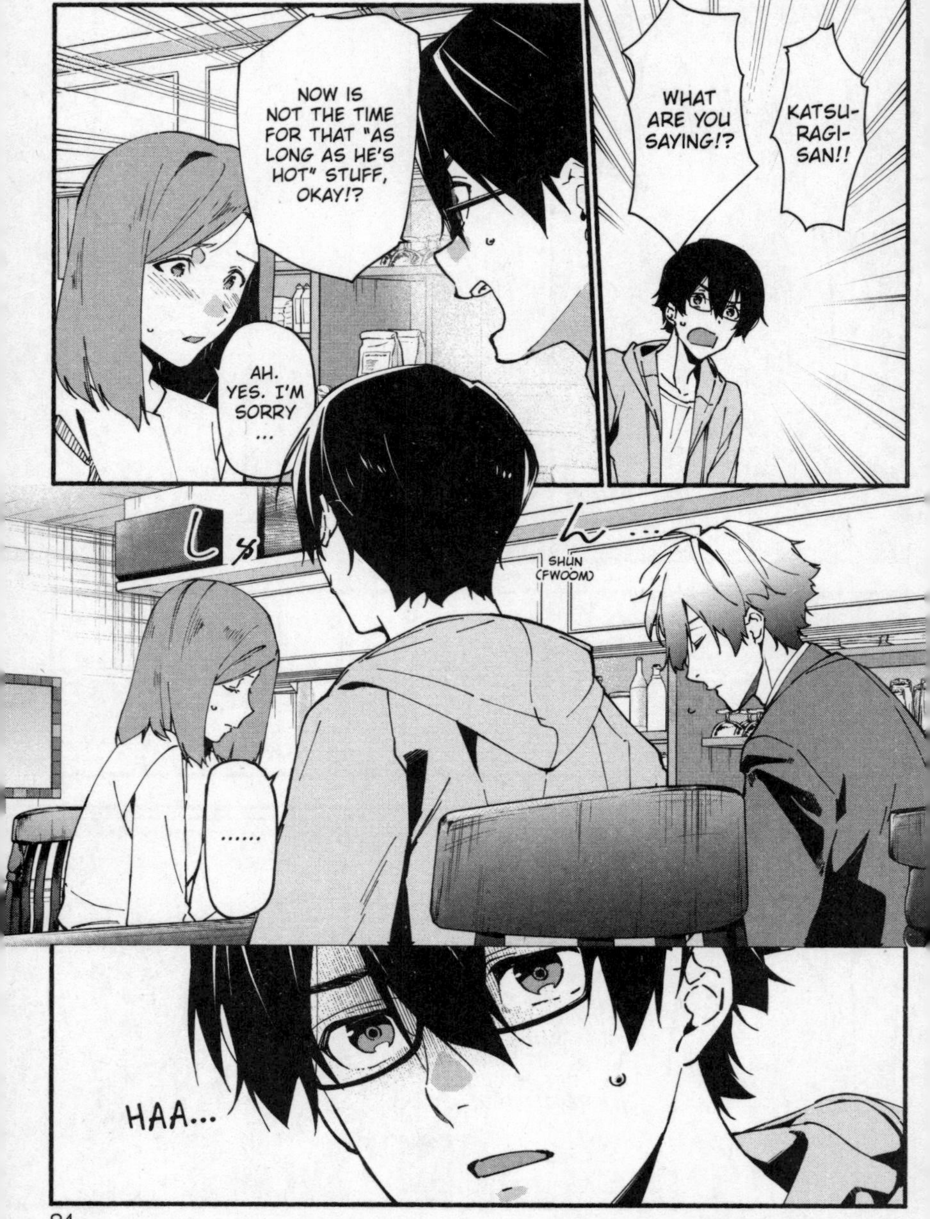
KATSU-RAGI-SAN!!
WHAT ARE YOU SAYING!?
NOW IS NOT THE TIME FOR THAT "AS LONG AS HE'S HOT" STUFF, OKAY!?
AH. YES. I'M SORRY ...
SHUN (FWOOM)
......
HAA...

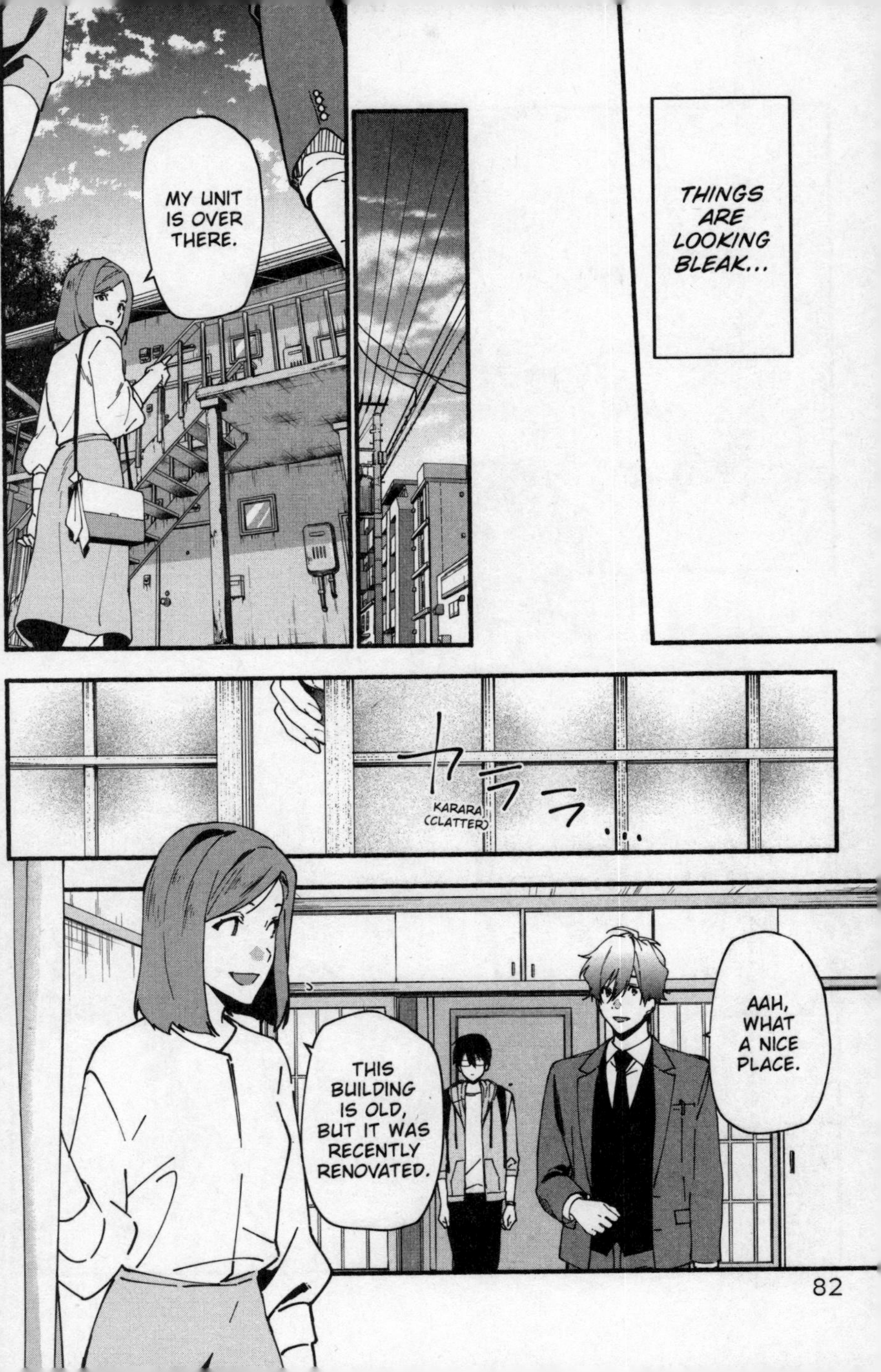
THINGS ARE LOOKING BLEAK...
MY UNIT IS OVER THERE.
KARARA (CLATTER)
AAH, WHAT A NICE PLACE.
THIS BUILDING IS OLD, BUT IT WAS RECENTLY RENOVATED.

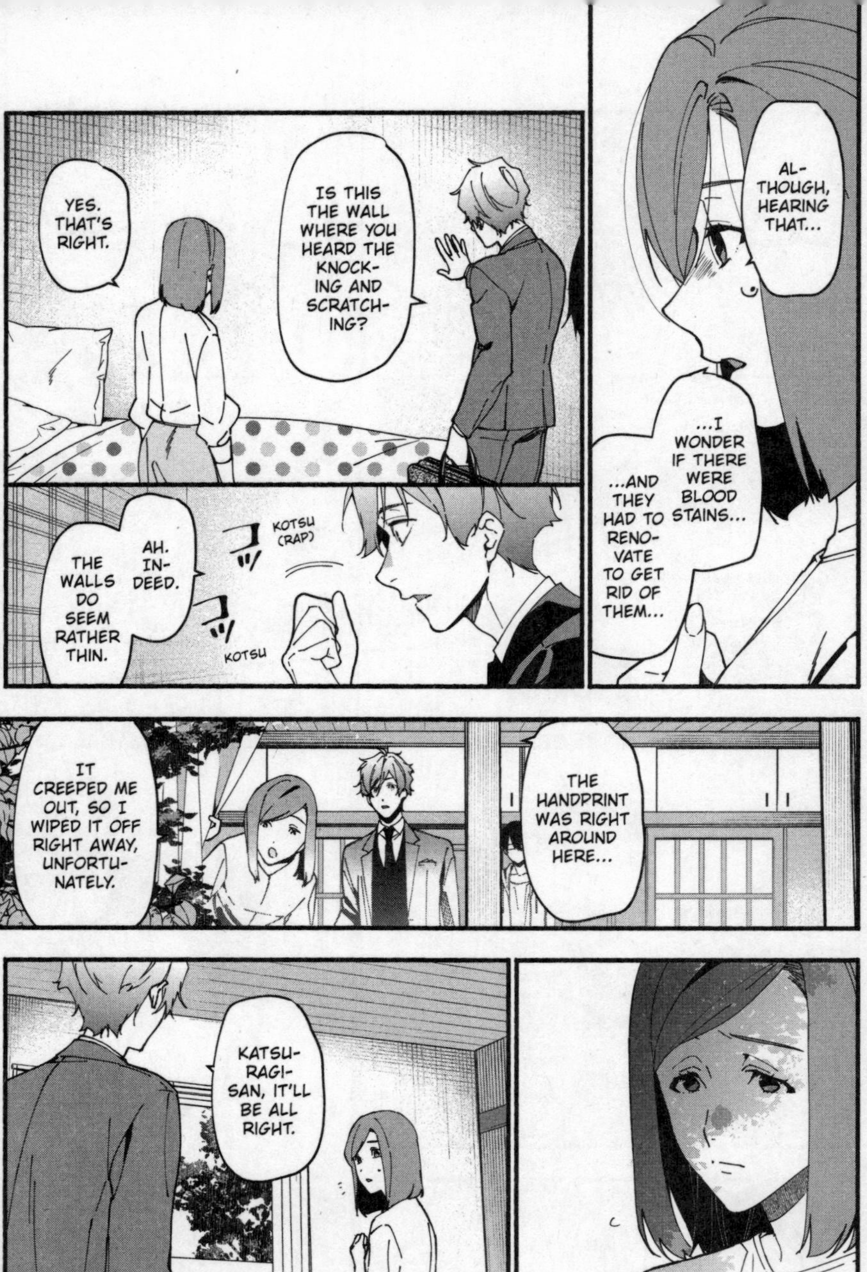
AL-THOUGH, HEARING THAT...
...I WONDER IF THERE WERE BLOOD STAINS...
...AND THEY HAD TO RENO-VATE TO GET RID OF THEM...
IS THIS THE WALL WHERE YOU HEARD THE KNOCK-ING AND SCRATCH-ING?
YES. THAT'S RIGHT.
KOTSU (RAP)
KOTSU
AH. IN-DEED.
THE WALLS DO SEEM RATHER THIN.
THE HANDPRINT WAS RIGHT AROUND HERE...
IT CREEPED ME OUT, SO I WIPED IT OFF RIGHT AWAY, UNFORTU-NATELY.
KATSU-RAGI-SAN, IT'LL BE ALL RIGHT.

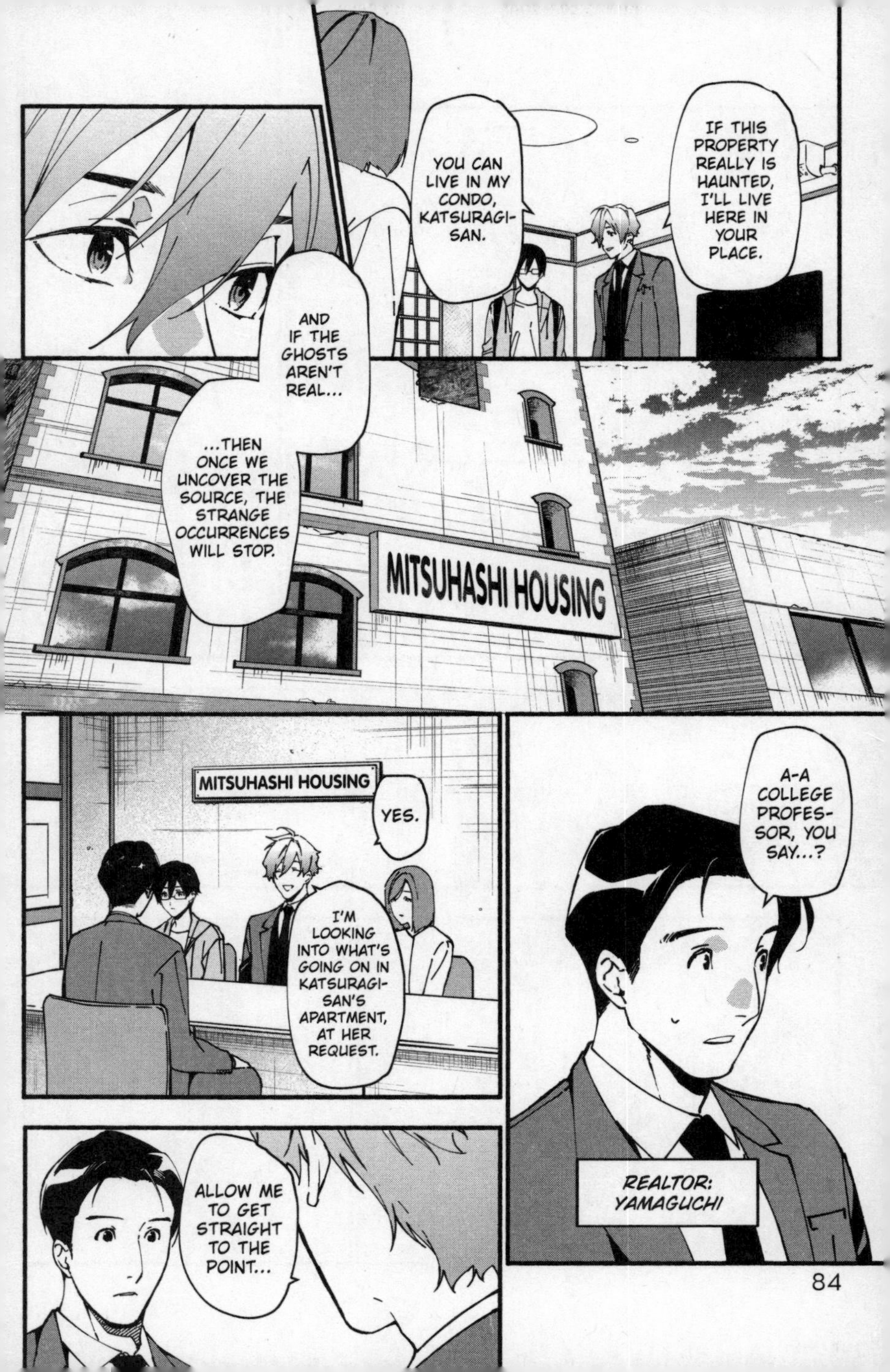
IF THIS PROPERTY REALLY IS HAUNTED, I'LL LIVE HERE IN YOUR PLACE.
YOU CAN LIVE IN MY CONDO, KATSURAGI-SAN.
AND IF THE GHOSTS AREN'T REAL...
...THEN ONCE WE UNCOVER THE SOURCE, THE STRANGE OCCURRENCES WILL STOP.
MITSUHASHI HOUSING
A-A COLLEGE PROFESSOR, YOU SAY...?
REALTOR: YAMAGUCHI
MITSUHASHI HOUSING
YES.
I'M LOOKING INTO WHAT'S GOING ON IN KATSURAGI-SAN'S APARTMENT, AT HER REQUEST.
ALLOW ME TO GET STRAIGHT TO THE POINT...

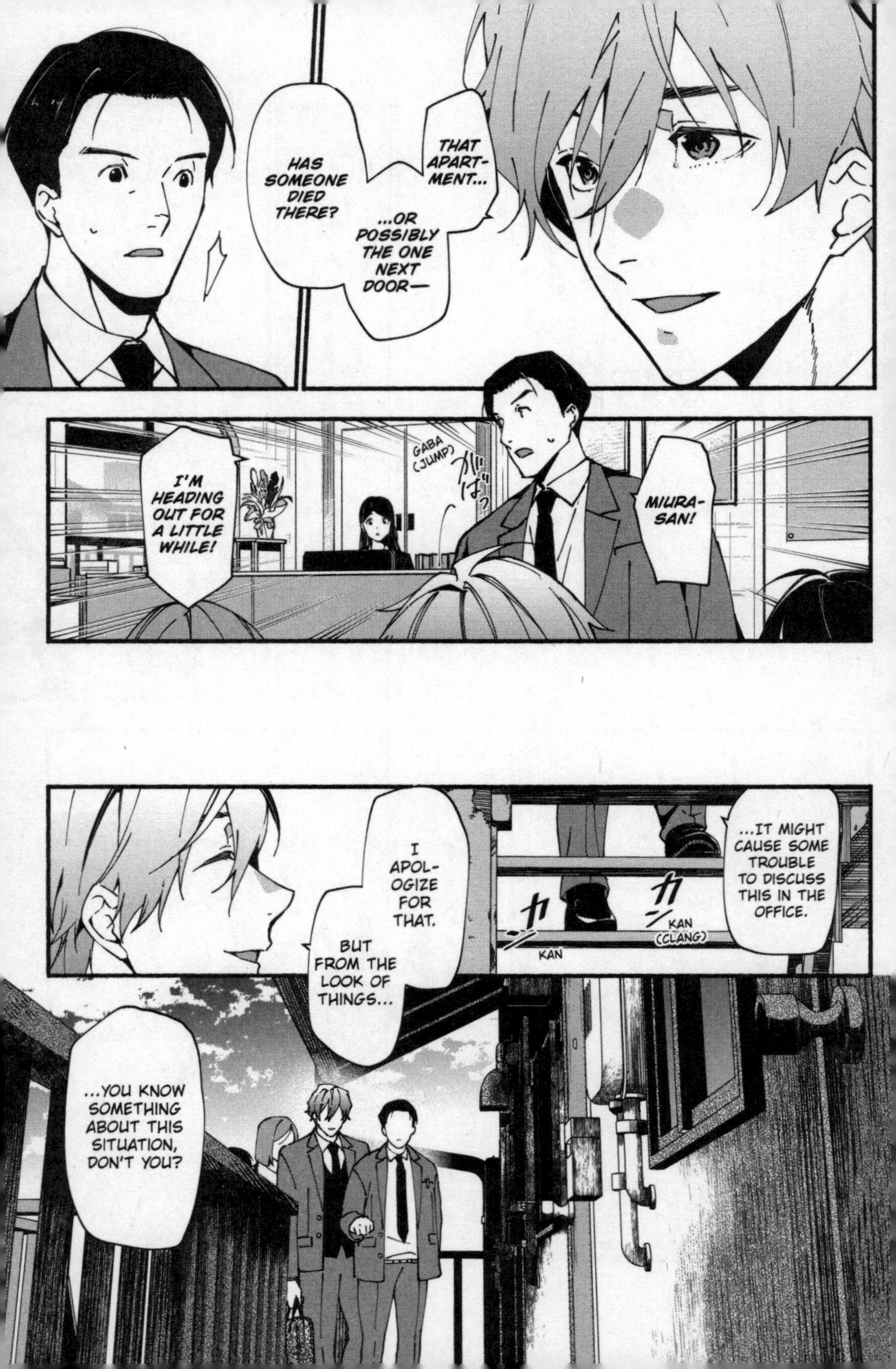
THAT APARTMENT...
...OR POSSIBLY THE ONE NEXT DOOR—
HAS SOMEONE DIED THERE?
MIURA-SAN!
GABA (JUMP)
I'M HEADING OUT FOR A LITTLE WHILE!
...IT MIGHT CAUSE SOME TROUBLE TO DISCUSS THIS IN THE OFFICE.
KAN (CLANG)
KAN
I APOLOGIZE FOR THAT.
BUT FROM THE LOOK OF THINGS...
...YOU KNOW SOMETHING ABOUT THIS SITUATION, DON'T YOU?

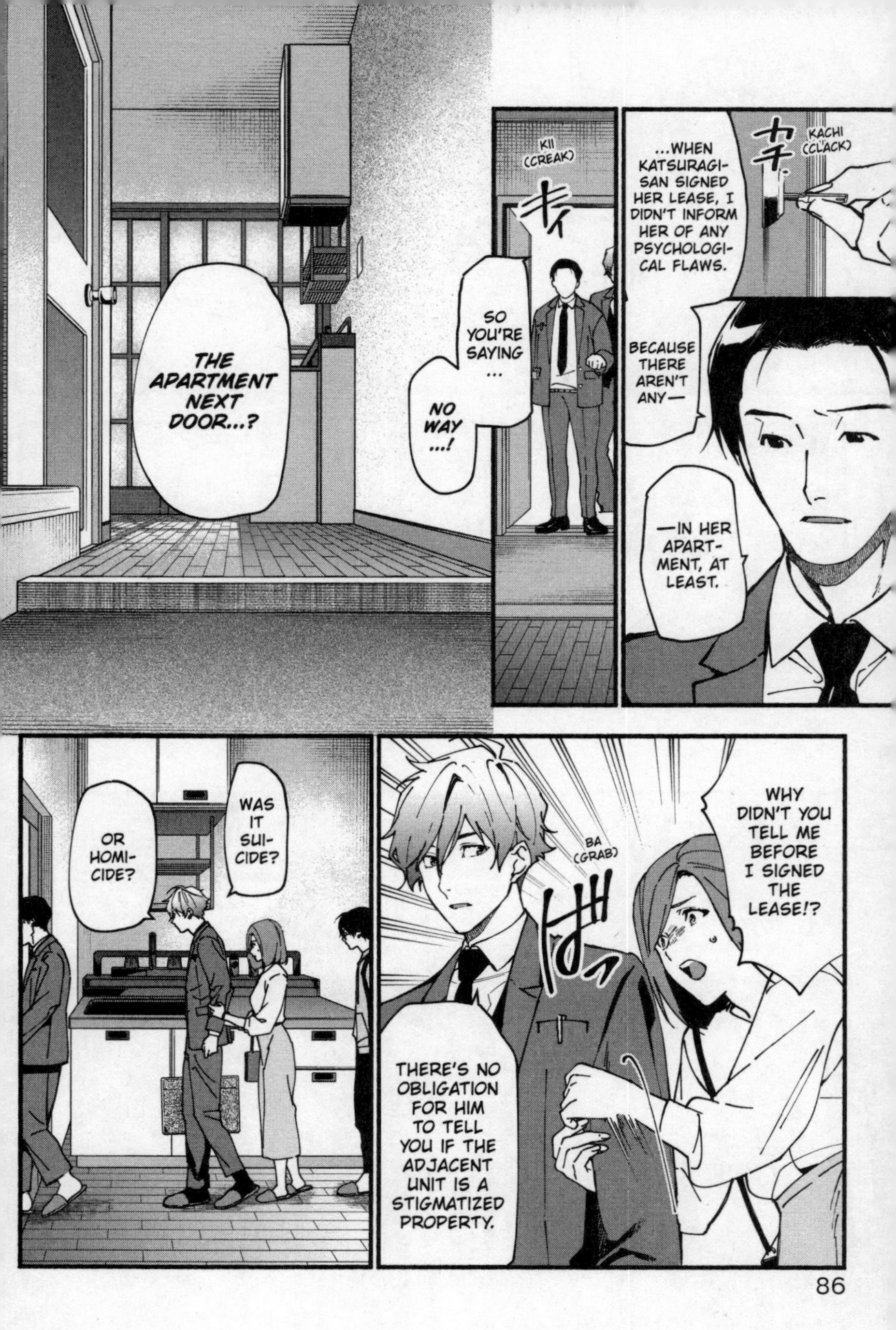

KACHI (CLACK)
...WHEN KATSURAGI-SAN SIGNED HER LEASE, I DIDN'T INFORM HER OF ANY PSYCHOLOGICAL FLAWS.
BECAUSE THERE AREN'T ANY—
—IN HER APARTMENT, AT LEAST.
KII (CREAK)
SO YOU'RE SAYING...
NO WAY...!
THE APARTMENT NEXT DOOR...?
WHY DIDN'T YOU TELL ME BEFORE I SIGNED THE LEASE!?
BA (GRAB)
THERE'S NO OBLIGATION FOR HIM TO TELL YOU IF THE ADJACENT UNIT IS A STIGMATIZED PROPERTY.
WAS IT SUICIDE?
OR HOMICIDE?

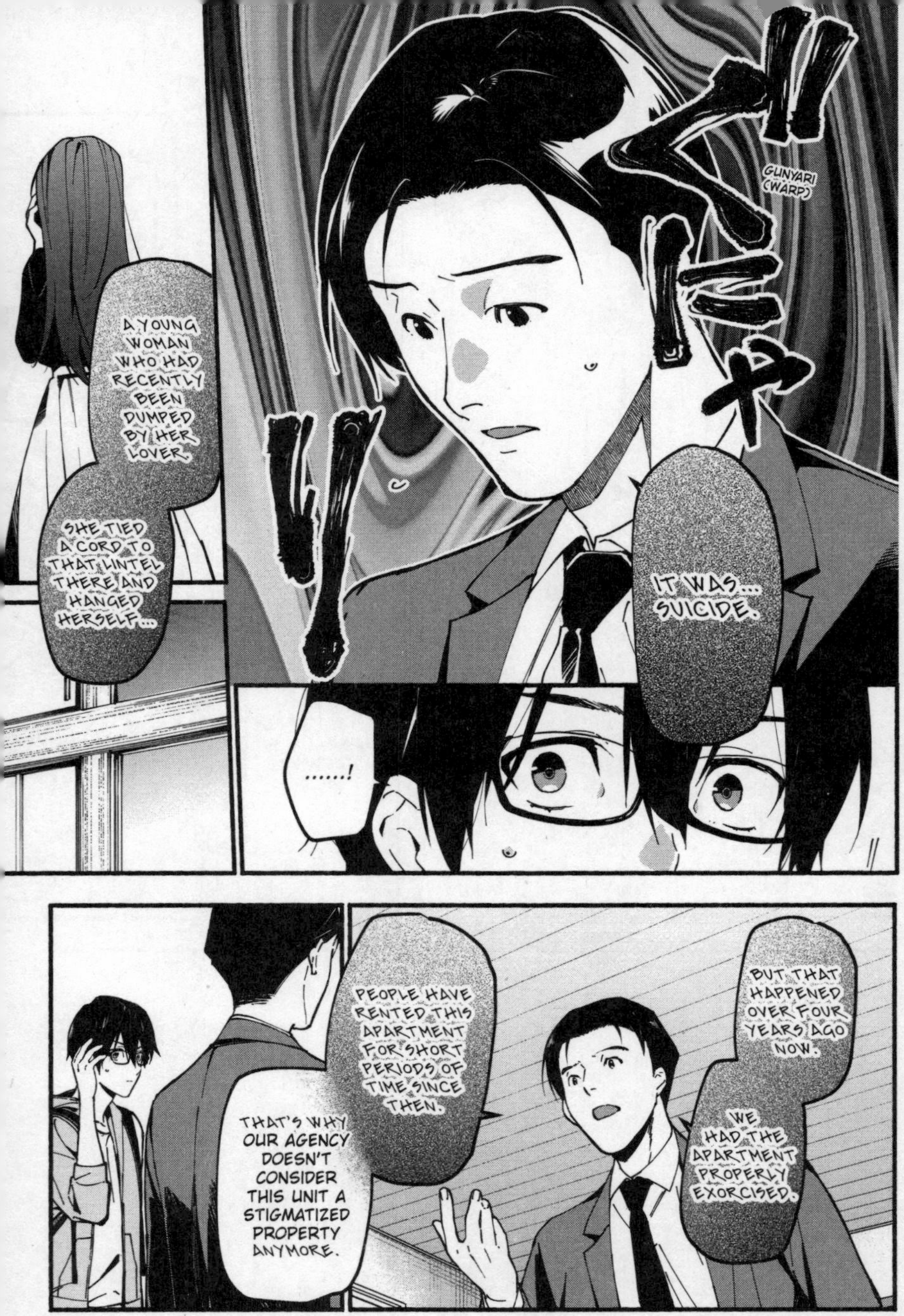
GUNYARI (WARP)
IT WAS... SUICIDE.
A YOUNG WOMAN WHO HAD RECENTLY BEEN DUMPED BY HER LOVER.
SHE TIED A CORD TO THAT LINTEL THERE AND HANGED HERSELF...
......!
BUT THAT HAPPENED OVER FOUR YEARS AGO NOW.
WE HAD THE APARTMENT PROPERLY EXORCISED.
PEOPLE HAVE RENTED THIS APARTMENT FOR SHORT PERIODS OF TIME SINCE THEN.
THAT'S WHY OUR AGENCY DOESN'T CONSIDER THIS UNIT A STIGMATIZED PROPERTY ANYMORE.

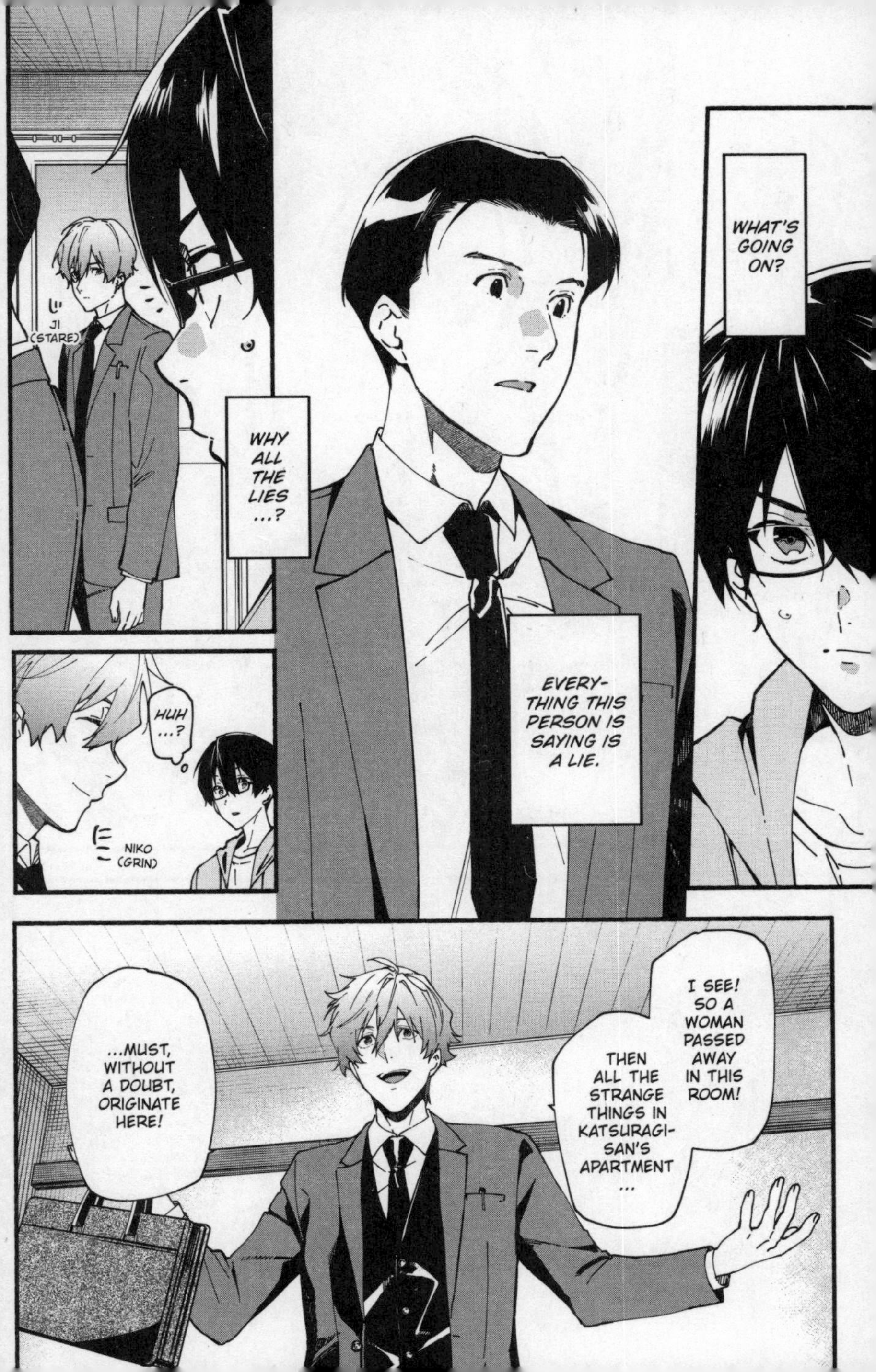

WHAT'S GOING ON?
EVERY-THING THIS PERSON IS SAYING IS A LIE.
WHY ALL THE LIES ...?
JI (STARE)
HUH ...?
NIKO (GRIN)
I SEE! SO A WOMAN PASSED AWAY IN THIS ROOM!
THEN ALL THE STRANGE THINGS IN KATSURAGI-SAN'S APARTMENT ...
...MUST, WITHOUT A DOUBT, ORIGINATE HERE!

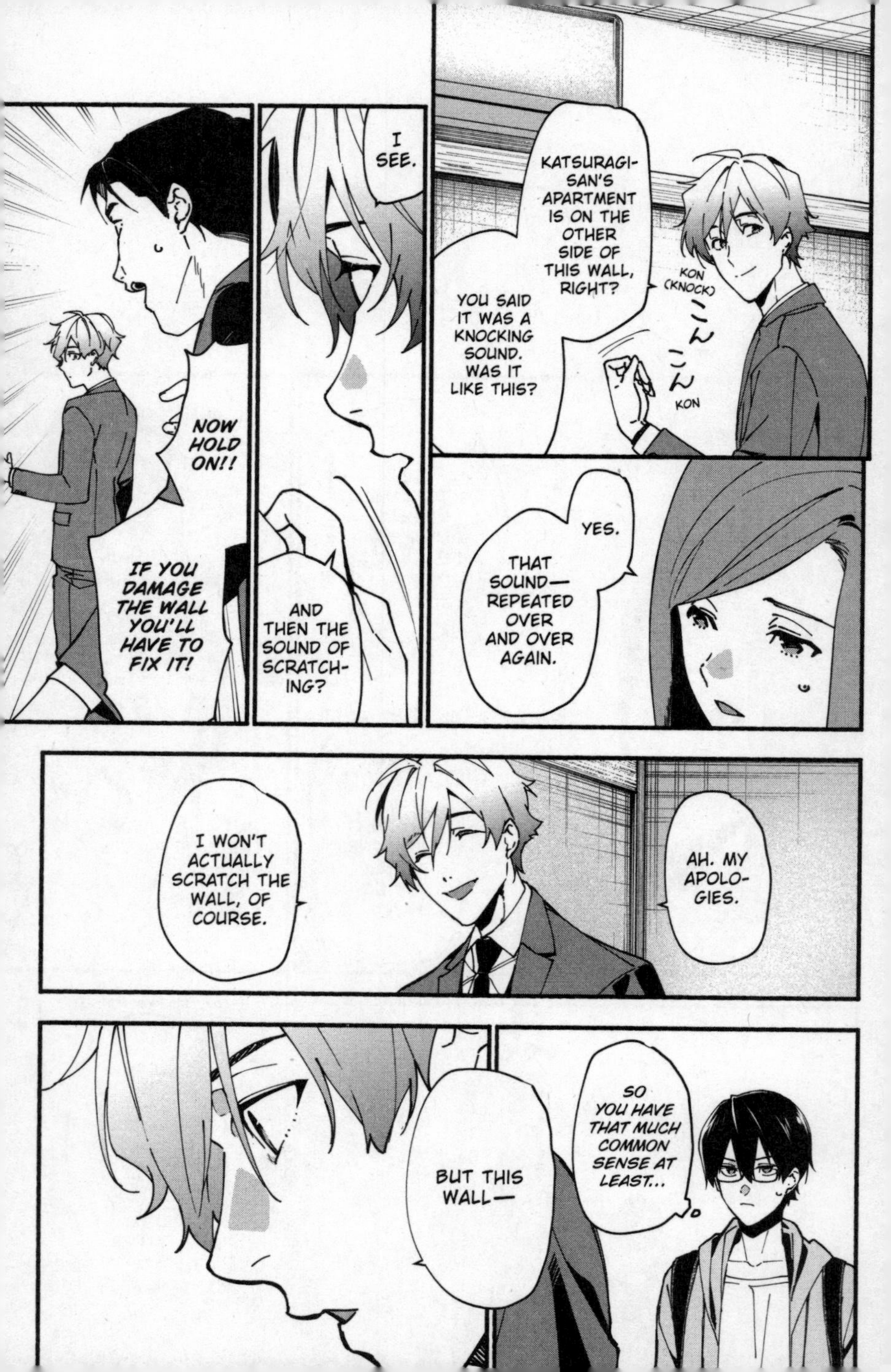
KATSURAGI-SAN'S APARTMENT IS ON THE OTHER SIDE OF THIS WALL, RIGHT?
KON (KNOCK) こん
こん KON
YOU SAID IT WAS A KNOCKING SOUND. WAS IT LIKE THIS?
YES.
THAT SOUND— REPEATED OVER AND OVER AGAIN.
I SEE.
AND THEN THE SOUND OF SCRATCHING?
NOW HOLD ON!!
IF YOU DAMAGE THE WALL YOU'LL HAVE TO FIX IT!
I WON'T ACTUALLY SCRATCH THE WALL, OF COURSE.
AH. MY APOLOGIES.
SO YOU HAVE THAT MUCH COMMON SENSE AT LEAST...
BUT THIS WALL—

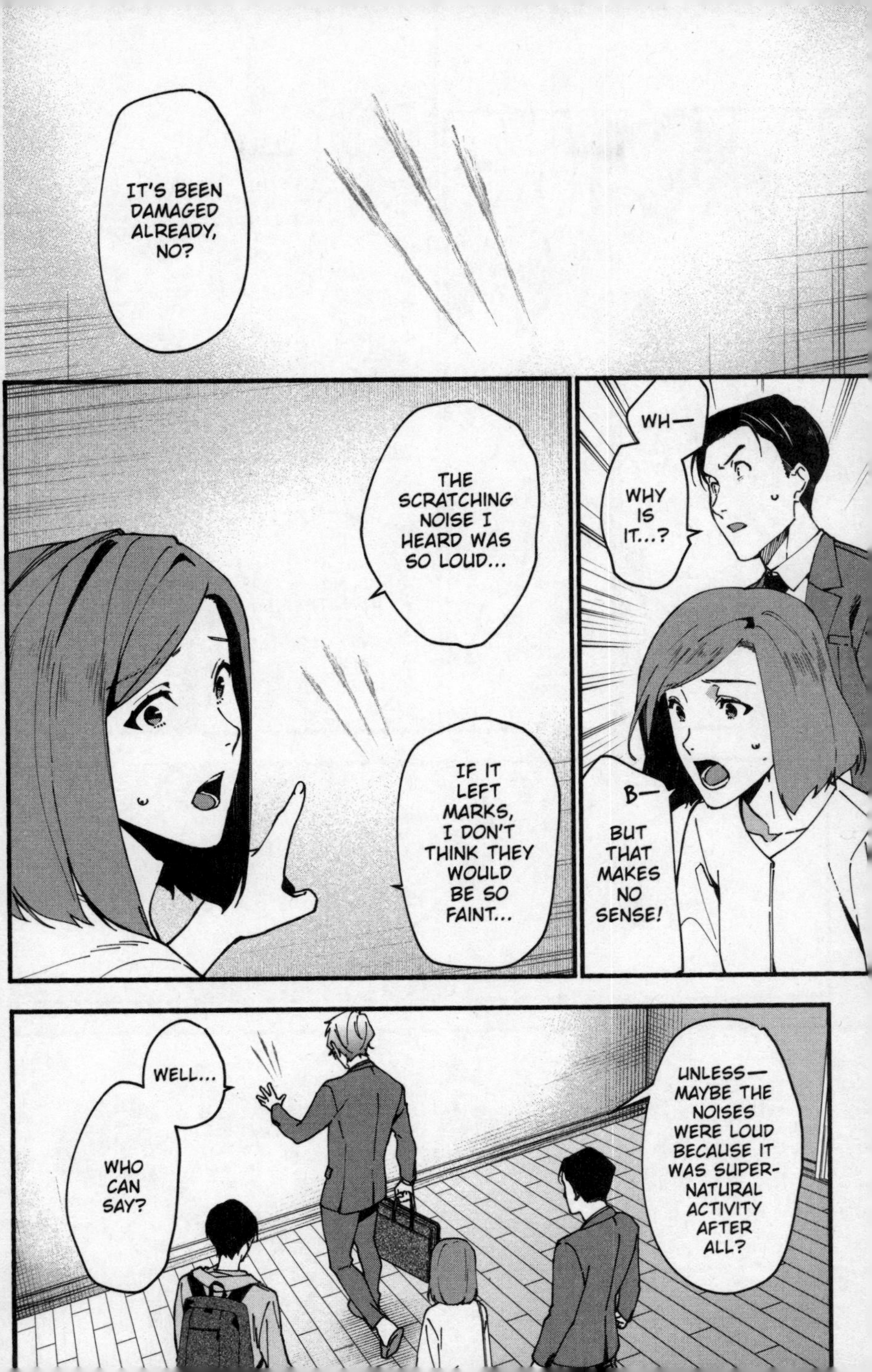
IT'S BEEN DAMAGED ALREADY, NO?
WH— WHY IS IT...?
B— BUT THAT MAKES NO SENSE!
THE SCRATCHING NOISE I HEARD WAS SO LOUD...
IF IT LEFT MARKS, I DON'T THINK THEY WOULD BE SO FAINT...
UNLESS— MAYBE THE NOISES WERE LOUD BECAUSE IT WAS SUPER-NATURAL ACTIVITY AFTER ALL?
WELL... WHO CAN SAY?

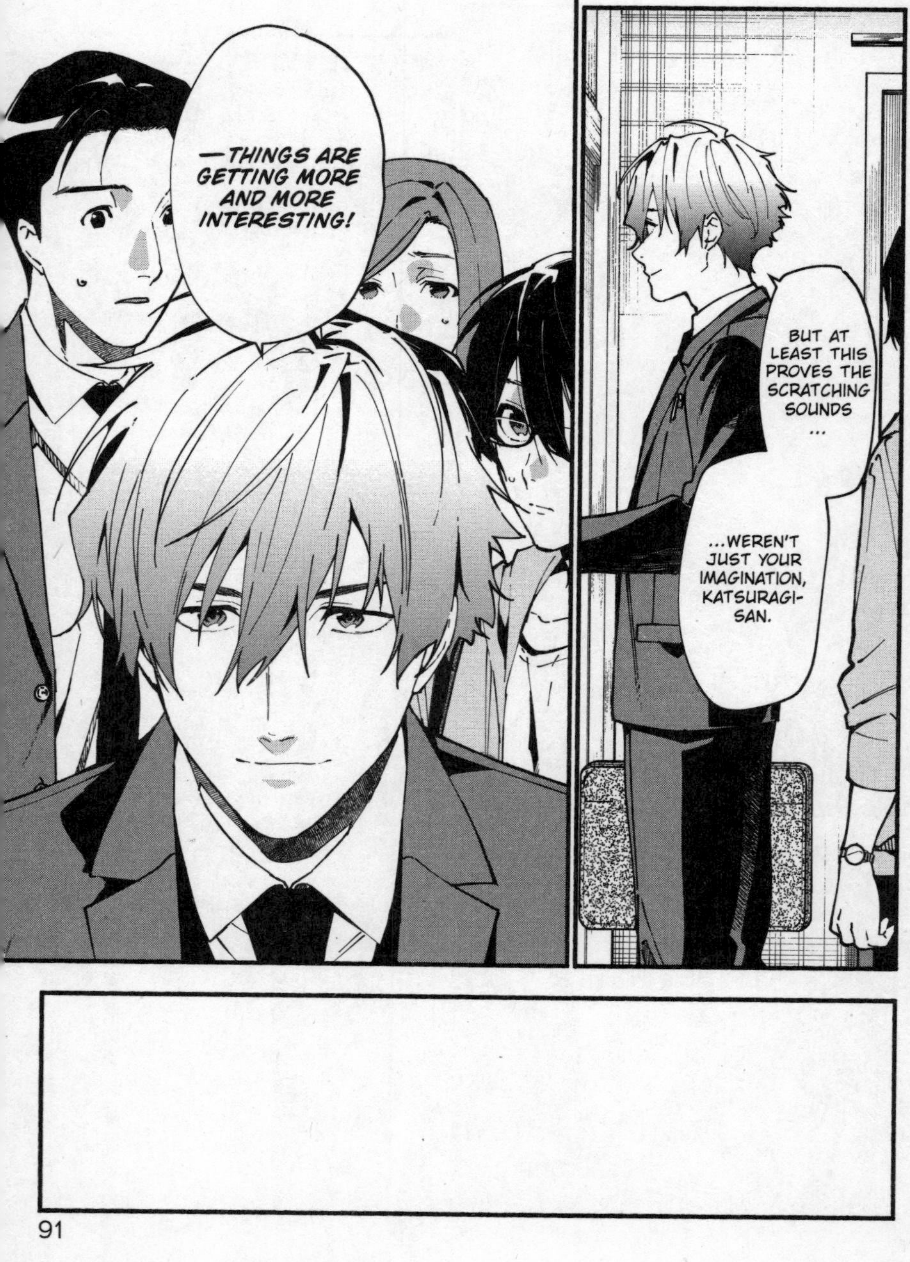
BUT AT LEAST THIS PROVES THE SCRATCHING SOUNDS ...
...WEREN'T JUST YOUR IMAGINATION, KATSURAGI-SAN.
—THINGS ARE GETTING MORE AND MORE INTERESTING!

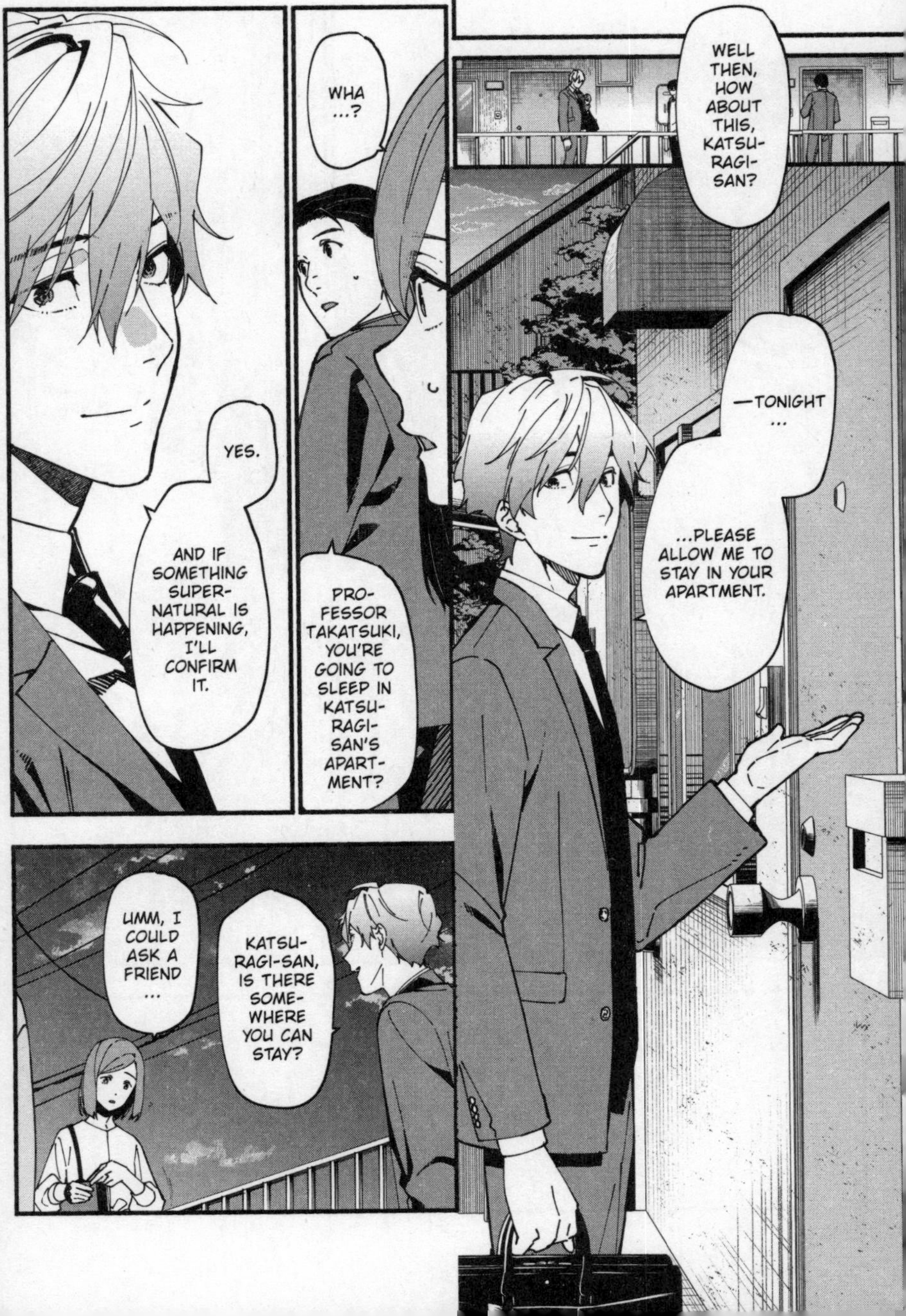

WELL THEN, HOW ABOUT THIS, KATSURAGI-SAN?
—TONIGHT ...
...PLEASE ALLOW ME TO STAY IN YOUR APARTMENT.
WHA ...?
PROFESSOR TAKATSUKI, YOU'RE GOING TO SLEEP IN KATSURAGI-SAN'S APARTMENT?
YES.
AND IF SOMETHING SUPERNATURAL IS HAPPENING, I'LL CONFIRM IT.
KATSURAGI-SAN, IS THERE SOMEWHERE YOU CAN STAY?
UMM, I COULD ASK A FRIEND ...

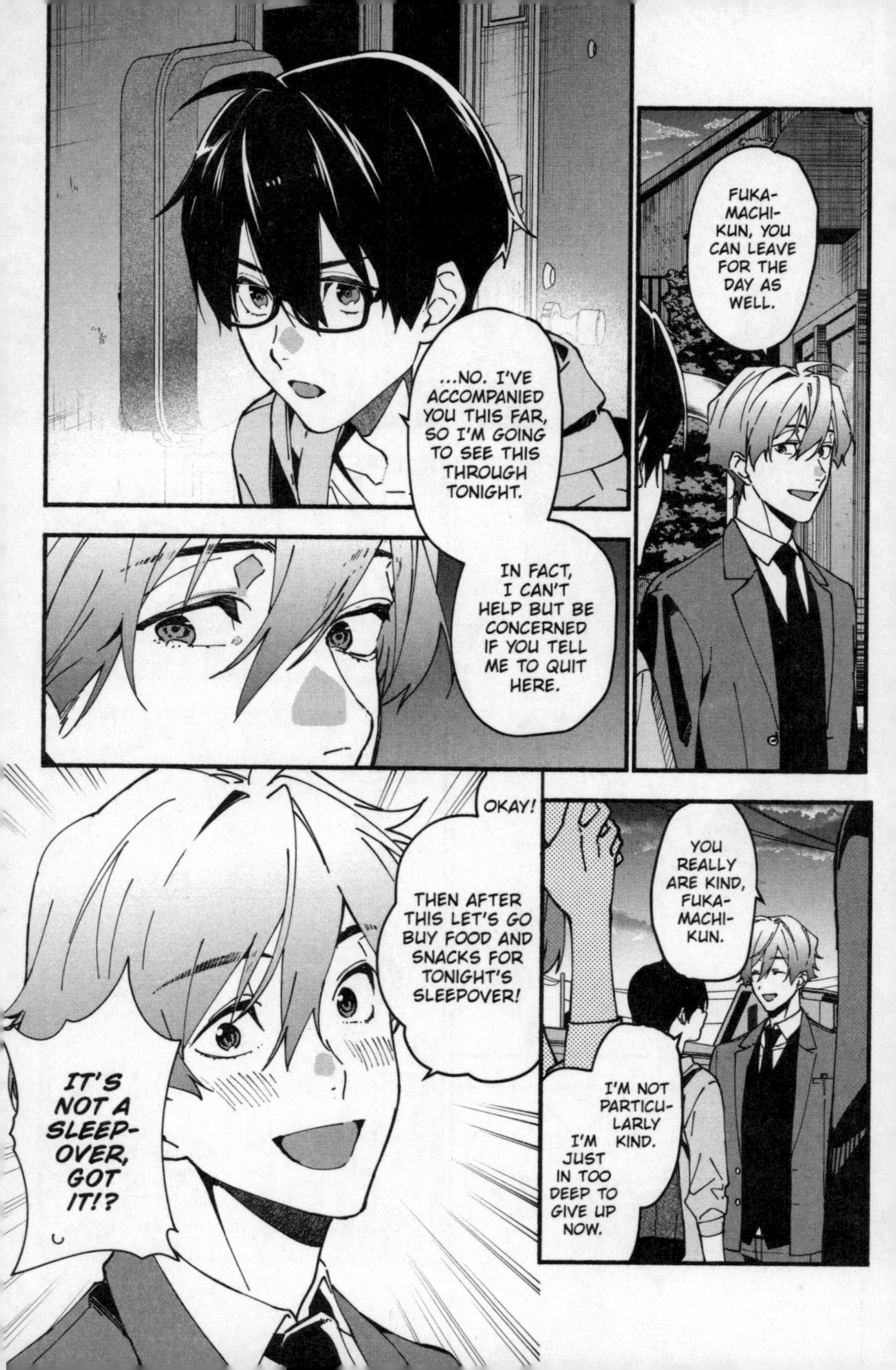
FUKA-MACHI-KUN, YOU CAN LEAVE FOR THE DAY AS WELL.
...NO. I'VE ACCOMPANIED YOU THIS FAR, SO I'M GOING TO SEE THIS THROUGH TONIGHT.
IN FACT, I CAN'T HELP BUT BE CONCERNED IF YOU TELL ME TO QUIT HERE.
YOU REALLY ARE KIND, FUKA-MACHI-KUN.
I'M NOT PARTICU-LARLY KIND.
I'M JUST IN TOO DEEP TO GIVE UP NOW.
OKAY!
THEN AFTER THIS LET'S GO BUY FOOD AND SNACKS FOR TONIGHT'S SLEEPOVER!
IT'S NOT A SLEEP-OVER, GOT IT!?

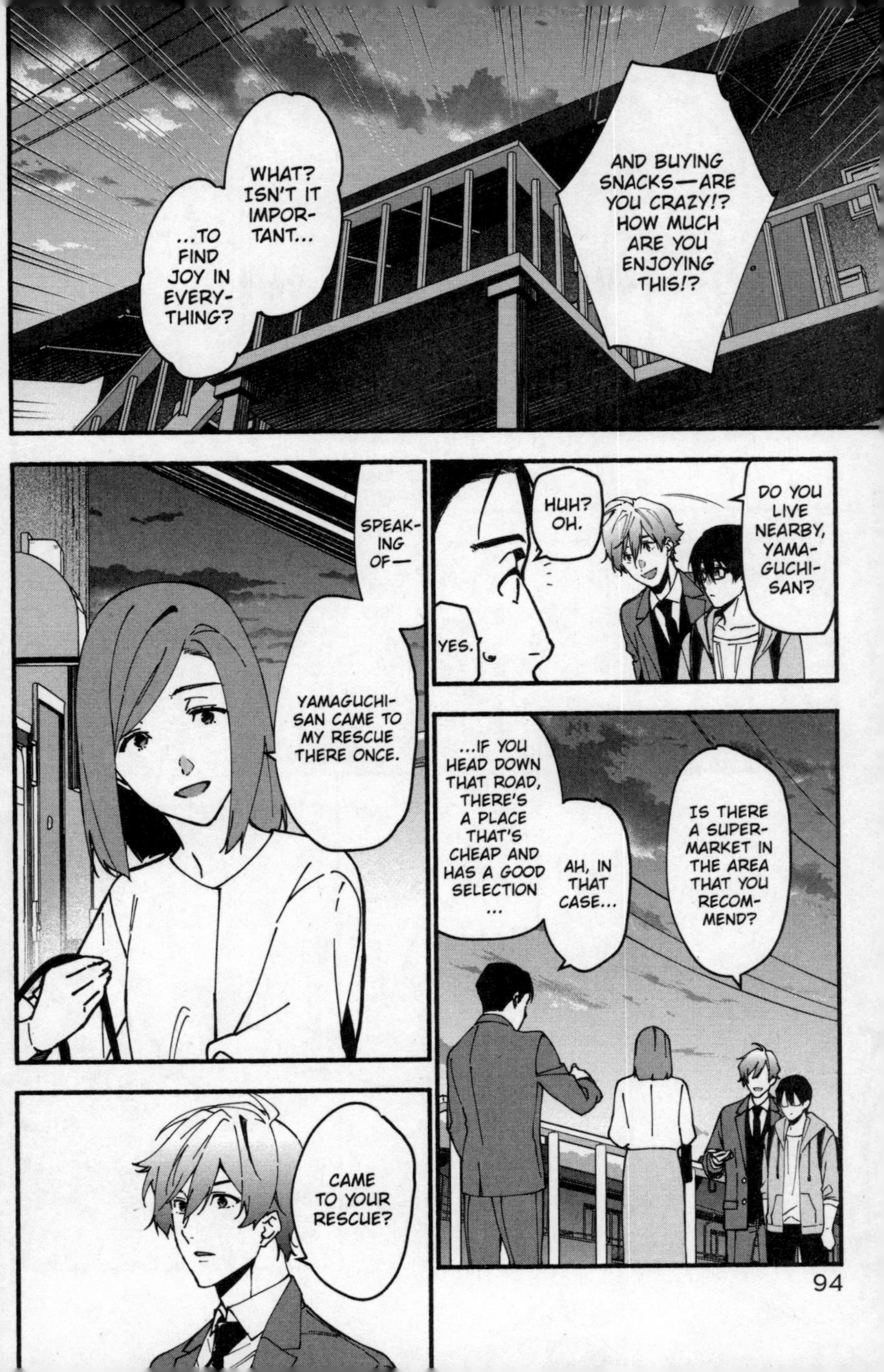
AND BUYING SNACKS—ARE YOU CRAZY!? HOW MUCH ARE YOU ENJOYING THIS!?
WHAT? ISN'T IT IMPORTANT...
...TO FIND JOY IN EVERYTHING?
DO YOU LIVE NEARBY, YAMAGUCHI-SAN?
HUH? OH.
YES.
IS THERE A SUPERMARKET IN THE AREA THAT YOU RECOMMEND?
AH, IN THAT CASE...
...IF YOU HEAD DOWN THAT ROAD, THERE'S A PLACE THAT'S CHEAP AND HAS A GOOD SELECTION...
SPEAKING OF—
YAMAGUCHI-SAN CAME TO MY RESCUE THERE ONCE.
CAME TO YOUR RESCUE?

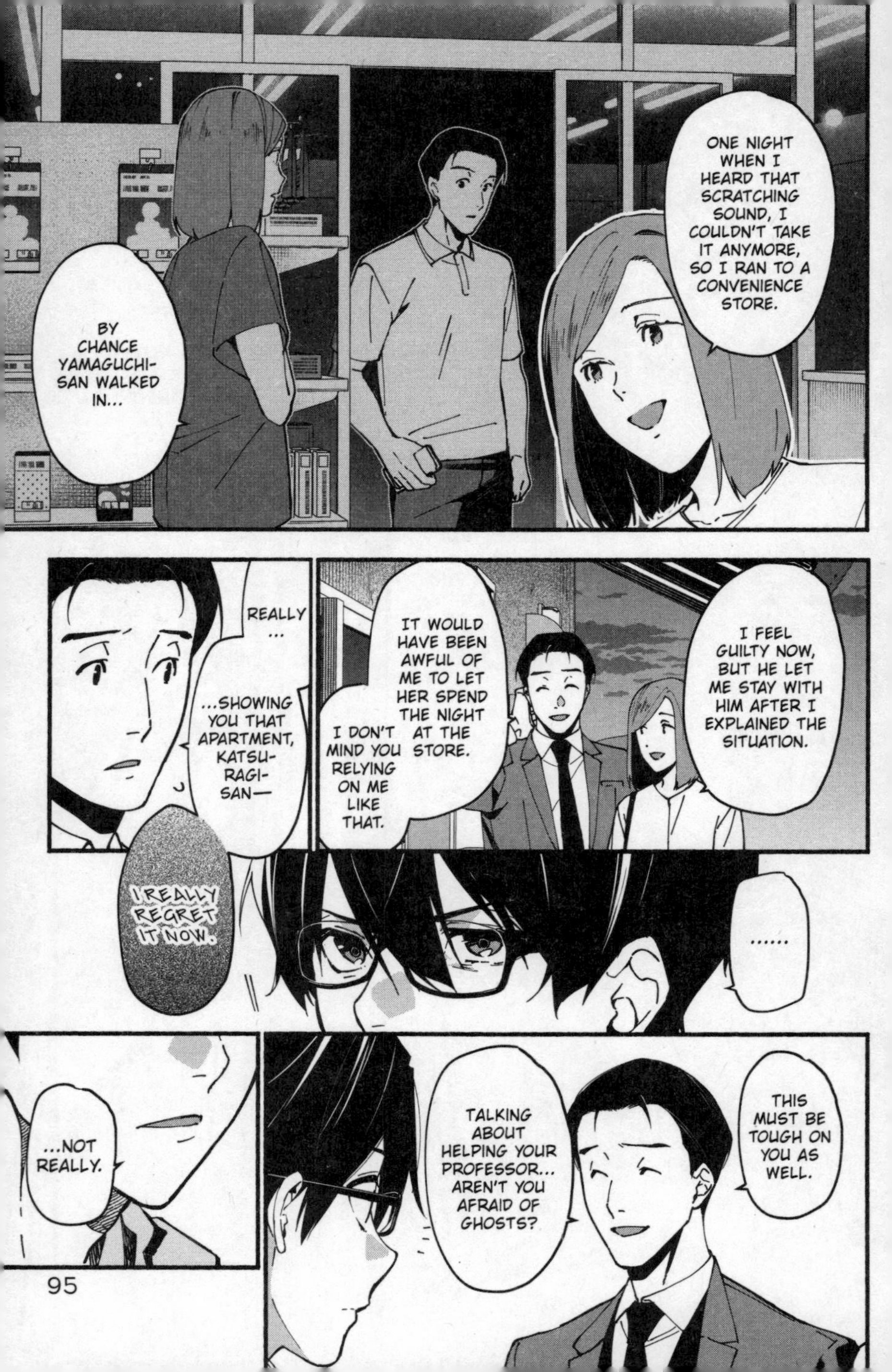
ONE NIGHT WHEN I HEARD THAT SCRATCHING SOUND, I COULDN'T TAKE IT ANYMORE, SO I RAN TO A CONVENIENCE STORE.
BY CHANCE YAMAGUCHI-SAN WALKED IN...
I FEEL GUILTY NOW, BUT HE LET ME STAY WITH HIM AFTER I EXPLAINED THE SITUATION.
IT WOULD HAVE BEEN AWFUL OF ME TO LET HER SPEND THE NIGHT AT THE STORE.
I DON'T MIND YOU RELYING ON ME LIKE THAT.
REALLY ...
...SHOWING YOU THAT APARTMENT, KATSURAGI-SAN—
......
I REALLY REGRET IT NOW.
THIS MUST BE TOUGH ON YOU AS WELL.
TALKING ABOUT HELPING YOUR PROFESSOR... AREN'T YOU AFRAID OF GHOSTS?
...NOT REALLY.

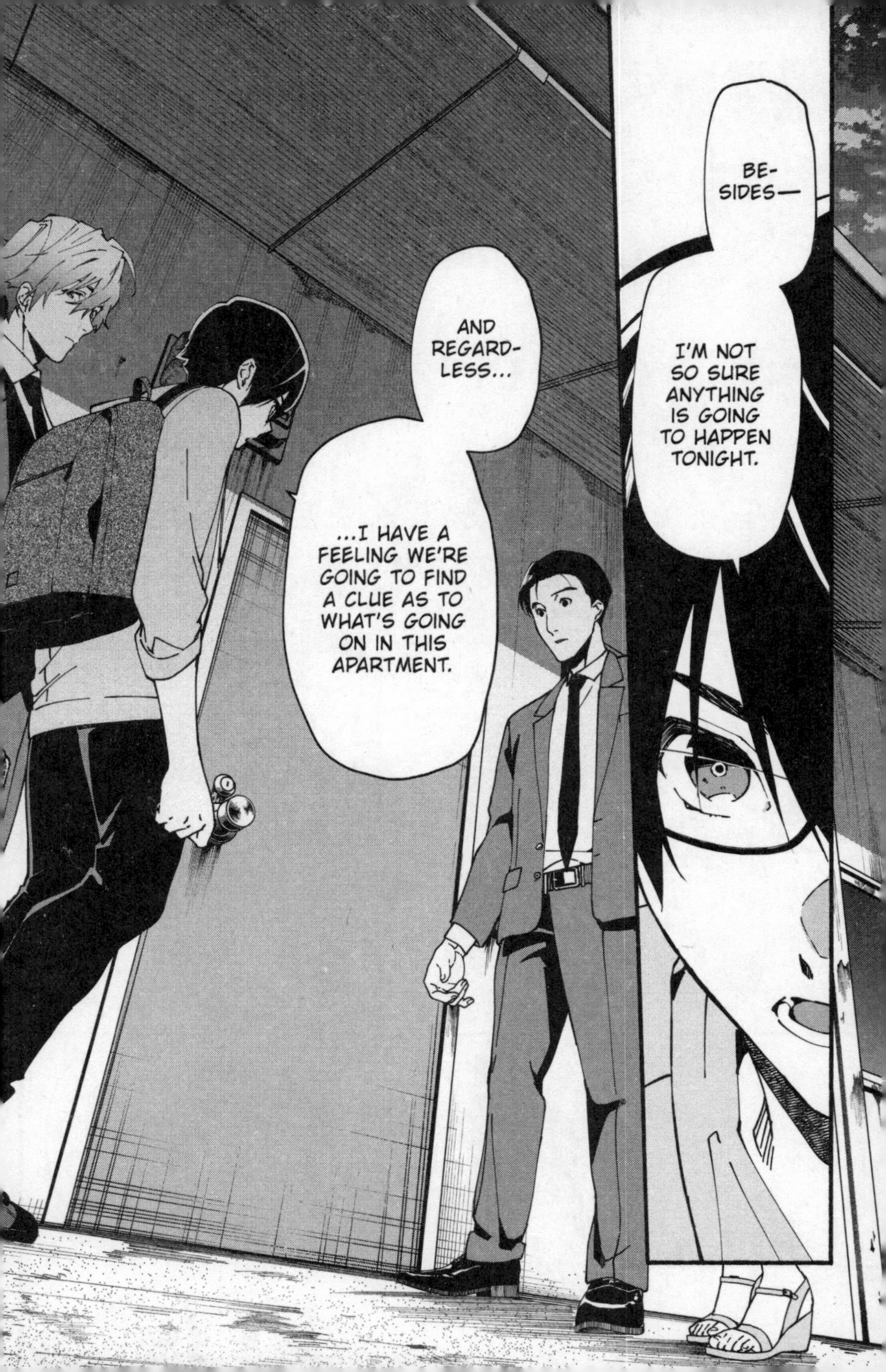
BE-SIDES—
I'M NOT SO SURE ANYTHING IS GOING TO HAPPEN TONIGHT.
AND REGARD-LESS...
...I HAVE A FEELING WE'RE GOING TO FIND A CLUE AS TO WHAT'S GOING ON IN THIS APARTMENT.

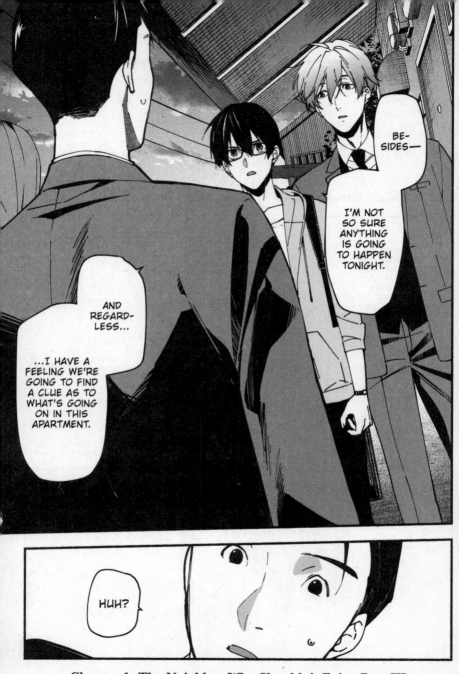

Chapter 1: The Neighbor Who Shouldn't Exist, Part III

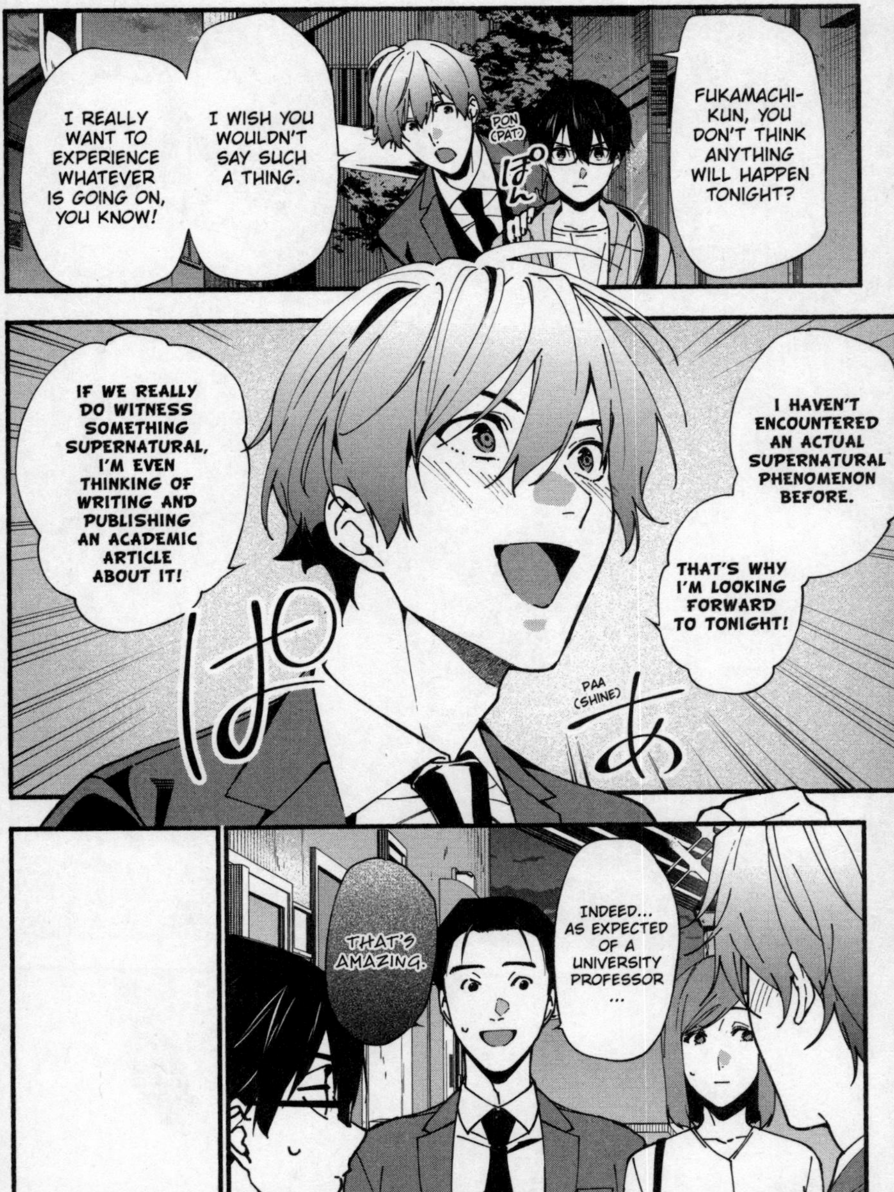
FUKAMACHI-KUN, YOU DON'T THINK ANYTHING WILL HAPPEN TONIGHT?
PON (PAT)
ぽん
I WISH YOU WOULDN'T SAY SUCH A THING.
I REALLY WANT TO EXPERIENCE WHATEVER IS GOING ON, YOU KNOW!
I HAVEN'T ENCOUNTERED AN ACTUAL SUPERNATURAL PHENOMENON BEFORE.
THAT'S WHY I'M LOOKING FORWARD TO TONIGHT!
PAA (SHINE)
ぱあ
IF WE REALLY DO WITNESS SOMETHING SUPERNATURAL, I'M EVEN THINKING OF WRITING AND PUBLISHING AN ACADEMIC ARTICLE ABOUT IT!
INDEED... AS EXPECTED OF A UNIVERSITY PROFESSOR ...
THAT'S AMAZING.

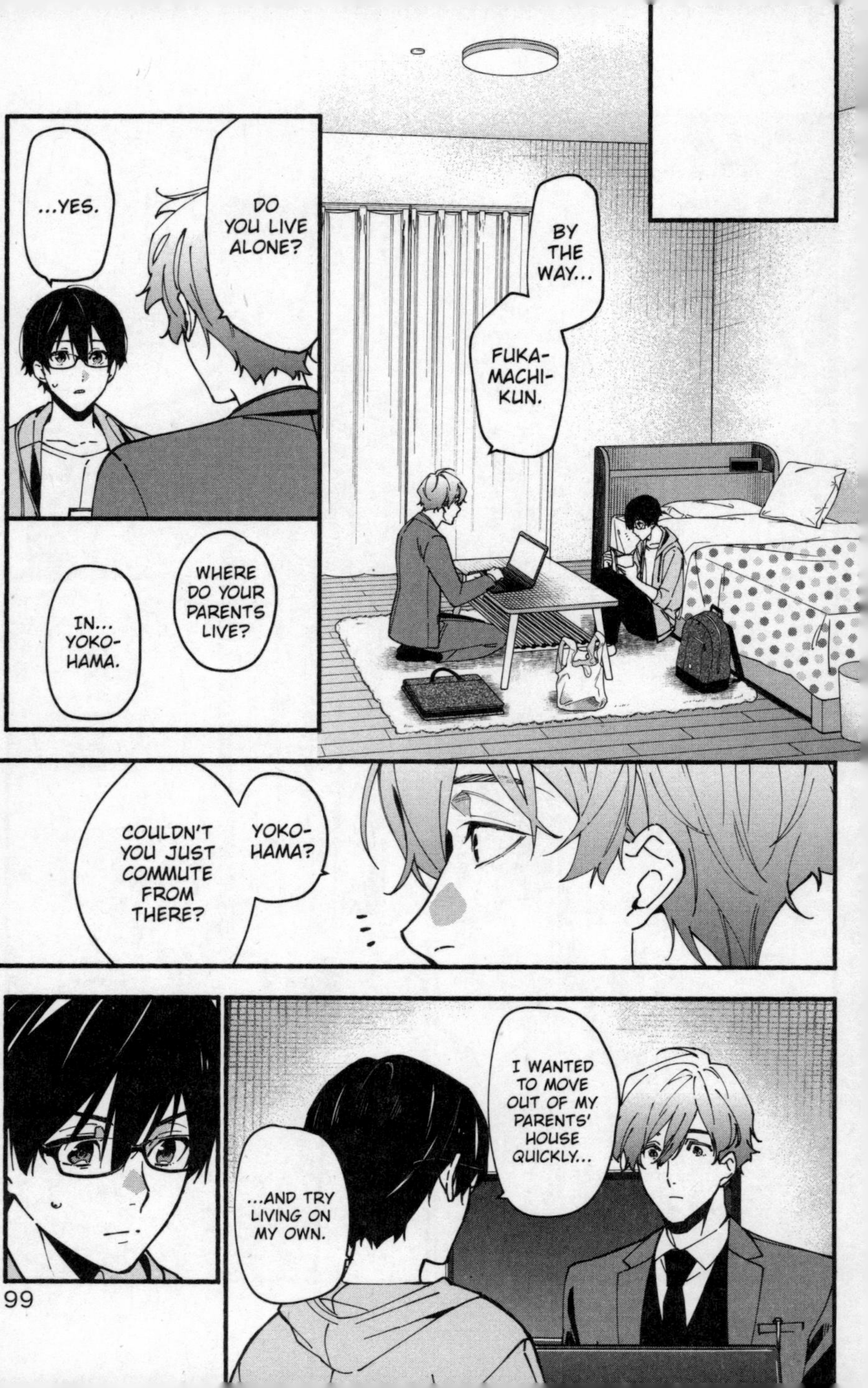

BY THE WAY...
FUKAMACHI-KUN.
DO YOU LIVE ALONE?
...YES.
WHERE DO YOUR PARENTS LIVE?
IN... YOKOHAMA.
YOKOHAMA?
COULDN'T YOU JUST COMMUTE FROM THERE?
I WANTED TO MOVE OUT OF MY PARENTS' HOUSE QUICKLY...
...AND TRY LIVING ON MY OWN.

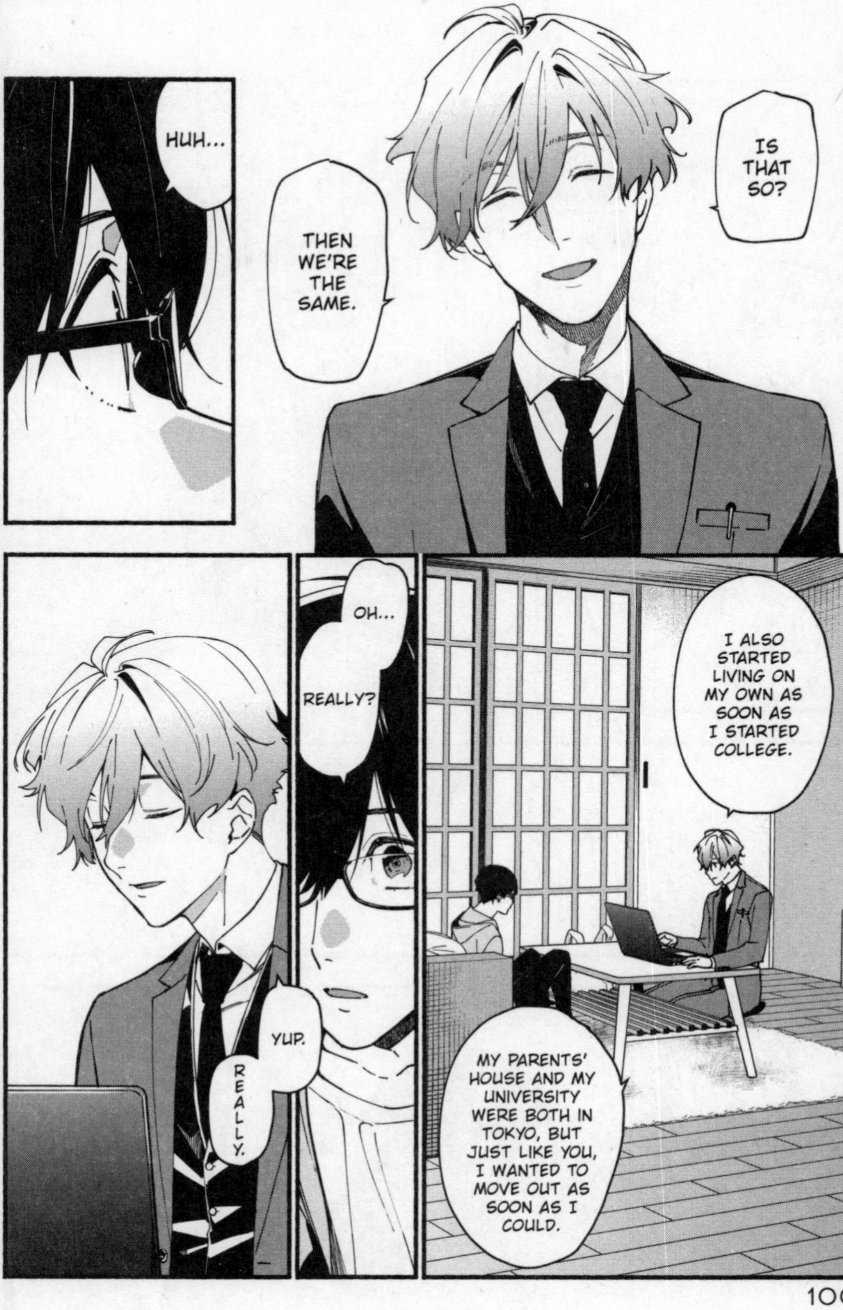
IS THAT SO?
THEN WE'RE THE SAME.
HUH...
I ALSO STARTED LIVING ON MY OWN AS SOON AS I STARTED COLLEGE.
MY PARENTS' HOUSE AND MY UNIVERSITY WERE BOTH IN TOKYO, BUT JUST LIKE YOU, I WANTED TO MOVE OUT AS SOON AS I COULD.
OH...
REALLY?
YUP.
REALLY.

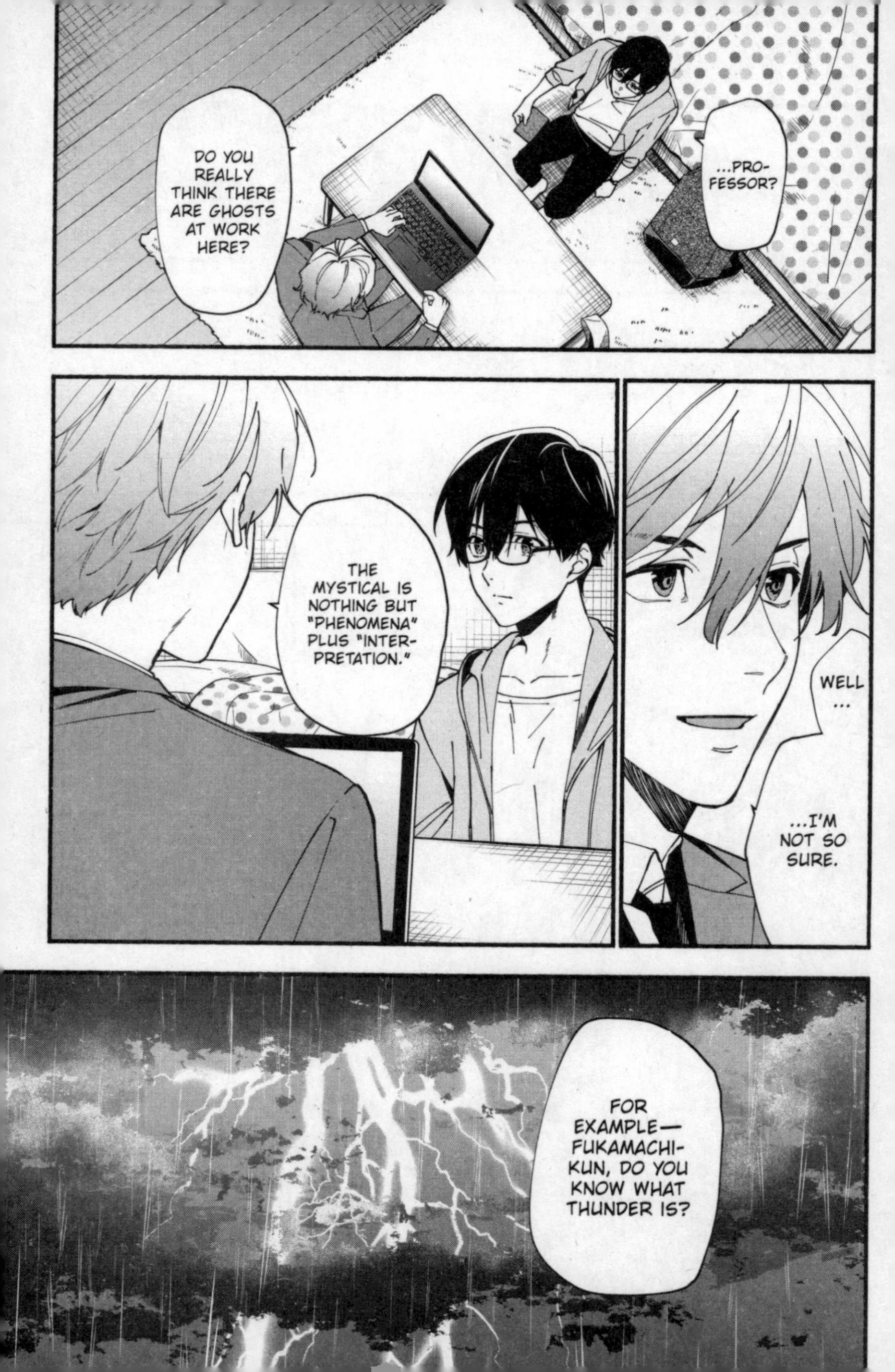
...PRO-FESSOR?
DO YOU REALLY THINK THERE ARE GHOSTS AT WORK HERE?
WELL ...
...I'M NOT SO SURE.
THE MYSTICAL IS NOTHING BUT "PHENOMENA" PLUS "INTER-PRETATION."
FOR EXAMPLE— FUKAMACHI-KUN, DO YOU KNOW WHAT THUNDER IS?

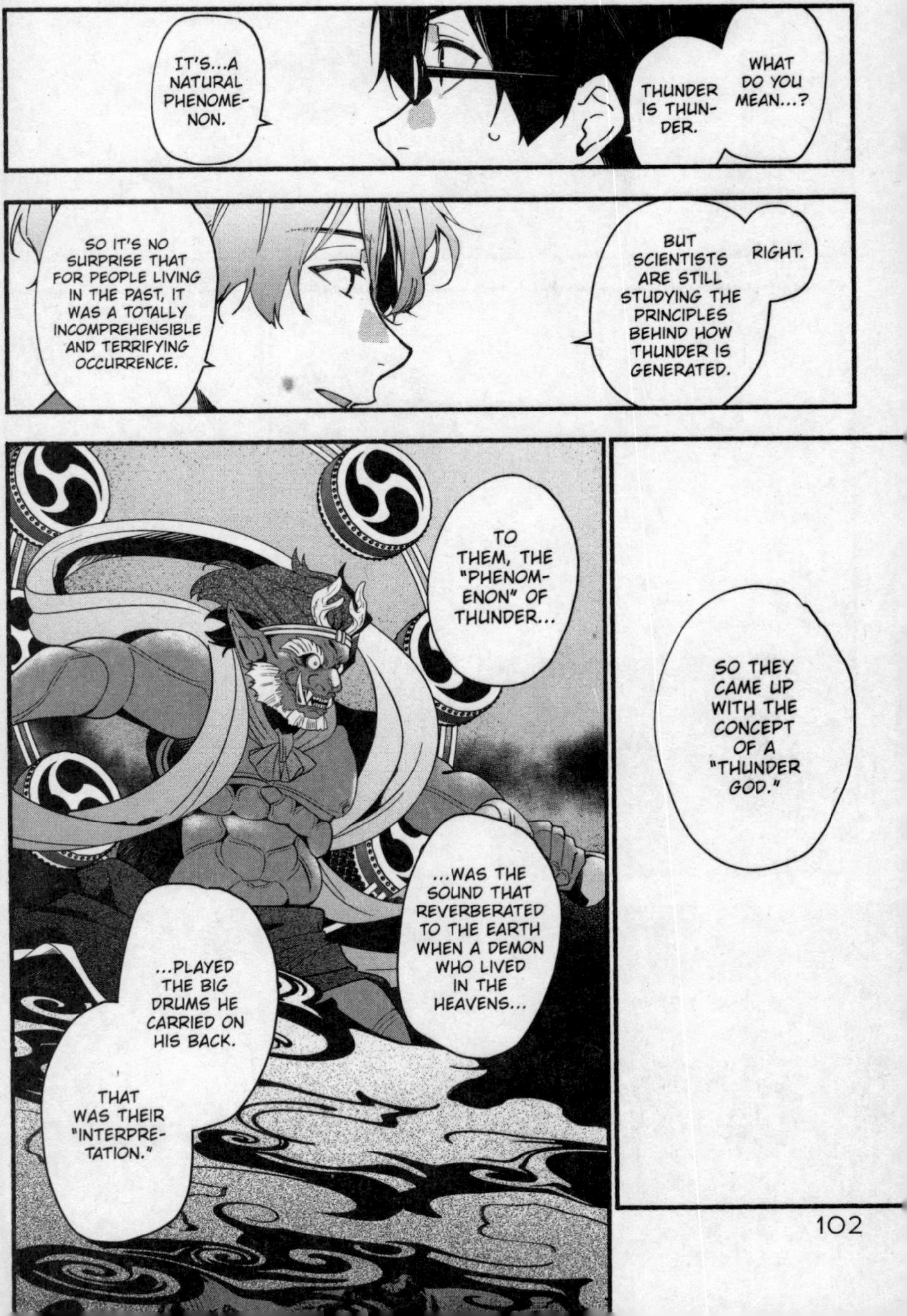
WHAT DO YOU MEAN...?
THUNDER IS THUNDER.
IT'S...A NATURAL PHENOMENON.
RIGHT.
BUT SCIENTISTS ARE STILL STUDYING THE PRINCIPLES BEHIND HOW THUNDER IS GENERATED.
SO IT'S NO SURPRISE THAT FOR PEOPLE LIVING IN THE PAST, IT WAS A TOTALLY INCOMPREHENSIBLE AND TERRIFYING OCCURRENCE.
SO THEY CAME UP WITH THE CONCEPT OF A "THUNDER GOD."
TO THEM, THE "PHENOMENON" OF THUNDER...
...WAS THE SOUND THAT REVERBERATED TO THE EARTH WHEN A DEMON WHO LIVED IN THE HEAVENS...
...PLAYED THE BIG DRUMS HE CARRIED ON HIS BACK.
THAT WAS THEIR "INTERPRETATION."

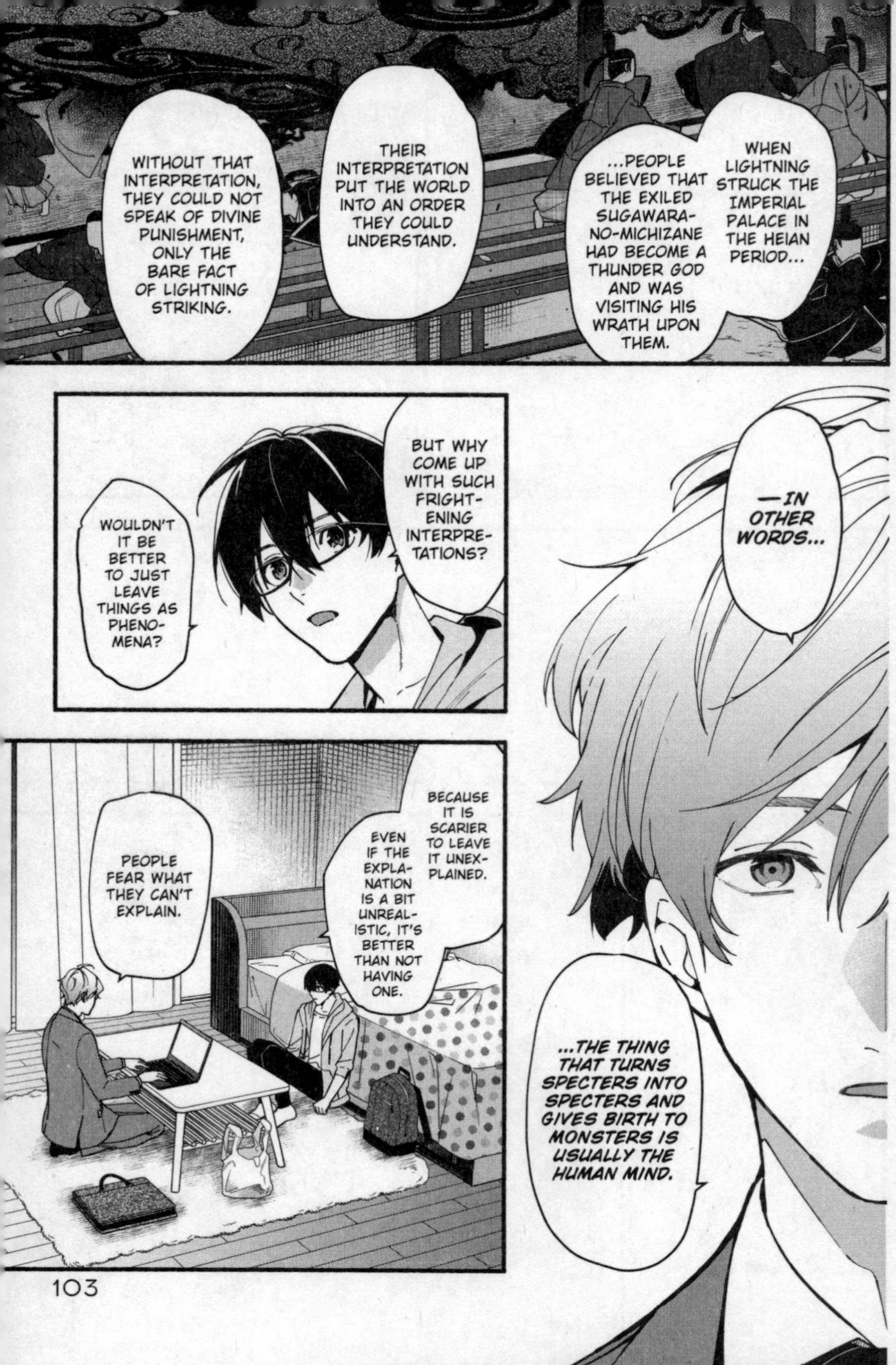
WHEN LIGHTNING STRUCK THE IMPERIAL PALACE IN THE HEIAN PERIOD...
...PEOPLE BELIEVED THAT THE EXILED SUGAWARA-NO-MICHIZANE HAD BECOME A THUNDER GOD AND WAS VISITING HIS WRATH UPON THEM.
THEIR INTERPRETATION PUT THE WORLD INTO AN ORDER THEY COULD UNDERSTAND.
WITHOUT THAT INTERPRETATION, THEY COULD NOT SPEAK OF DIVINE PUNISHMENT, ONLY THE BARE FACT OF LIGHTNING STRIKING.
BUT WHY COME UP WITH SUCH FRIGHT-ENING INTERPRE-TATIONS?
WOULDN'T IT BE BETTER TO JUST LEAVE THINGS AS PHENO-MENA?
BECAUSE IT IS SCARIER TO LEAVE IT UNEX-PLAINED.
EVEN IF THE EXPLA-NATION IS A BIT UNREAL-ISTIC, IT'S BETTER THAN NOT HAVING ONE.
PEOPLE FEAR WHAT THEY CAN'T EXPLAIN.
—IN OTHER WORDS...
...THE THING THAT TURNS SPECTERS INTO SPECTERS AND GIVES BIRTH TO MONSTERS IS USUALLY THE HUMAN MIND.

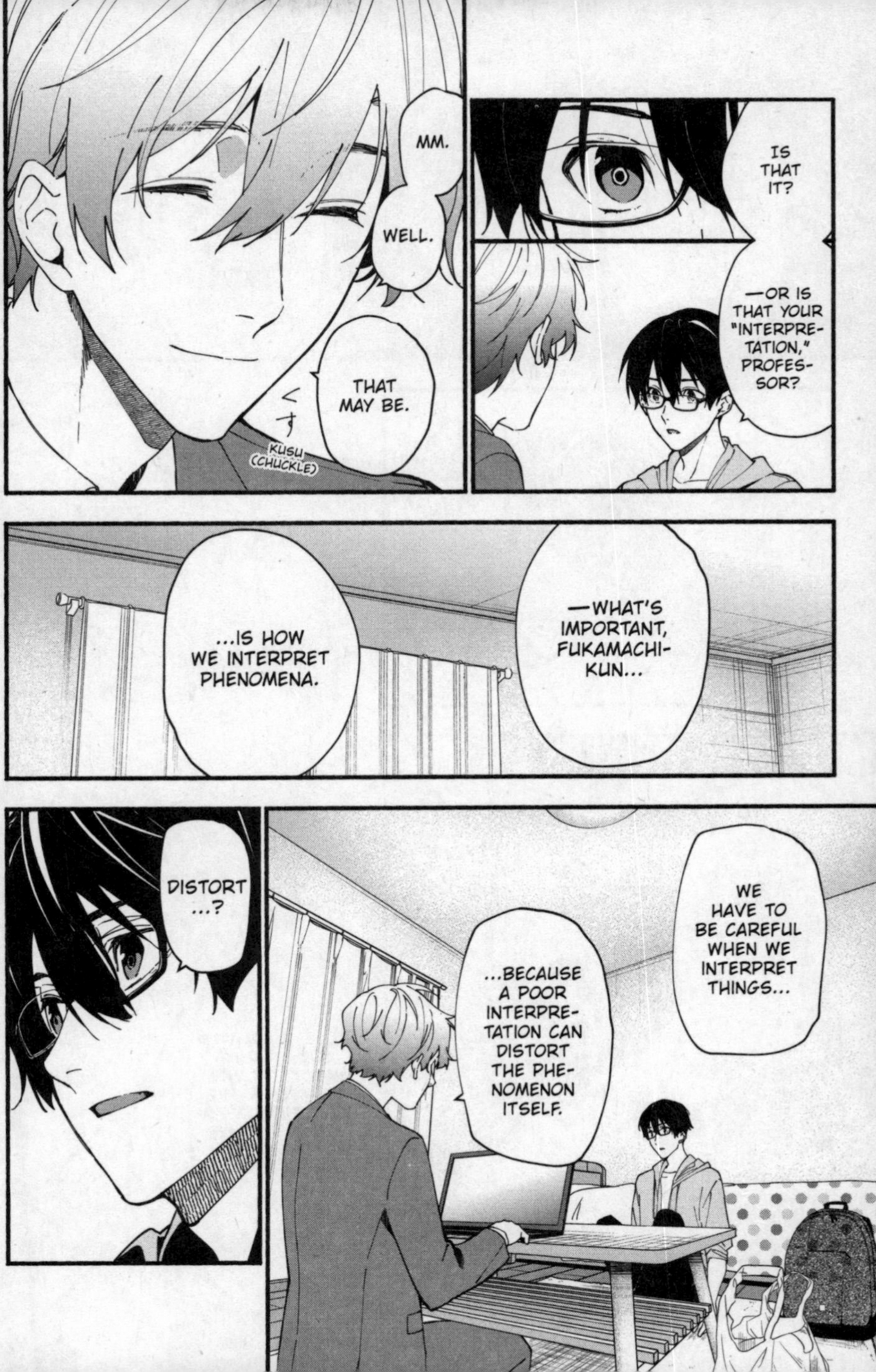
IS THAT IT?
—OR IS THAT YOUR "INTERPRETATION," PROFESSOR?
MM.
WELL.
THAT MAY BE.
くす
KUSU (CHUCKLE)
—WHAT'S IMPORTANT, FUKAMACHI-KUN...
...IS HOW WE INTERPRET PHENOMENA.
WE HAVE TO BE CAREFUL WHEN WE INTERPRET THINGS...
...BECAUSE A POOR INTERPRETATION CAN DISTORT THE PHENOMENON ITSELF.
DISTORT...?

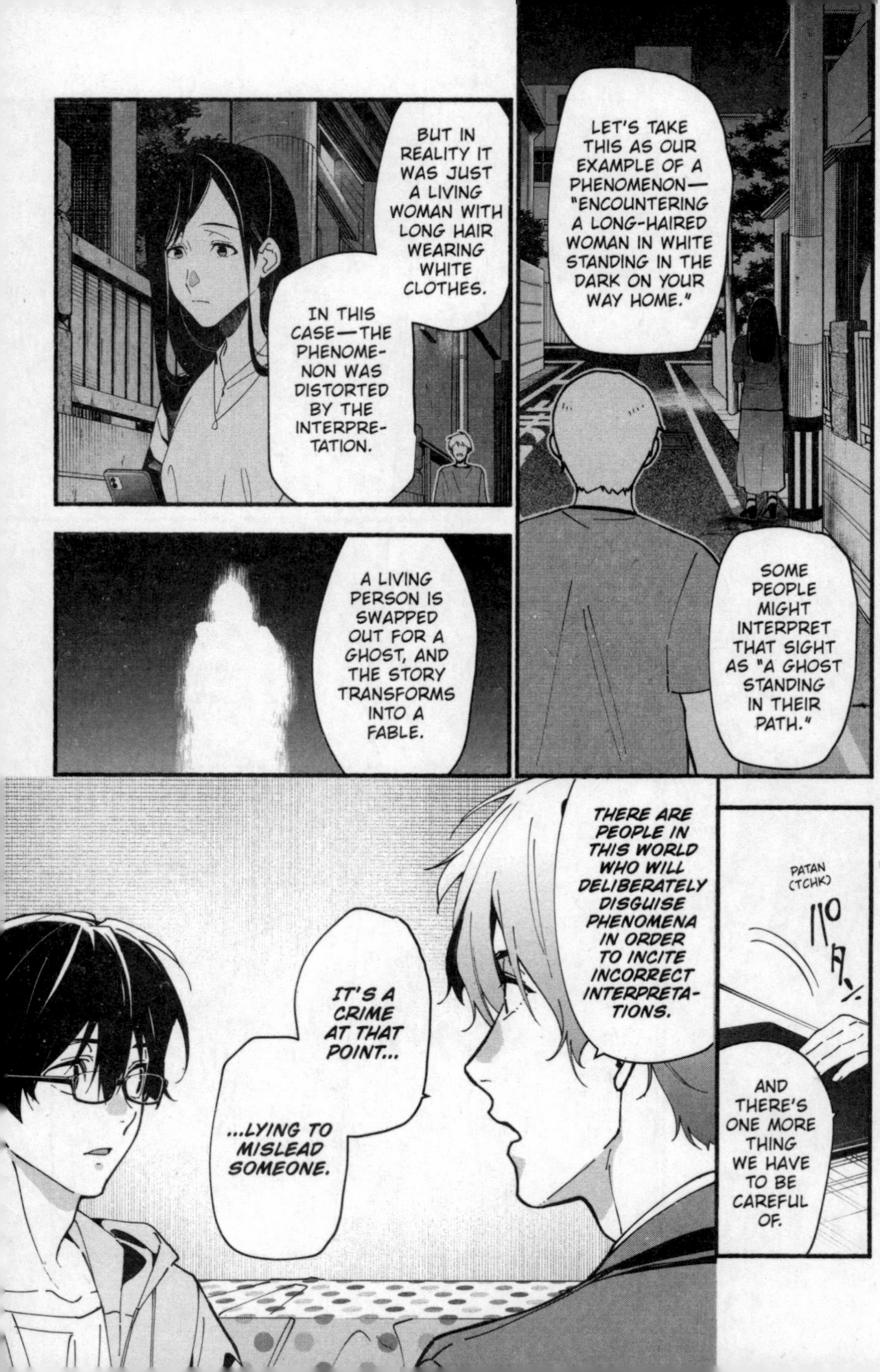
LET'S TAKE THIS AS OUR EXAMPLE OF A PHENOMENON—"ENCOUNTERING A LONG-HAIRED WOMAN IN WHITE STANDING IN THE DARK ON YOUR WAY HOME."
SOME PEOPLE MIGHT INTERPRET THAT SIGHT AS "A GHOST STANDING IN THEIR PATH."
BUT IN REALITY IT WAS JUST A LIVING WOMAN WITH LONG HAIR WEARING WHITE CLOTHES.
IN THIS CASE—THE PHENOMENON WAS DISTORTED BY THE INTERPRETATION.
A LIVING PERSON IS SWAPPED OUT FOR A GHOST, AND THE STORY TRANSFORMS INTO A FABLE.
PATAN (TCHK)
パタ
AND THERE'S ONE MORE THING WE HAVE TO BE CAREFUL OF.
THERE ARE PEOPLE IN THIS WORLD WHO WILL DELIBERATELY DISGUISE PHENOMENA IN ORDER TO INCITE INCORRECT INTERPRETATIONS.
IT'S A CRIME AT THAT POINT...
...LYING TO MISLEAD SOMEONE.

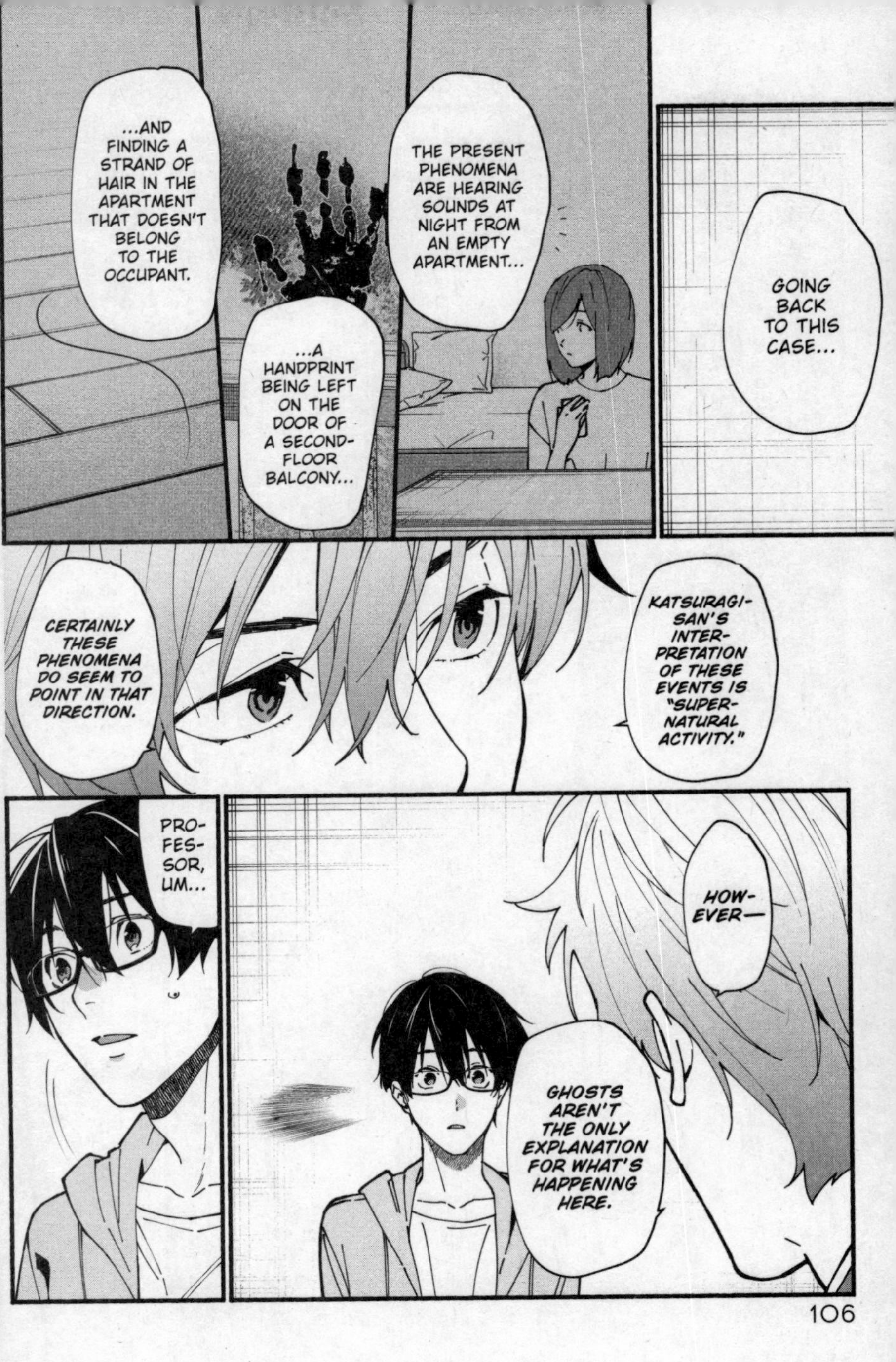
GOING BACK TO THIS CASE...
THE PRESENT PHENOMENA ARE HEARING SOUNDS AT NIGHT FROM AN EMPTY APARTMENT...
...A HANDPRINT BEING LEFT ON THE DOOR OF A SECOND-FLOOR BALCONY...
...AND FINDING A STRAND OF HAIR IN THE APARTMENT THAT DOESN'T BELONG TO THE OCCUPANT.
KATSURAGI-SAN'S INTERPRETATION OF THESE EVENTS IS "SUPERNATURAL ACTIVITY."
CERTAINLY THESE PHENOMENA DO SEEM TO POINT IN THAT DIRECTION.
HOWEVER—
GHOSTS AREN'T THE ONLY EXPLANATION FOR WHAT'S HAPPENING HERE.
PROFESSOR, UM...

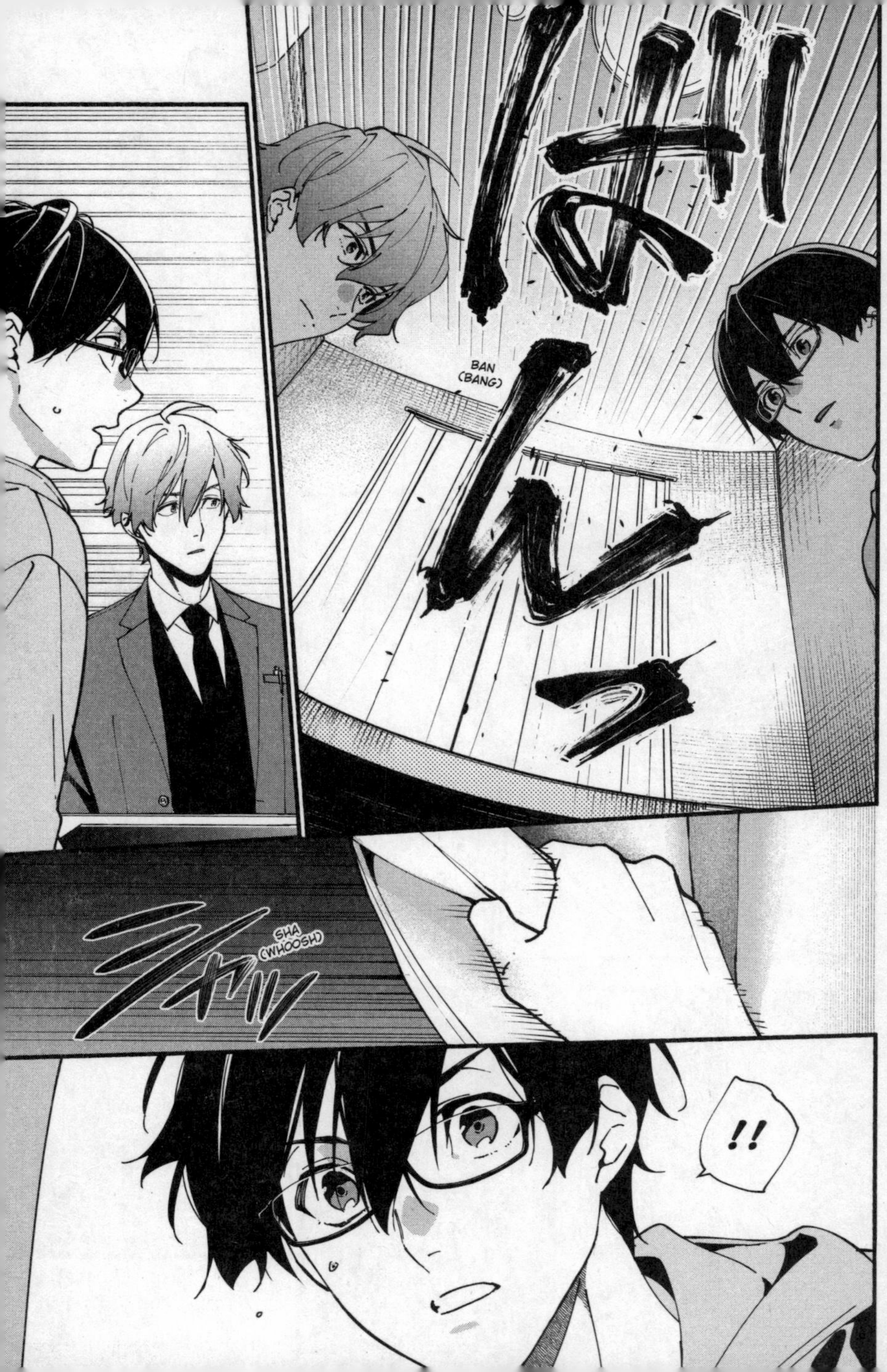
ばんっ
BAN (BANG)
シャッ
SHA (WHOOSH)
!!

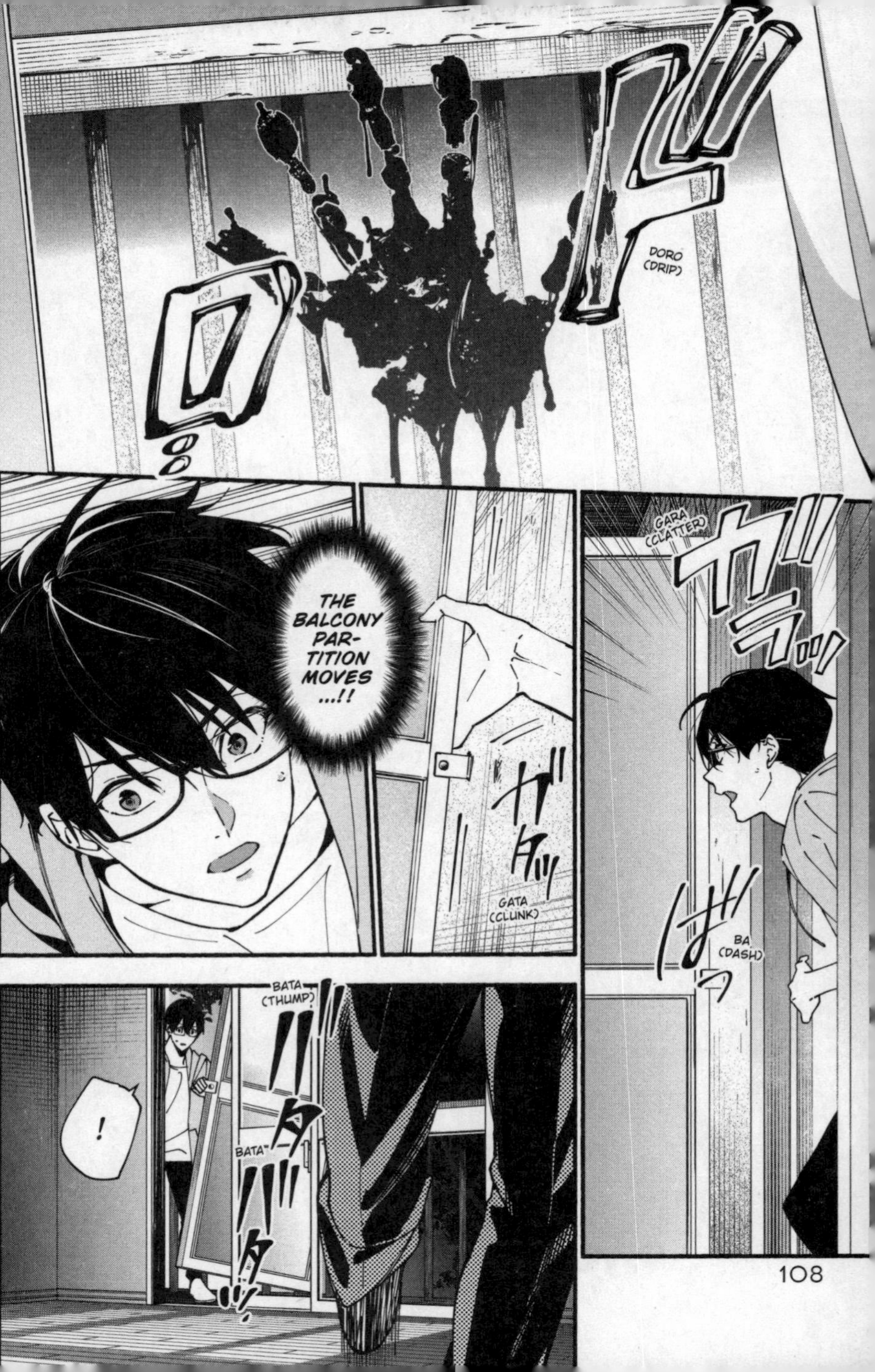
DORO (DRIP)
GARA (CLATTER)
BA (DASH)
GATA (CLUNK)
THE BALCONY PARTITION MOVES...!!
BATA (THUMP)
BATA
!

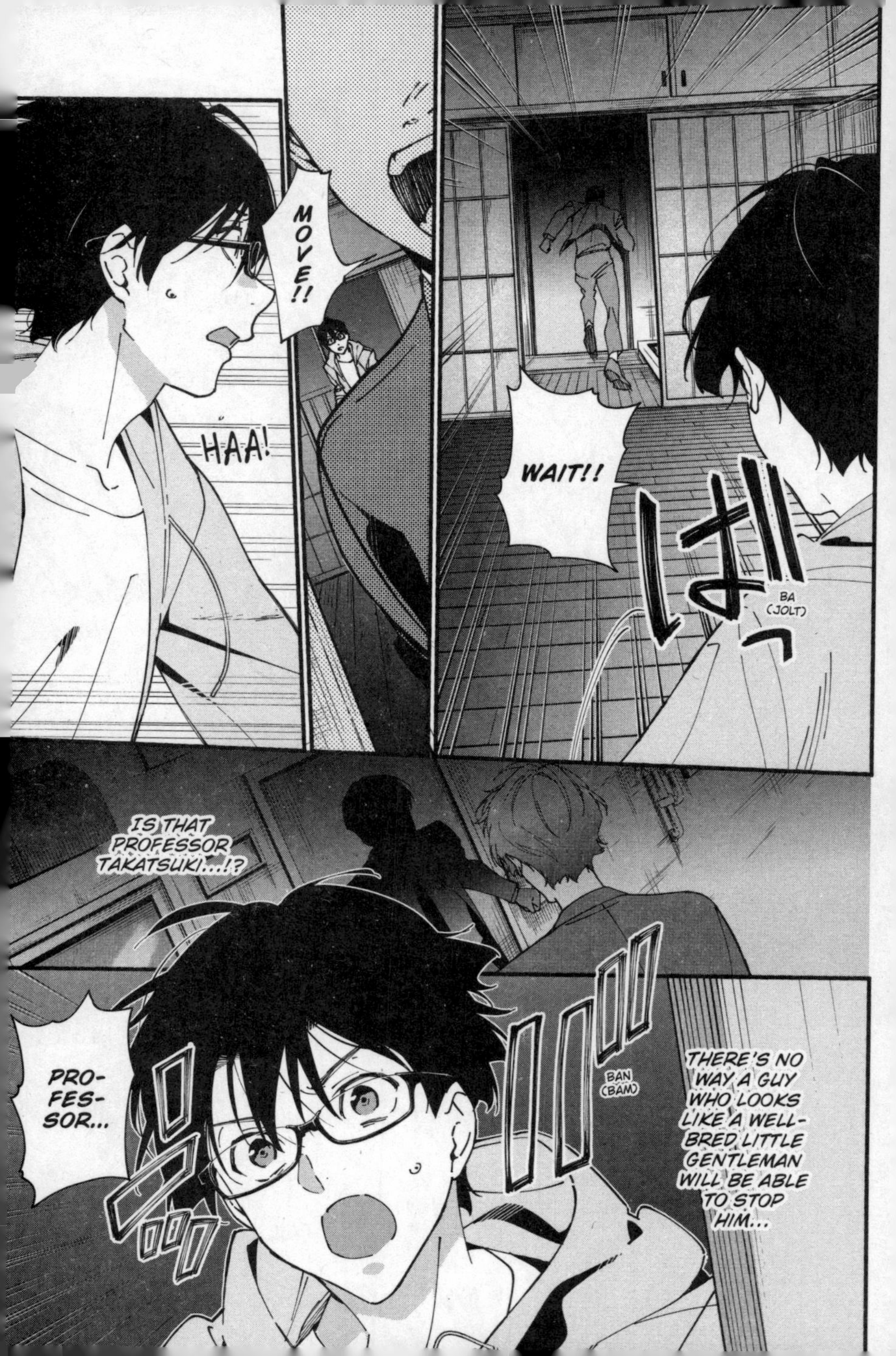
WAIT!!
BA (JOLT)
MOVE!!
HAA!
IS THAT PROFESSOR TAKATSUKI...!?
THERE'S NO WAY A GUY WHO LOOKS LIKE A WELL-BRED LITTLE GENTLEMAN WILL BE ABLE TO STOP HIM...
BAN (BAM)
PRO-FES-SOR...

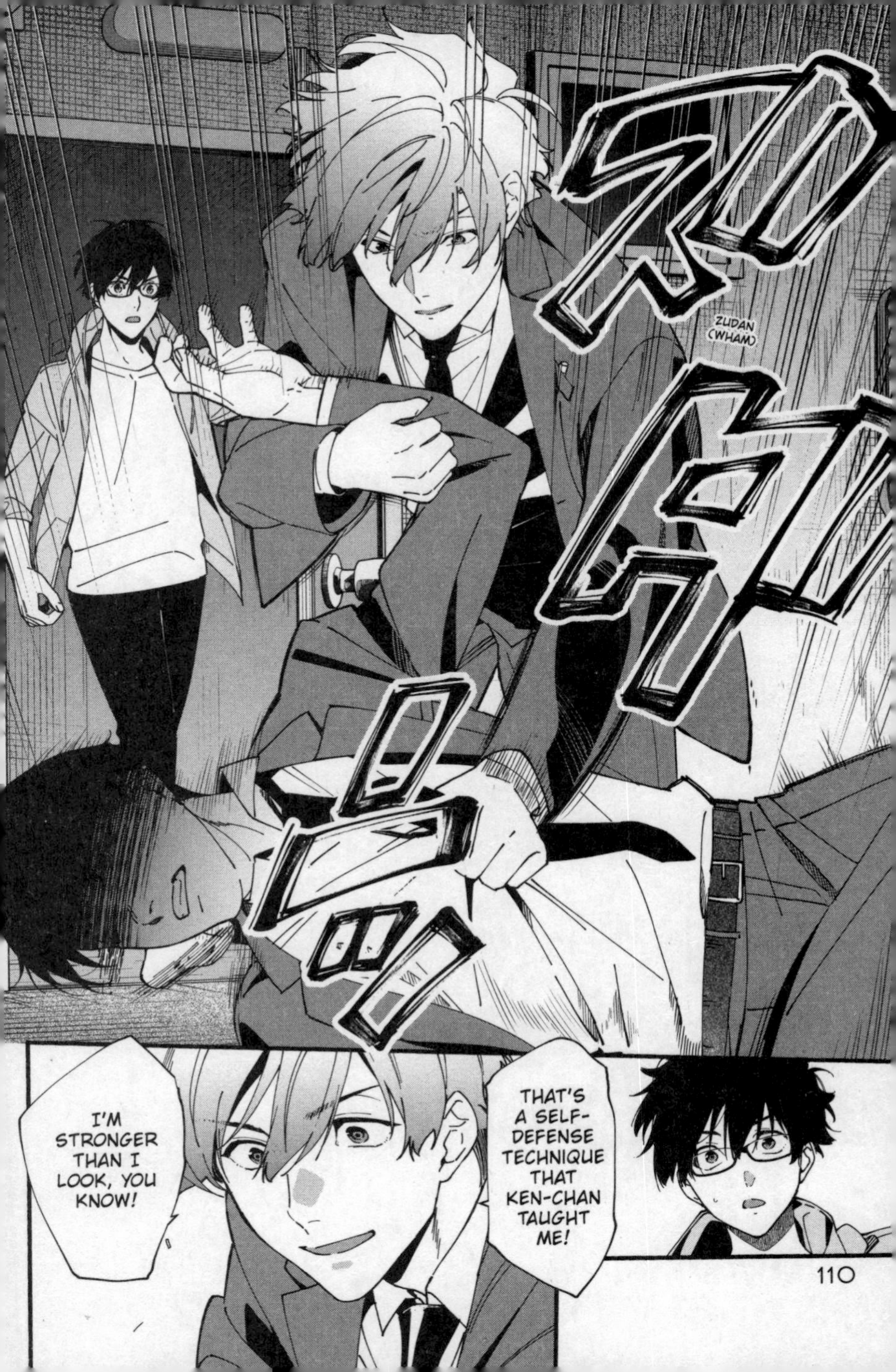
ZUDAN
(WHAM)
THAT'S A SELF-DEFENSE TECHNIQUE THAT KEN-CHAN TAUGHT ME!
I'M STRONGER THAN I LOOK, YOU KNOW!

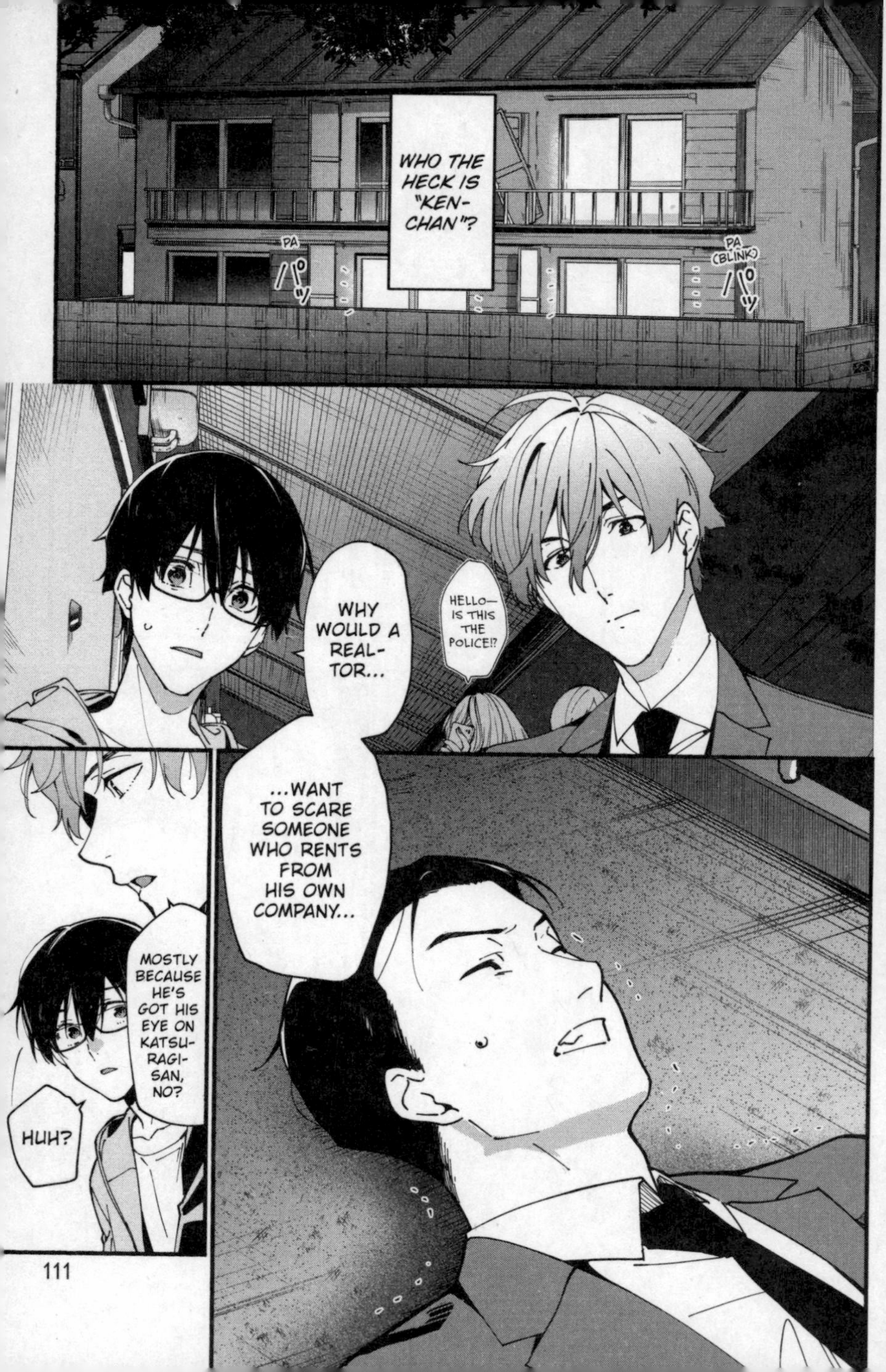
WHO THE HECK IS "KEN-CHAN"?
PA (BLINK)
PA
HELLO— IS THIS THE POLICE!?
WHY WOULD A REALTOR...
...WANT TO SCARE SOMEONE WHO RENTS FROM HIS OWN COMPANY...
MOSTLY BECAUSE HE'S GOT HIS EYE ON KATSURAGI-SAN, NO?
HUH?

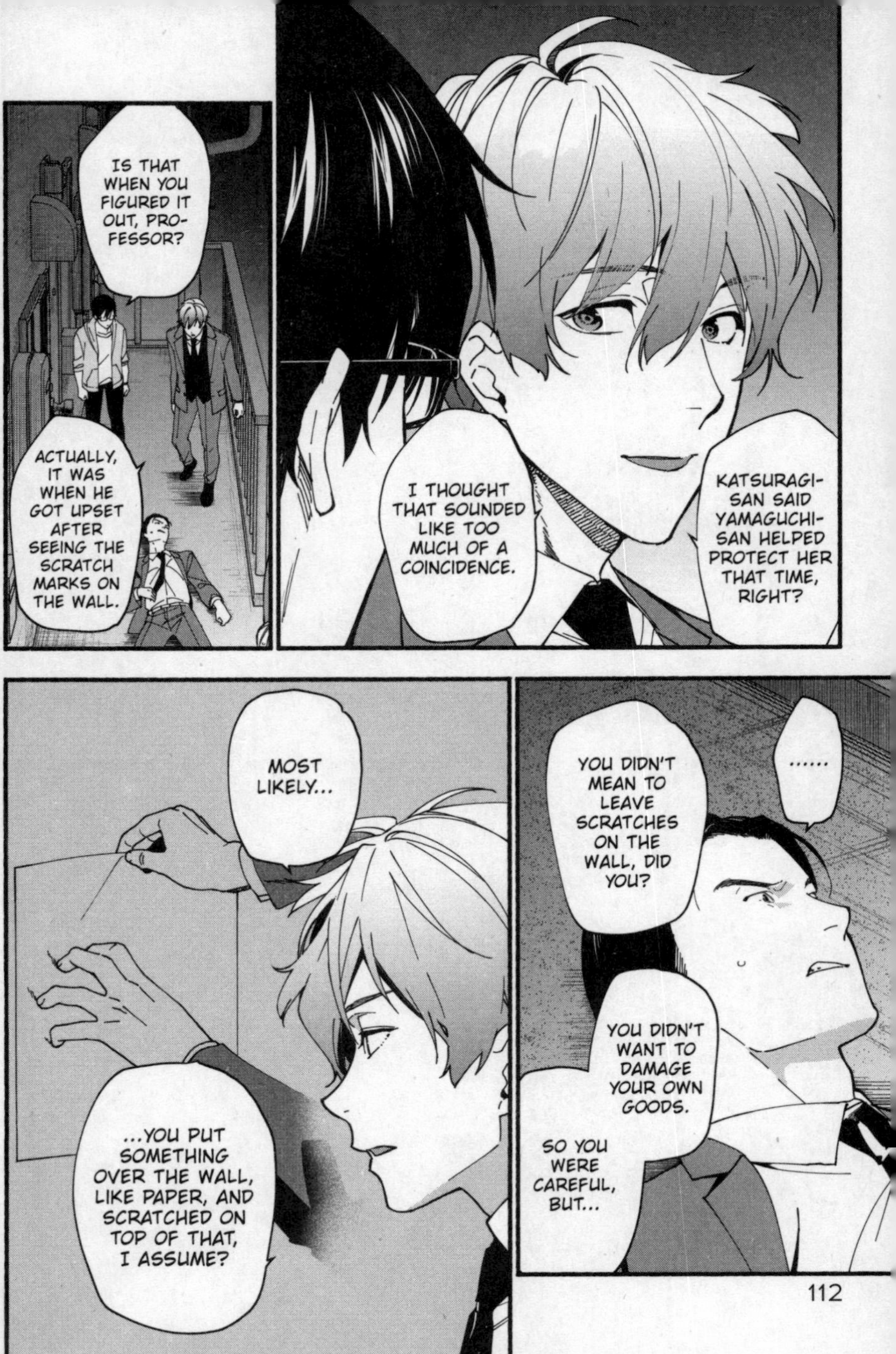
KATSURAGI-SAN SAID YAMAGUCHI-SAN HELPED PROTECT HER THAT TIME, RIGHT?
I THOUGHT THAT SOUNDED LIKE TOO MUCH OF A COINCIDENCE.
IS THAT WHEN YOU FIGURED IT OUT, PRO-FESSOR?
ACTUALLY, IT WAS WHEN HE GOT UPSET AFTER SEEING THE SCRATCH MARKS ON THE WALL.
......
YOU DIDN'T MEAN TO LEAVE SCRATCHES ON THE WALL, DID YOU?
YOU DIDN'T WANT TO DAMAGE YOUR OWN GOODS.
SO YOU WERE CAREFUL, BUT...
MOST LIKELY...
...YOU PUT SOMETHING OVER THE WALL, LIKE PAPER, AND SCRATCHED ON TOP OF THAT, I ASSUME?

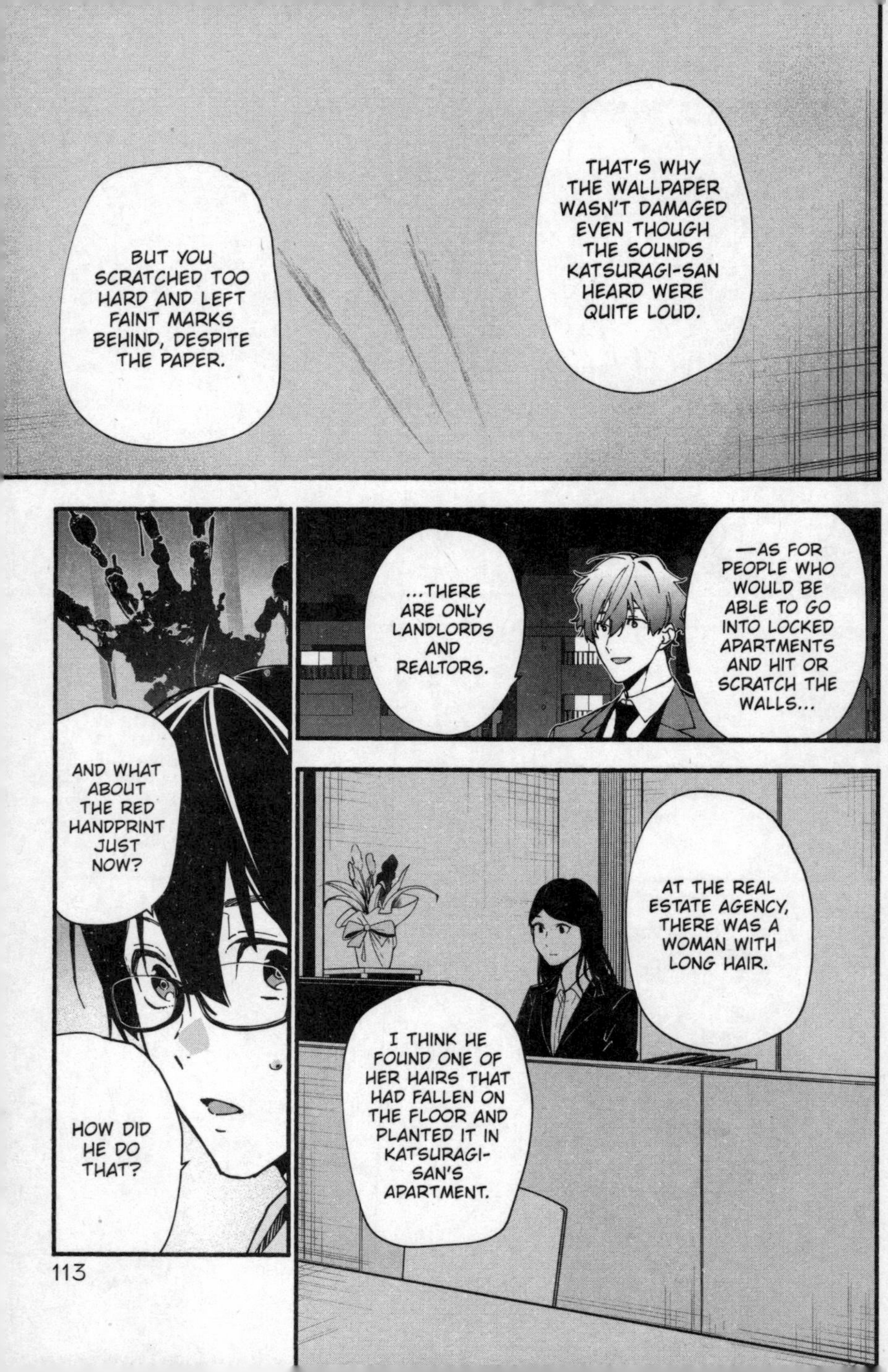
THAT'S WHY THE WALLPAPER WASN'T DAMAGED EVEN THOUGH THE SOUNDS KATSURAGI-SAN HEARD WERE QUITE LOUD.
BUT YOU SCRATCHED TOO HARD AND LEFT FAINT MARKS BEHIND, DESPITE THE PAPER.
—AS FOR PEOPLE WHO WOULD BE ABLE TO GO INTO LOCKED APARTMENTS AND HIT OR SCRATCH THE WALLS...
...THERE ARE ONLY LANDLORDS AND REALTORS.
AT THE REAL ESTATE AGENCY, THERE WAS A WOMAN WITH LONG HAIR.
I THINK HE FOUND ONE OF HER HAIRS THAT HAD FALLEN ON THE FLOOR AND PLANTED IT IN KATSURAGI-SAN'S APARTMENT.
AND WHAT ABOUT THE RED HANDPRINT JUST NOW?
HOW DID HE DO THAT?

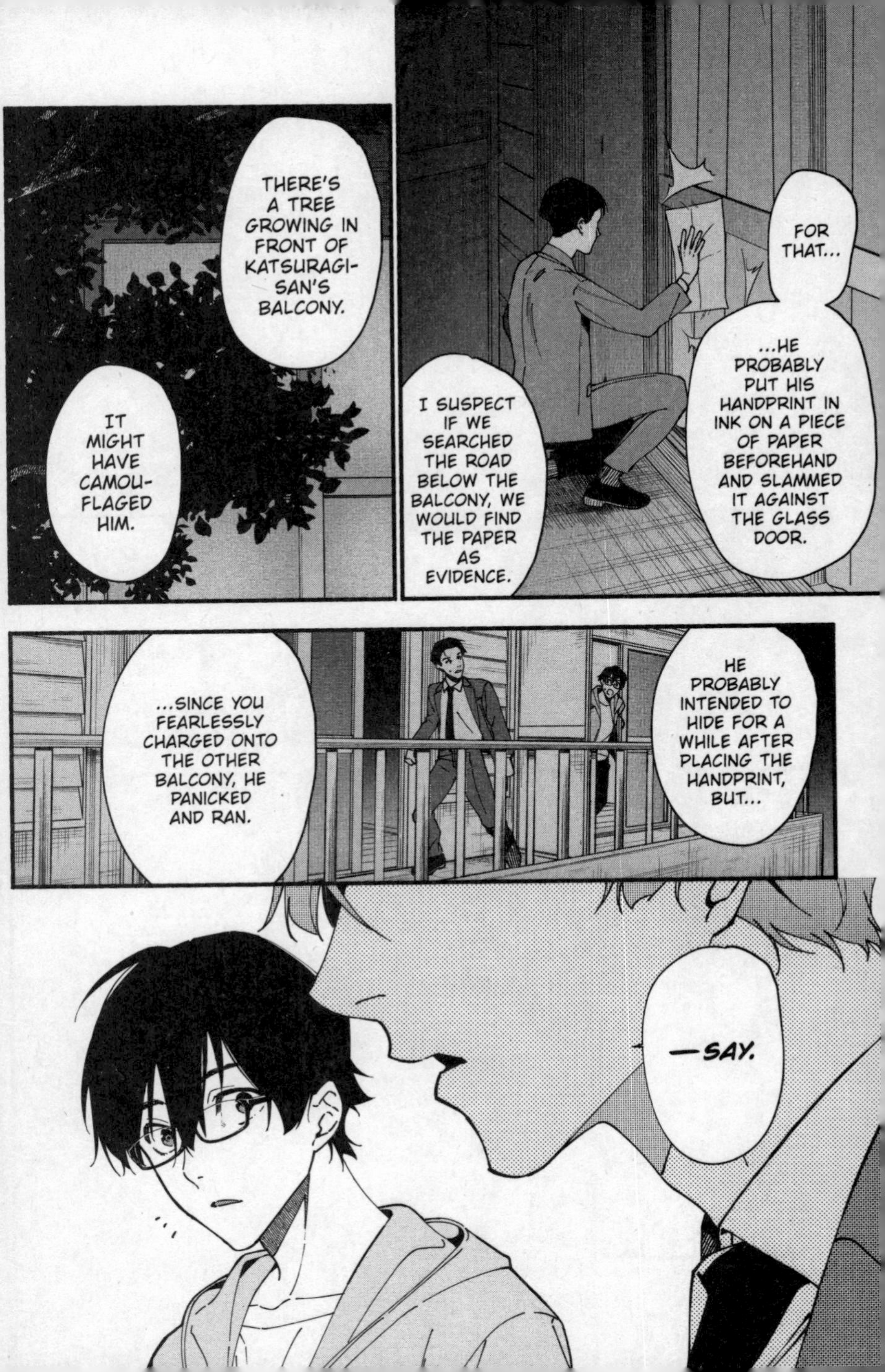
FOR THAT...
...HE PROBABLY PUT HIS HANDPRINT IN INK ON A PIECE OF PAPER BEFOREHAND AND SLAMMED IT AGAINST THE GLASS DOOR.
I SUSPECT IF WE SEARCHED THE ROAD BELOW THE BALCONY, WE WOULD FIND THE PAPER AS EVIDENCE.
THERE'S A TREE GROWING IN FRONT OF KATSURAGI-SAN'S BALCONY.
IT MIGHT HAVE CAMOU-FLAGED HIM.
HE PROBABLY INTENDED TO HIDE FOR A WHILE AFTER PLACING THE HANDPRINT, BUT...
...SINCE YOU FEARLESSLY CHARGED ONTO THE OTHER BALCONY, HE PANICKED AND RAN.
—SAY.
...

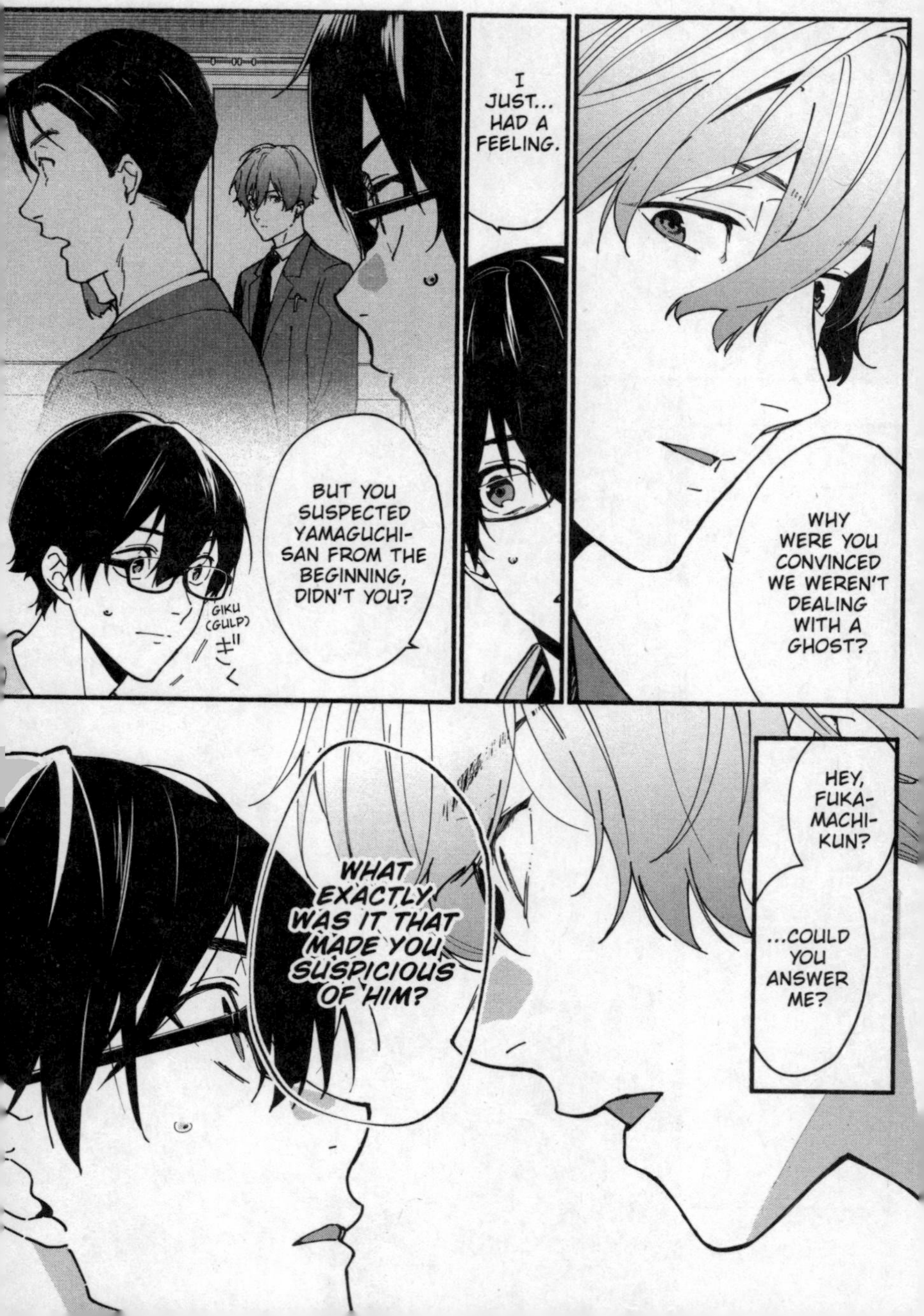
WHY WERE YOU CONVINCED WE WEREN'T DEALING WITH A GHOST?
I JUST... HAD A FEELING.
BUT YOU SUSPECTED YAMAGUCHI-SAN FROM THE BEGINNING, DIDN'T YOU?
GIKU (GULP)
ぎく
HEY, FUKA-MACHI-KUN?
WHAT EXACTLY WAS IT THAT MADE YOU SUSPICIOUS OF HIM?
...COULD YOU ANSWER ME?

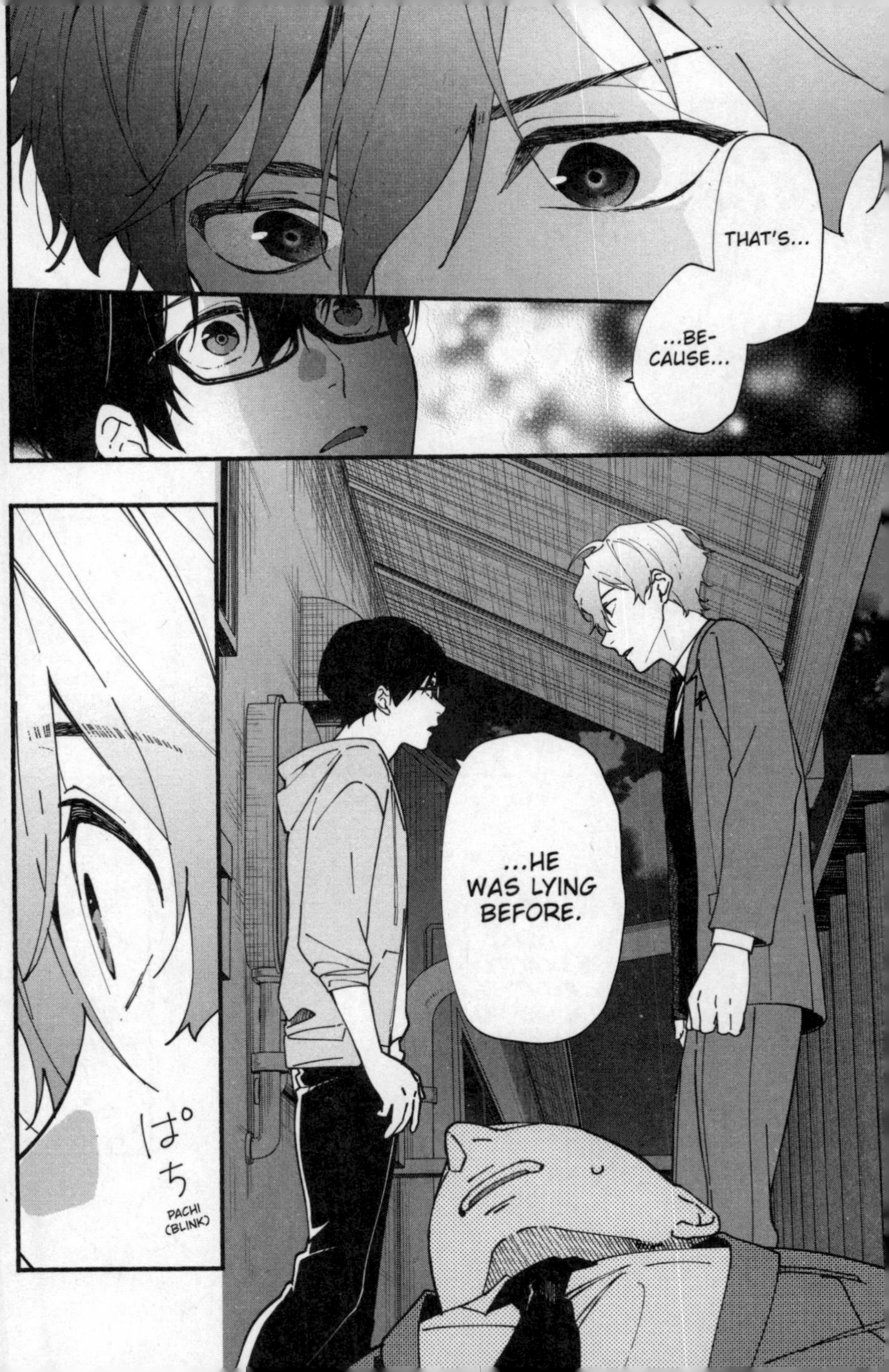
THAT'S...
...BE-
CAUSE...
...HE WAS LYING BEFORE.
ぱち
PACHI (BLINK)

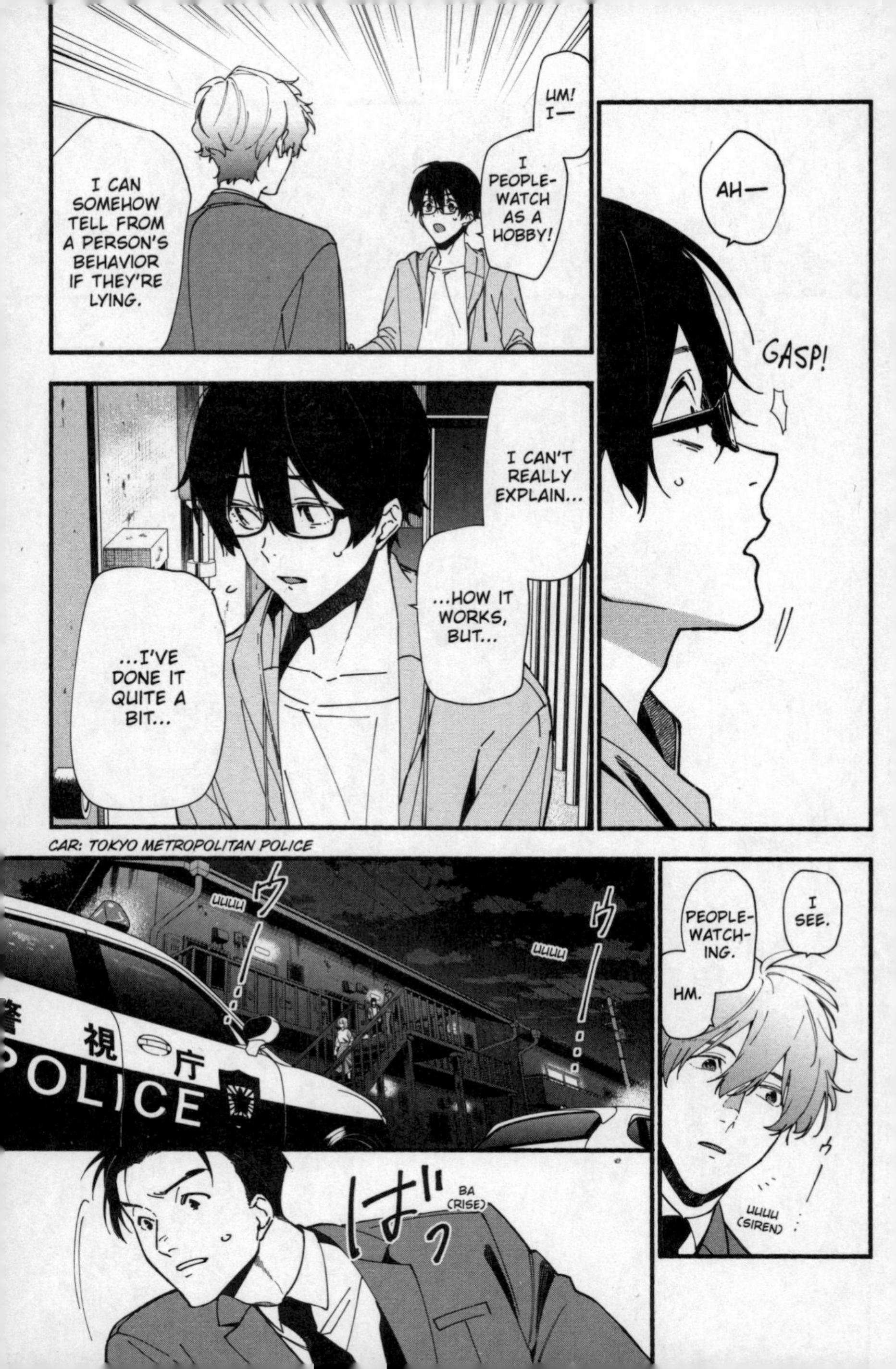
AH—
GASP!
UM! I—
I PEOPLE-WATCH AS A HOBBY!
I CAN SOMEHOW TELL FROM A PERSON'S BEHAVIOR IF THEY'RE LYING.
I CAN'T REALLY EXPLAIN...
...HOW IT WORKS, BUT...
...I'VE DONE IT QUITE A BIT...
CAR: TOKYO METROPOLITAN POLICE
I SEE.
PEOPLE-WATCHING.
HM.
UUUU (SIREN)
UUUU
UUUU
警視庁
POLICE
BA (RISE)

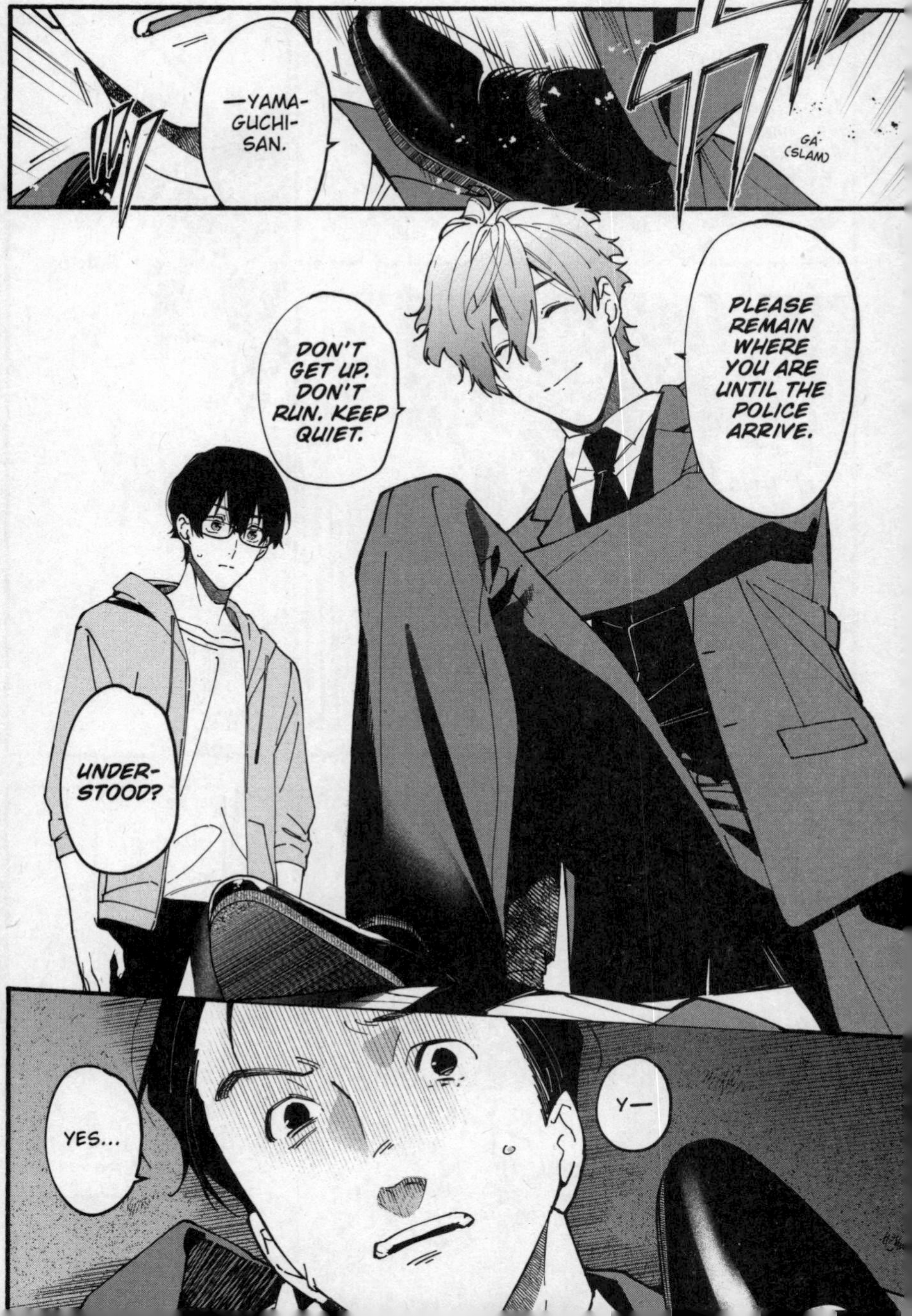
GA (SLAM)
—YAMA-GUCHI-SAN.
PLEASE REMAIN WHERE YOU ARE UNTIL THE POLICE ARRIVE.
DON'T GET UP. DON'T RUN. KEEP QUIET.
UNDER-STOOD?
Y—
YES...

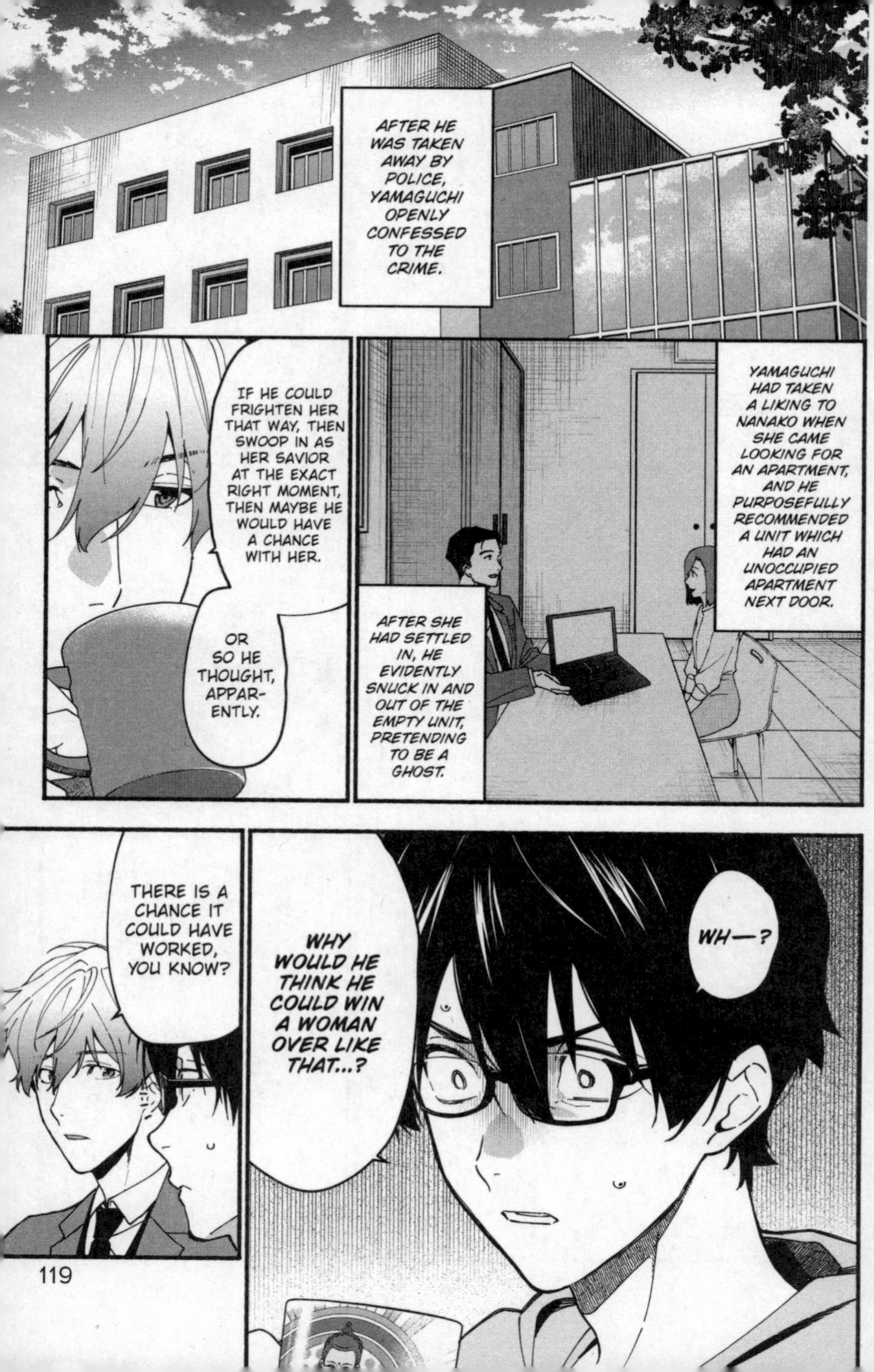
AFTER HE WAS TAKEN AWAY BY POLICE, YAMAGUCHI OPENLY CONFESSED TO THE CRIME.
YAMAGUCHI HAD TAKEN A LIKING TO NANAKO WHEN SHE CAME LOOKING FOR AN APARTMENT, AND HE PURPOSEFULLY RECOMMENDED A UNIT WHICH HAD AN UNOCCUPIED APARTMENT NEXT DOOR.
AFTER SHE HAD SETTLED IN, HE EVIDENTLY SNUCK IN AND OUT OF THE EMPTY UNIT, PRETENDING TO BE A GHOST.
IF HE COULD FRIGHTEN HER THAT WAY, THEN SWOOP IN AS HER SAVIOR AT THE EXACT RIGHT MOMENT, THEN MAYBE HE WOULD HAVE A CHANCE WITH HER.
OR SO HE THOUGHT, APPARENTLY.
WH—?
WHY WOULD HE THINK HE COULD WIN A WOMAN OVER LIKE THAT...?
THERE IS A CHANCE IT COULD HAVE WORKED, YOU KNOW?

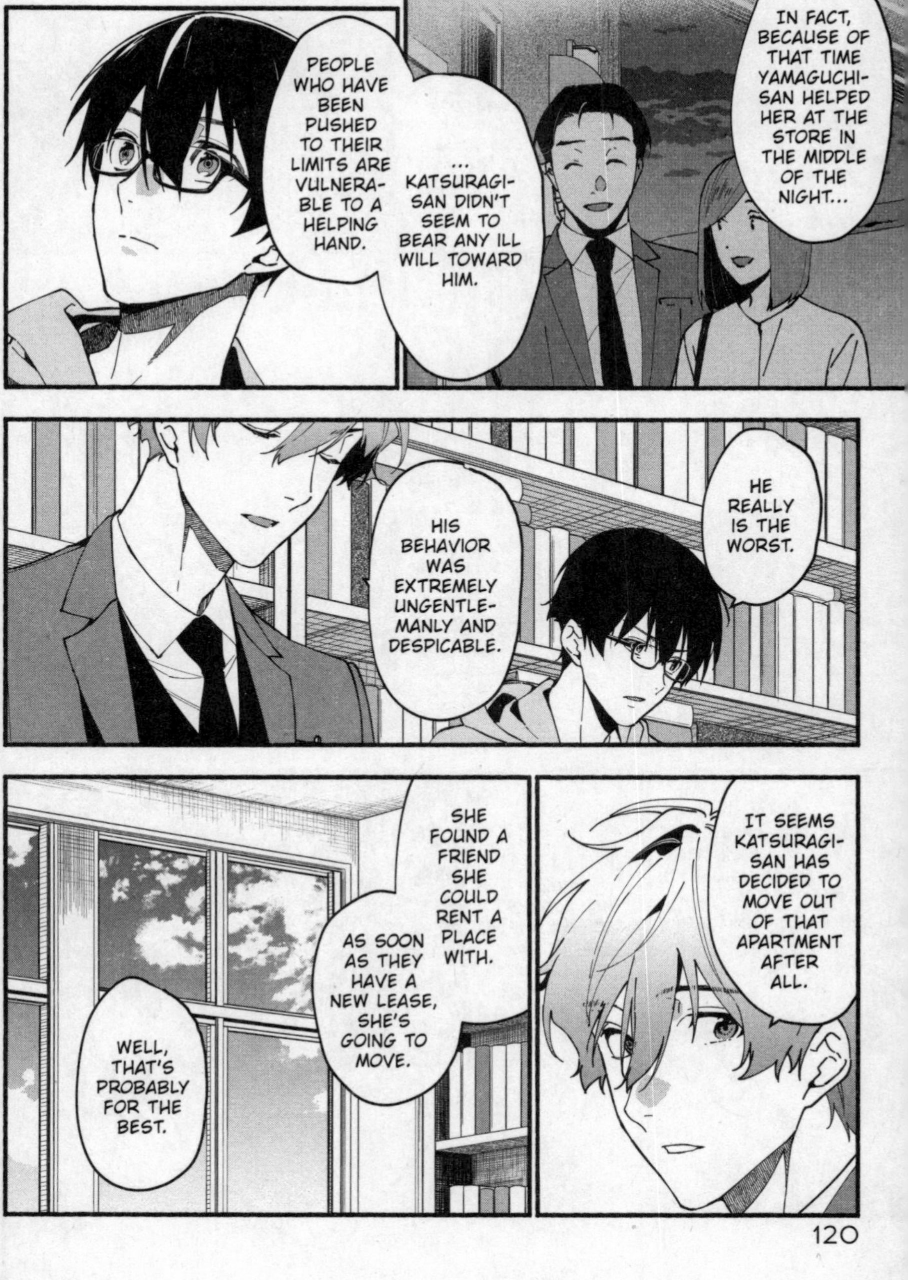
IN FACT, BECAUSE OF THAT TIME YAMAGUCHI-SAN HELPED HER AT THE STORE IN THE MIDDLE OF THE NIGHT...
... KATSURAGI-SAN DIDN'T SEEM TO BEAR ANY ILL WILL TOWARD HIM.
PEOPLE WHO HAVE BEEN PUSHED TO THEIR LIMITS ARE VULNERA-BLE TO A HELPING HAND.
HE REALLY IS THE WORST.
HIS BEHAVIOR WAS EXTREMELY UNGENTLE-MANLY AND DESPICABLE.
IT SEEMS KATSURAGI-SAN HAS DECIDED TO MOVE OUT OF THAT APARTMENT AFTER ALL.
SHE FOUND A FRIEND SHE COULD RENT A PLACE WITH.
AS SOON AS THEY HAVE A NEW LEASE, SHE'S GOING TO MOVE.
WELL, THAT'S PROBABLY FOR THE BEST.

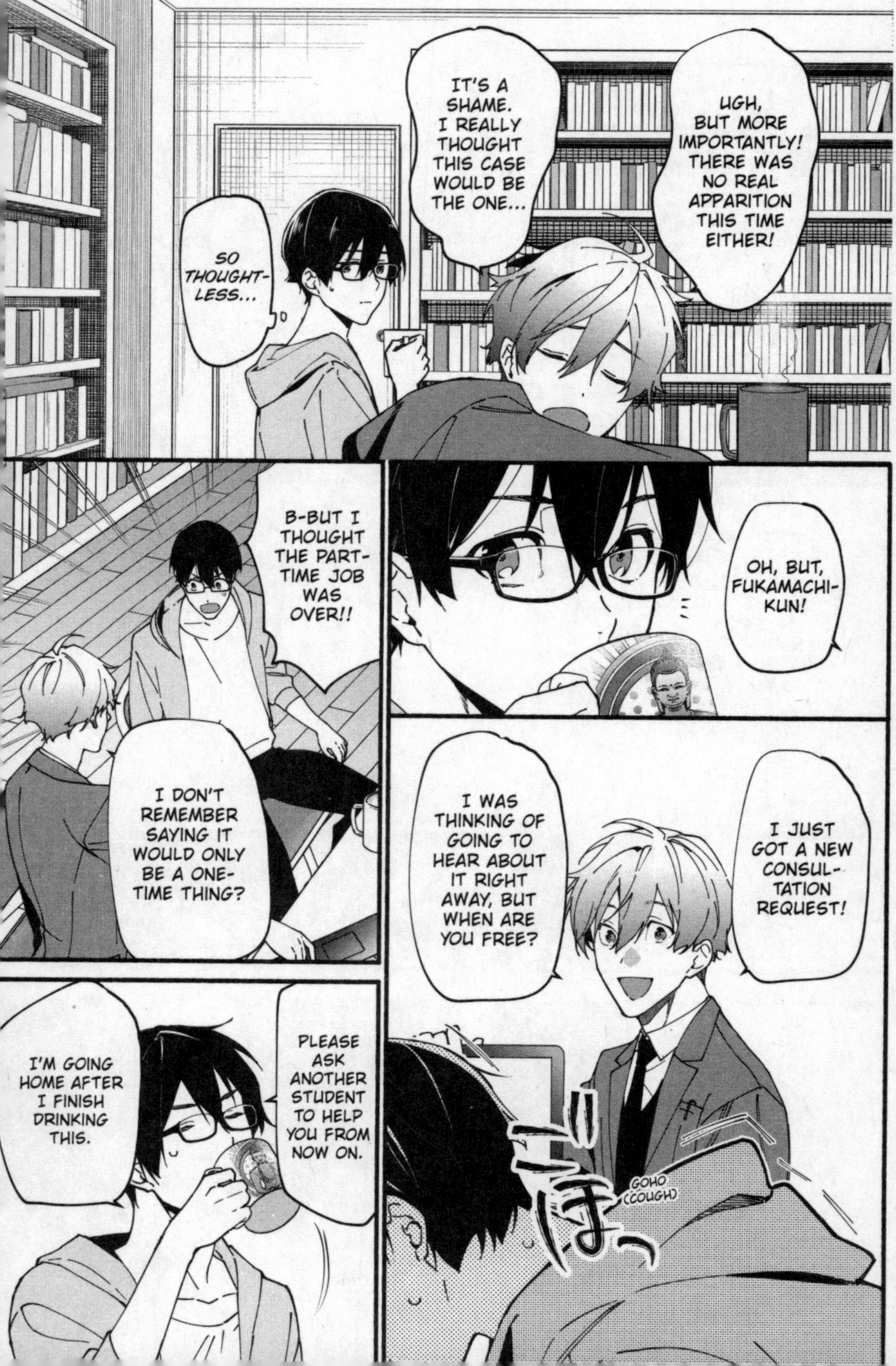
UGH, BUT MORE IMPORTANTLY! THERE WAS NO REAL APPARITION THIS TIME EITHER!
IT'S A SHAME. I REALLY THOUGHT THIS CASE WOULD BE THE ONE...
SO THOUGHTLESS...
OH, BUT, FUKAMACHI-KUN!
I JUST GOT A NEW CONSULTATION REQUEST!
I WAS THINKING OF GOING TO HEAR ABOUT IT RIGHT AWAY, BUT WHEN ARE YOU FREE?
GOHO (COUGH)
B-BUT I THOUGHT THE PART-TIME JOB WAS OVER!!
I DON'T REMEMBER SAYING IT WOULD ONLY BE A ONE-TIME THING?
PLEASE ASK ANOTHER STUDENT TO HELP YOU FROM NOW ON.
I'M GOING HOME AFTER I FINISH DRINKING THIS.

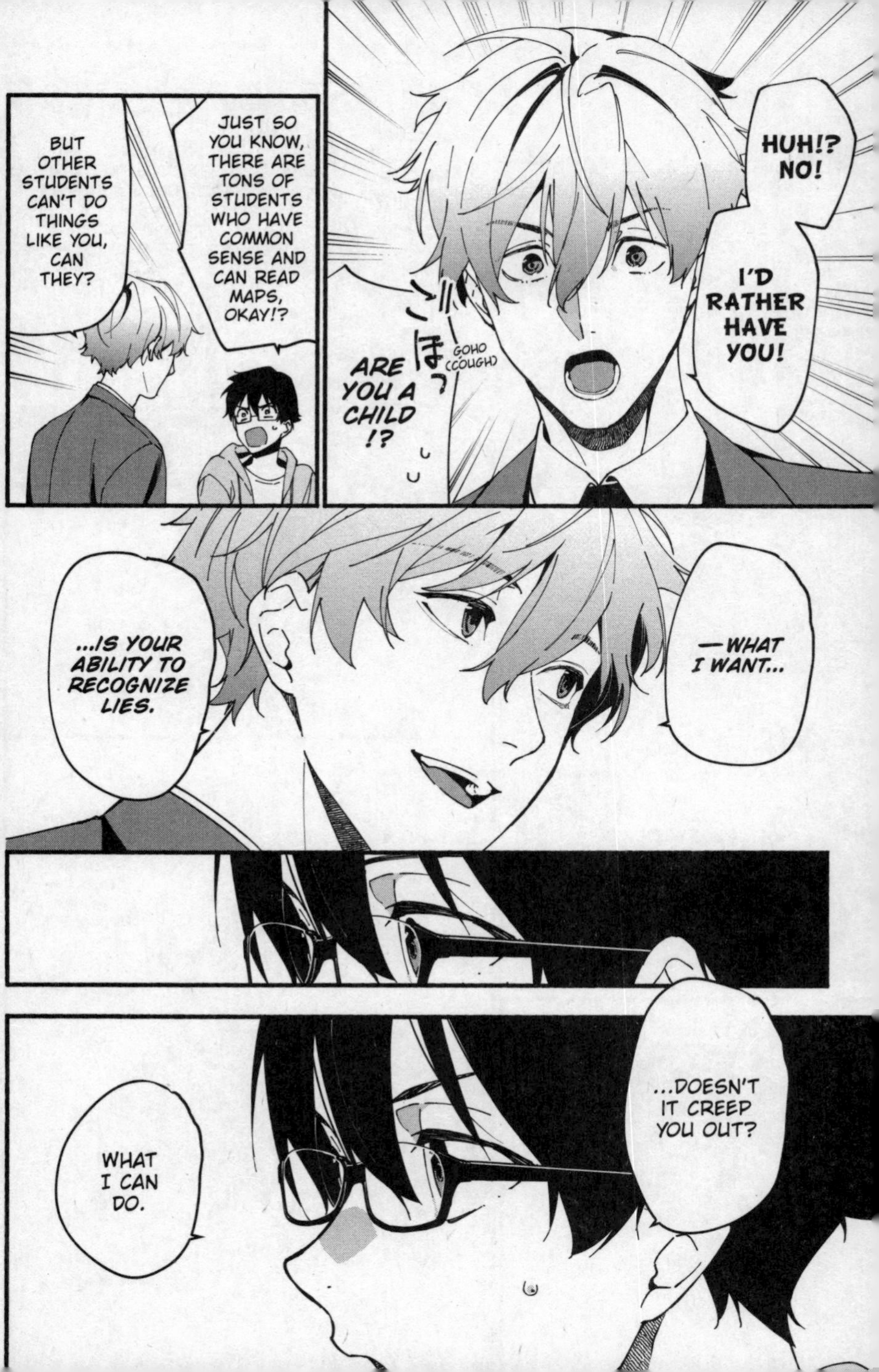
HUH!? NO!
I'D RATHER HAVE YOU!
ごほっ
GOHO (COUGH)
ARE YOU A CHILD!?
JUST SO YOU KNOW, THERE ARE TONS OF STUDENTS WHO HAVE COMMON SENSE AND CAN READ MAPS, OKAY!?
BUT OTHER STUDENTS CAN'T DO THINGS LIKE YOU, CAN THEY?
—WHAT I WANT...
...IS YOUR ABILITY TO RECOGNIZE LIES.
...DOESN'T IT CREEP YOU OUT?
WHAT I CAN DO.

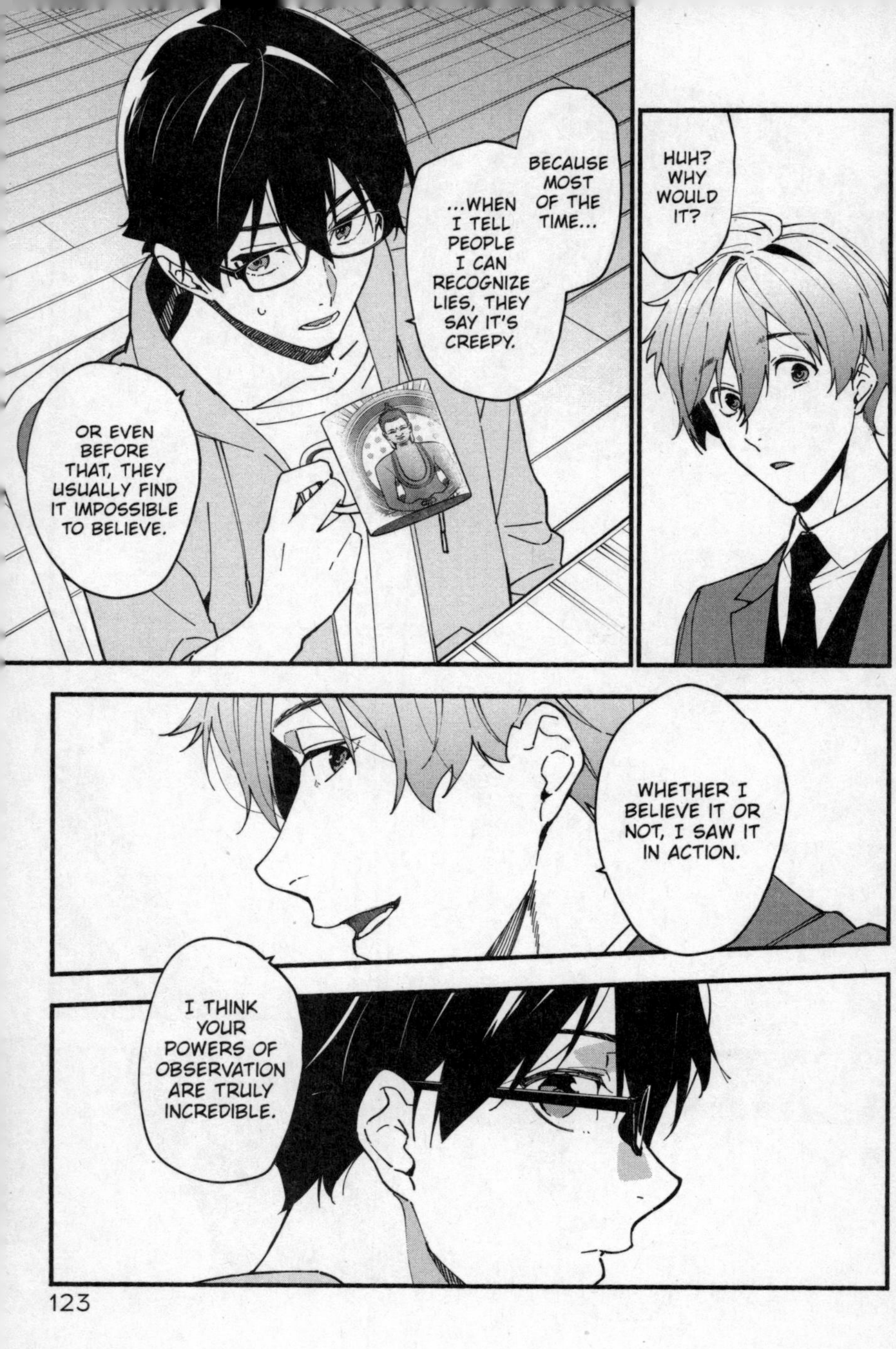
HUH? WHY WOULD IT?
BECAUSE MOST OF THE TIME...
...WHEN I TELL PEOPLE I CAN RECOGNIZE LIES, THEY SAY IT'S CREEPY.
OR EVEN BEFORE THAT, THEY USUALLY FIND IT IMPOSSIBLE TO BELIEVE.
WHETHER I BELIEVE IT OR NOT, I SAW IT IN ACTION.
I THINK YOUR POWERS OF OBSERVATION ARE TRULY INCREDIBLE.

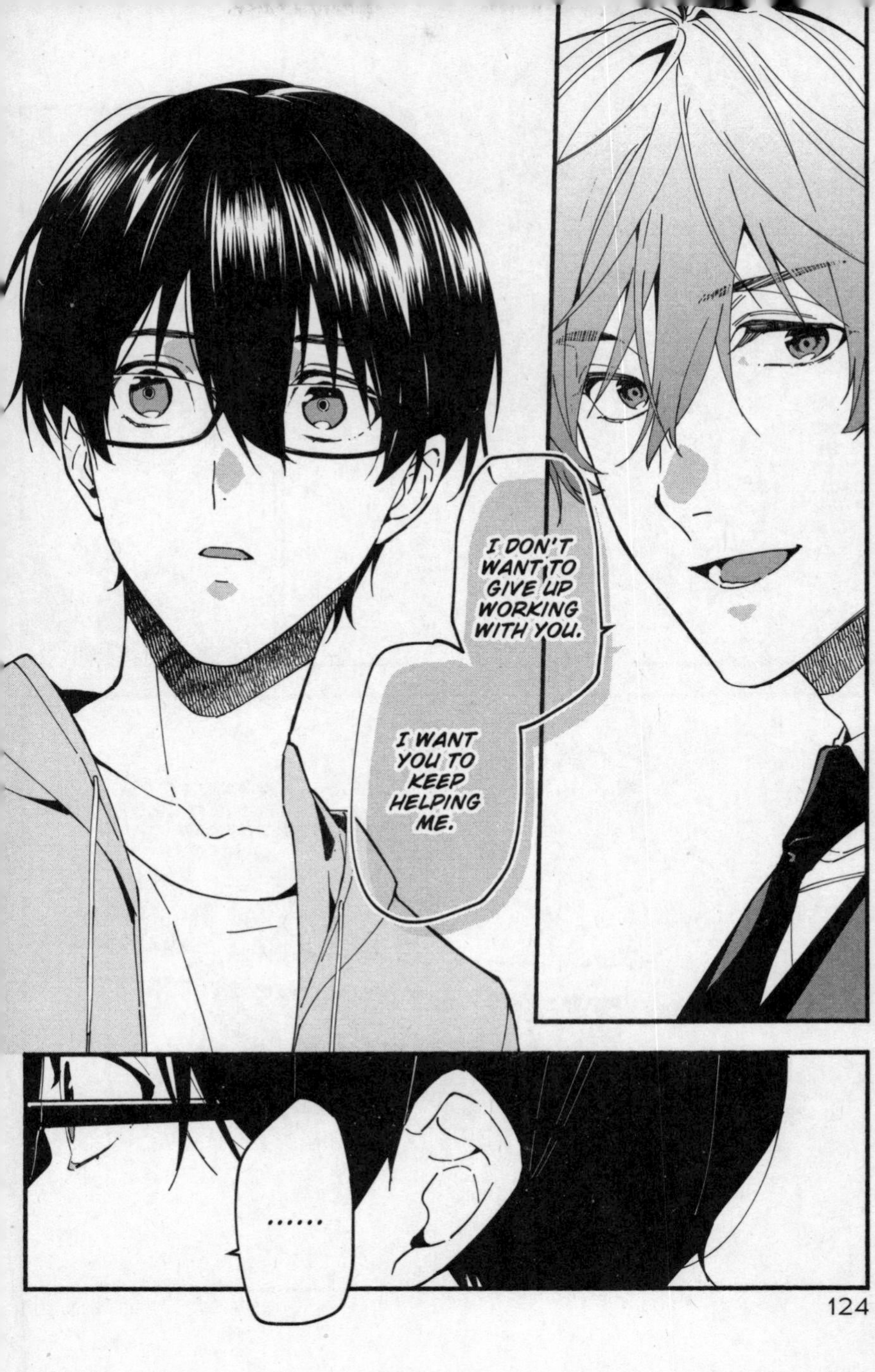
I DON'T WANT TO GIVE UP WORKING WITH YOU.
I WANT YOU TO KEEP HELPING ME.
......

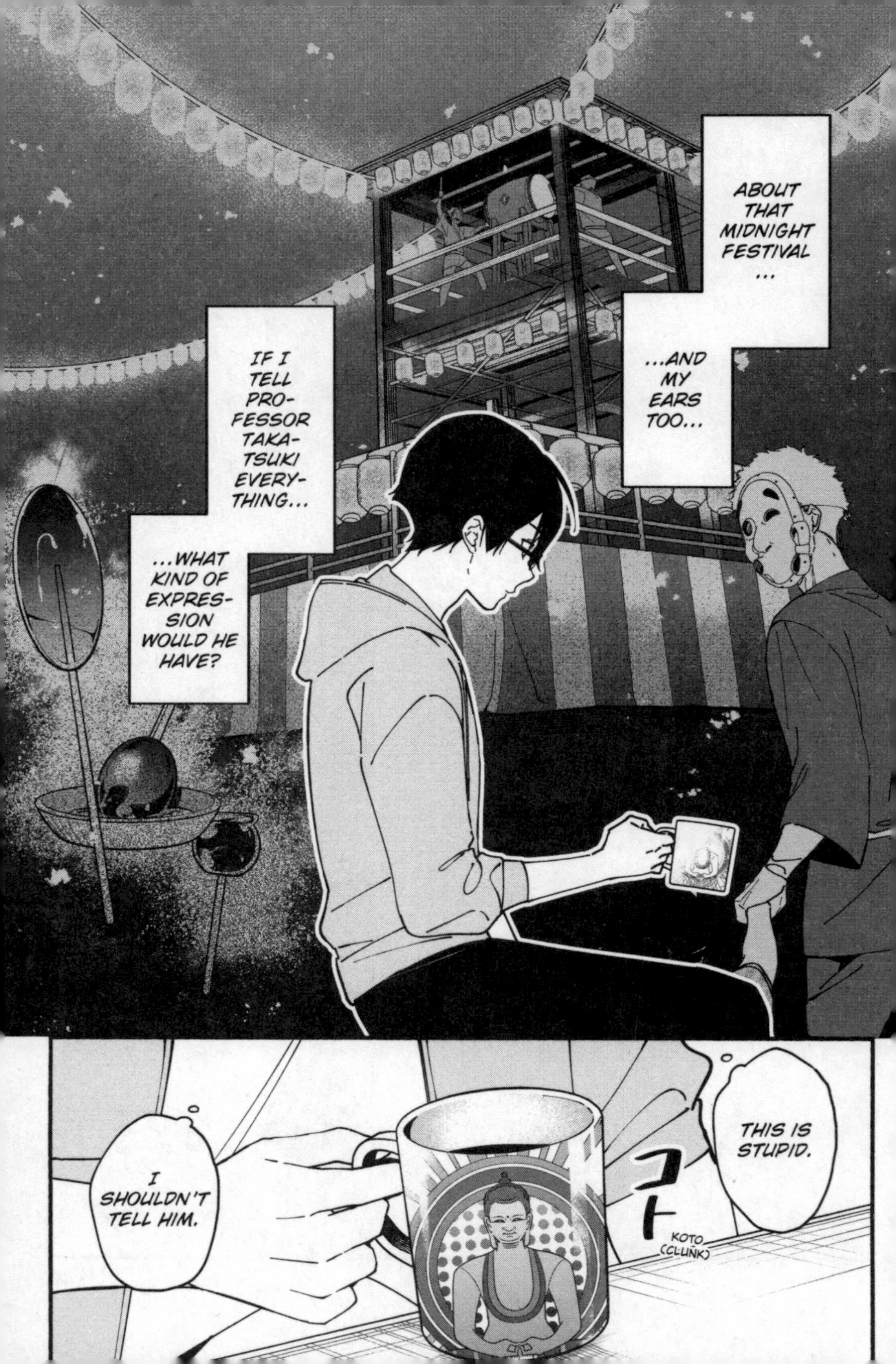
ABOUT THAT MIDNIGHT FESTIVAL...
...AND MY EARS TOO...
IF I TELL PRO-FESSOR TAKA-TSUKI EVERY-THING...
...WHAT KIND OF EXPRES-SION WOULD HE HAVE?
THIS IS STUPID.
コト
KOTO (CLUNK)
I SHOULDN'T TELL HIM.

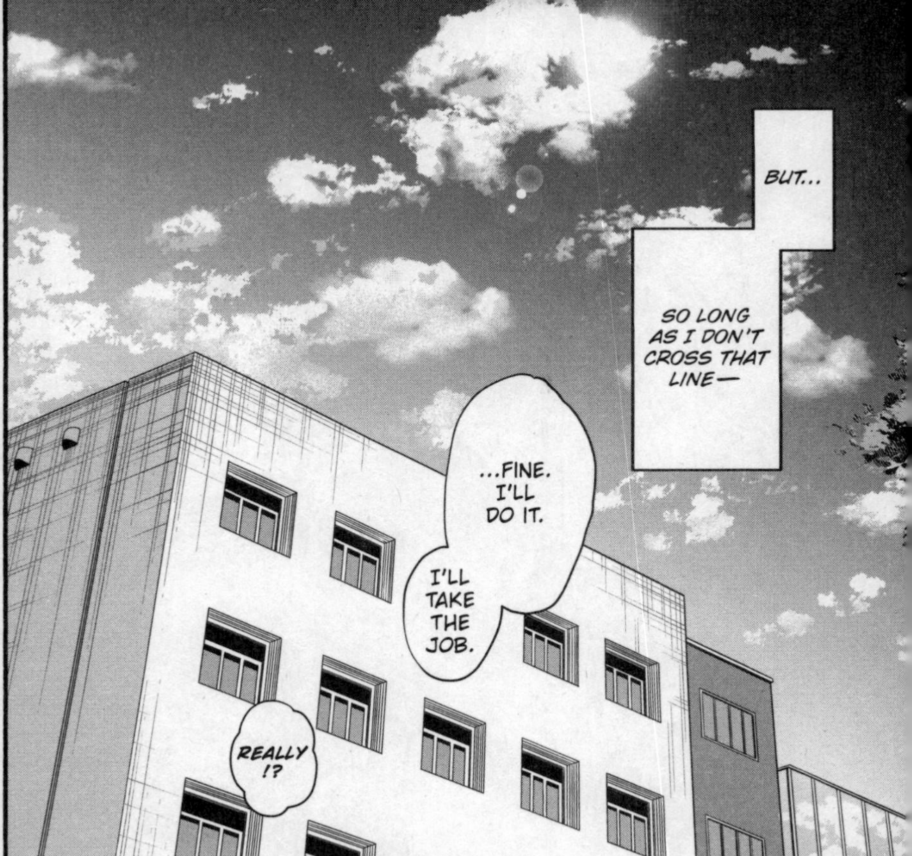
BUT...
SO LONG AS I DON'T CROSS THAT LINE—
...FINE. I'LL DO IT.
I'LL TAKE THE JOB.
REALLY!?

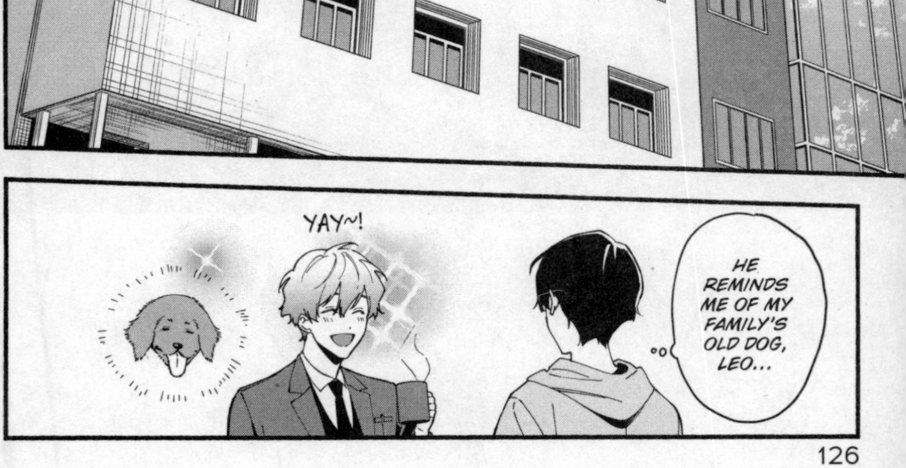
HE REMINDS ME OF MY FAMILY'S OLD DOG, LEO...
YAY~!

Associate Professor Akira Takatsuki's Conjecture

Associate Professor Akira Takatsuki's Conjecture

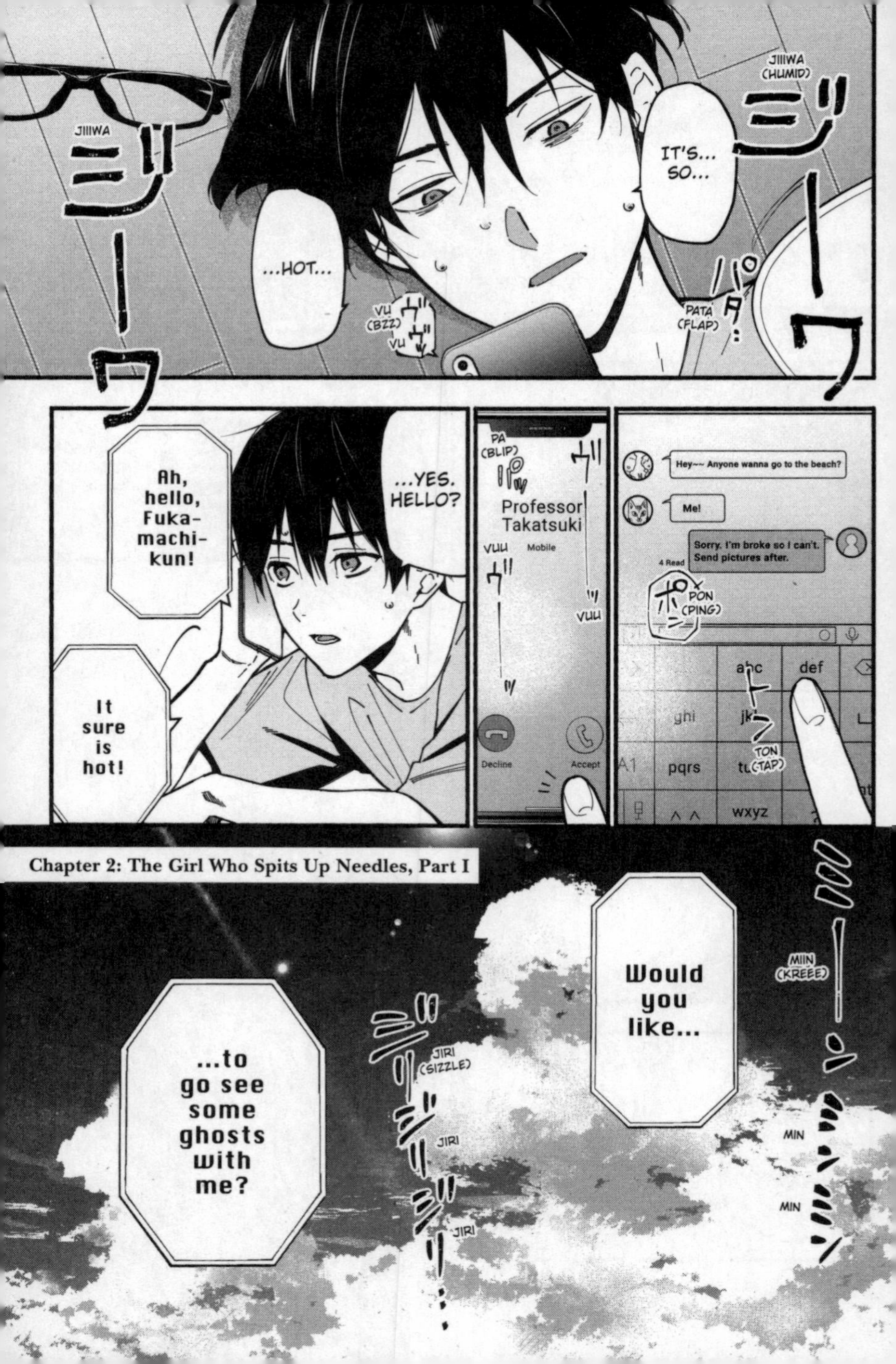
JIIIWA (HUMID)
IT'S... SO...
...HOT...
PATA (FLAP)
VU (BZZ) VU
JIIIWA
Hey~~ Anyone wanna go to the beach?
Me!
Sorry. I'm broke so I can't. Send pictures after.
4 Read
PON (PING)
abc
def
ghi
pqrs
wxyz
TON (TAP)
PA (BLIP)
Professor Takatsuki
Mobile
VUU
VUU
Decline
Accept
...YES. HELLO?
Ah, hello, Fukamachi-kun!
It sure is hot!
Chapter 2: The Girl Who Spits Up Needles, Part I
MIIN (KREEE)
Would you like...
MIN
MIN
JIRI (SIZZLE)
JIRI
JIRI
...to go see some ghosts with me?

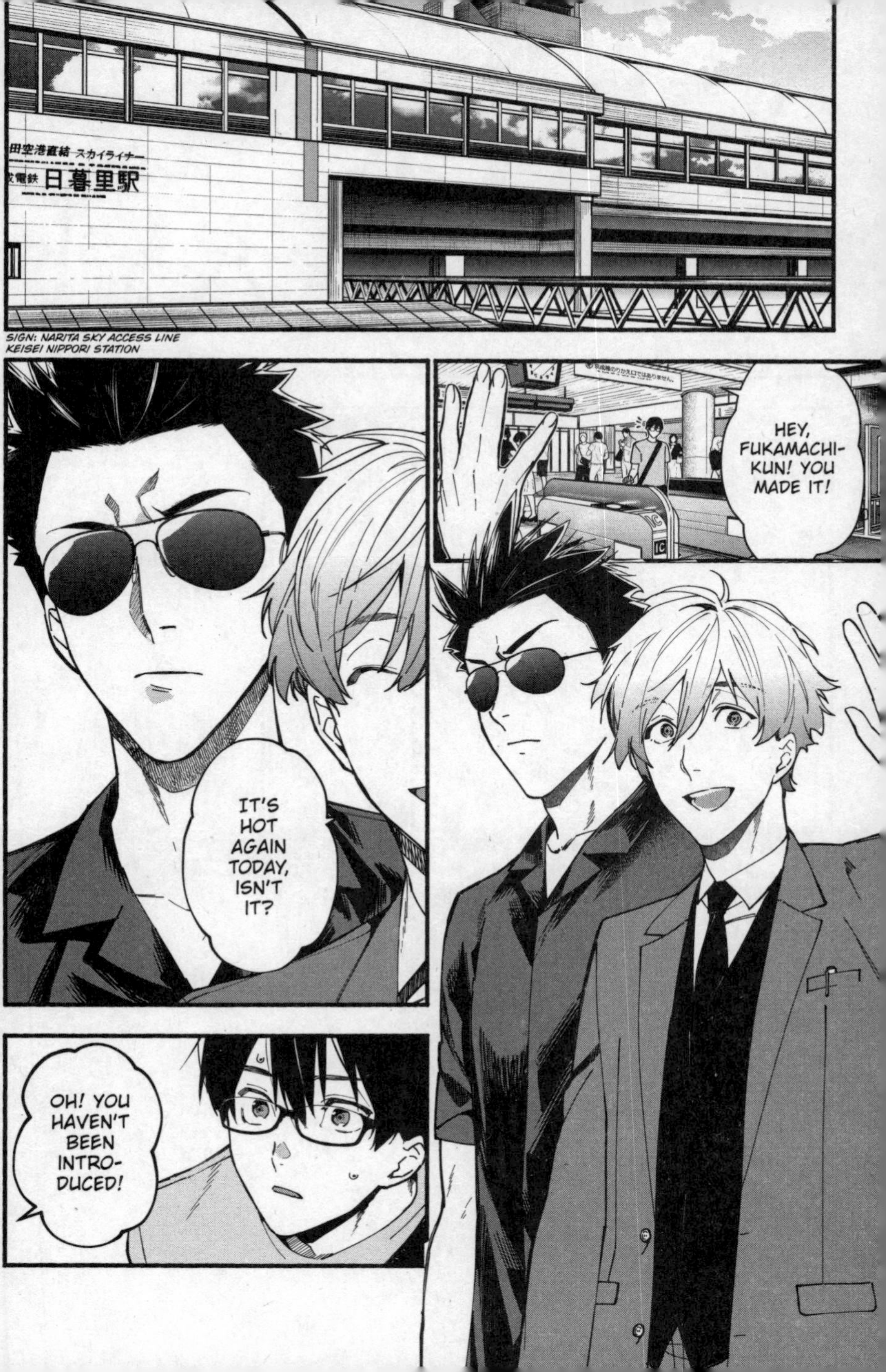
田空港直結 スカイライナー
成電鉄 日暮里駅
SIGN: NARITA SKY ACCESS LINE
KEISEI NIPPORI STATION
HEY, FUKAMACHI-KUN! YOU MADE IT!
IT'S HOT AGAIN TODAY, ISN'T IT?
OH! YOU HAVEN'T BEEN INTRO-DUCED!

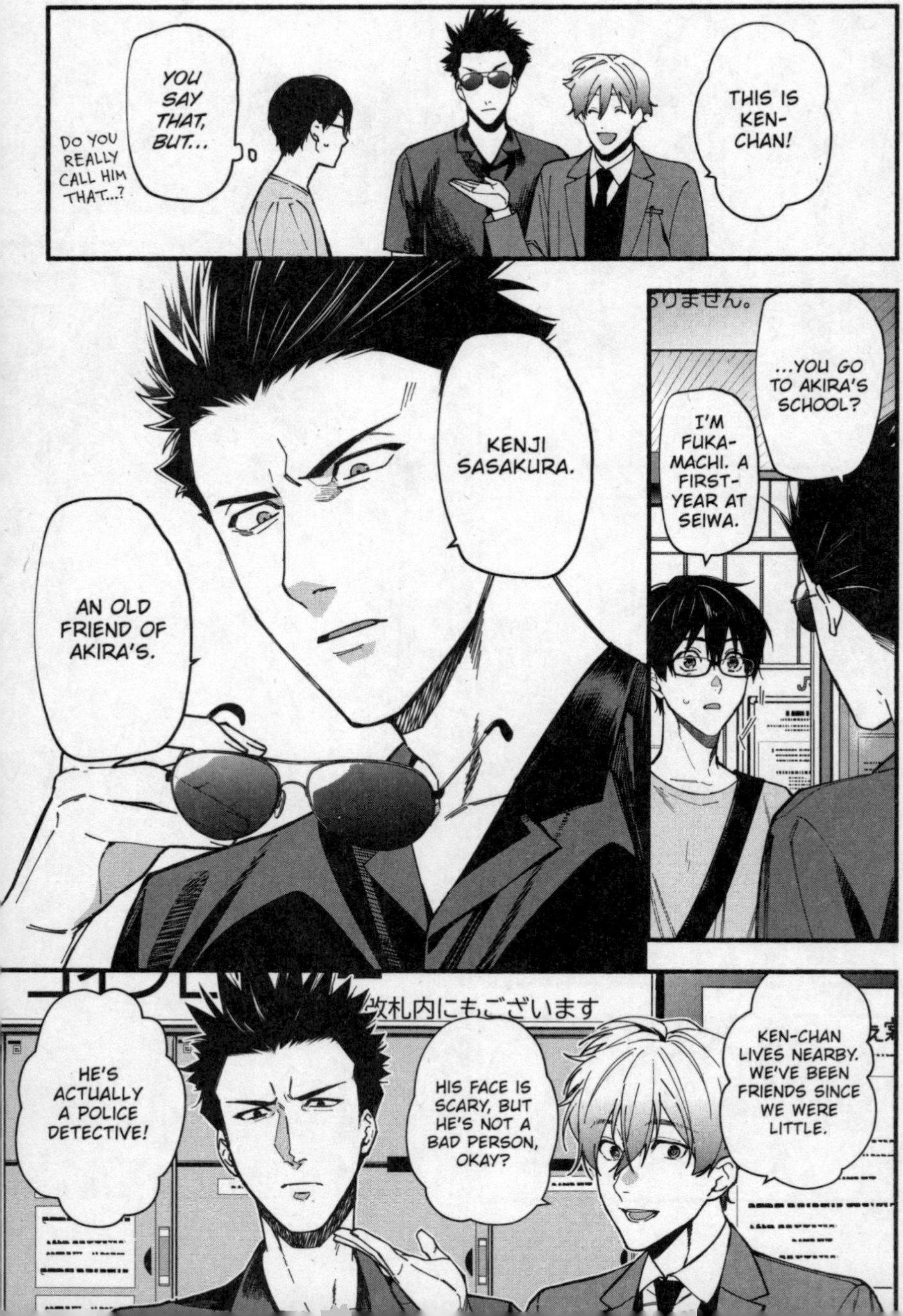
THIS IS KEN-CHAN!
YOU SAY THAT, BUT...
DO YOU REALLY CALL HIM THAT...?
りません。
...YOU GO TO AKIRA'S SCHOOL?
I'M FUKAMACHI. A FIRST-YEAR AT SEIWA.
KENJI SASAKURA.
AN OLD FRIEND OF AKIRA'S.
改札内にもございます
KEN-CHAN LIVES NEARBY. WE'VE BEEN FRIENDS SINCE WE WERE LITTLE.
HIS FACE IS SCARY, BUT HE'S NOT A BAD PERSON, OKAY?
HE'S ACTUALLY A POLICE DETECTIVE!

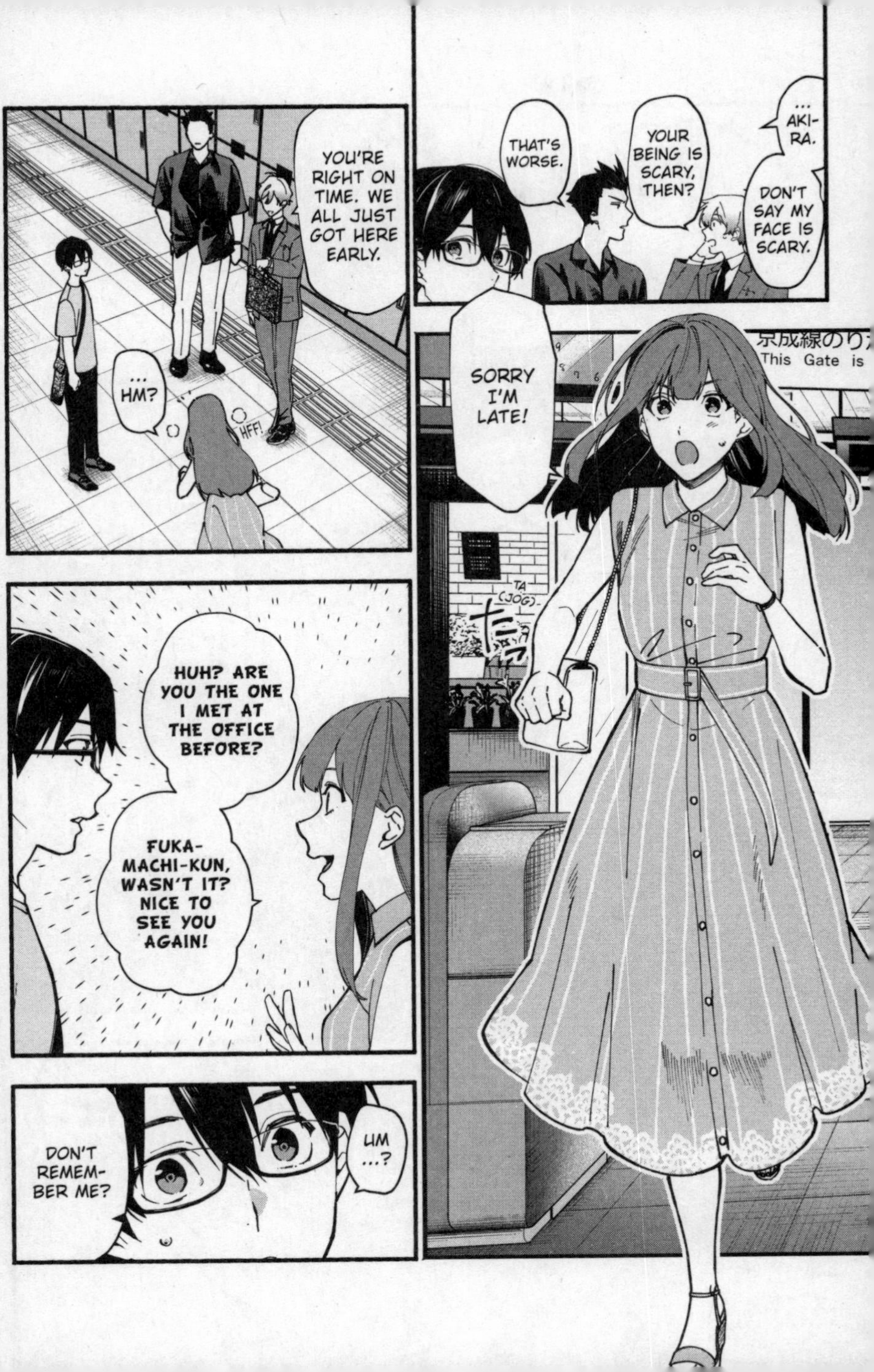
... AKI- RA.
DON'T SAY MY FACE IS SCARY.
YOUR BEING IS SCARY, THEN?
THAT'S WORSE.
YOU'RE RIGHT ON TIME. WE ALL JUST GOT HERE EARLY.
... HM?
HFF!
京成線のり
This Gate is
SORRY I'M LATE!
TA (JOG)
HUH? ARE YOU THE ONE I MET AT THE OFFICE BEFORE?
FUKA-MACHI-KUN, WASN'T IT? NICE TO SEE YOU AGAIN!
UM ...?
DON'T REMEM-BER ME?

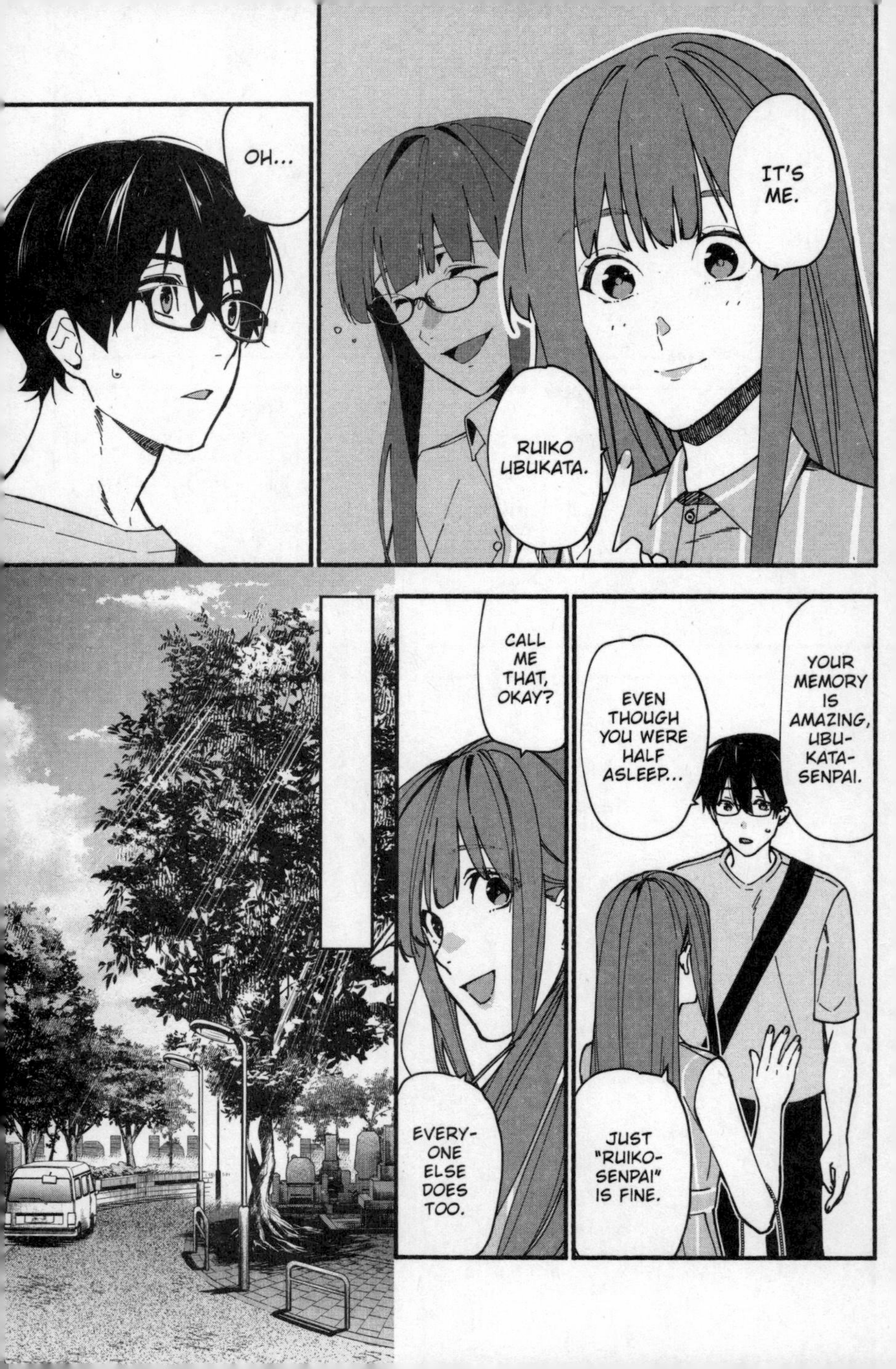
IT'S ME.
RUIKO UBUKATA.
OH...
YOUR MEMORY IS AMAZING, UBUKATA-SENPAI.
EVEN THOUGH YOU WERE HALF ASLEEP...
JUST "RUIKO-SENPAI" IS FINE.
CALL ME THAT, OKAY?
EVERYONE ELSE DOES TOO.

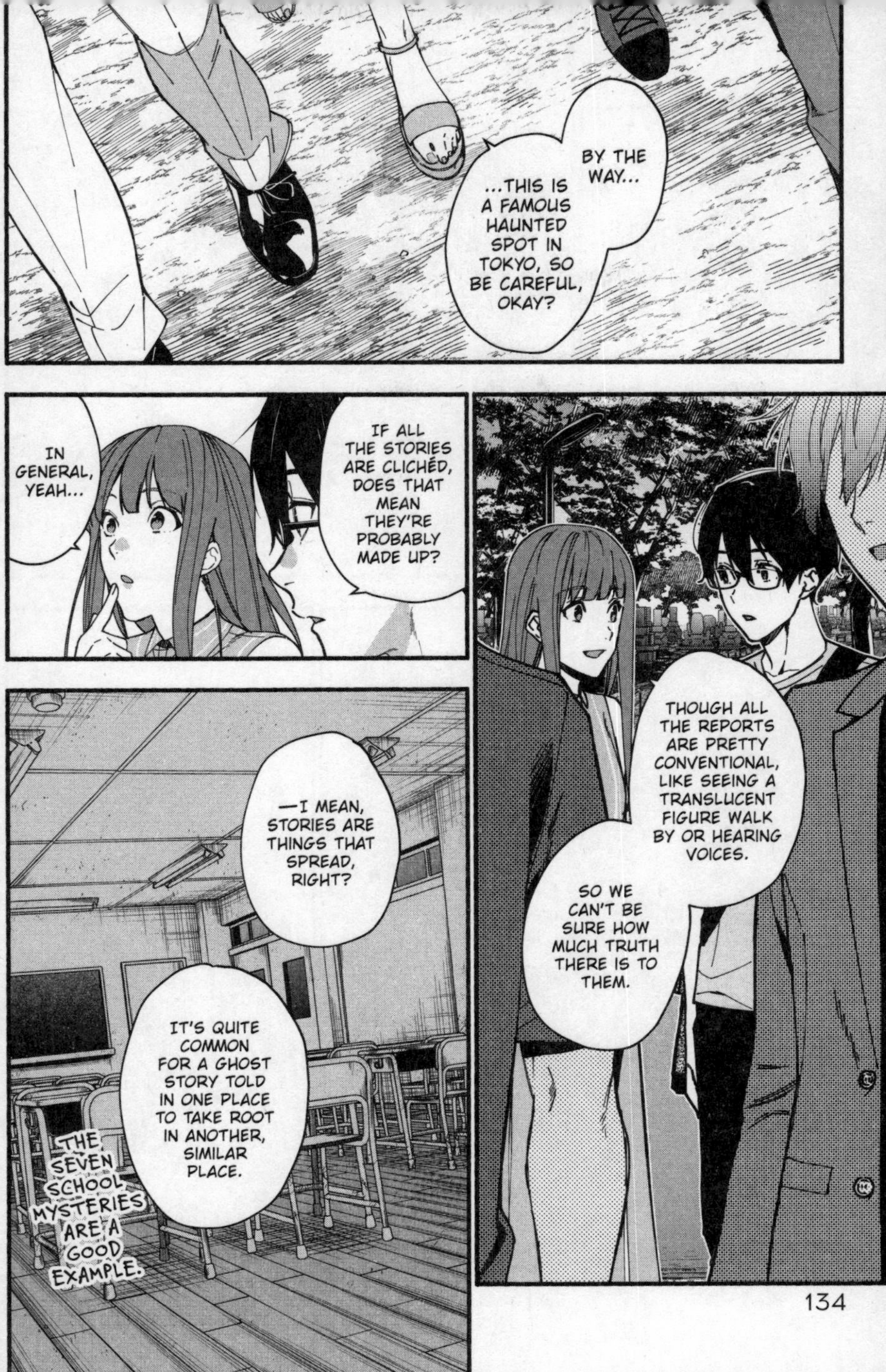
BY THE WAY...
...THIS IS A FAMOUS HAUNTED SPOT IN TOKYO, SO BE CAREFUL, OKAY?
THOUGH ALL THE REPORTS ARE PRETTY CONVENTIONAL, LIKE SEEING A TRANSLUCENT FIGURE WALK BY OR HEARING VOICES.
SO WE CAN'T BE SURE HOW MUCH TRUTH THERE IS TO THEM.
IF ALL THE STORIES ARE CLICHÉD, DOES THAT MEAN THEY'RE PROBABLY MADE UP?
IN GENERAL, YEAH...
—I MEAN, STORIES ARE THINGS THAT SPREAD, RIGHT?
IT'S QUITE COMMON FOR A GHOST STORY TOLD IN ONE PLACE TO TAKE ROOT IN ANOTHER, SIMILAR PLACE.
THE SEVEN SCHOOL MYSTERIES ARE A GOOD EXAMPLE.

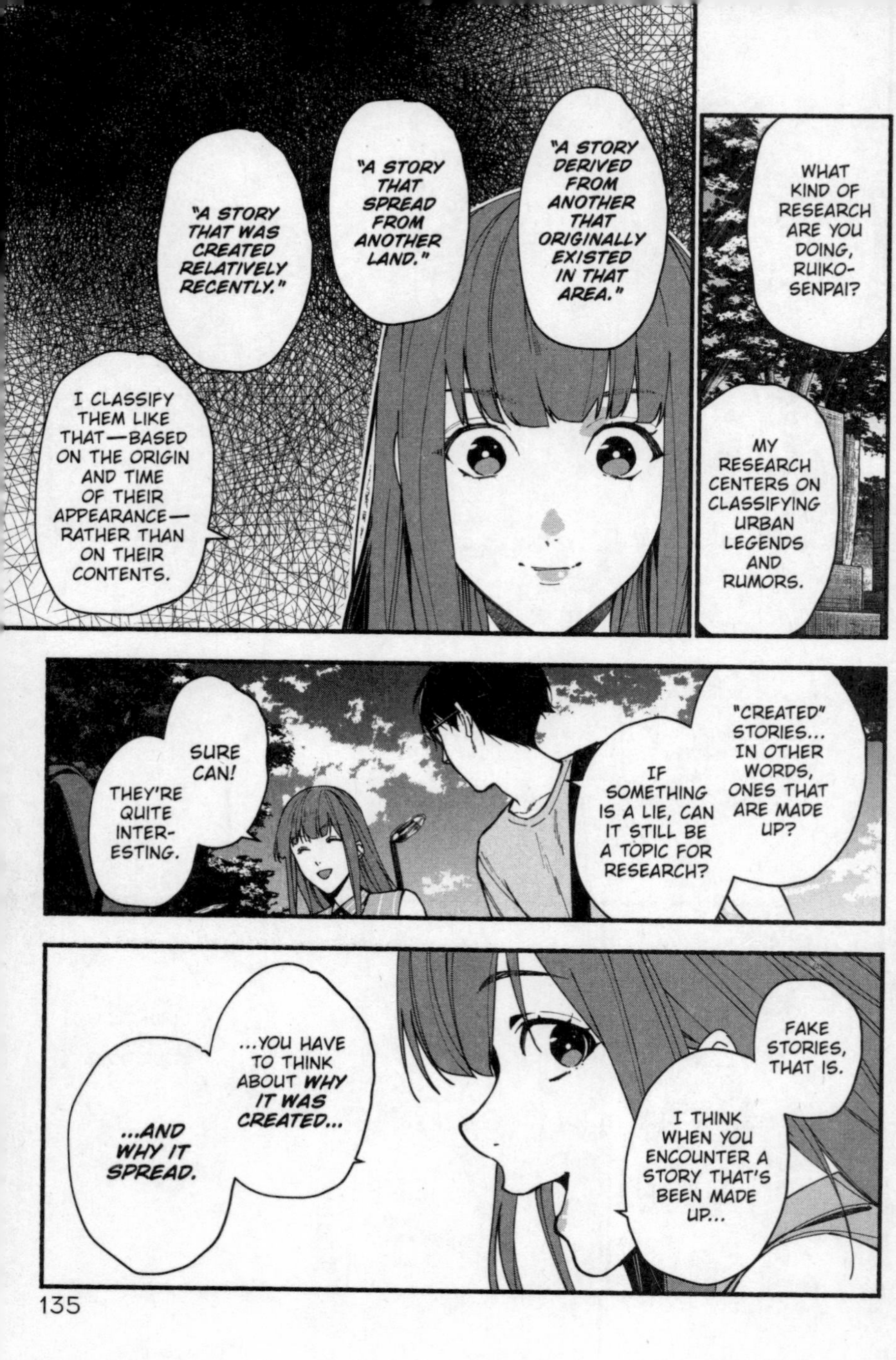

WHAT KIND OF RESEARCH ARE YOU DOING, RUIKO-SENPAI?
MY RESEARCH CENTERS ON CLASSIFYING URBAN LEGENDS AND RUMORS.
"A STORY DERIVED FROM ANOTHER THAT ORIGINALLY EXISTED IN THAT AREA."
"A STORY THAT SPREAD FROM ANOTHER LAND."
"A STORY THAT WAS CREATED RELATIVELY RECENTLY."
I CLASSIFY THEM LIKE THAT—BASED ON THE ORIGIN AND TIME OF THEIR APPEARANCE—RATHER THAN ON THEIR CONTENTS.
"CREATED" STORIES... IN OTHER WORDS, ONES THAT ARE MADE UP?
IF SOMETHING IS A LIE, CAN IT STILL BE A TOPIC FOR RESEARCH?
SURE CAN!
THEY'RE QUITE INTER-ESTING.
FAKE STORIES, THAT IS.
I THINK WHEN YOU ENCOUNTER A STORY THAT'S BEEN MADE UP...
...YOU HAVE TO THINK ABOUT *WHY IT WAS CREATED...*
...AND WHY IT SPREAD.

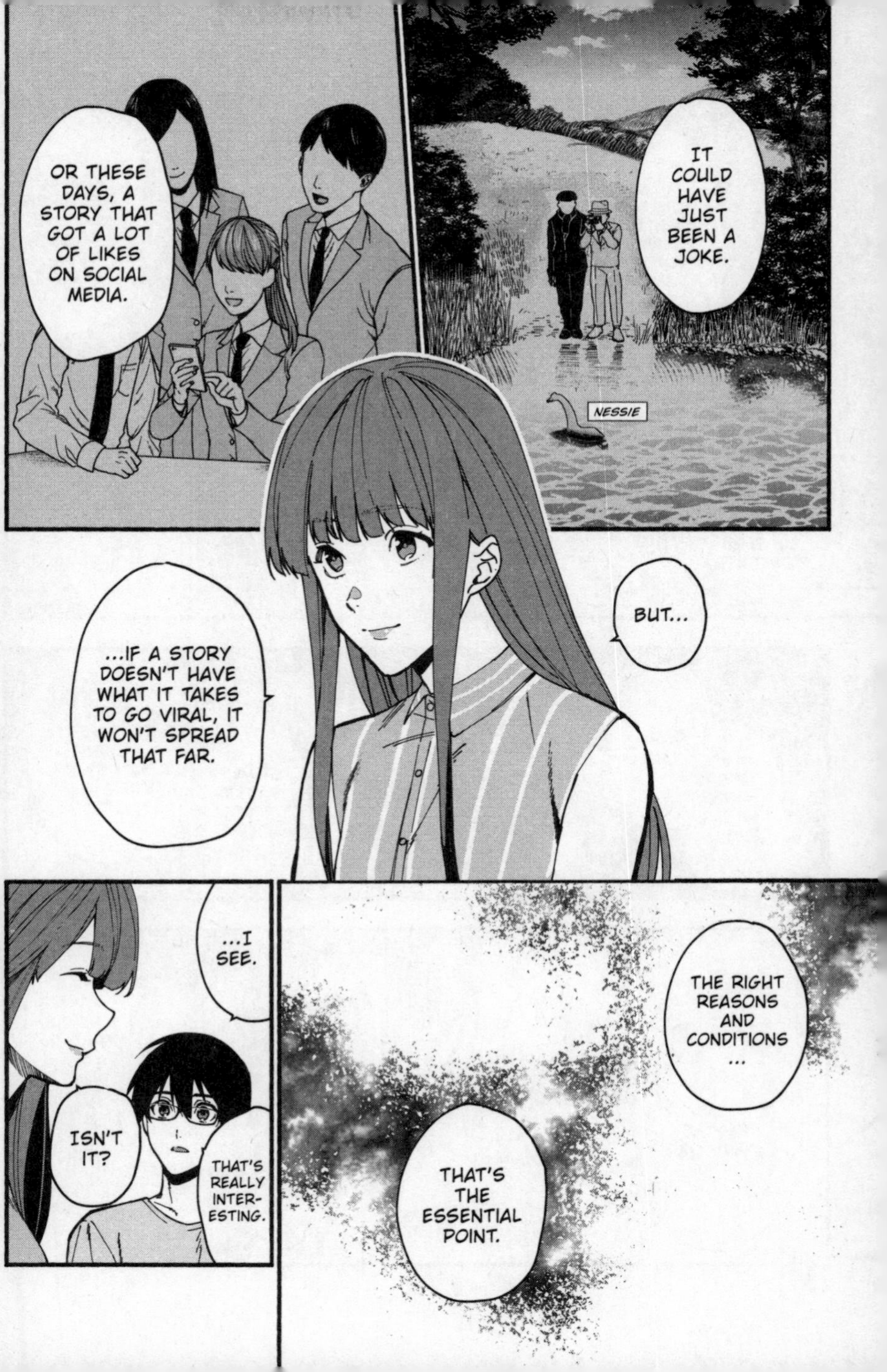
IT COULD HAVE JUST BEEN A JOKE.
NESSIE
OR THESE DAYS, A STORY THAT GOT A LOT OF LIKES ON SOCIAL MEDIA.
BUT...
...IF A STORY DOESN'T HAVE WHAT IT TAKES TO GO VIRAL, IT WON'T SPREAD THAT FAR.
THE RIGHT REASONS AND CONDITIONS ...
THAT'S THE ESSENTIAL POINT.
...I SEE.
THAT'S REALLY INTER-ESTING.
ISN'T IT?

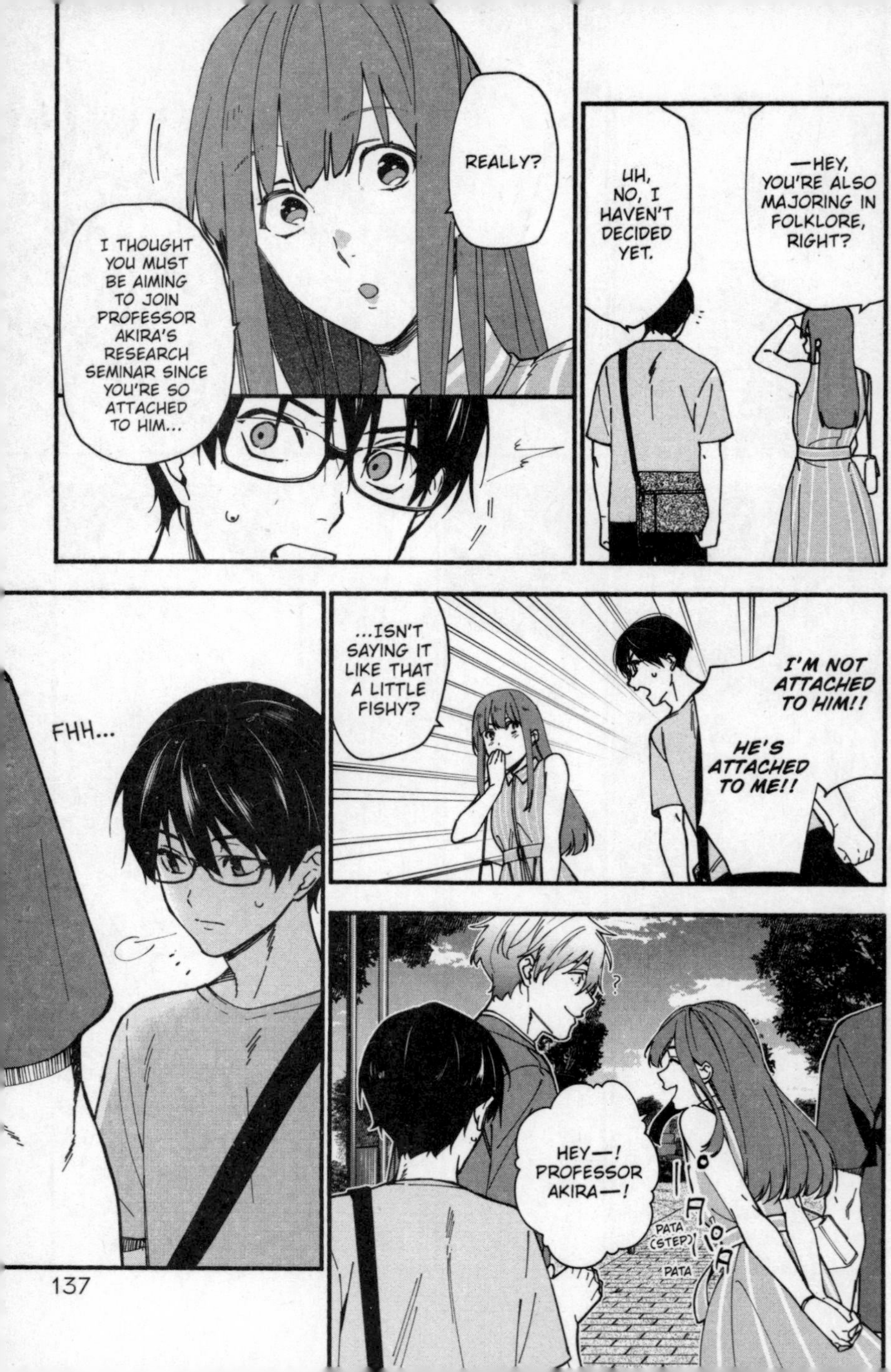
—HEY, YOU'RE ALSO MAJORING IN FOLKLORE, RIGHT?
UH, NO, I HAVEN'T DECIDED YET.
REALLY?
I THOUGHT YOU MUST BE AIMING TO JOIN PROFESSOR AKIRA'S RESEARCH SEMINAR SINCE YOU'RE SO ATTACHED TO HIM...
I'M NOT ATTACHED TO HIM!!
HE'S ATTACHED TO ME!!
...ISN'T SAYING IT LIKE THAT A LITTLE FISHY?
HEY—! PROFESSOR AKIRA—!
PATA (STEP)
PATA
FHH...

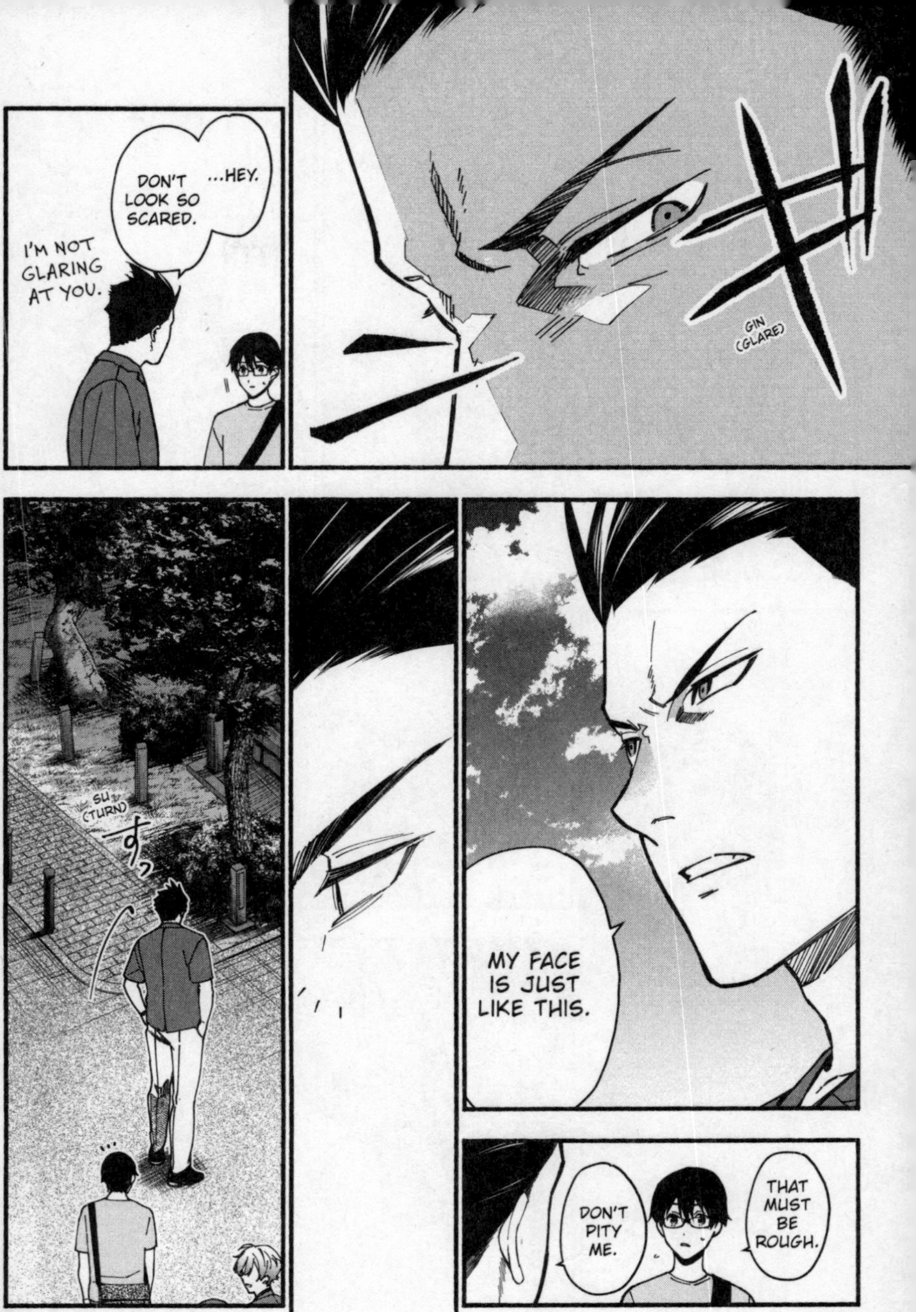
GIN (GLARE)
...HEY.
DON'T LOOK SO SCARED.
I'M NOT GLARING AT YOU.
MY FACE IS JUST LIKE THIS.
THAT MUST BE ROUGH.
DON'T PITY ME.
SU (TURN)
すっ

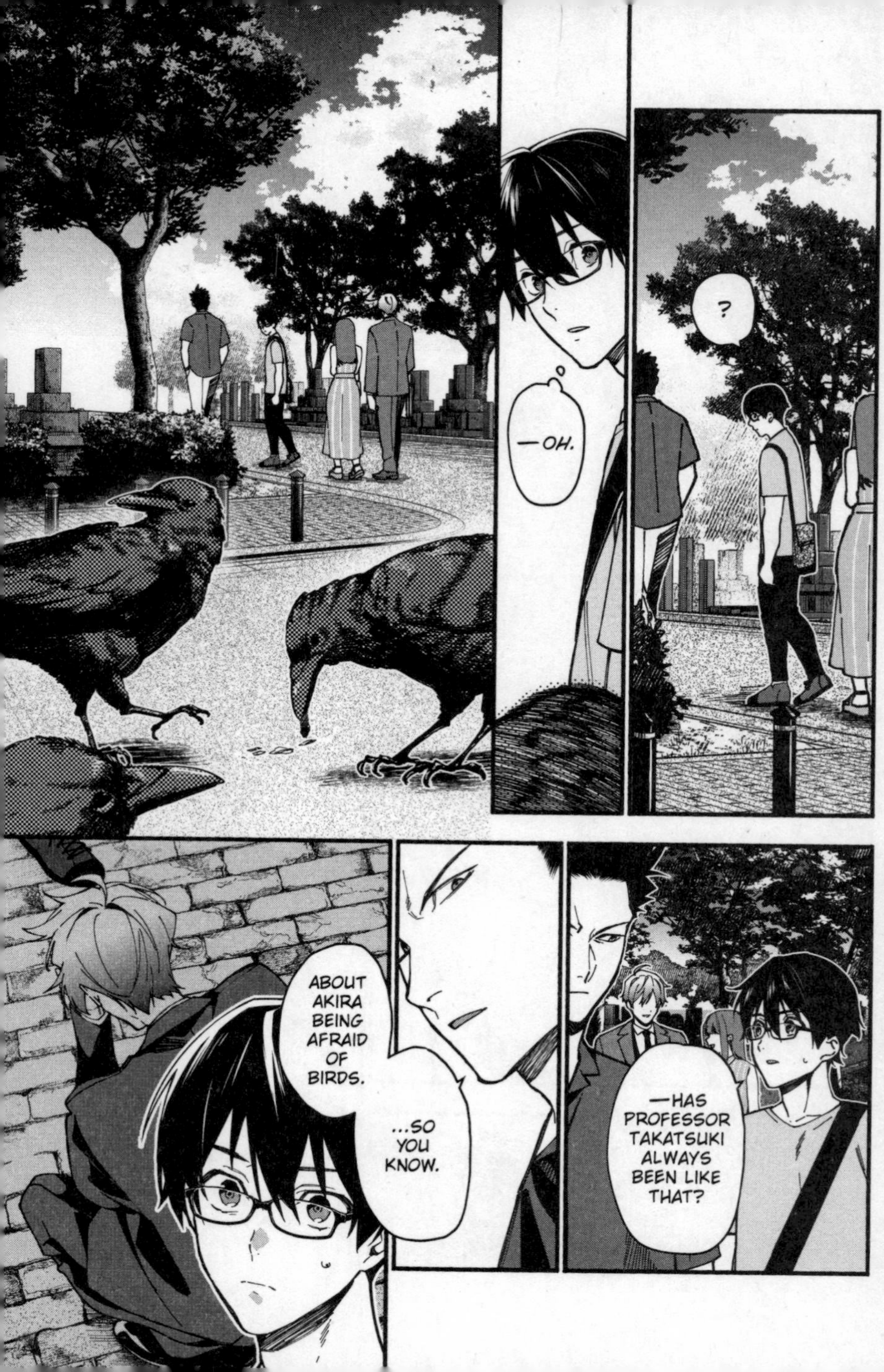
?
—OH.
—HAS PROFESSOR TAKATSUKI ALWAYS BEEN LIKE THAT?
...SO YOU KNOW.
ABOUT AKIRA BEING AFRAID OF BIRDS.

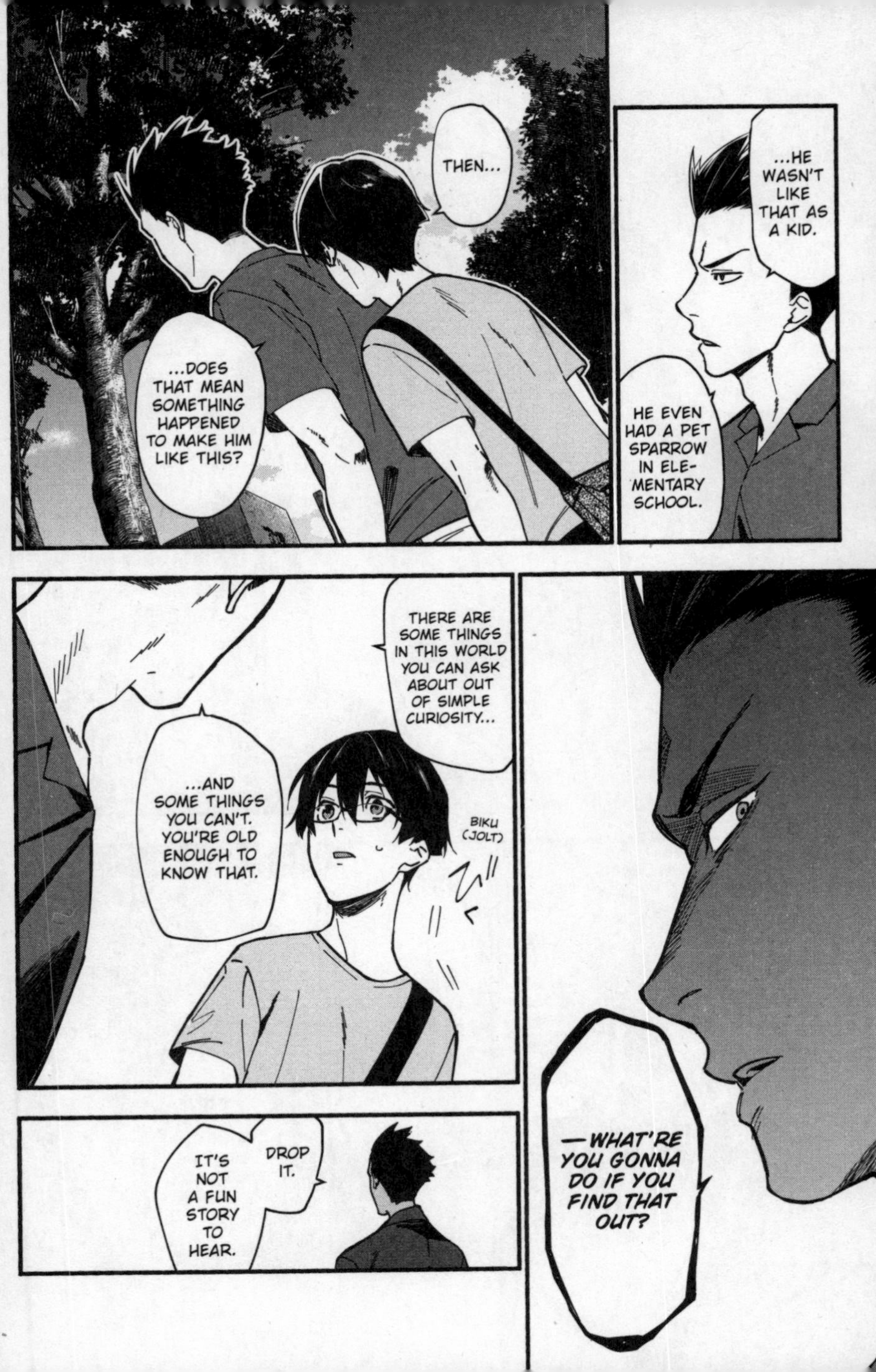
…HE WASN'T LIKE THAT AS A KID.
HE EVEN HAD A PET SPARROW IN ELE-MENTARY SCHOOL.
THEN…
…DOES THAT MEAN SOMETHING HAPPENED TO MAKE HIM LIKE THIS?
—WHAT'RE YOU GONNA DO IF YOU FIND THAT OUT?
THERE ARE SOME THINGS IN THIS WORLD YOU CAN ASK ABOUT OUT OF SIMPLE CURIOSITY…
…AND SOME THINGS YOU CAN'T. YOU'RE OLD ENOUGH TO KNOW THAT.
BIKU (JOLT)
DROP IT.
IT'S NOT A FUN STORY TO HEAR.

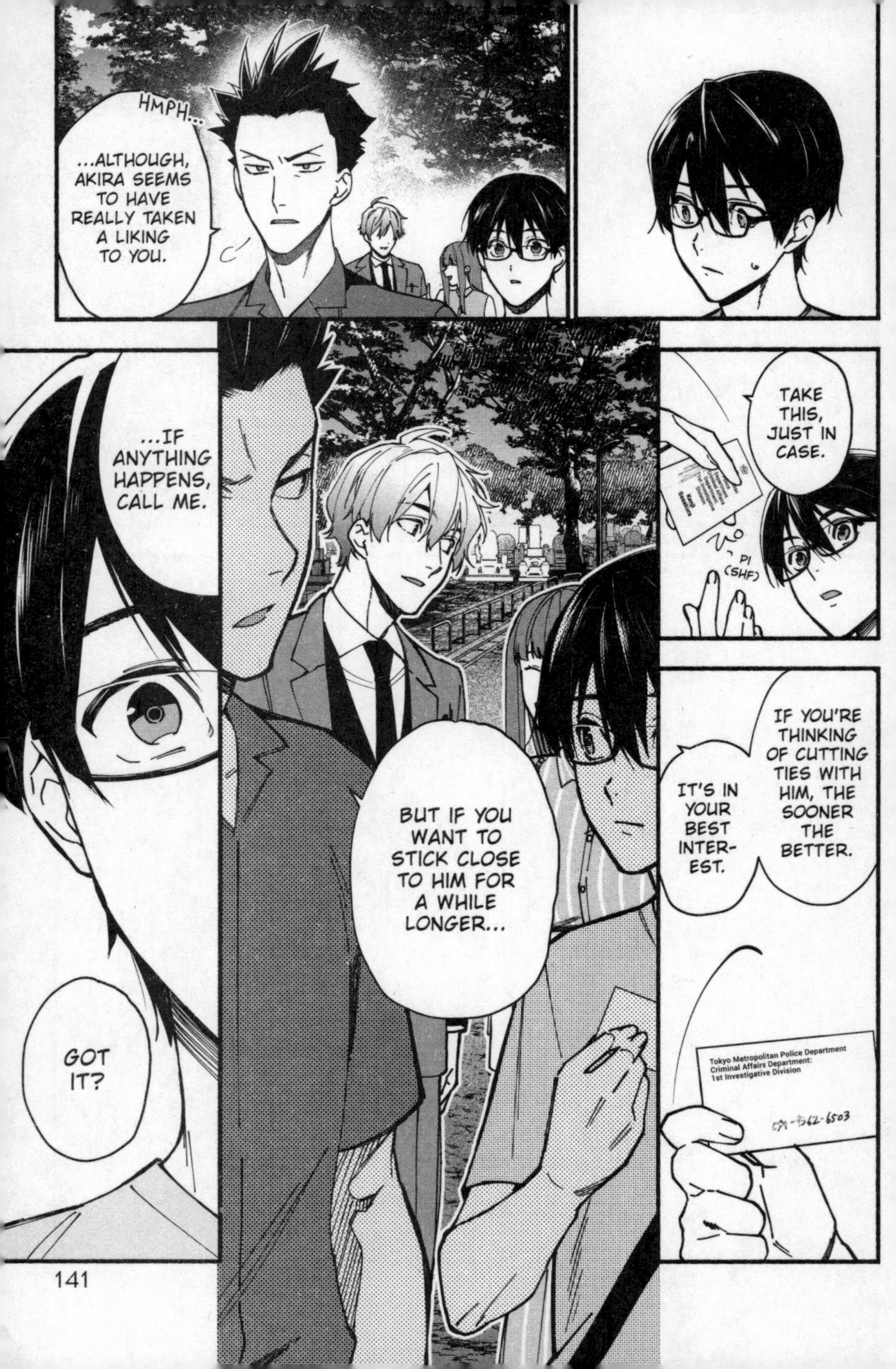
HMPH...
...ALTHOUGH, AKIRA SEEMS TO HAVE REALLY TAKEN A LIKING TO YOU.
TAKE THIS, JUST IN CASE.
PI (SHF)
IF YOU'RE THINKING OF CUTTING TIES WITH HIM, THE SOONER THE BETTER.
IT'S IN YOUR BEST INTER-EST.
Tokyo Metropolitan Police Department
Criminal Affairs Department:
1st Investigative Division
BUT IF YOU WANT TO STICK CLOSE TO HIM FOR A WHILE LONGER...
...IF ANYTHING HAPPENS, CALL ME.
GOT IT?

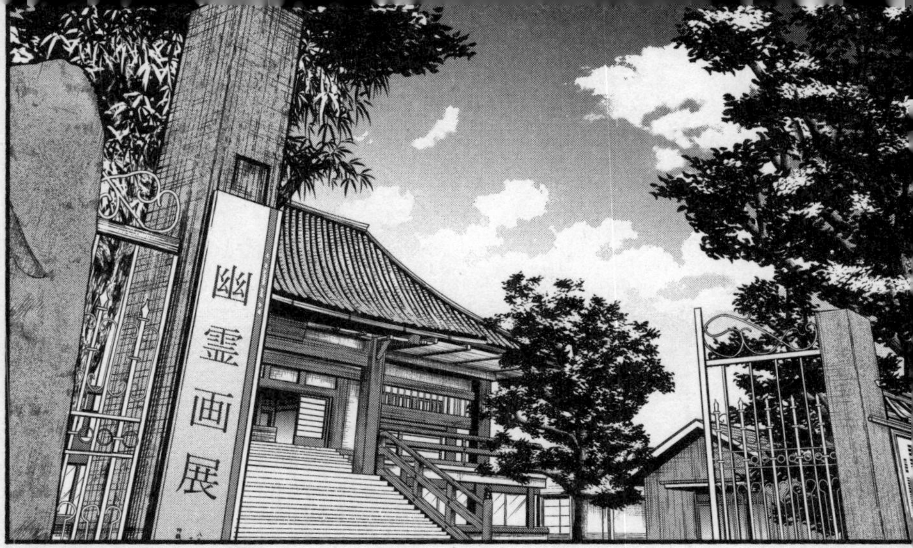
幽霊画展

SIGN: GHOST SCROLLS EXHIBITION

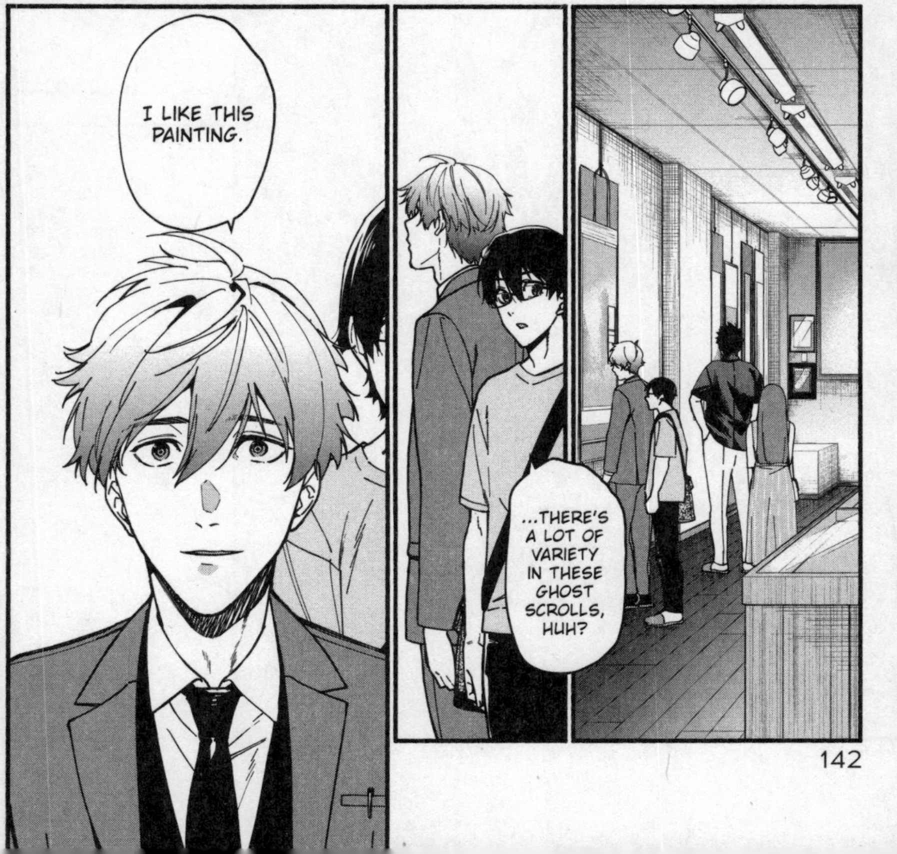
...THERE'S A LOT OF VARIETY IN THESE GHOST SCROLLS, HUH?
I LIKE THIS PAINTING.

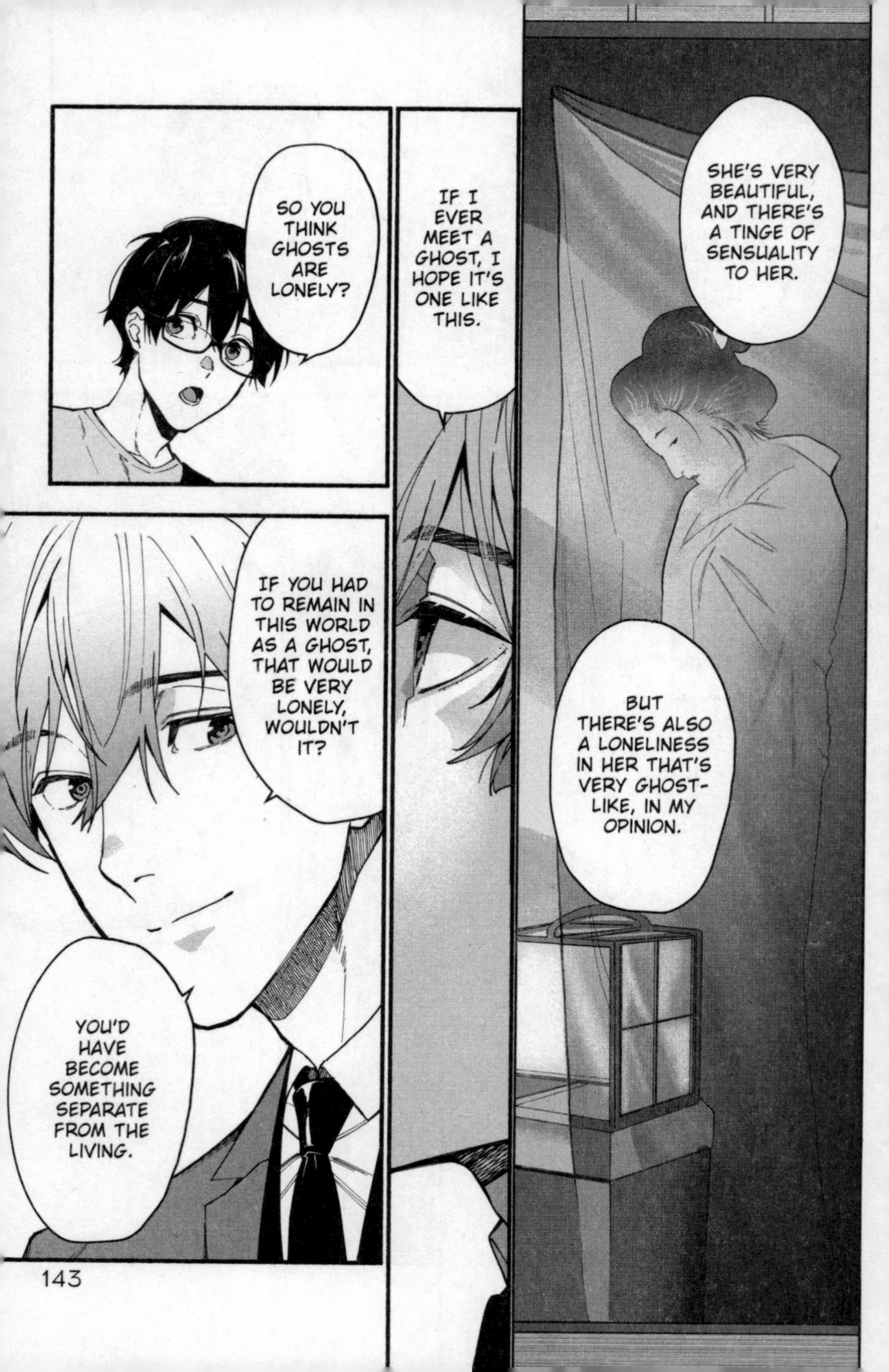
SHE'S VERY BEAUTIFUL, AND THERE'S A TINGE OF SENSUALITY TO HER.
BUT THERE'S ALSO A LONELINESS IN HER THAT'S VERY GHOST-LIKE, IN MY OPINION.
IF I EVER MEET A GHOST, I HOPE IT'S ONE LIKE THIS.
SO YOU THINK GHOSTS ARE LONELY?
IF YOU HAD TO REMAIN IN THIS WORLD AS A GHOST, THAT WOULD BE VERY LONELY, WOULDN'T IT?
YOU'D HAVE BECOME SOMETHING SEPARATE FROM THE LIVING.

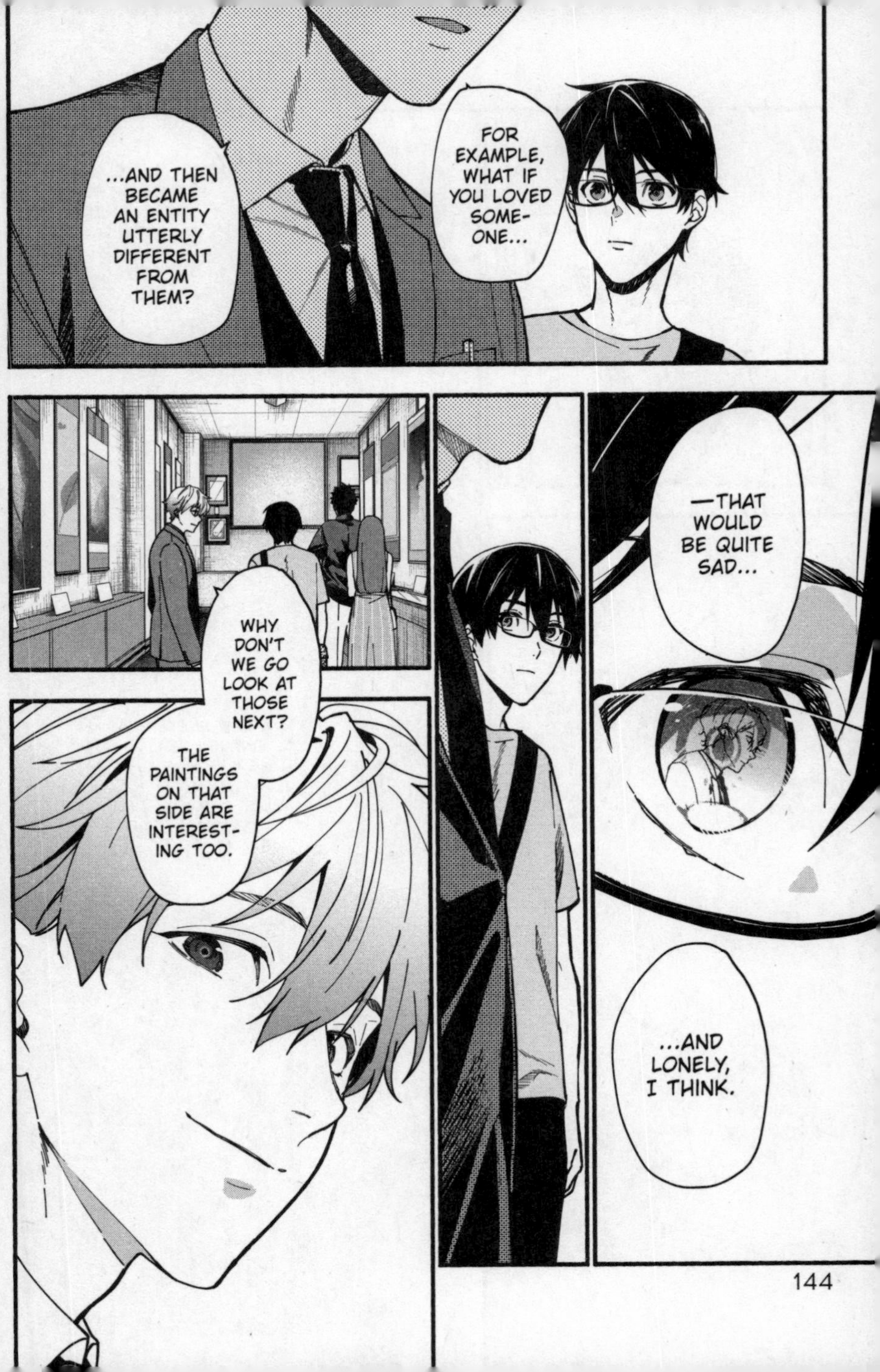
FOR EXAMPLE, WHAT IF YOU LOVED SOME-ONE...
...AND THEN BECAME AN ENTITY UTTERLY DIFFERENT FROM THEM?
—THAT WOULD BE QUITE SAD...
...AND LONELY, I THINK.
WHY DON'T WE GO LOOK AT THOSE NEXT?
THE PAINTINGS ON THAT SIDE ARE INTERESTING TOO.

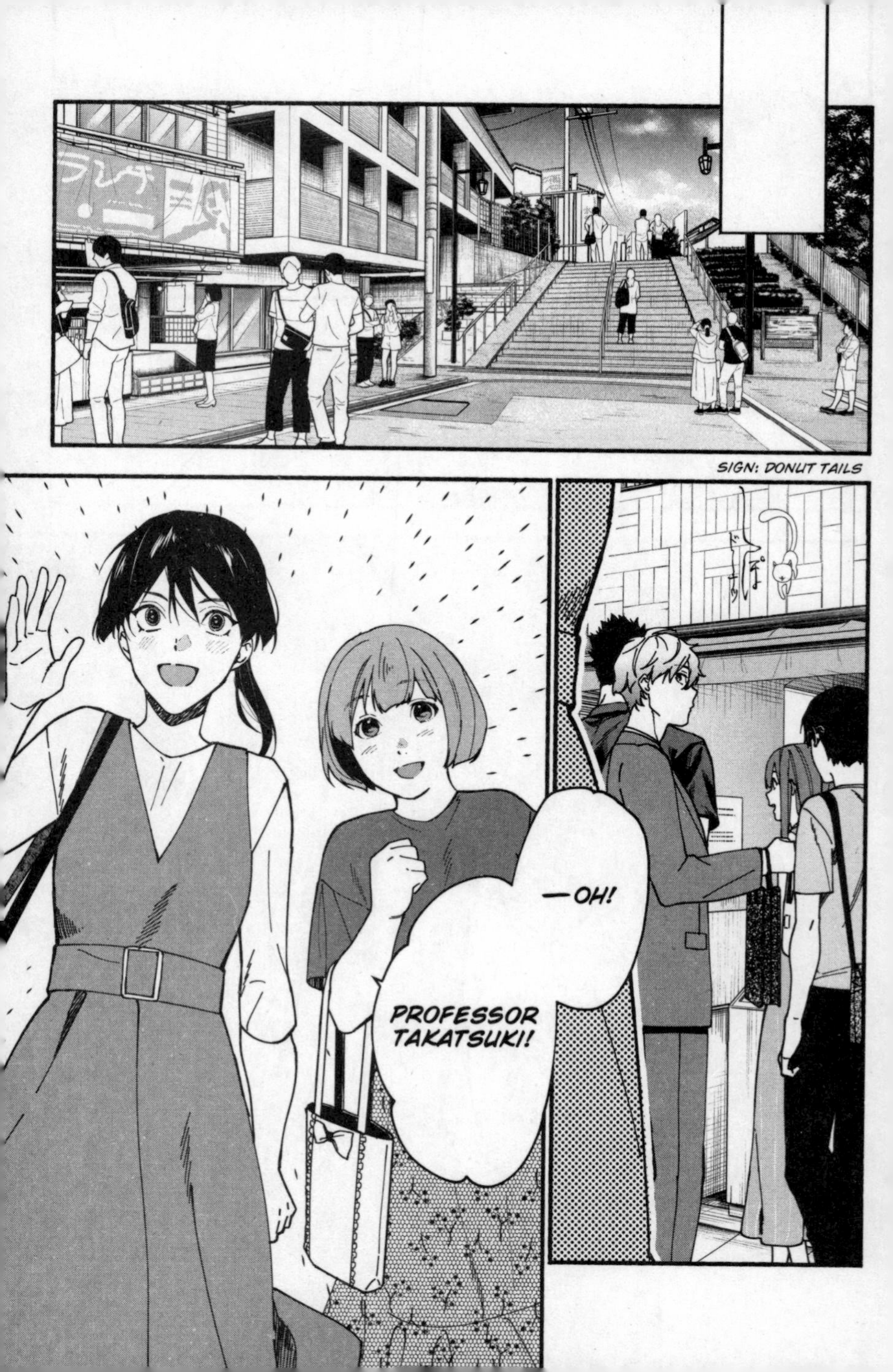
SIGN: DONUT TAILS
—OH!
PROFESSOR TAKATSUKI!

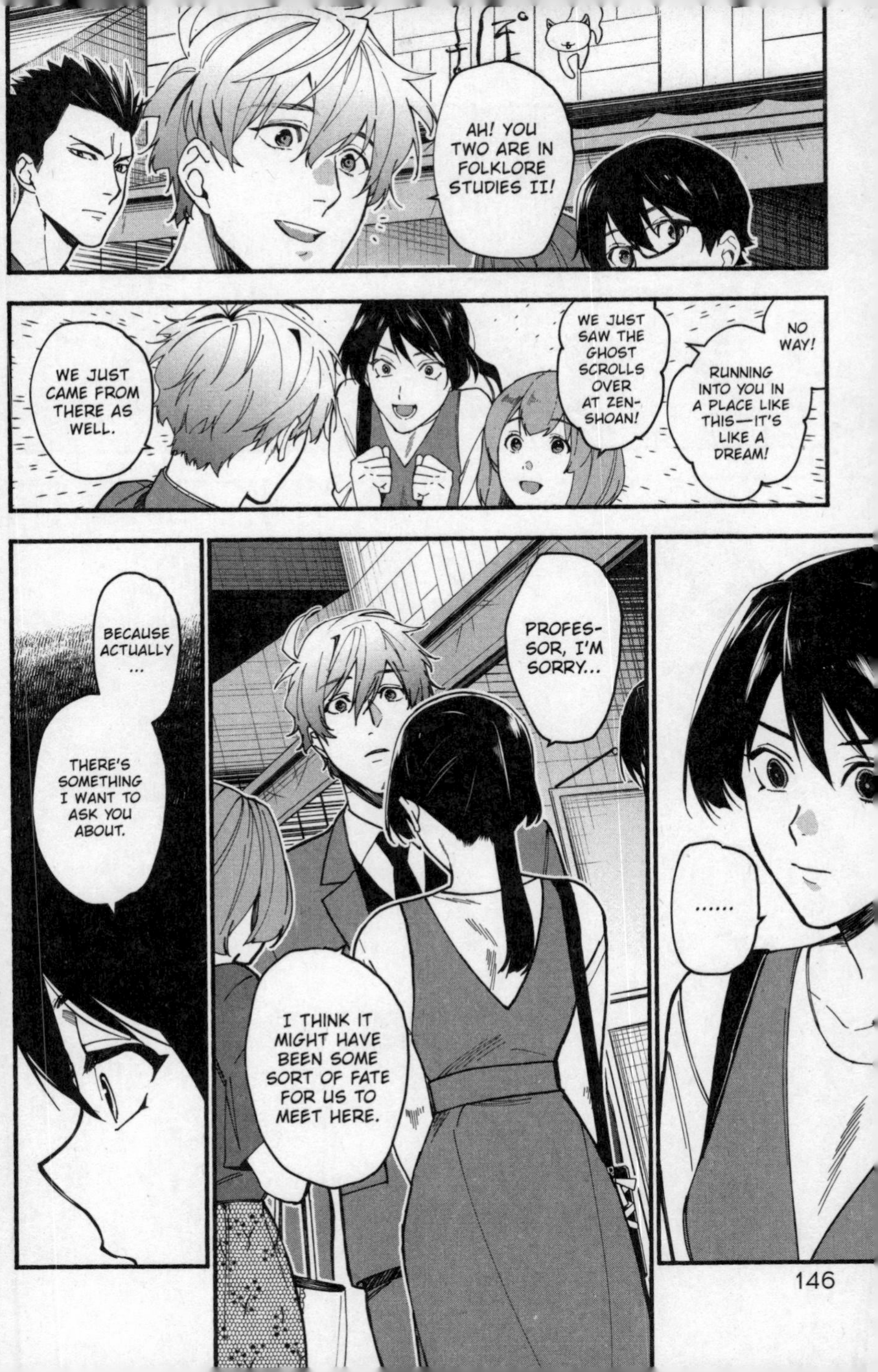
AH! YOU TWO ARE IN FOLKLORE STUDIES II!
NO WAY!
RUNNING INTO YOU IN A PLACE LIKE THIS—IT'S LIKE A DREAM!
WE JUST SAW THE GHOST SCROLLS OVER AT ZEN-SHOAN!
WE JUST CAME FROM THERE AS WELL.
......
PROFES-SOR, I'M SORRY...
I THINK IT MIGHT HAVE BEEN SOME SORT OF FATE FOR US TO MEET HERE.
BECAUSE ACTUALLY ...
THERE'S SOMETHING I WANT TO ASK YOU ABOUT.

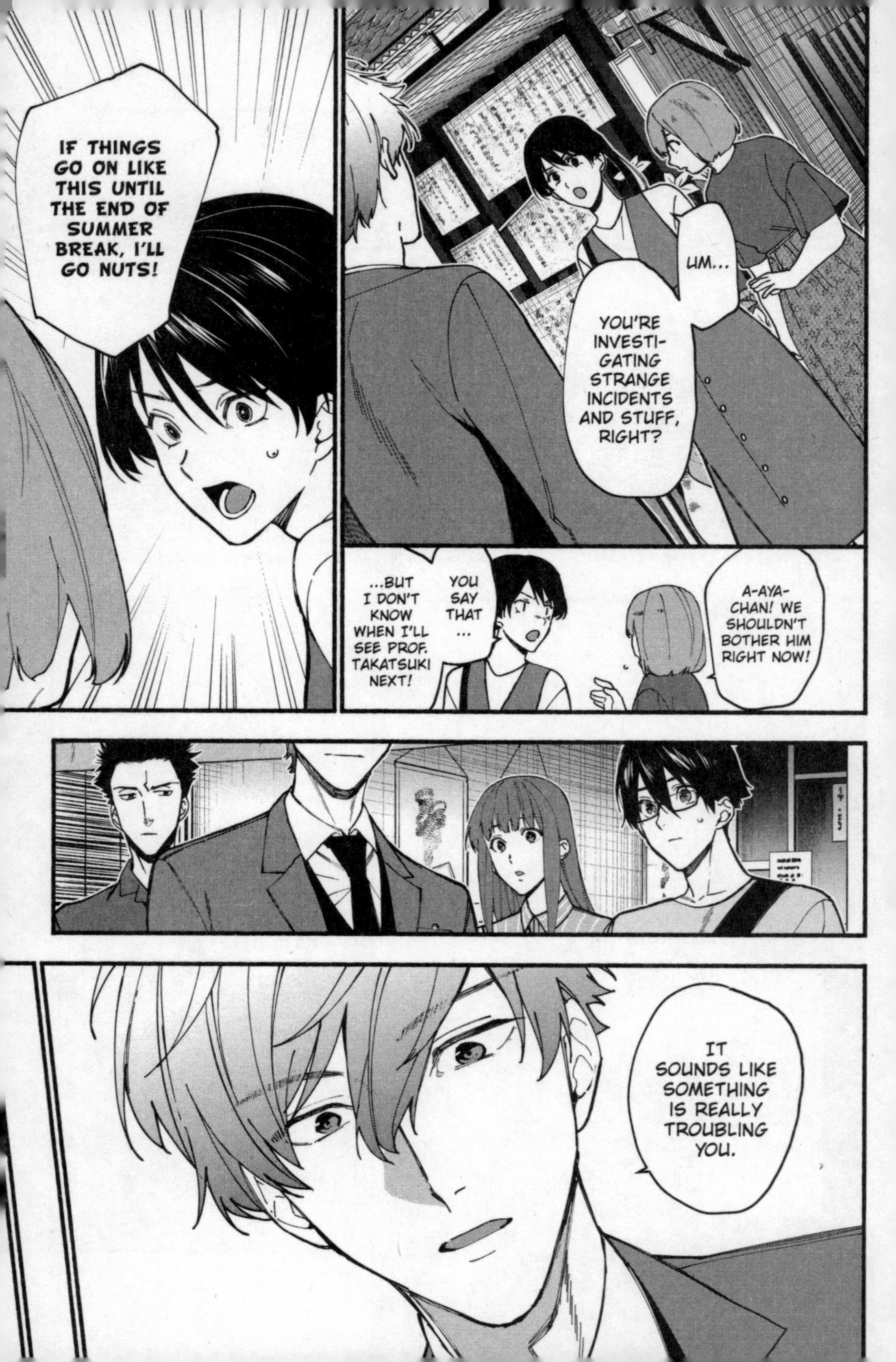
UM...
YOU'RE INVESTIGATING STRANGE INCIDENTS AND STUFF, RIGHT?
A-AYA-CHAN! WE SHOULDN'T BOTHER HIM RIGHT NOW!
YOU SAY THAT ...
...BUT I DON'T KNOW WHEN I'LL SEE PROF. TAKATSUKI NEXT!
IF THINGS GO ON LIKE THIS UNTIL THE END OF SUMMER BREAK, I'LL GO NUTS!
IT SOUNDS LIKE SOMETHING IS REALLY TROUBLING YOU.

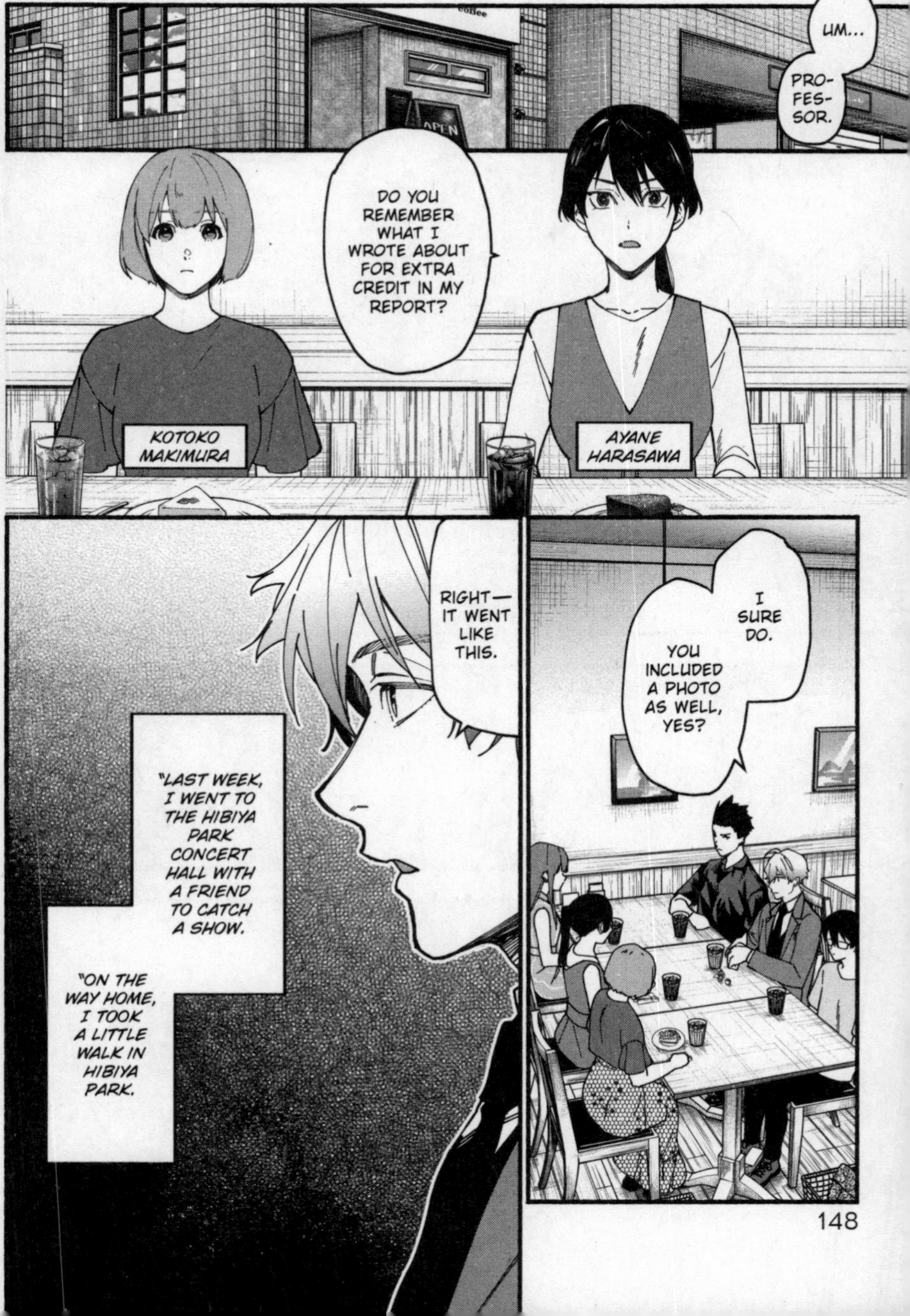
UM... PRO-FES-SOR.
DO YOU REMEMBER WHAT I WROTE ABOUT FOR EXTRA CREDIT IN MY REPORT?
AYANE HARASAWA
KOTOKO MAKIMURA
I SURE DO.
YOU INCLUDED A PHOTO AS WELL, YES?
RIGHT— IT WENT LIKE THIS.
"LAST WEEK, I WENT TO THE HIBIYA PARK CONCERT HALL WITH A FRIEND TO CATCH A SHOW.
"ON THE WAY HOME, I TOOK A LITTLE WALK IN HIBIYA PARK.

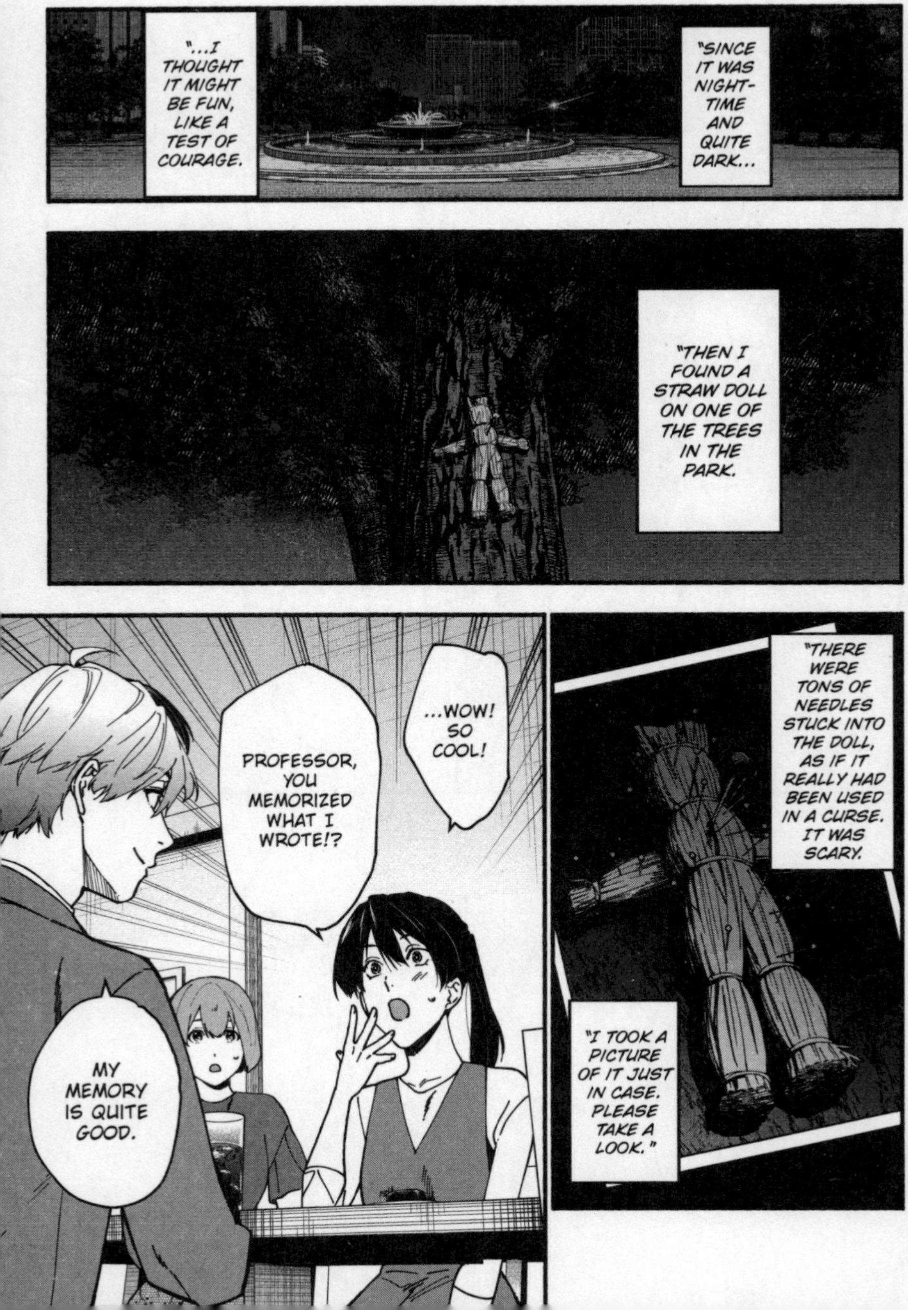
"SINCE IT WAS NIGHT-TIME AND QUITE DARK...
"...I THOUGHT IT MIGHT BE FUN, LIKE A TEST OF COURAGE.
"THEN I FOUND A STRAW DOLL ON ONE OF THE TREES IN THE PARK.
"THERE WERE TONS OF NEEDLES STUCK INTO THE DOLL, AS IF IT REALLY HAD BEEN USED IN A CURSE. IT WAS SCARY.
"I TOOK A PICTURE OF IT JUST IN CASE. PLEASE TAKE A LOOK."
...WOW! SO COOL!
PROFESSOR, YOU MEMORIZED WHAT I WROTE!?
MY MEMORY IS QUITE GOOD.

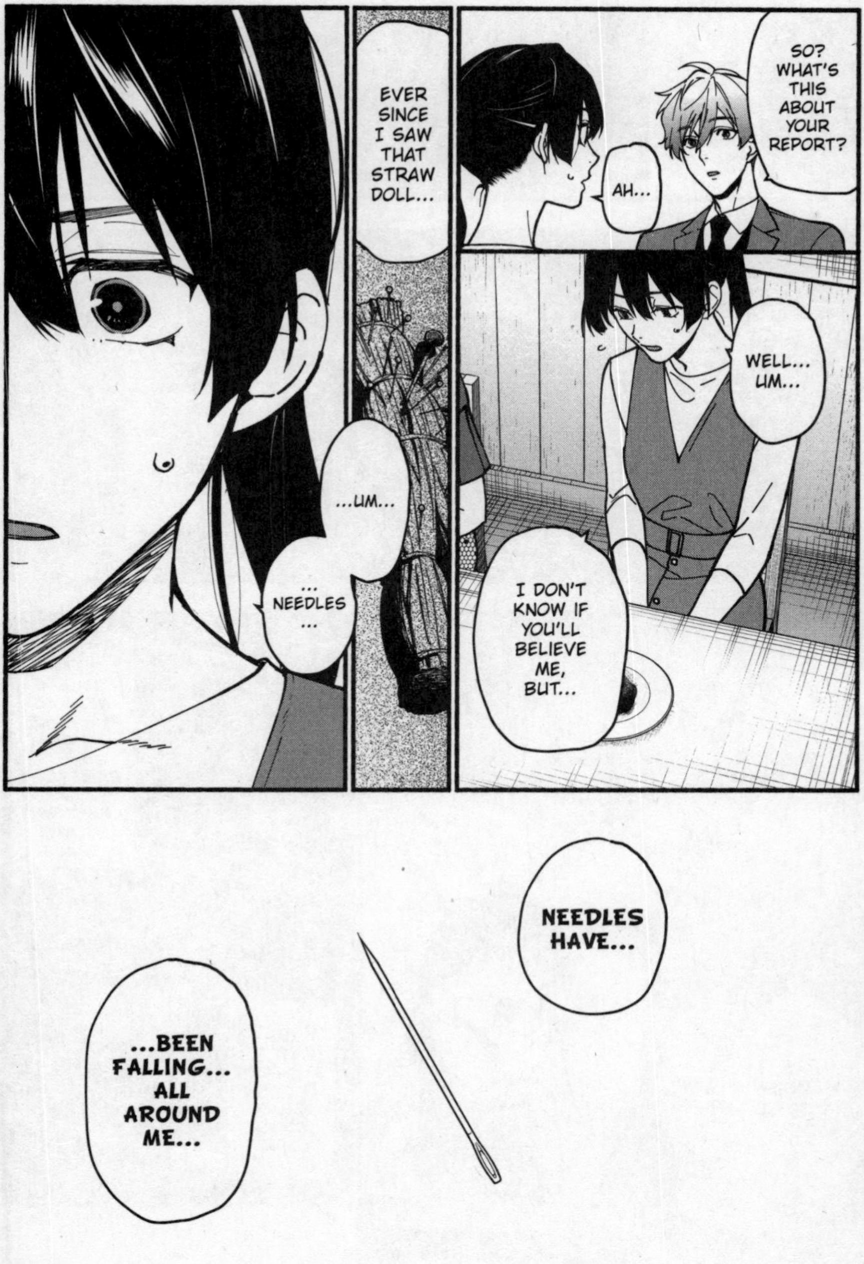
SO? WHAT'S THIS ABOUT YOUR REPORT?
AH...
WELL... UM...
I DON'T KNOW IF YOU'LL BELIEVE ME, BUT...
EVER SINCE I SAW THAT STRAW DOLL...
...UM...
... NEEDLES ...
NEEDLES HAVE...
...BEEN FALLING... ALL AROUND ME...

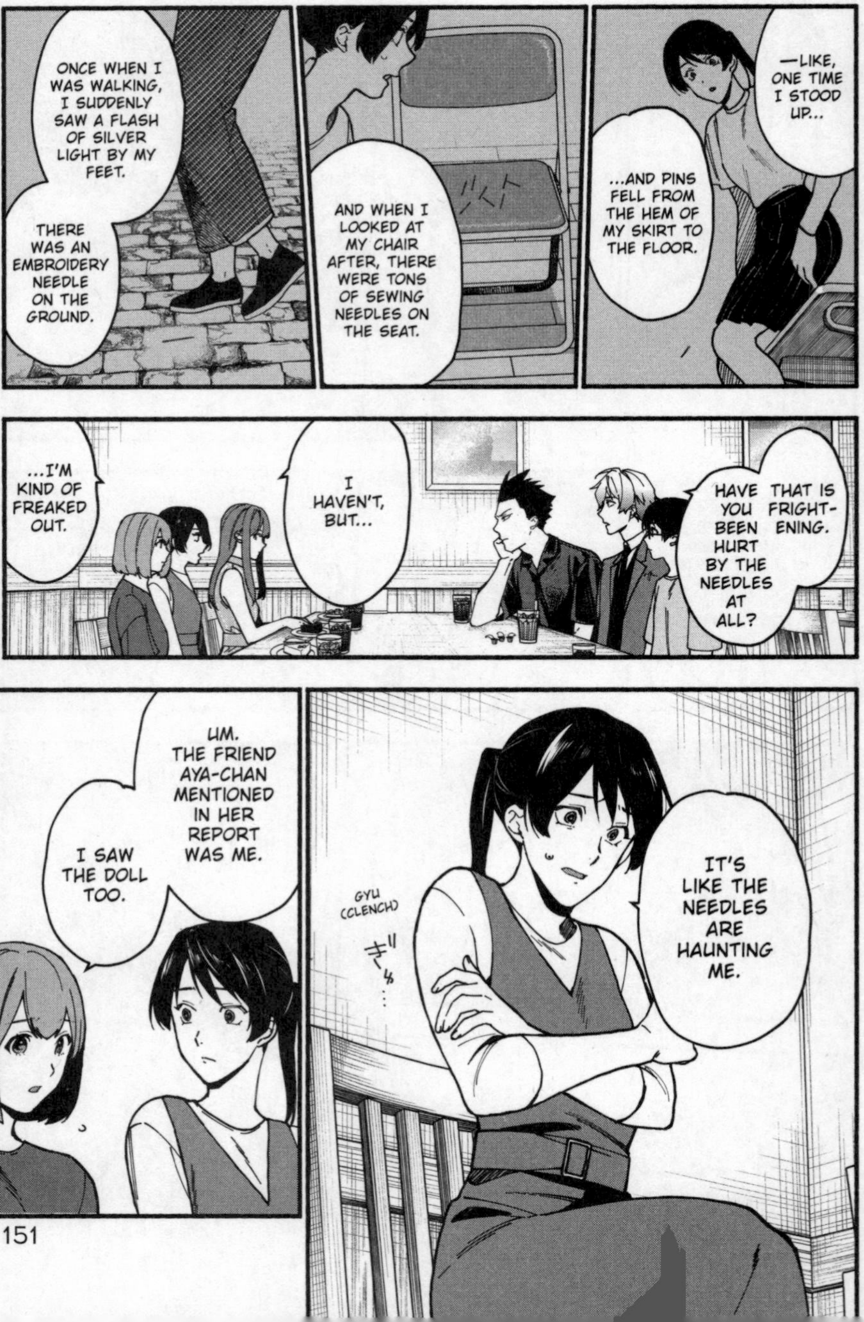
—LIKE, ONE TIME I STOOD UP...
...AND PINS FELL FROM THE HEM OF MY SKIRT TO THE FLOOR.
AND WHEN I LOOKED AT MY CHAIR AFTER, THERE WERE TONS OF SEWING NEEDLES ON THE SEAT.
ONCE WHEN I WAS WALKING, I SUDDENLY SAW A FLASH OF SILVER LIGHT BY MY FEET.
THERE WAS AN EMBROIDERY NEEDLE ON THE GROUND.
THAT IS FRIGHTENING.
HAVE YOU BEEN HURT BY THE NEEDLES AT ALL?
I HAVEN'T, BUT...
...I'M KIND OF FREAKED OUT.
IT'S LIKE THE NEEDLES ARE HAUNTING ME.
GYU (CLENCH)
UM. THE FRIEND AYA-CHAN MENTIONED IN HER REPORT WAS ME.
I SAW THE DOLL TOO.

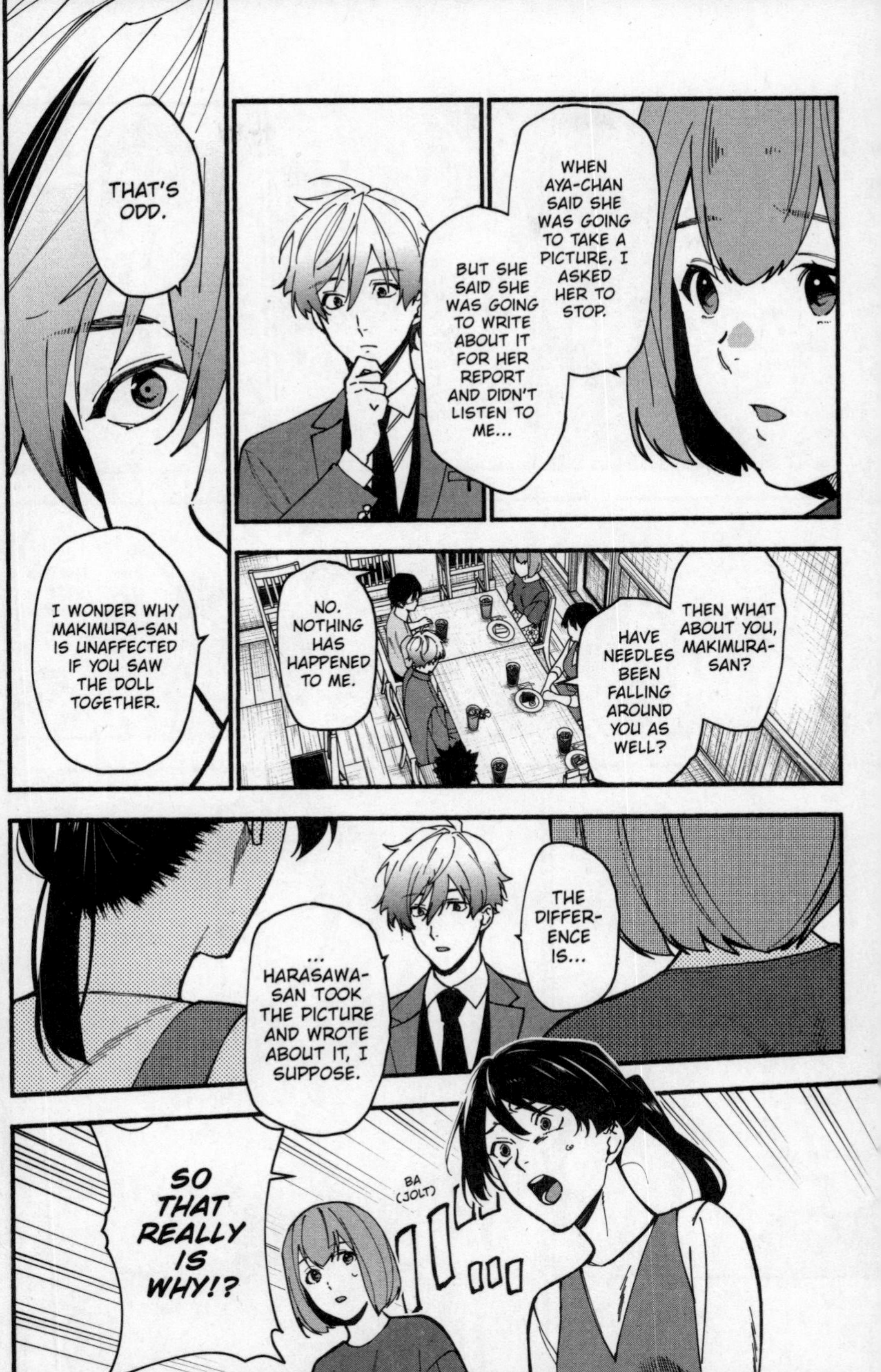
WHEN AYA-CHAN SAID SHE WAS GOING TO TAKE A PICTURE, I ASKED HER TO STOP.
BUT SHE SAID SHE WAS GOING TO WRITE ABOUT IT FOR HER REPORT AND DIDN'T LISTEN TO ME...
THEN WHAT ABOUT YOU, MAKIMURA-SAN?
HAVE NEEDLES BEEN FALLING AROUND YOU AS WELL?
NO. NOTHING HAS HAPPENED TO ME.
THAT'S ODD.
I WONDER WHY MAKIMURA-SAN IS UNAFFECTED IF YOU SAW THE DOLL TOGETHER.
THE DIFFERENCE IS...
...HARASAWA-SAN TOOK THE PICTURE AND WROTE ABOUT IT, I SUPPOSE.
BA (JOLT)
SO THAT REALLY IS WHY!?

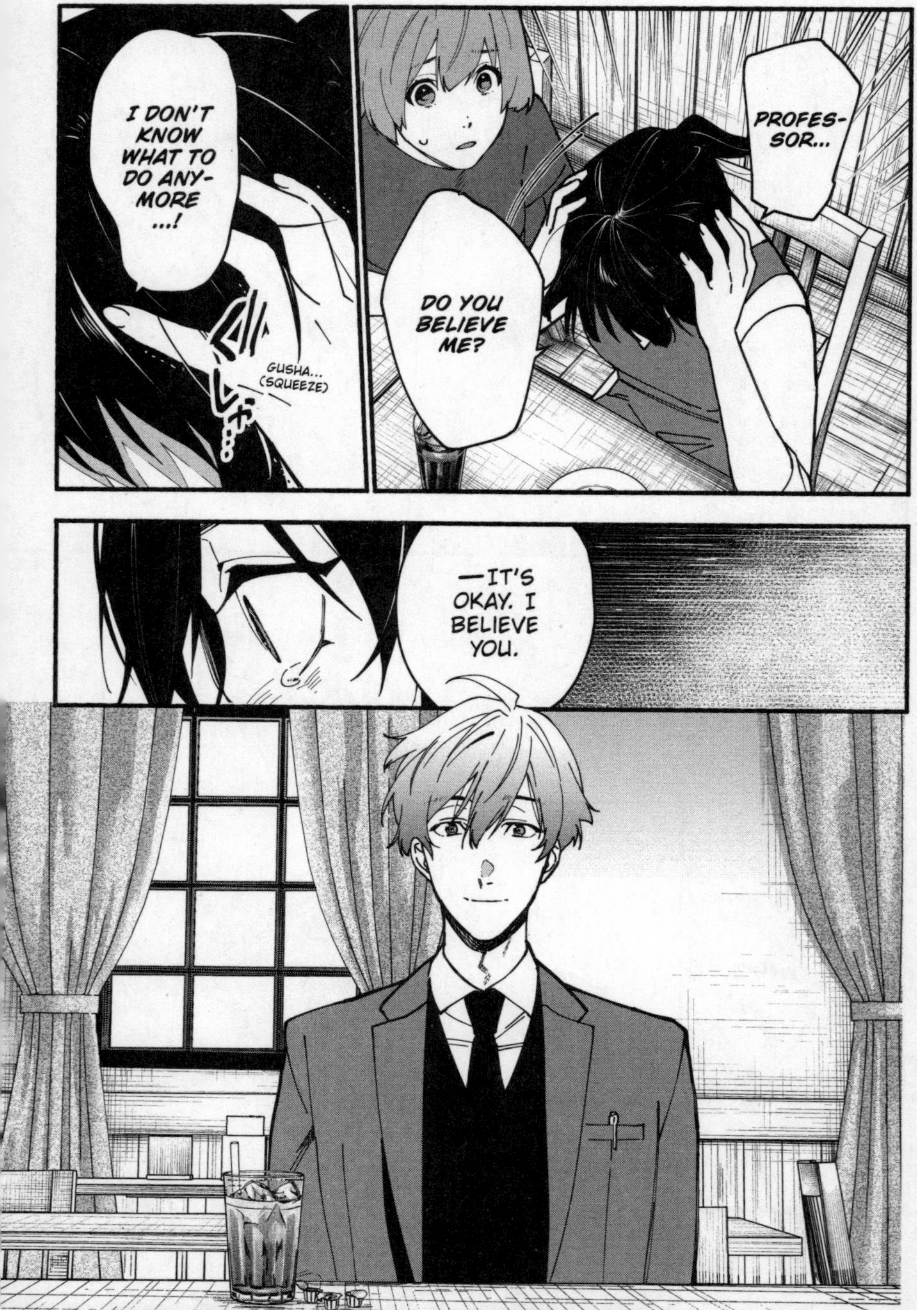
PROFES-SOR...
DO YOU BELIEVE ME?
I DON'T KNOW WHAT TO DO ANY-MORE ...!
GUSHA... (SQUEEZE)
—IT'S OKAY. I BELIEVE YOU.

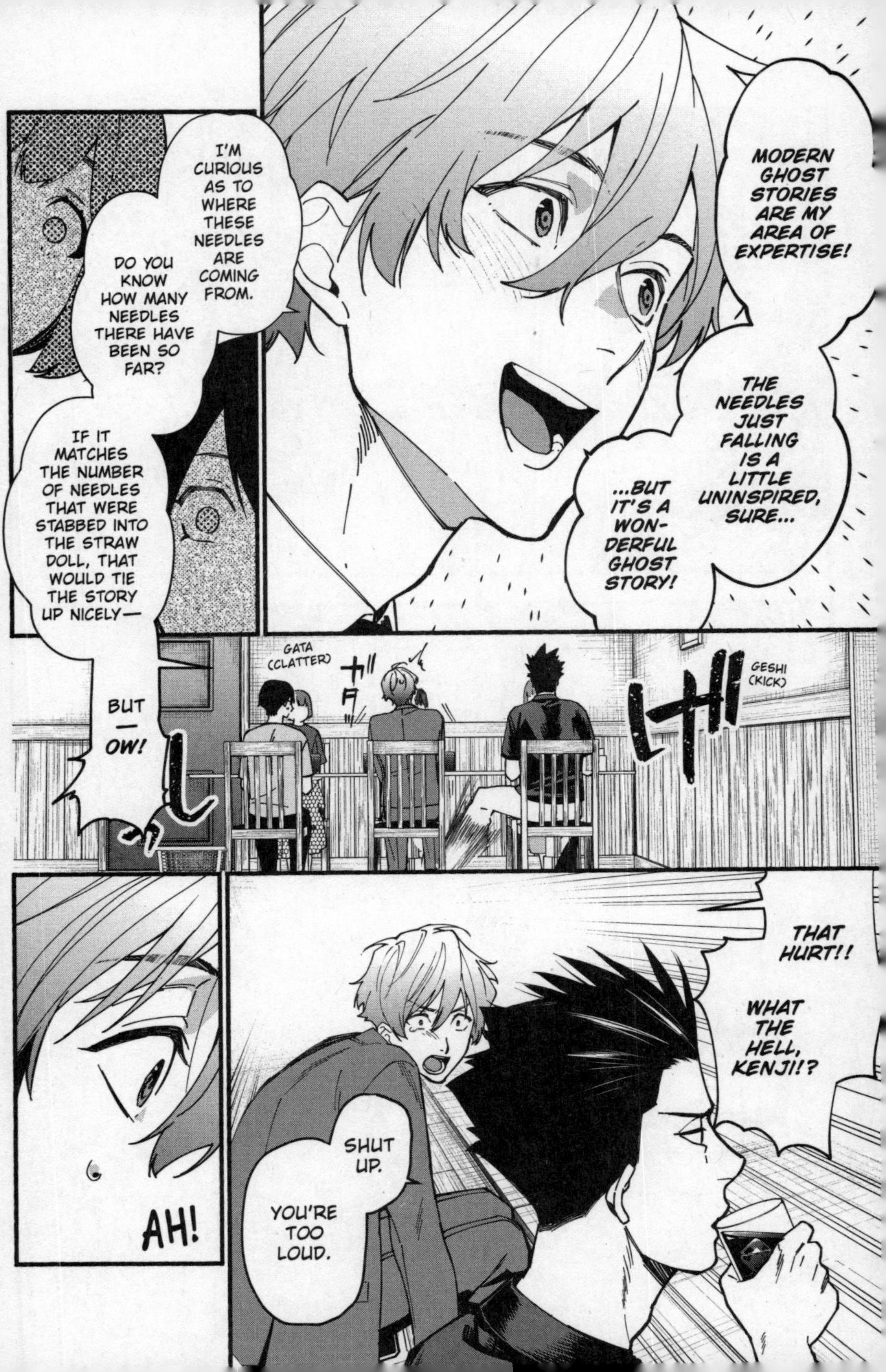

MODERN GHOST STORIES ARE MY AREA OF EXPERTISE!
THE NEEDLES JUST FALLING IS A LITTLE UNINSPIRED, SURE...
...BUT IT'S A WON-DERFUL GHOST STORY!
I'M CURIOUS AS TO WHERE THESE NEEDLES ARE COMING FROM.
DO YOU KNOW HOW MANY NEEDLES THERE HAVE BEEN SO FAR?
IF IT MATCHES THE NUMBER OF NEEDLES THAT WERE STABBED INTO THE STRAW DOLL, THAT WOULD TIE THE STORY UP NICELY—
GESHI (KICK)
ゲシ
GATA (CLATTER)
ガタ
BUT — OW!
THAT HURT!!
WHAT THE HELL, KENJI!?
SHUT UP.
YOU'RE TOO LOUD.
AH!

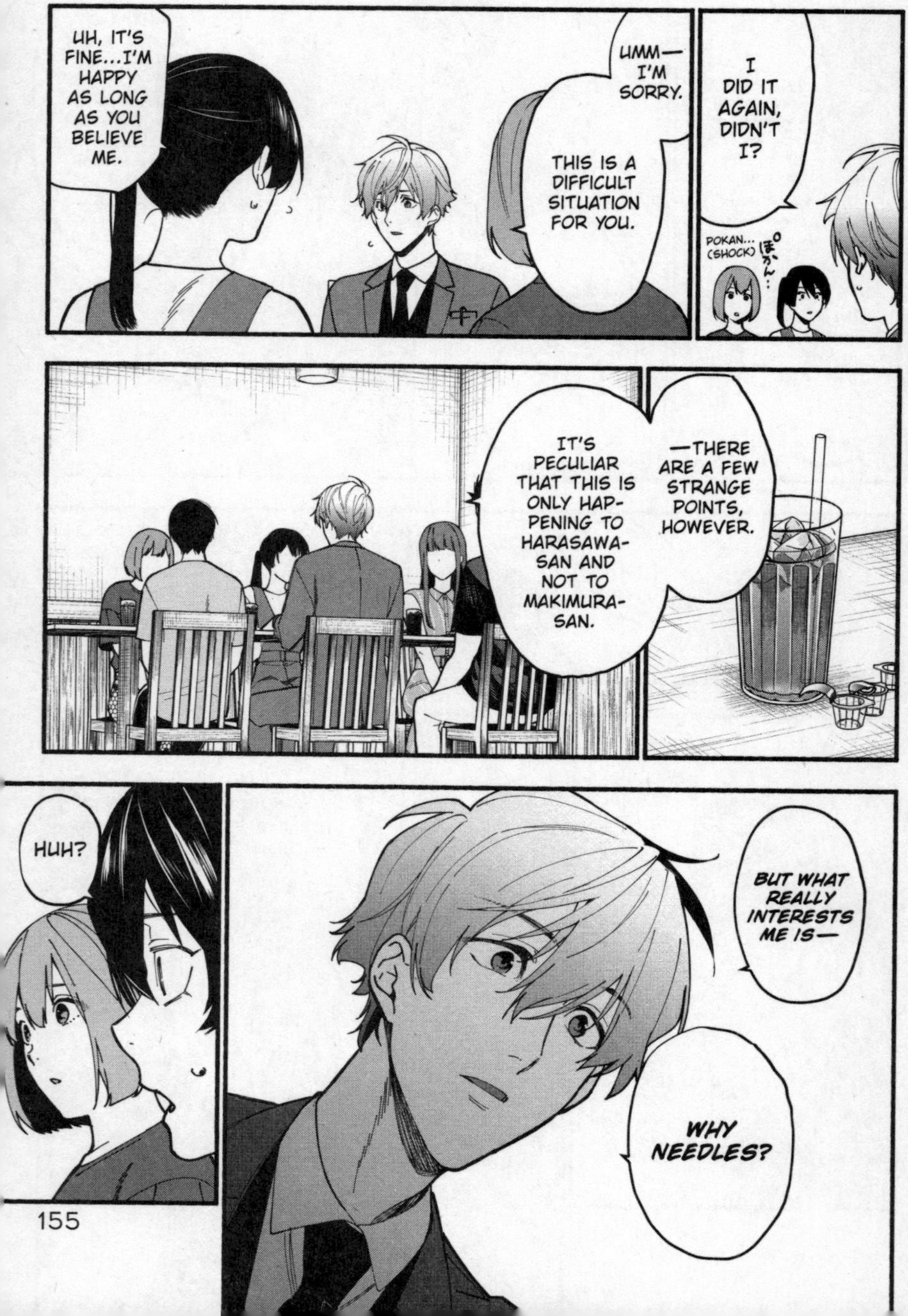
I DID IT AGAIN, DIDN'T I?
POKAN... (SHOCK)
ぽかん…
UMM— I'M SORRY.
THIS IS A DIFFICULT SITUATION FOR YOU.
UH, IT'S FINE...I'M HAPPY AS LONG AS YOU BELIEVE ME.
—THERE ARE A FEW STRANGE POINTS, HOWEVER.
IT'S PECULIAR THAT THIS IS ONLY HAP-PENING TO HARASAWA-SAN AND NOT TO MAKIMURA-SAN.
BUT WHAT REALLY INTERESTS ME IS—
WHY NEEDLES?
HUH?

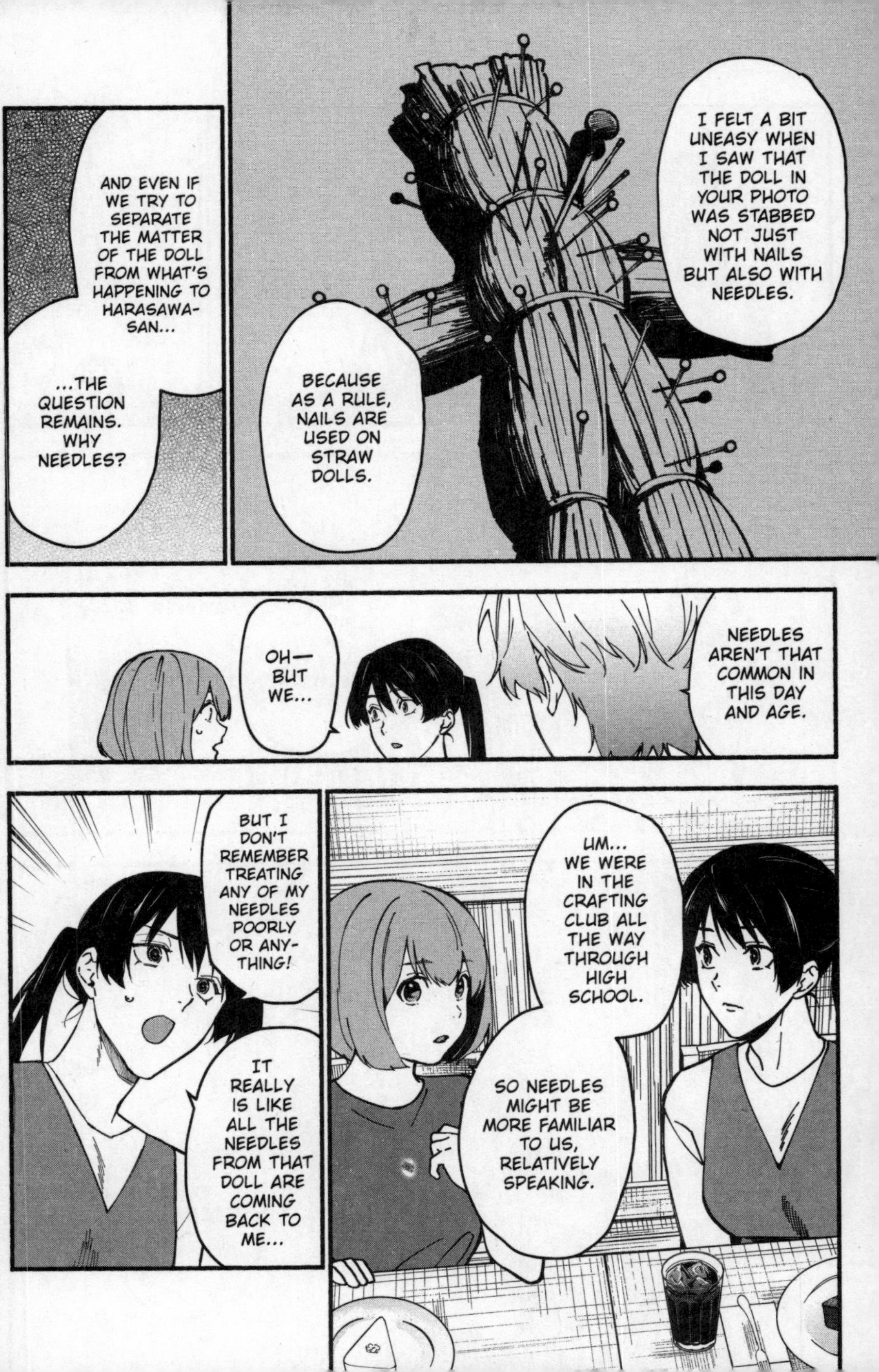
I FELT A BIT UNEASY WHEN I SAW THAT THE DOLL IN YOUR PHOTO WAS STABBED NOT JUST WITH NAILS BUT ALSO WITH NEEDLES.
BECAUSE AS A RULE, NAILS ARE USED ON STRAW DOLLS.
AND EVEN IF WE TRY TO SEPARATE THE MATTER OF THE DOLL FROM WHAT'S HAPPENING TO HARASAWA-SAN...
...THE QUESTION REMAINS. WHY NEEDLES?
NEEDLES AREN'T THAT COMMON IN THIS DAY AND AGE.
OH— BUT WE...
UM... WE WERE IN THE CRAFTING CLUB ALL THE WAY THROUGH HIGH SCHOOL.
SO NEEDLES MIGHT BE MORE FAMILIAR TO US, RELATIVELY SPEAKING.
BUT I DON'T REMEMBER TREATING ANY OF MY NEEDLES POORLY OR ANY-THING!
IT REALLY IS LIKE ALL THE NEEDLES FROM THAT DOLL ARE COMING BACK TO ME...

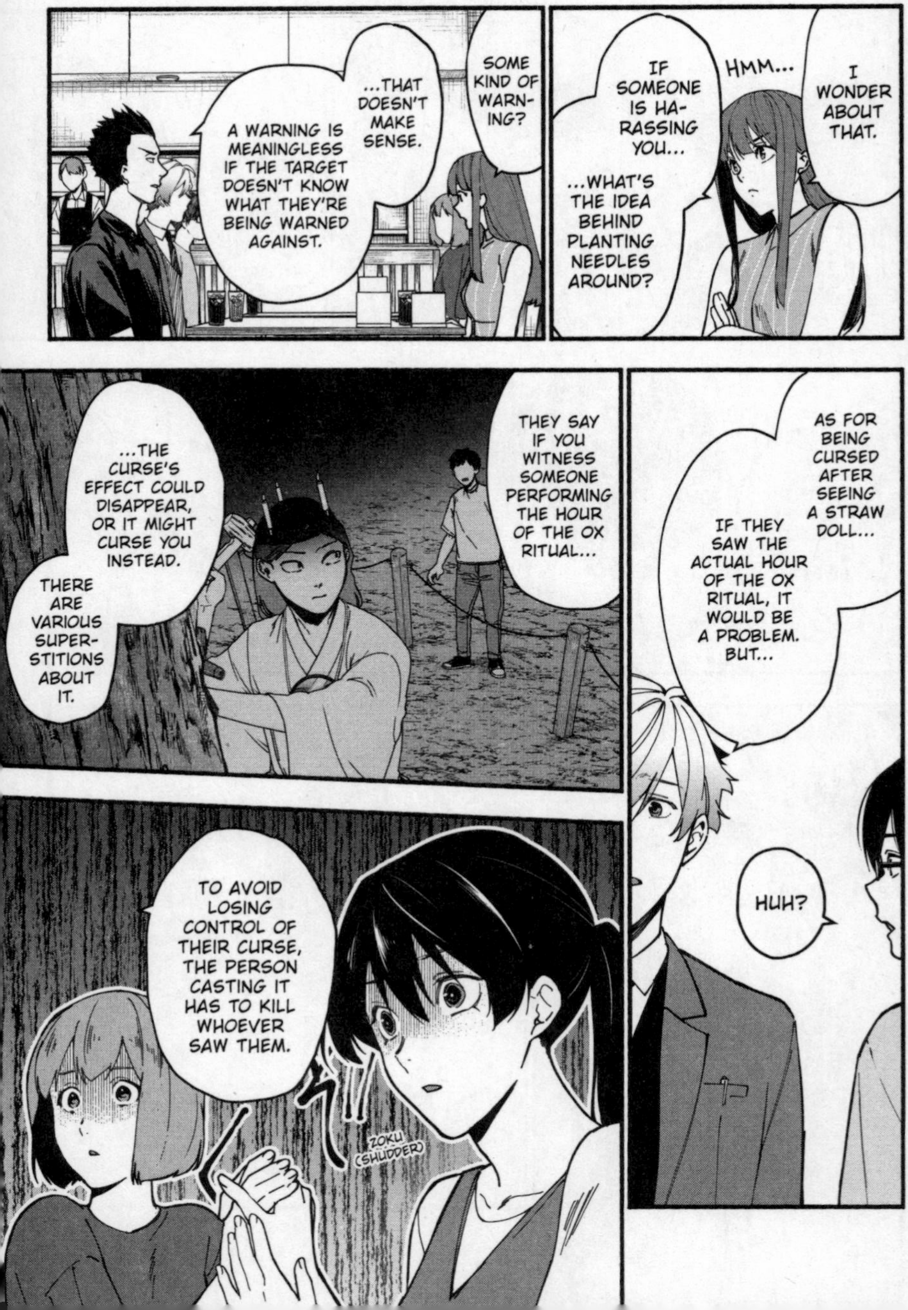
I WONDER ABOUT THAT.
HMM...
IF SOMEONE IS HA-RASSING YOU...
...WHAT'S THE IDEA BEHIND PLANTING NEEDLES AROUND?
SOME KIND OF WARN-ING?
...THAT DOESN'T MAKE SENSE.
A WARNING IS MEANINGLESS IF THE TARGET DOESN'T KNOW WHAT THEY'RE BEING WARNED AGAINST.
AS FOR BEING CURSED AFTER SEEING A STRAW DOLL...
IF THEY SAW THE ACTUAL HOUR OF THE OX RITUAL, IT WOULD BE A PROBLEM. BUT...
HUH?
THEY SAY IF YOU WITNESS SOMEONE PERFORMING THE HOUR OF THE OX RITUAL...
...THE CURSE'S EFFECT COULD DISAPPEAR, OR IT MIGHT CURSE YOU INSTEAD.
THERE ARE VARIOUS SUPER-STITIONS ABOUT IT.
TO AVOID LOSING CONTROL OF THEIR CURSE, THE PERSON CASTING IT HAS TO KILL WHOEVER SAW THEM.
ZOKU (SHUDDER)

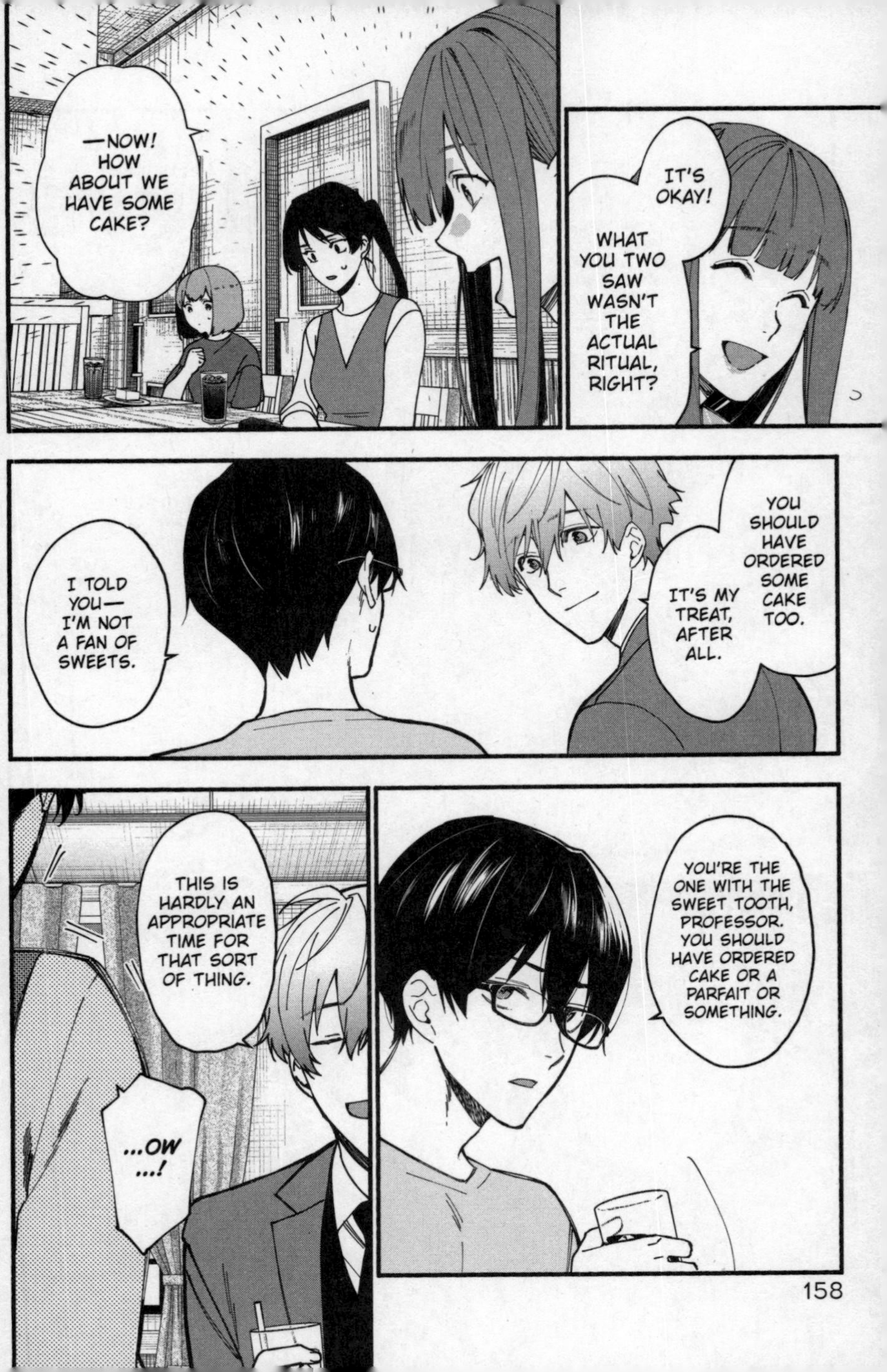
IT'S OKAY!
WHAT YOU TWO SAW WASN'T THE ACTUAL RITUAL, RIGHT?
—NOW! HOW ABOUT WE HAVE SOME CAKE?
YOU SHOULD HAVE ORDERED SOME CAKE TOO.
IT'S MY TREAT, AFTER ALL.
I TOLD YOU— I'M NOT A FAN OF SWEETS.
YOU'RE THE ONE WITH THE SWEET TOOTH, PROFESSOR. YOU SHOULD HAVE ORDERED CAKE OR A PARFAIT OR SOMETHING.
THIS IS HARDLY AN APPROPRIATE TIME FOR THAT SORT OF THING.
...OW ...!

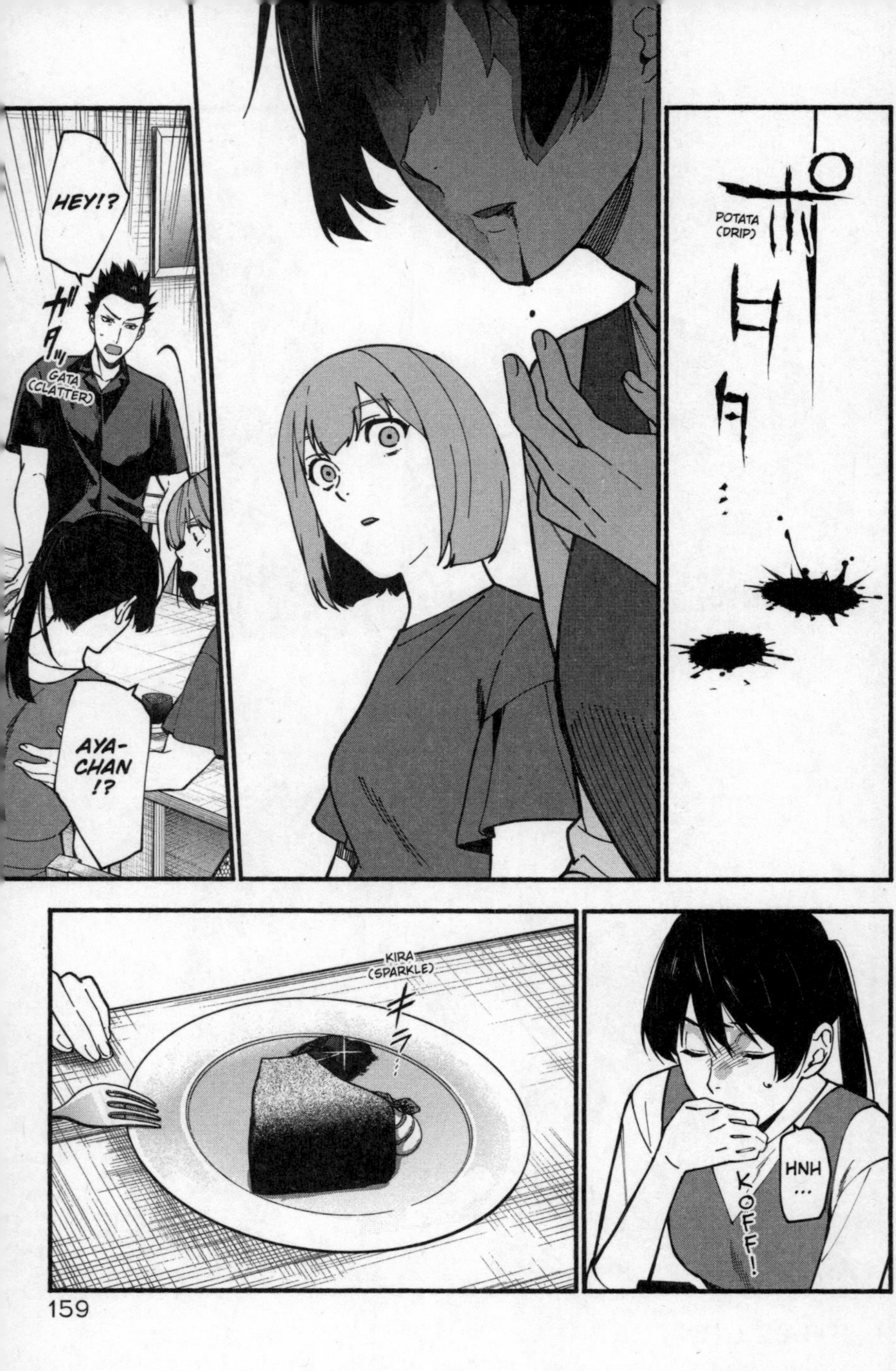
POTATA (DRIP)
HEY!?
GATA (CLATTER)
AYA-CHAN!?
HNH...
KOFF!
KIRA (SPARKLE)

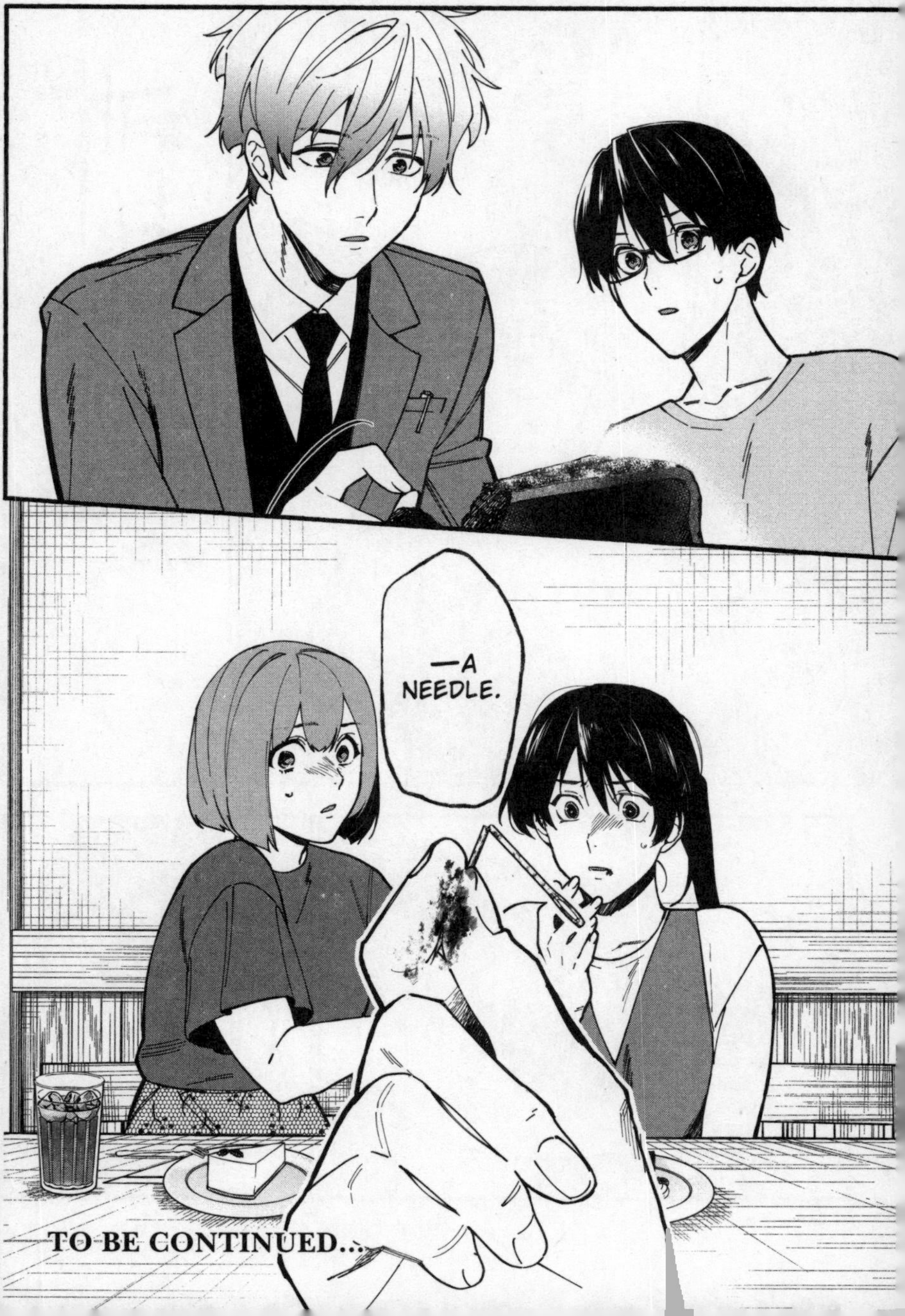

—A NEEDLE.
TO BE CONTINUED...

Translation Notes

Page 14
Rakugo is a form of traditional Japanese comedy storytelling.

Page 26
Daijisen is a major dictionary in Japan, frequently used by students. Its name means "great fountain of words." The *Digital Daijisen* is the electronic version.

Page 27
Hanako-san and the **Slit-Mouthed Woman** are a pair of well-known Japanese urban legends. As Professor Takatsuki would tell you, their exact elements can vary widely, but each has core features. Hanako-san is the ghost of a girl who haunts school toilets, while the otherwise beautiful Slit-Mouthed Woman approaches victims with her disfigured mouth obscured to ask them what they think of her appearance. The response determines how she treats her victim, but generally, most outcomes are not congenial. Hanako-san dates back to the 1950s but remains extraordinarily popular to this day, while the Slit-Mouthed Woman is likely hundreds of years old but experienced a burst of popularity in the late 1970s and early 1980s.

Page 29
Tsuchinoko is a Japanese cryptid, typically understood to be a short snake with a thick, flat body. They can jump exceptionally high. The modern cryptid developed its identity and gained its popularity in the latter half of the twentieth century, but there are arguably much older legends and accounts that prefigure it.

Page 48
Clay figures and **flame-style pottery** are characteristic artifacts of the Jomon period in Japan, which stretches from prehistoric times to approximately 300 BCE. The flame-style pots date from the Middle Jomon period, around the fourth to third millennium BCE, and feature ornate fire-like forms around the rim. The exact purpose of the distinctive *dogu* clay figures remains unknown.

Page 48
Ichimatsu dolls are a type of traditional Japanese doll, often a baby doll or child doll played with by young girls. Their glass eyes and placid faces can be rather creepy, hence the fear evoked by a mysterious burnt doll.

Page 53
The festival where Fukamachi had his strange experience was a **Bon festival**. Held in the summer, *Bon* or *Obon* is the Japanese manifestation of a highly syncretic holiday that exists in much of East Asia, focused on the veneration of ancestors.

Page 73
Stigmatized properties, *jiko bukken* in Japan, are real estate properties where something distasteful like a crime or death has occurred. Realtors and landlords are expected and sometimes legally obligated to disclose that a property is stigmatized due to something that took place there or another "psychological flaw," such as being previously owned by someone who committed a crime.

Page 136
The **Nessie hoax** depicted here is the famous 1934 "surgeon's photograph."

Page 156
When Ayane says **didn't treat her needles poorly**, she is not suggesting that she might have somehow lost needles years ago, and they are now falling out of her clothes, but is rather ruling out another supernatural explanation— that the spirits of her needles themselves are displeased with her. In the light novel, she even points out that she attends *Hari-Kuyo*, the Japanese ceremony for needles broken or used up through the year.

Page 157
The Hour of the Ox ritual is an ancient Japanese curse, in which the caster, typically a woman, visits a shrine while wearing a crown of iron and candles and hammers nails into a sacred tree. The deed must be done between one and three a.m., the Hour of the Ox by traditional Chinese timekeeping. A doll was not necessarily involved in the older versions, but modern accounts invariably feature one.

Afterword

Thank you for reading Volume 1 of the *Associate Professor Akira Takatsuki's Conjecture* manga! I'm Mikage Sawamura, the author of the original novel. I never thought something I wrote would become a manga... When I first received the proposal for its comic adaptation, I remember replying with a rather serious face: "The *Takatsuki* series is basically a story about handsome guys talking for long periods of time. Would that read well in a manga? Is that okay?" I mean, Takatsuki really does just blather on endlessly during lecture scenes and when he's giving his interpretations. I kept wondering if the manga would turn out all right...and it absolutely did!

Every time I see the storyboards and rough drafts, I really enjoy them! Even though I wrote the original story and know everything that's going to happen, it's still fun! The lengthy dialogue was consolidated so well, and I could really tell that the manga team read the novel carefully before making the comic. I just kept writing "Thank you so much!" in my notes to the supervising editor (lol). I'm just so pleased! I can't stop being excited about how the rest of the story will turn out in manga form. Let's enjoy it together, everyone! (Oh, and if possible, please read the original novel as well!)

Mikage Sawamura

AFTERWORD

My name is Toji Aio, and I'm in
charge of the manga adaptation of
Associate Professor Akira Takatsuki's Conjecture.
I really wanted to draw the tale of the middle-aged
man in black full-body tights that was posted on
Neighborhood Stories. So when the storyboard was
approved and Sawamura-sensei told me,
"I'm glad you drew it in a surreal but cute way,"
I was really happy.
I feel like it's a huge luxury to be able not only
to enjoy reading Professor Takatsuki's stories
but also to enjoy drawing them as well. If those
of you who read this book also enjoy it,
I'll be so fortunate.

TOJI AIO

ASSISTANTS
Yuzuki Inaba
Egami
Makoto Ohno
Peace Lit
Funatsumaru
Haru Yanagi
Profile Picture Illustration
(Japanese version): MASA

Thank you very much!

Associate Professor
Akira Takatsuki's Conjecture

Art: Toji Aio • Original Story: Mikage Sawamura • Character Design: Jiro Suzuki
Translation: Katelyn Smith • Lettering: Arbash Mughal

JUNKYOJU・TAKATSUKIAKIRA NO SUISATSU Vol.1
©Toji Aio 2020
©Mikage Sawamura 2020
First published in Japan in 2020 by KADOKAWA CORPORATION, Tokyo. English translation rights arranged with KADOKAWA CORPORATION, Tokyo through TUTTLE-MORI AGENCY, INC., Tokyo.

English translation © 2023 by Yen Press, LLC

Yen Press
150 West 30th Street, 19th Floor
New York, NY 10001

Visit us at yenpress.com · facebook.com/yenpress · twitter.com/yenpress · yenpress.tumblr.com · instagram.com/yenpress

First Yen Press Edition: August 2023
Edited by Yen Press Editorial: Rory Nevins, Carl Li
Designed by Yen Press Design: Madelaine Norman

Yen Press is an imprint of Yen Press, LLC.
The Yen Press name and logo are trademarks of Yen Press, LLC.

Library of Congress Control Number: 2023938732

ISBNs: 978-1-9753-6117-4 (paperback)
978-1-9753-6118-1 (ebook)

1 3 5 7 9 10 8 6 4 2

WOR

Printed in the United States of America